הדרך יהוה

THE WAY

An introduction to modern
'Jewish-Christianity' (Talmidaism)

Book 2: Teaching Talmidi Ethics and Outlook through the Words of the 'Our Father'

Shmuel ben Naftali

Other books by the same author in this series:
THE WAY – An Introduction to Modern 'Jewish-Christianity' (Talmidaism) Book 1: Re-Interpreting Jesus of Nazareth and the History of his first Jewish Followers in the light of Israelite Theology

To be published (prospective title):
THE WAY – An Introduction to Modern 'Jewish-Christianity' (Talmidaism) Book 3: Applying an Ancient Faith to the Issues of the Modern World

This edition published May 2018
published under the auspices of
'LAMP HOUSE BOOKS'
(a private, non-profit foundation of
The World Fellowship of Followers of the Way)

Published through KDP on Amazon

email: **shmuliq.parzal@googlemail.com**

website : **www.talmidi.co.il**

ISBN: 9781982958084

PLEASE TREAT THIS BOOK WITH
RESPECT, AS IT CONTAINS THE HOLY
NAME OF GOD.

PLEASE THEREFORE
DO NOT DESTROY IT.
IF YOU NO LONGER REQUIRE IT,
PLEASE GIVE IT TO SOMEONE ELSE
WHO MIGHT BE INTERESTED IN
READING IT.

DEDICATION

I once again dedicate these books to Yahveh our God, for the sake of whose Kingdom and Message these sermons and articles were collected over the course of the last 30 years; and to the memory of the prophet Yeshua˘ of Nazareth, of his cousins Ya'aqov the Pious and Shim'on bar Qlofas, of the line of Nasis[a] who succeeded them, and to the memory of those ancient Followers of the Way whose faith has too long been forgotten, but whose faith we try to remember in the conduct of our lives.

---

[a] pronounced nah-SEEZ (singular Nasi – nah-SEE) – religious presidents of the ancient community of the Way

Contents

למה קרון אתון לי מרי ברם
ית מה די אמרית לא עבדון
אתון

"Why do you call me 'Master', and yet do
nothing that I say?"

(Sefer Yeshua` 106:2, Gospel of Luke 6:46)

לא כל נשא די קרא לי ואמר
מרי מרי יעל הוא למלכותיה
דאלהא אלא אינון די עבדון
ית רעותיה דאבוהון דבשמייא

"Not everyone who calls out to me, saying
'Master! Master!' will find the kingdom of
God, but rather those who do the will of
their heavenly Father."

(Sefer Yeshua` 107:2; Gospel of Matthew 7:21)

(I have done my best to translate these verses into the Standard Jewish
Aramaic of the 1st century CE; if anyone can correct them, or provide
better translations, please contact me at the email address on the last page
of this book)

A NOTE ON THE AUTHOR

(reproduced from Book 1)
Shmuel Parzal was born in Sri Lanka (then Ceylon) in 1961, and emigrated to England in February 1962 with his parents and grandparents.

He was born of mixed ancestry, mostly of Dutch, Portuguese *Converso*[a] and English lineage. He was raised as a Catholic, and during his late teenage years felt a calling to become a priest. However, due to internal spiritual doubts and a realisation that he was not yet ready to enter into ministry, he concluded that this was not to be his vocation.

Later, he spent some years with the Unitarians, during which time he acted as a lay preacher, travelling around congregations in the southeast of England to take services. He describes this time as "an important turning point in my spiritual development, when I learned to question everything, and accept nothing as given". He eventually converted to Judaism, beginning the process with the Reform Movement, and completing it with the Liberal Jewish community in London.

He now acts as Moderator for the moderate wing of the Talmidi Israelite community, a role that he has fulfilled since 1998.

A long-time researcher in early Christian and Jewish history, he has focussed his private studies not only on early 'Jewish-Christianity' (that is, Talmidaism), but also on the pre-Exile Israelite faith and its theology, as distinct from post-Exile Rabbinic theology.

---

[a] Jews who were forcibly converted to Christianity under pain of death, during the Portuguese Inquisition in the 16th and 17th centuries.

PREFACE

Out of the three books in this series on Talmidaism, the book you now hold in your hands is the pinnacle of the precious project. The first and third parts of the series were after-thoughts that grew into books in their own right.

This second book in the series is intended for those who wish to explore how to apply the ethics, values and beliefs of the earliest followers of Yeshua` in their everyday lives. It explores those beliefs and precepts which are unhelpful to God's Kingdom, as well as those beliefs and teachings which bring us nearer into the Presence of our Heavenly Father. This means not only expanding on the teachings of Yeshua` of Nazareth and Jacob the Pious ('St. James the Just'), but also the principles and values of God that were practised by Abraham, Moses, David and the Hebrew prophets of Israel. As the earliest community that followed the Jewish prophet Yeshua`, we have our own emphases, and these I will explore in depth.

In pursuit of this endeavour, I wanted to collect together all the sermons and articles that I have written over the last 30 years – most of them anyway – since my spiritual conversion to the Way in 1987. I also needed a medium of teaching the Talmidi Israelite faith in a structured way. As I mentioned in my previous book, in 1998 I related the story of my reconstruction of the Jewish Aramaic 'Our Father', and in that book, I had briefly given some historical and theological information to help readers understand the intent and cultural medium of the prayer. I came to realise that the prayer's structure and themes were an ideal scaffold onto which I could order my articles.

These books are my life's work. I genuinely feel called by God to deliver a message, but I have always felt that I am the wrong person to deliver that message. Having Asperger's Syndrome, I have always had difficulty expressing myself, both in spoken and in written language. As a child, I could barely write short paragraphs, let alone a book! My natural inclination to shy away from publicity and self-promotion, has always made me think that I am the wrong person to deliver the message. However, having seen how evangelical preachers and self-promoters make God's message all about themselves, reluctantly I have to admit that perhaps God does actually know what God is doing. I am not a professional writer, I have no academic qualifications or degrees to put after my name, and so I can only ask you to forgive the literary inadequacies of this book. Give this message a chance to the end of the book, and I promise you, your heart will be opened in awe to the Presence of God.

During most of the years between 1987 and today, I never thought these books would ever get published. In 2012 I developed PTSD; for legal reasons, I cannot talk about the circumstances. Then in 2014, a manipulative NHS therapist so entrenched and magnified my PTSD with her gas-lighting tactics, that until the Autumn of 2017, I have been completely unable to function – either to read or write anything, look after myself, or live anywhere near a normal life. I finally received appropriate therapy in 2017, and I thank my EMDR therapist, Nigel Vincent, for my ascent out of a darkness I never thought it was possible to escape from. I also have him to thank for the finished product you hold in your hands; I have him to thank for suggesting that I get my books published on Amazon, and how that could realistically be achieved in practical terms.

I would also like to thank two brothers in faith: Mike Clarke, for his enthusiastic reception of this book, who told me that he was 'pumped' after reading it! And Paul Robbins, whose intelligent questions taught me the true value of our faith. Also my sister in faith Gill Guest, who has supported and encouraged me over many years.

Shmuel Parzal
Lincoln, England
June 2017

GENERAL INTRODUCTION

Where religion has failed, and where it can do better

One of the biggest problems that Religion itself faces today, is the mind-set that the whole earth must follow the same religion in order to solve its problems – that all human beings must convert to share the same ideology and system of beliefs. However, the nature of humanity is such that this is never going to happen. What *can* change though, is in a willingness of religious people of all faiths to work towards the same set of values – this is the underlying, practical purpose behind spreading the Kingdom of God on earth.

Due to the destructive phenomenon of religious fundamentalism, as well as the spiritual and physical violence that ensues from it, most human beings have come to see religion as the very thing that drives people apart; many fair-minded people abandon religion for this very reason. This is one major problem that modern Talmidaism is greatly concerned with, and one it seeks to redress in its moderate outlook, and in its intellectually responsible theology.

For most decent people, religious fundamentalism and religious intolerance are the unacceptable faces of modern religion. It is not the strictness of theology that modern Talmidaism would object to, but rather its use of hatred and discord, the psychological harm it does to people's minds, and that fundamentalists lack any basic godly compassion and empathy *for those who are not their own*.

Some religious communities have made religion so much about belief, that one's moral behaviour becomes irrelevant. The emphasis on 'salvation through faith alone', and the notion of 'once saved, always saved', has created a class of individuals who see nothing wrong with greed or hatred, as long as they 'accept Christ as their lord and saviour'. They ignore the immoral behaviour of their politicians, and see nothing wrong with corrupting and twisting the truth if it suits their own ends. They eagerly look forward to a time of universal conflict and collapse, and the end of the world has become their ultimate goal of faith. However, the only real outcome of their blinkered fight will be the fracturing and collapse of their own society. Talmidi Israelite theology places emphasis instead on thought, word and action that does not harm the sacred reputation of God. In so doing, Talmidaism brings personal responsibility and accountability back into the realm of spiritual life.

There are also some religious people who want to return their faith to a supposedly idealised point of time in the far distant past, and effectively fossilise it there. They imagine that converting the world to the same religion is the only plan that God can possibly have. However, the fossilisation of faith and society ensures that God's ultimate plans are *never* fulfilled (and that there is no spiritual growth or evolution towards the eventual perfection of humanity).

This is like ensuring that a seed never grows, that a field of wheat never produces grain, or that a tree never bears fruit. The reality is that there never was a perfect period in the past; that is yet to come. Truly good and spiritually holy people enter the world-stage at times of crisis, encourage us to remember God's noble ideals, and exhort us to labour towards a time of human betterment. A wise people of faith learn and grow from their ongoing experience of life – there is nothing wrong with sticking to your values, but your society should never set itself in stone, because a fossilised society is essentially a dead society.

The Israelite faith therefore encourages the betterment and stability[a] of human society, by passing on its values from generation to generation so that it improves and evolves, explaining not only what needs to be done, but also *why*. It promotes an adaptable and evolving society, to encourage humanity towards becoming the amazing beings God created us to be. This is the reason why in my first chapter, I take you through the evolution of our faith, from the time of Abraham to the modern day.

Yet other religious communities believe that the solution to the world's problems is for the whole of humanity to come under the political control of their religion. Such people vainly believe their religion is the perfect religion, the natural religion of all humanity; they believe their scriptures to be perfect and infallible, and their founding leaders to be perfect examples of human virtue, who never once did anything wrong. The natural consequence of this, is the condescending mind-set that all other religions are to be looked down on with scorn, are sub-standard, and that other religions have to *submit* to it. The only outcome of this religious stance is *eternal* conflict with all other faiths – a self-destructive and corrupting struggle to dominate and control.

The eradication of all other religions will not stop human conflict – consider those countries where one religion completely dominates, but which are still plagued with seemingly unending violence and war; at

---

[a] The stability of society was an important virtue in the ancient Israelite religion, Prov 29:4 – *'A king who rules by justice brings stability to the Land, but he who imposes heavy tolls upon it brings it to ruin'.* see also Isa 33:6, where wisdom and knowledge are seen as the sure foundation of a stable society. Lev 18:5 describes God's laws as *'the pursuit by which people shall live'.* They are laws by which Israelite society shall remain stable, by which the Israelite people shall be governed and prosper.

this point I am reminded of the saying, 'absolute power corrupts absolutely'.

The true heart of a religion is shown by the fruit it bears in human society. In practice, no human being can possibly fully know the One, True religion of heaven,[a] which can never be fully understood or followed perfectly by the imperfect beings of this mortal plane. True humility before God understands this; true submission to God means acknowledging that our lives are about seeking and engaging with the will of a living God, rather than with just a book (whatever that scripture might be).

This means having the humility to realise that all human beings are sons and daughters of God, regardless of their religion, or lack of it. It means having the humility to acknowledge that doing God's will isn't enough; one has to be willing also to be *changed* by the will of God. This is one of the emphases of Talmidaism that I shall be examining in the course of this book.

Then there are those who look at the peace and prosperity that a spiritual way of life promises and hopes for, and are utterly bored by it. They would prefer conflict, because it is supposedly more stimulating and interesting. For them, dystopia is more fulfilling than utopia, because war and fighting give them a stronger sense of purpose – just look at the current proliferation of novels about warring, militaristic, dystopian societies! For them, perpetual conflict and 'survival of the fittest' is the only natural way of existence (which actually only works in the short term; such a philosophy stifles growth and expansion of the species in the long run). To an extent, this is also a failing of Religion itself, because it has singularly failed to convince humanity of the idea that the struggle to create a better world and a better humanity, is in itself a fulfilling, affirming and worthwhile task. Religion in general has failed to give humanity anything realistic and pragmatic to believe in.

What is different about the Israelite religion compared to any other religion, is that it is about discovering and engaging with the **living** will of Yahveh, living a life that shows that God's will and future plans *matter*; it's about sanctifying the good reputation of Yahveh through the fruit our faith bears; it's about working for a better, healed world, and uplifting humanity to the kind of beings that God intended us to be, so that the division between heaven and earth falls away; ultimately, Yahwism is about preparing humanity for heaven on earth – the next step in the evolution of the human species. It acknowledges that nothing created by human beings will ever be perfect – our ancient heroes were

---

[a] According to Israelite theology, the true religion of the human soul is *Tsedeq* (Righteousness or Uprightness) - Prov 8:20, 12:28, 16:31; cf Isa 40:14.

never perfect, nor were our ancestors ever perfect – but what mattered is that they *tried*, and God blessed them for that.

Talmidaism – the Talmidi Israelite faith – is not an inflexible or fundamentalist faith. It brings together scripture with the living wisdom of Yahveh, and what has been learnt from the ongoing human experience of human life.[a] It is a rational, reasoning and just faith that is not in conflict with science. Moderate Talmidis have no problem with evolution, archaeological research, modern medicine, or geological studies and the great age of the Earth.

These three books are by no means a complete description of modern Talmidaism. However, I hope that their contents will provide a new starting point, and provoke a renewed debate about the community of Yeshua`'s ancient Jewish followers, and the foundations of both the Jewish and Christian faiths.

---

[a] We take into account truisms and principles derived from the observable wisdom of God in the human experience of life (*liqachim*, singular *léqach*; this is, after all, the essence of the Book of Proverbs and the Wisdom books of the Hebrew Bible).

CHAPTER ONE: Where Talmidaism came from, and the purpose of this book

Introduction

The teachings of the prophet Yeshua` give us the emphases of our faith – the hallmarks of what our faith represents. However, we do not restrict ourselves solely to Yeshua`'s teaching by ignoring other Hebrew prophets and sages. We believe that Yeshua` was a thoroughly Hebrew prophet whose faith, values and culture were founded on the teachings of Yahveh expounded throughout the Hebrew Bible – the Miqra;[a] I will therefore regularly examine issues derived not from the teachings of Yeshua`, but from the teachings of other Hebrew prophets and biblical writers. I will examine modern issues from the mind-set of their values too – because their faith was the *Israelite* faith, and we believe that part of Yeshua`'s ministry was to restore the values, concepts and mind-set of the Israelite faith of Abraham, Moses and Solomon.

Once you have finished reading this book, you will by then have noticed that I did not talk much about Israelite customs and traditions – such as the festivals, passage-of-life customs or communal worship. I will leave all that to another book; the focus of this book is the life of the healthy Israelite mind and heart, by examining beliefs that promote a healthy, spiritual outlook on life, and turning away from those false attitudes that hinder spiritual growth. In this book, I focus on attitude, values and mind-set, rather than customs and traditions.

Modern religion has gone awry, because it focuses either on fossilised belief systems, or ritual practice by rote, and completely ignores values and outlook applicable to real, everyday life. As a result, Religion has abandoned the reason why God created her in the first place, and turned itself into something negative and destructive, under which humanity has submitted itself in a form of voluntary slavery. Religion is now about what only exists in the human mind, rather than about what is concrete, tangible and verifiable in the real world, and applicable to real life.

For those of us who have come from a Christian background, it is

---

[a] This is the oldest known term for the Hebrew Bible (pronounced mik-RAA). The more usual term *Tánakh*, is a rabbinic abbreviation (T.N.K.) taken from the 3 parts of the Hebrew Bible: **T**orah, Prophets (**N**evi'im) and Writings (**K**etuvim). Ancient rabbinic culture had a propensity for using a huge number of abbreviations for all manner of things, even for whole sentences in the Talmud. I personally prefer the non-rabbinic term Miqra.

1

something of a shock to find that religion is not just about what you believe. And not all religions share the same ethics or morals either; what is acceptable in one religion may be completely abhorrent in another – this was especially true in ancient times. For example, Greek and Roman religion considered it perfectly acceptable to use child abandonment – leaving new-borns to die in some remote place – as an acceptable form of birth control.

Nor is religion necessarily about believing in God; Buddhism, in its truest form, has no place for any god, although certain Buddhist societies have retained their ancestral gods in a somewhat modified form. And even now, there are groups forming fully atheist 'churches' – providing all the trappings of religion, like gathering together, singing together, and discussing life's meaning together, but without any belief in God, heaven, or the supernatural.

It is true that even in ancient times there were religious conflicts, but they weren't necessarily about what people believed. Rather, they were because the life-values of a particular group posed a threat to the accepted norms and values of a particular society. For example, the insistence of early Followers on social justice, and our criticism of the moral values of the Sadducean priesthood, proved a danger to that elite group of priests. Earlier, in the Hellenist period of Judean history, Judaism posed a political threat, not a theological one. And in ancient times, Jews in the Holy Land experienced wars and invasions not for *who* they were, but because of *where* they were.

So what is the essence of religion? What makes a religion a religion? If not beliefs, then what? From the dawn of human history until the advent of Paullist Christianity, religion was about the cultural framework of a society, and how it passed its collective knowledge and wisdom from generation to generation; it was about giving society meaning and purpose within certain parameters set by each culture. Religion was what enabled large groups of people to come together in the spirit of co-operation, and provided a framework for settling differences; it was the glue that held society together, and what got them through the various stages of life together. It consoled them in difficult times, and helped them celebrate in joyous times. Paullist theology rejected everything that was relevant in religion to the living conduct of real life here and now, for the beliefs of what someone else had taught them on faith alone, and about what might be in the future.

The religion of heaven, and the Universal Covenant

So how far back does one go for one's first point of reference? Is Yeshua''s teaching sufficient? The prophets of the First Temple period?

Solomon? Moses? Adam? I would posit we need to go even further back in time – to the very first system of values that God gave us – *Tsedeq* (or 'Righteousness')[a] – the religion of heaven that God first imprinted on our souls.

Imagine if you can, the highest good, the noblest values, the greatest goals, and purest spiritual outlook. If you can do that, you can imagine the religion of heaven – the first religion that we were all created with. This is the religion we all followed in heaven, before we ever came to earth; it is the religion we have most of us forgotten, the values of goodness we can only weakly defend in the face of religious fundamentalism.

There has been some criticism of Talmidaism online, in that we apparently project back onto Yeshua` the values of the Gentile West – for example reason, humaneness and tolerance.[b] This mostly comes from a lack of understanding of what Talmidaism is – or what the Israelite faith hoped for. As Talmidis we realise that Yeshua` had a limited mission – to call people back to God's ways, so that as many as possible could be saved from the tribulation about to hit the land of Israel.

You see, Talmidaism is much more than Yeshua`, Jacob the Pious and his early community in Jerusalem; Talmidaism is the sum of the best of Yahwist Israelite values, and that set of values presents a God who is against superstition, who instils within us a discernment for wisdom, justice and understanding, and who teaches us to be fair and just towards our neighbours. Much of this is to bring out from within us what God has already placed there – a reasoning, humane and understanding heart, that places importance on individual responsibility, and enables us to draw on our inner courage and strength to get through the difficulties of life. Anyone who thinks Torah has nothing to do with reason or social justice, doesn't understand Torah!

In Hebrew, there is a term, ברית עולם *brit `olam*. It literally means, 'eternal covenant'. Every time this phrase is used, it refers to the Covenant with Israel – except for one time. That one occasion occurs in Isaiah 24:5. There, the prophet describes how the earth will be ravaged and laid waste. This will not be for breaking the laws of Torah, but because *". . . the earth is defiled by her inhabitants, because they have transgressed* [humane] *laws, they have violated* [moral] *principles, and broken the universal covenant* (brit `olam)." This covenant is referring

---

[a] The Essene Book of Jubilees seems to have been aware of this concept. At 7:20–28, Noah teaches his sons the way of Righteousness, and then goes on to list several laws that are not part of the Rabbinic list of Noachide laws.

[b] I would guess that such people have never read the Book of Proverbs or Ecclesiastes, or understood the universality in the latter parts of the Book of Isaiah.

to a covenant that covers **the whole of humanity**.

Now, there are some who say that this covenant is the one with Noah[a] or even the one with Adam.[b] However, this cannot be the case, because there are some things for which the Hebrew prophets criticise other nations, that would not be covered by either one of these two covenants. For example, Amos[c] criticises the people of Moab for burning the bones of the King of Edom,[d] and for this, God would mete out His divine justice against them. But this act is not covered under either the Adamic or Noachide laws or covenants.

The Universal Covenant is in fact the natural moral law that exists between Yahveh and the whole of humanity. It is not written on any scroll or parchment, nor are its terms recorded in any book. The only place it is written is on the human heart – the human conscience. The Universal Covenant is what gives all human beings the sense of moral outrage when any human being does something wrong. Even though an act might not be outlawed by any biblical mitsvah[e] or proclamation, we inherently know that a word or deed is wrong. For the ancient Israelites, the unwritten laws of hospitality, which appear nowhere in Torah, were part of this Universal Covenant too. All decent people would also consider the psychological and physical abuse of children to be wrong, but this is not covered by the written Torah either.

Take also the question of, 'What law or covenant were the people of the earth judged under before the Great Flood, *before* the Noachide laws?'[f] Gen 6:11-13 reads like an indictment in a court of law. However, without the universal covenant – without that set of unwritten laws – no righteous judgment could be made by a just God against humanity. Without the Universal Covenant, in God's court of law, humanity could otherwise legitimately have said, 'But you gave us no law or code to live by, so how could we be accused of breaking any laws?'

---

[a] which are the 7 so-called Noachide laws, which Rabbinic teaching says are the only laws incumbent on the entire human race: 1. Not to worship idols, 2. Not to curse God, 3. to establish courts of justice, 4. Not to commit murder, 5. Not to engage in sexual immorality, 6. Not to steal, 7. Not to eat the flesh torn from a living animal.

[b] this covers the fact that God gave every green thing to us as food, in return for acting as stewards over creation - Gen 1:28-30, 2:16-17.

[c] Amos 2:1

[d] presumably this king was a much-loved or respected monarch, and the action caused a deep sense of outrage amongst those who heard of it.

[e] a biblical commandment

[f] Humanity is charged with having brought creation to ruin (*hišḥit*), for having become corrupt (*nišḥat*), and for violence (*ḥamas*). Only 'bringing creation to ruin' would have been against the Adamic Covenant in place at the time; the other two would not. They would be against *Tsedeq*, however.

The prophet Yeshua` taught us that 'the Kingdom of God is within you.'[a] The prophet Jeremiah[b] also speaks about God writing God's laws on our hearts, and Deuteronomy tells us that God's Word is written on our hearts.[c] If we ignore the natural religion of heaven that God has placed within us, we ignore an important part of what God requires of us as religious people. Neglecting the holiness of the way of the heart and mind, leaving human souls to descend into hatefulness, injustice and selfishness, profanes the Sanctity of Yahveh just as much as neglecting the spiritual reverence due to God, within the context of ritual observance and tradition.

In the Israelite religion, the natural religion of the human soul is *Tsedeq* – Righteousness (or Justice / Uprightness).[d] The laws that govern natural human religion have been written on the human heart – the human conscience, not on any parchment or scrolls; these are the laws that Noah followed and taught to his sons, the laws by which God judged him blameless[e] - after all, he didn't have a bible or Torah to refer to (and neither did Abraham, Isaac, Jacob etc).

So, even though other nations do not have Torah, they **do** have God's heavenly law of *Tsedeq* – the Way of Righteousness,[f] which from the day we gained sentience, was written on the human heart, giving us the knowledge to be able to tell the difference between good and evil. Knowing as we do, that no additions to God's covenant can override what is previously given, it is important to be stated here that *even the written Torah cannot override Tsedeq* – the written Torah cannot override what God has written on the human heart. If it does appear to do so, then we must be interpreting Torah incorrectly (and if anyone says that Torah can overrule *Tsedeq*, what they are effectively saying is that Torah is not righteous or just)!

Righteousness and Wisdom – both of which are from God – are the two guide-stones by which we apply and interpret Torah; just as priests entered the Temple of Solomon between 2 pillars, so also humankind should practice their religion, approaching God between the twin pillars of Righteousness and Wisdom. If we apply written religious law without wisdom or righteousness, we turn our faces against God, and set ourselves up for judgment.

The terms of the Universal Covenant are simple: the positive

---

[a] S.Yesh 20:3, 21:3 (Lk 17:20-21)
[b] Jer 31:33
[c] Dt 30:14, "But the Word is very near to you, in your mouth **and in your heart**, that you may observe it."
[d] Prov 8:20, 12:28, 16:31; cf Isa 40:14. cf also Book of Jubilees 7:20-28
[e] Gen 6:9
[f] Prov 8:20, 12:28, 16:31.

instructions are, 'Act justly, love mercy, and walk humbly with your God.'[a] The punishment for violating this is also simple: 'As you have done, so will God do to you.'[b]

This is the covenant that the people of Nineveh broke, and necessitated Jonah being sent to call them to repent (otherwise, tell me by what religious law were they being judged under – they certainly weren't condemned for breaking the Torah of Moses)! They were judged under the Universal Covenant – the covenant under which the Philistines were condemned by Amos, because of the cruelty they had shown to other nations (i.e. not just Israel); this is the covenant under which all the prophets condemn other nations for their unjust actions, regardless of which people their cruelty is directed against.

The Universal Covenant applies to *all* humanity, even the Jewish people. It preceded the Torah given at Sinai, and the covenant cut there. Since no covenant can be revoked or cancelled, this covenant of natural moral law applies even to the Jewish people – something that fundamentalist Jews who ignore the good that is unwritten tend to forget. As I previously mentioned, the implication of this is that no Torah law should be applied in such a way that it causes a deep sense of moral outrage in the human soul. I personally believe that the Universal Covenant was meant to be the ultimate moderating influence *against all subsequent covenants and laws*. In other words, I believe that God never expected any human being to apply their religion in such a way that it violates their God-given conscience.

Sometimes fundamentalist, extremist Jews will do something wrong that provokes our natural sense of moral outrage – the covenant that Yahveh has written on the human heart. These fundamentalists will say to us, 'We have done nothing wrong – show me where it says I cannot do this!' And there will be occasions where their actions are not explicitly forbidden by Torah, and they have not broken the Sinai Covenant. But they *have* broken God's natural principles of *Tsedeq*, as well as the Universal Covenant, and God will demand an accounting for what they have done; *as they have done, so God will do to them.*

The first, humane and natural laws of the Universal Covenant have not been written down or codified by sages, nor have they been subject to the rulings of rabbis – no religious teacher can ever rule against *Tsedeq*. Any human being can appeal directly to God for justice under it, Jew and Gentile alike, and any man or woman who has been wronged, can raise their voice to God and call for justice against their adversaries,

---

[a] Micah 6:8; This instruction, although addressed to Israelites, applies to all humanity, to follow religion with humility'.
[b] Obadiah 1:15

saying, 'May Yahveh judge between you and me!'[a]

To conclude this section on *Tsedeq* and the Universal Covenant, it needs to be said that *Tsedeq* is not a way of avoiding following the written Torah. Allegiance to *Tsedeq* ensures that we, as Followers of the Way of Yahveh, apply all the written Torah with wisdom, justice, compassion, mercy, and above all, with God's Love. Acknowledging the rôle of the Universal Covenant in our lives, means that we hold ourselves to the highest spiritual standard that our Heavenly Father has ever set us – the very first, humane laws that Yahveh our God created us to follow.

Religious fundamentalists will hate the Universal Covenant, because it is the only religious writ that they cannot corrupt and deliberately misrepresent for their own ends. When a religious person does something that fires the human sense of outrage, and they answer you and say, 'Point out to me where it is written in scripture that what I have done is wrong,' you can legitimately say to them, 'Read my heart – the eternal words that God has written there – and they say that what you have done is wrong!'

The evolution of Yahwism, Judaism and Talmidaism

Throughout this book, I will be using various theological terms to define our faith. Now, other writers will have their own definitions of these terms, but in order to understand what *I* am trying to get at, I need to explain to you what I myself mean by those terms.

Occasionally I hear people debate the question of, 'How far back in theological history should we go to find our point of origin, the so-called "root" of the truth of faith?' Now, God has a long-term plan to take us forward on a particular path. Unfortunately, human error has invariably taken us on a different path. Over the millennia, Hebrew religion has taken on various beliefs and practices which were not part of God's original plan. As a movement, we therefore needed to go backwards first, retracing where we have come from, in order to then go forwards again – this time, evolving on the path which God has ordained for us. Defining what terms cover what beliefs and time periods, helps us to see where our starting point was, and where we should have been heading.

Yes, there was a starting point, and there were truths we had at the very start. But then, as time went on, Hebrew religion learned new things. However, at each fork in the road, the Hebrew faith sometimes took turns we felt were not the best roads to have taken.

---

[a] Sarah's words calling for divine justice in Gen 16:5 – otherwise, what other covenant or law was Sarah asking for justice under?

Most Jews today would use the terms 'Judaism' or 'the Jewish faith' to cover absolutely everything from the time of Abraham, right through to Moses, David and Solomon. However, if you look at how the terms were historically applied, 'Judaism' is technically only 'the religion of the Judeans' – that is, the religion of the Judeans returning from exile in Babylon in the 6th century BCE. By such a definition, it could be argued that David and Solomon were Jews, since they were both of the tribe of Judah. However, Abraham was not a Jew (he was a Sumerian by birth), and Moses was not a Jew (since he was of the tribe of Levi). They were not Jews as history would understand the term, but rather what I would call, 'Yahwists'.

The semantic differences between 'Yahwism', 'the Israelite religion' and 'Judaism' need to be grasped, in order to understand the evolution of Talmidaism, and where it stands on the theological family tree of Abrahamic religions. The point of this is not to create division, but rather to gain a realistic overview of the past, present and future of Talmidaism – where it came from and, more importantly, where it is going.

***Tsedeq ('Righteousness')*:**[a] I have already talked about this – the law of heaven, the original, highest and truest religion, and the natural law that God has written on all human hearts. It is the basis of what the Israelite faith called the Universal Covenant[b] – the first Covenant of conscience, mercy and compassion that no subsequent covenant can ever revoke or nullify. It is never expanded on in scripture, because it is assumed that the reader is already familiar with it – *"Love mercy, do justice and walk humbly with God"*.[c] This sacred covenant precedes the so-called 'Noachide' laws and the Adamic covenant, and is referring to the very first, heavenly covenant instilled within all of us at the very creation of our souls.

By this covenant, all successive covenants are measured and interpreted. If the wording of successive Covenants appear to go against the human conscience, then we must be interpreting or applying them wrongly.

Pure monotheism also begins with *Tsedeq* – that is, the eternal understanding that there is no god but Yahveh. Exclusive worship of Yahveh (as *El Shadday*) began with Abraham nearly 4,000 years ago, but our Hebrew ancestors did not always worship Yahveh exclusively; we are constantly reminded by atheists that many Israelites were polytheists. The exclusive worship of Yahveh is therefore not an

---

[a] Prov 8:20, 12:28, 16:31; cf Isa 40:14.
[b] cf Isaiah 24:5 – *brit 'olam*, not 'eternal covenant' but rather 'universal covenant'; see Essay 10 in this book.
[c] Micah 6:8

innovation of post-exile Judaism – as some academics claim – but rather a return to the original, heavenly ideal of *Tsedeq*.

Yahwism: When I use the term 'Yahwism',[a] I am referring to 'the religion of Abraham' – specifically 'the exclusive worship of Yahveh, along with the ethical system given by Yahveh'.[b] This is the manner of faith that Abraham and his descendants followed, right up until the revelation at Sinai. Any beliefs and principles that they might realistically have held, can logically be termed as 'Yahwist'. For example, the belief that Yahveh alone is the Creator, is the primary Yahwist belief, along with the understanding of Israel's covenantal relationship[c] with God; also, the opposition to superstition and idol worship is Yahwist; so too, that God is neither male nor female; that Yahveh is everywhere but unseen, and is without physical form; that Yahveh is all-powerful, all-knowing and all-sovereign; also, even the understanding that a righteous person might not always be perfect.[d]

The distaste for the Canaanite practice of ritual intercourse and religious prostitution is also 'Yahwist'; also the understanding that places of the dead are *not* suitable places of Yahwist worship; and that there are no such things as demons and devils; finally, that at certain times God intervenes in human affairs, and that God's will is knowable[e] (otherwise, how would we know what constitutes a righteous way of life)? Talmidaism places great emphasis on Yahwist beliefs and principles – after heavenly *Tsedeq*, Abraham's faith truly is the earthly bedrock of our faith to which we return, and from which a Talmidi cannot afford to depart.

I would have to mention at this point, that an awareness of the two concepts of '*Tsedeq*' and 'Yahwism' is essential, since Islam claims to be the only natural religion of humanity. It claims that Abraham and all Hebrew prophets were actually Muslims i.e. that they were not Yahwists

---

[a] Academia defines Yahwism differently, as simply 'the worship of Yahweh' [sic], without going any further.

[b] While Christianity and Islam are Abrahamic religions – considering Abraham as the founder of monotheistic faith – they are not Yahwist faiths, as they do not hold the Name of Yahveh as holy, and do not have the same understanding of the concepts of holiness, *Kavodh* (Divine radiance), *Davar* (Divine ethos), what a prophet is for, or the purpose of the Israelite religion.

[c] a covenantal relationship is a relationship built upon agreed obligations between God and Israel, where God and Israel *both* have responsibilities, and there are agreed benefits and blessings for keeping to that agreement (or 'Covenant').

[d] Whereas the ancestors of pagan nations were portrayed as perfect, godlike beings, the ancestors of the Israelites are portrayed as basically good people, who sometimes made mistakes, and were not perfect.

[e] admittedly, not completely or perfectly, but nevertheless knowable.

following *Tsedeq*. Talmidaism has a sensible response to such a claim. Beliefs such as the one that a messiah will save us instead of God ('messianism'), is not Yahwist, and why we have therefore abandoned the belief. Messianism resulted from later Jewish contact with the Zoroastrian religion, which held a similar belief in a saviour-king sent from heaven.

In the ancient world, you would describe your religious allegiance by saying that you were the son or daughter of a particular god. So an adherent of the Israelite religion was called a *ben Yahveh* – literally, 'a son of Yahveh' (or for a woman, *bat Yahveh* – a 'daughter of Yahveh'). Our modern English equivalent of these terms would be 'Yahwist'. The period of pure Yahwism would be from the time of Abraham until just before the revelation at Horeb (c. 2000-1445 BCE). However, its influence has obviously extended through the Israelite and Jewish periods to the present day.

The Israelite religion: The revelation of the Torah on Mt Horeb, marks the beginning of the Israelite religion. The introduction of the concept of a codified, written Torah into our faith, is the defining feature of this period. Before this, the ethical and moral code followed by Abraham and his immediate descendants was *Tsedeq*. The Sinai Torah gives us the egalitarian nature of Israelite society, the just and fair rule of law, legal protections for the poor, and the notion of Yahveh as Israel's King. The codifying of the rights of animals e.g. to rest on the Sabbath, and not to be treated with cruelty, is way beyond any other culture of its time.

Beliefs such as the cleansing power of the glory of Yahveh (the fire of the 'Divine Radiance') stem from this period; so also the power of the holiness of Yahveh. During this period, the symbolism underlying animal sacrifice is given to the priests of Israel – we learned about Azza Zeil[a] at this point, and the understanding that we are cleansed of the stain of sin by the fire of Yahveh's glory, not by blood; we gained the understanding that the physical body cannot withstand the fire of God's glory, but that the human soul can – especially in a state of repentance. These are all concepts that modern Judaism has lost – likely because of

---

[a] Lev 16:8 - not 'scapegoat', but a proto-Semitic term meaning, 'Fortress of Shadow' (the Hebrew would be *Azzat Tzeil*). This is the dark place where souls undergo trial after death, to be purified of unrepented sins before entering heaven. It is the meaning behind the symbolism of the 2 goats at Yom Kippur; the one sent into the wilderness, represents the sins that are separated from the soul and left in *Azza Zeil*; and the goat sacrificed represents the purified soul that returns to God, to receive its final purification by the glory of God. The prophet Yeshua''s name for this place was, 'the Outer Darkness'.

times of exile, but which are still present in scripture if you know where to look for them.

The Middle Israelite period (the time of David and Solomon), is spiritually the golden age of the Israelite faith. This is the period where reverence for Wisdom and Knowledge becomes an essential part of the Israelite faith. The notion of 'Davar'[a] enters at this stage – that the Message, Wisdom and Knowledge which come from Yahveh are not separate parts of God, but are an integral part of the very nature of God. The ideals of Yahwism come to their greatest fruition during this period of Israelite thought.

We tend to think of ideals such as reason,[b] humaneness and tolerance as being products solely of modern Western nations, but these ideals are there in the Book of Proverbs, and in the universality of the latter portions of the Book of Isaiah. God's ethos allows us to learn wisdom from the lessons of life – known in Hebrew as *liqachim*.[c] God's life-lessons fall like rain on fresh grass, and refresh us like dew on the earth.[d] What God teaches us through life itself nourishes our human souls. Anyone who says that one can learn nothing from real life, and that we are just to mechanically follow the commandments of Torah by rote, does not understand the beautiful Wisdom writings of the Hebrew Bible.

The late Israelite period is the period of the majority of the biblical prophets – the understanding of prophets as messengers of warnings (and consolations) from God. During this time, the Israelite religion split into the Judean form and the Ephrathite form (the forms practised in the southern and northern kingdoms respectively). Social justice and inner holiness become emphasised, along with the new concept of 'the Day of Yahveh'.[e] With the realisation that Israel and Judah's anointed kings were not the ideals of Yahwist virtue they were supposed to be, the hope arose that a re-united Israel would one day see a good and virtuous anointed king, who remained faithful to Yahveh.

The period of the Israelite religion would be from 1445-539 BCE.

---

[a] literally, 'Word' – referring to the whole corpus of ethical and moral teaching that is an innate and intrinsic part of what Yahveh is; it can also mean 'Message', 'revered teaching', 'all-encompassing philosophy', 'just precepts', and 'wise advice', as well as 'proclamation', 'commandment' and 'edict'.

[b] Ecclesiastes 7:25

[c] singular *léqach* – a moral lesson or life-lesson learned from perceiving the observable wisdom of God in everyday life, and gaining benefit from it (cf Prov 1:5, 9:9, Isa 29:24.

[d] cf Dt 32:2.

[e] that when human society cruelly ignores God's laws, and corrupts religion into something perverse, then a time of tribulation ('the Day of Yahveh') will come upon us when God puts things right. For Israel, that usually means exile.

Most academics lump the Yahwist and Israelite periods together, renaming it, 'biblical Judaism'.

Judaism: After the Judeans ('Jews' – the descendants of the three southern tribes)[a] began returning to Judea, the Israelite religion became more Judeo-centric. The centrality and fate of the people of Judea ('Jews') became an important concern of the faith. Exile theology became more refined, and the text of the five books of Torah was committed to writing. The existing idea of the universality of Yahveh came to fruition at this time – much of the latter portions of the universalist Book of Isaiah were written shortly after the exile.

During this period, the institution of the synagogue began to develop, and the idea of local government through the synagogue. The unfortunate – and unbiblical – belief that there are no more prophets also stems from this period. Political, social and economic problems caused ordinary people to lose faith in the active presence of God (Talmidaism, in contrast, seeks to restore people's faith in the active, daily Presence of Yahveh).

It was in this period that certain non-Yahwist concepts started creeping into Judaism. The two most pernicious and damaging being the idea of a messiah king-saviour, and the idea of Satan – both of which came from the Zoroastrian religion of Persia (where many Jews lived before returning to the Holy Land). Since the texts of many books of the bible were being redacted at this very time, these beliefs were back-edited retrospectively into those texts, at a time when their oral forms were being set down into their more permanent, written form. The idea of a final, eschatological fight between good and evil – as equal and opposite forces – also comes from dualist Zoroastrianism.

Judaism obviously extends right through to the present day. For the purposes of understanding the lineage and descent of Talmidaism, the early Judaic period would be from 539 BCE to 70 CE (also known as the Second Temple period). During this time, one section of the Jewish community continued to uphold and pass on the ideals of the Israelite faith – Common Judaism.[b] For the purposes of my writings, I use the term 'Common Judaism' to refer to the non-sectarian religion of ordinary Jewish people. It was the only section of the Jewish community that still believed in the idea of prophets – an important concept in ancient Talmidaism.

The historian Josephus never mentions this section of Jewish society when he described the four schools of Jewish philosophy

---

[a] that is, Judah, Benjamin and Shimon.
[b] I am aware that other writers use this term differently, to mean 'that which is common to all forms of Judaism'. I use it to mean 'non-sectarian' Judaism'.

(Pharisees, Sadducees, Essenes and Zealots), because Common Judaism was not an officially organised grouping – more of a phenomenon or fact on the ground. Both Karaite and Talmidi Judaism are descended theologically from Common Judaism; it is the reason we are so similar.

Ancient Talmidaism: This is what most academics would call, 'Jewish-Christianity'. It applies to the Jewish community of Yeshua`'s followers, centred on the leadership of Jacob the Pious and his successors, from Jerusalem to Pella. It covers specifically that part of historical 'Jewish-Christianity' which held Yeshua` to have been a human prophet, born of natural human birth.[a] A defining difference between the 'James-community' and mainstream Christianity, is that it rejected the apostleship of Paul of Tarsus.

The ancient concept of personal, inner holiness came to the fore once more in Yeshua`'s teaching, as did social justice and concern for the poor. Also during this period, Judaism still accepted the notion of 'Godfearers' – non-Jews who followed the God of Israel and Jewish customs, but did not go through the full process of conversion. At that stage, Judaism was still tolerant of the concept of plurality in the overall faith of the Assembly of Israel.

In Hebrew, a Follower of the Way is called, *ben ha-dérekh* – literally, 'a son of the Way'; and so for a woman, *bat ha-dérekh* ('a daughter of the Way').

Modern Talmidaism: This is the modern revival (1960's-80's) of ancient, historical 'Jewish-Christianity', which holds to the *same* beliefs and line of authority as that of the ancient community, as well as the same stance on Paul (things which distinguish us from 'Messianic Judaism', which we are not a part of). On the understanding that Yeshua` sought to restore the original faith of Abraham and Moses, our faith restored many Yahwist/Israelite concepts and principles that have been lost from mainstream Judaism; we also abandoned those alien beliefs which were foreign to the faith of Abraham.

I hope that, by this relation of the various stages of Jewish religious history, you now understand that we did not learn everything all at once, but that God has been teaching us over a long period of time, and that faith *evolves*. Just as a ripe fruit does not suddenly appear from nowhere out of the ground, so also spiritual development does not come upon the human race fully formed; like a plant that is tended carefully in a garden – being fed and watered by God – human spiritual growth takes place gradually too. Like a plant, there will one day be a flowering and fruition

---

[a] We know these are beliefs held by the Jewish followers of Yeshua`, because these are beliefs that the early Christian Church Fathers criticised them for.

in the human race – which is the perfection of humanity,[a] and the fulfilment of God's kingdom with heaven on earth.

Using the words of the 'Our Father' to teach Talmidi Israelite values

Yeshua˙ was asked how his followers should pray. His reply was the *Our Father*. His reply does not necessarily mean that we should specifically use *this* prayer, although as a model of prayer it is an excellent one. What he was doing was using it as a model of the naturally free and open way we should pray.

Now, Judaism has some very beautiful prayers. Some are very formal, some are more open and natural. By his answer, Yeshua˙ implied that he preferred the second of these types. He was telling us that it's all right to pray about our real, daily needs. It's all right not to restrict ourselves to the ancient prayers of our ancestors. He once told his followers, *'When you pray, don't babble and repeat your prayers over and over like Gentiles do, for they think that their prayers will be answered because of their many words and repetitions.'*[b] He was saying that we should not be stuffy, verbose or pompous in the way we pray, but rather that we should pray from the heart – after all, that is what God sees: our hearts. God will instantly see through any longwinded insincerity at once, so we might as well dispense with it right from the start.

There are a number of important themes and emphases that Yeshua˙ taught us, that are contained within the words of the prayer. For many a long year, I tried to think of a way of how to teach Talmidi values in a structured way, and eventually, I decided on the framework of the *'Our Father'* as the best pattern of teaching I could use.

So let us begin!

---

[a] this understanding comes from Daniel's 'son of man' teachings, where he explains that the son of man actually represents perfected humanity – see Dan 7:18-27; the son of man is not just one person, but many people, known as 'holy ones' – the name of human souls in heaven.
[b] S.Yesh. 153:1 - cf Mt 6:7

CHAPTER TWO: Sanctifying God's Name – A Call to Action on God's Behalf

אבון דבשמייא
יתקדש שמך

*aboon de-bishmayya,
yitkadesh shmakh*

*Our Father, who is in heaven,
Sanctified be Your Name!*

Before I begin, I would like to reiterate that I am not using the words of the *'Our Father'* used in the King James Bible, or any other translation for that matter. I am using the reconstructed, Jewish Aramaic words of the prayer I translated about 20 years ago. This is the first time, as far as I am aware, that this had ever been done – translating the prayer back into Jewish Aramaic. We do of course have the words in Syriac, but this is a completely different dialect (as different as the American dialect of Alabama is to the dialect of Glasgow, Scotland). To read the complete words of the reconstructed prayer in English, see appendix 3; the Aramaic version is appendix 1.

The prayer itself is divided up into couplets (sets of two lines each). Now, to understand the relevance of each couplet, you have to be aware of the troubles that were going on in Yeshua`'s day. Yeshua` could have included absolutely anything in this model prayer. However, there had to be pressing, contemporary reasons for including these six, specific petitions in the prayer he taught his followers. He wanted certain emphases to be at the forefront of his followers' minds whenever they prayed to their heavenly Father.

Line 1: Our Father, who is in heaven,

This line is not unusual in Jewish prayer; it is found in prayers recorded throughout the Talmud.[a] In the mainstream Jewish community, there is a lot of reluctance nowadays to address God as 'Father' because of its association with Christianity. However, there is nothing un-Jewish about it at all. In fact, there is nothing in *any* part of the prayer that goes against anything in the original Israelite faith.

In Yeshua`'s day, one of the titles given to some religious teachers was *abba*. Now, in modern Hebrew, it means 'daddy', but in ancient Aramaic, it simply meant 'father' – it didn't imply any degree of intimacy *per se*. It would seem that Yeshua` had a dislike for giving titles to religious clerics, such as 'rabbi', 'father' or 'teacher': *"And do not call anyone 'Father' on earth, for you have but one Father – the One in Heaven."*[b]

Today there are mega-churches, whose pastors are accomplished performers, raking in millions of dollars. Their message isn't what Yeshua` taught, but their own words, and their own ministry. The pastor doesn't teach you how to live one's life in accordance with the way of life Yeshua` taught, but rather, the importance of giving money to his or her ministry.

In the first line of the prayer, Yeshua` was, in a way, trying to emphasise that he is referring to our Father – the one in heaven, as opposed to the ones who took on the title on earth – haughty religious teachers who were often full of their own importance.

Let's look now at the individual words of the prayer.

Father...

This was meant more as a title of respect and affection, rather than as a statement of God's gender. Yahveh has no body, no human form,[c] and therefore no gender. This is a basic and fundamental tenet of the Israelite religion. You remember all those human bodily functions the ancient Israelites had to be cleansed of before they could approach any sacred area? Like contact with the dead, intercourse, menstruation, sickness and so on? The list of human physical functions that we were to separate and cleanse ourselves from before attending Temple, was **not** intended to give us the impression that these physical functions were bad or sinful; rather, they were to impress upon us that God has no physical functions, and therefore no corporeal body. This includes the fact that God has no human gender.

Now, Yeshua` was by no means the first prophet to call God

---

[a] (Ber. v. 1; Tosef., Demai, ii. 9; Soṭah ix, 15; Abot v. 20; Yoma viii. 9

[b] S.Yesh. 161:8; cf Mt 23:9

[c] Dt 4:12-15

'Father'. The prophet Isaiah twice called God 'Father':

'Surely You are our Father; though Abraham regard us not, and Israel recognise us not; You, O Yahveh, are our Father; from of old, Your Name is 'Our Redeemer'[a]

'Yet now, O Yahveh, You are our Father; we are the clay, and You are the Potter – we are all the work of Your hands'.[b]

This verse leads us to the first aspect of how God is our Father. In Hebrew, the 'father' of anything is its creator – for example, the father of a book is the author; so also is God the Author of all the unwritten laws of the physical Universe. Acknowledging God as Father means acknowledging God as our Creator. As God's creations, we are naturally meant to take on certain aspects and qualities of our Creator – this is a consequence of being made in the image and likeness of God.

For example, just as God cares for and looks after God's creation, so also as God's children, we are meant to take on the same rôle. We are stewards of God's creation, and are therefore meant to look after the land and everything on it and in it. To abuse the earth is to walk away from our responsibility towards God's creation.

This leads us onto the second aspect of how God is our Father. Just as God is compassionate, just, forgiving and merciful, so should we also be, as sons and daughters of our Heavenly Father. We were meant to become more than mere humans, who simply do what everyone else does. This is why Yeshua` taught us to forgive even our enemies and those who hate us, so that we could rightly be called 'children of our Father in heaven.'[c]

A Follower of the Way is called to show who their heavenly Father is by their way of life – by the way they are considerate of others, and by the way that they are kind and fair towards others. By doing this, our way of life shines before others, so that other people see that light, and give glory to our Father in heaven.[d]

Call no one 'Father', 'Rabbi' or 'Master'

As I mentioned earlier, Yeshua` instructed his followers to call no one 'Father', 'Teacher', or 'Master'.[e] This translates in Hebrew and Aramaic to titles such as *Abba*, *Rabbi* and *Mari* (*Moreh* – 'Teacher' or 'Guide' – was also used as a title in ancient times). The understanding that our community should not give our leaders honorific titles stem

---

[a] Isa 63:16
[b] Isa 64:7
[c] S.Yesh. 70:2; cf Mt 5:44
[d] S.Yesh. 74:3; cf Mt 5:16
[e] S.Yesh. 161:7-9; cf Mt 23:8-10

from this. In the modern Talmidi community, we can have job titles to describe what we do, but we do not address our leaders with honorific titles. Like the ancient Israelites, Talmidaism is egalitarian; if we were ever to have a Nasi to lead our community once more, then even he or she would not be addressed with a title – we would simply use his or her personal name (no matter how 'undeferential' that may sound to a non-Talmidi).

I recall a fundamentalist literalist once saying that we should not even call our parents 'father' or 'mother', 'mum' or 'dad' – because Yeshua` told us to *'call no one father on earth'.*[a] He obviously believed this because he was unaware of the cultural and historical background to this teaching of the prophet Yeshua`. If we do not address our parents as father or mother, mum or dad or some other similar words, this breaks the commandment to respect our father and our mother. And besides, calling your parents 'dad' or 'mum' is often a way of expressing one's love for them. Some common sense has to be used here therefore.

What Yeshua` was alluding to and speaking out against, was the habit of the leaders of various Jewish sects of his time to use titles, as if the titles in and of themselves gave their words legitimacy (whereas our parents have a legitimate right to be called father and mother). They would insist that everyone – even those who were not their followers – address them using an honorific title. *Abba, Rabbi, Mari* and *Moreh* were all titles given to some Jewish leader or other in the 1st century CE. It is a form of haughtiness and vain-glory which Yeshua` spoke out against. If you are addressing someone in our community for the first time, and you do not know their name, I think it is sufficient to open by calling them 'brother' or sister', and then using their first name once it is known.

Yeshua` would not have had the intention of dishonouring one's parents by going so far as to apply this rule even to one's natural parents – because calling them father and mother is justified. Rather, the intent of his teaching was to direct us as Followers of the Way to avoid giving titles to our leaders, or addressing them with honorific titles – because a title doesn't make what you say true. Understanding the cultural and historical background to this, helps us to apply this teaching sensibly. In Yeshua`'s teaching, leaders were not there to be raised up on a pedestal and be served, but render service themselves to the people they lead.

God is neither male nor female

Calling God 'Father' is not assigning God a gender. In a cultural environment which unfortunately banned and blotted out the personal

---

[a] S.Yesh. 161:8; cf Mt 23:9

name of God – Yahveh[a] – it was the only other way of making God close and personal. It was the only way to make God intimately 'real' to the ordinary, working class poor that the prophet Yeshua` originally spoke to.

It is unfortunate that the Hebrew language has no separate neuter pronouns – everything is either a 'he' or a 'she'. The best that Hebrew can do, is use the pronoun 'he' as a neuter pronoun for something with no gender (therefore, 'he' actually does not automatically assign a male gender in Hebrew). But as soon as the Hebrew for 'she' is used, it *immediately* has an unquestionable gender – *exclusively* female. That is why the male pronoun *hū* ('he') is used in Hebrew to refer to God in preference to *hī* ('she').

A good example of this 'gender assignment' becomes more obvious with plural pronouns. If you have a mixed group of men and women, then even if you have 99 women, and only one man, you still use the *male* pronoun for 'they' – *heim,* simply because it can be gender-neutral in Hebrew. However, once you have a group made up *exclusively* of women, then you have to use the female pronoun for 'they' – *hein.* In Hebrew, male pronouns do not immediately assign gender to what is being spoken about. However, as soon as you use a female pronoun, that makes it *exclusively* female.

I can fully sympathise with women who feel excluded from modern forms of worship because of the exclusion of feminine language with reference to God. I can understand that it can even feel oppressive and hurtful. In my personal opinion, if human language were not so restrictive, the male aspects of God would *also* be dispensed with when referring to Yahveh. It might be interesting to note here that the practice of more liberal Talmidis is to remove all gender references to God, as is the case also with Liberal Judaism.

At this point I feel the need to state categorically, that it is misleading to masculinise God, and project male images onto God; it would equally be misleading to *feminise* God, and project *female* images onto God. If the full impact of the Yahwist concept of God were to be realised, then because of the language we would then have to use, not only would women feel excluded, but *men* would feel excluded too!

It is not the case that God is both male and female; it is rather the case that Yahveh is *neither* male nor female. To see Yahveh as *both* male and female is to see God in human terms – to create God in our own image. It is easy to fall into the misleading trap of saying that Yahveh

---

[a] We do not know the exact pronunciation of God's name – some use Yehovah. My advice is to use whichever form of the name is sacred and meaningful to you.

has both male and female attributes. Doing this would be looking at God as if God were a human being, albeit of mixed gender. There is no point in looking for the male side of God, *or* the female side of God, because that would be attempting to divide God up into something that God cannot be divided into. Yahveh is not a conjoined being, nor part one thing and part another; *rather it is we who are halflings of what God is.*

Some people have tried to use both male and female language when referring to God, but all this succeeds in doing is make God into a 'duo-inity' (instead of a 'trinity'), with a **definite** male and female aspect. This would be reverting to the Canaanite experience of God, which always portrayed their main deities in male-female couples. Our God would end up as a male-female couple – 'two persons in one God'.[a]

Language – and more than that, the human experience – is inadequate to define God. The male and female aspects of Yahveh are inseparable and inextricably intertwined. That's why I say that it is better to say that Yahveh is neither male nor female.

Maleness and femaleness are limited *human* concepts that we need to put behind us if we want to even begin to understand God. Therefore, we need to redefine ourselves in terms of what *God* is, not define God in terms of what *we* are. Yahveh is a whole; it is we humans who are imperfect fractions of God's personality. It is we humans who are divided into halves of what God is, not the other way round.

If we look at God's personality, describing it in divine rather than human terms, I think we end up coming to the same point but from different directions. God is capable of unconditional, nourishing, tender love, which in our limited human way of looking at things, is mostly – but not exclusively – a female quality. The Israelite experience of Yahveh is also as a mighty warrior-defender who stands up for the voiceless, the weak and oppressed, which in our limited human way of looking at things, is mostly, but not exclusively, a male quality.

Men need to deal with a God who, in human terms, also has feminine qualities. If men need to have a male God in order to be able to identify with God, and if women need a *female* God in order to be able to identify with God, then *both* are doing their respective spiritualities an unhelpful disservice; it is a sign of the inadequacy of our image of ourselves, rather than any failure on the part of the nature of God.

Both men and women need to get to grips with a God who has what we humans perceive to be *both* male and female qualities, and stop trying to make God human in order to be able to identify with God as men or women – because you can't humanise God. God isn't human;[b] therefore,

---

[a] as compared to the trinitarian refrain: 'Three persons in one God'.

[b] Hos 11:9b 'For I am God, and not a man - the Holy One among you.'

men should stop looking for the maleness in God, and women should stop looking for the femaleness in God. Yahveh is unlike any human either in form or in personality,[a] so there is no point in giving God human attributes in order to feel comfortable with God, or in order to be able to identify with God. Otherwise, we would be remaking God in our own image, rather than acknowledging that God made us – 'male and female'[b] – in God's image. In a sense, God divided Himself in order to create us.

We define human qualities in God in order to identify with God or to relate better to God, but of course God is not human and never can be. We're looking at this issue the wrong way round. The only spiritual journey worth making in this respect, is one that seeks out the heavenly self within us. Rather than looking for our human qualities in God, the more profitable journey is to connect with God by defining *what are God's heavenly qualities within us*.

In the past, feminist historians have looked at ancient Israelite history, and come to the conclusion that it is a catalogue of expunging the femaleness of God. However, in the ancient, pagan sanctuaries of the Canaanites, there were representations of both male *and* female deities. The Asherah pole, which took the place of a natural tree, represented the female deity, and the Baal stone, or *matzéivah*, represented the male god. Most people are aware that the ancient Israelites were told to burn and destroy the Asherah poles, and feminists take this as the oppression of the female side of God. However, few are aware that the *matzéivah* – the symbol of the male pagan gods – *also* had to be removed.[c] In a sense, we could say that both femaleness *and* maleness, which were an essential part of the Canaanite way of seeing their gods, were being renounced completely by the Yahwist Israelite faith.

People also look at religious ritual, claiming that this vulgarises female aspects too. For example, when a woman has finished her menstruation, she is supposed to immerse in a *miqveh*[d] before she attends anything that requires a person to be in a state of ritual purity. However, the same also applies to a man when he has had a seminal emission.[e] This is nothing to do with either instance being bad, sinful or unwholesome; it is more to do with the ancient Yahwist practise of

---

[a] Num 23:19 'God is not a man, that he should have to lie, nor a human being, that he should have to change His mind.'.

[b] Gen 1:27 – 'God created humanity in His own image, in the image of God He created him *(i.e. humanity)*; male and female He created them.

[c] Deut 16:21-22

[d] a ritual immersion pool, with steps leading down one side, and more steps leading up out of the water on the other.

[e] Lev 15:16-18

emphasising that Yahveh has no bodily functions – neither of the male kind, nor of the female kind. The ritual immersion therefore marks a separation between what is human, and what is divine.

Nevertheless, admittedly the Hebrew bible does contain both male and female allusions to God, which don't come out in English. In Numbers 11:15, when Moses addresses God as 'You', he uses the feminine form of the word. And in Isaiah 49:15, God describes Himself as a mother who will not forget her children.

In Hebrew, the word 'father' is used both for male and female ancestors (*avot*); in Hebrew, masculine verbs are used to cover groups of both genders – it's not as clear-cut as it is in English. And in the Dead Sea Scrolls, when the pronoun 'He' (in Hebrew 'hū', spelt he-vav-alef) is used of God, it is often written with an ambiguous vav that looks half-way between a vav and a yod, so that it could be read as either hī (She) or hū (He).

There is a strength of 'bothness' that exists in biblical Hebrew language that we miss in English translations, and I think that causes problems. At the end of it all, as long as we instil in our hearts the wholeness of what God is, and acknowledge that whatever kind of language we use to describe God will always be inadequate, I think God will not hold this against us. God knows our limitations, and loves us in spite of them (or maybe even, because of them).

On the position of women in the community

Early on in the development of our modern community, there was a desire to improve the image and position of women in our groups. For centuries, Religion has not been kind to women – primarily because men have run the show for most of human history; given power, men will become drunk on it, and promulgate the most unjust rules and regulations. The unjustness of many of religion's rules, indicate to the innermost human soul – which was created by Yahveh – that these rules do not come from God. For example, Paul of Tarsus wrote that it was improper for a woman to speak in church,[a] and that a woman was created for the sake of a man;[b] that a woman was subordinate to a man,[c] and was to be obedient to her husband.[d]

The Quran teaches that the testimony of a woman is worth half that

---

[a] 1Cor 14:5
[b] 1Cor 11;7, 11:9
[c] 1Cor 11:3
[d] 1Tim 2:11-12

of a man's,[a] that men are in charge of women,[b] that a woman is there to satisfy a man's sexual needs,[c] that a husband is allowed to beat his wife into submission,[d] and that most women will go to hell.[e]

The prophet Yeshua` on the other hand, engaged with women. He didn't segregate himself from them – they were an integral part of his community of followers, and he called them to join with him in meals, as he did with Mary and Martha in Bethany. However, he wasn't doing something new – he wasn't instituting a new ruling overturning Torah, he was actually returning us to Yahveh's original way of thinking: *'male and female he created them'*.

Genesis says that God made a woman out of a man's rib. Now, I personally don't take this literally. In fact, science suggests that it was female creatures which came first – that is, primitive creatures early on in the evolution of life that could bear and bring forth offspring; and that males arose only afterwards as a way of enabling genes to mix. Nevertheless, the story in Genesis still has something valuable to say to us.

Eve (*Chavah* in Hebrew) is described as being created out of Adam's rib, and flesh was enclosed over it. In a midrash[f] from the *Targum*[g] *Yonatan*, the flesh used is said to have been part of Adam's heart. Now, to the modern, Western mind, the bible story seems to say that woman is made only of a small, insignificant part of a man. However, to an ancient Israelite – and even to a modern Hebrew speaker – this choice of a rib near the heart is significant.

---

[a] *All the references below from the Quran are from David Wood's YouTube channel, Acts17Apologetics.* Surah 2:282 – if 2 men are not available as witnesses, then 1 man and 2 women are acceptable. Mohammed taught this was due to the deficiency of a woman's mind (Sahih al-Bukhari 2658).

[b] Surah 4:34 – because God made man to excel over women.

[c] Surah 2:223 – that a woman cannot object to or refuse her husband's demands for sex – see also Sunan ibn Majah 1853 and Jami at-Tirmidhi 1160. Surah 4:24 says that a man can force the wife of another man to have sex with him if she has been captured in war; it's not considered adultery (see also Abu Dawud 2150).

[d] Surah 4:34 – a man should beat a rebellious wife until she submits to him. In Sahih al-Bukhari 5825, Mohammed's wife Aisha complained to Mohammed that Muslim women were being treated even worse than pagan women; Mohammed's response was to rebuke the beaten woman for being a bad wife.

[e] Mohammed said that most of the people in hell are women (Sahih al-Bukari 1052), because women curse too much, lack common sense and are ungrateful to their husbands (Sahih Muslim 142).

[f] a midrash is an explanatory story and commentary contained within a translation of the bible.

[g] A Targum is an Aramaic translation of the Bible

To the ancients, the seat of human personality and emotion was not the brain, but the heart (in Hebrew, the word *lev* means both 'heart' and 'mind'). It was exceedingly significant that a bone **near the heart** was taken, as well as flesh from the heart itself. This implies that much more than just a small, insignificant piece of a man was taken to make a woman.

If the original human personality was created to be in the image of God, then like God, we are given to assume that originally, the human personality **was also a balance of male and female qualities**; psychologically, Adam was not 'man' as a man is now. When God took Adam's rib, and enclosed it with the flesh of his heart, God in effect *divided the human personality in two*, giving some of God's traits to the woman, and giving the man what was left of God's traits. Woman, in effect, was given what was close to God's 'heart'.

In Israelite tradition, the matriarchs are just as important in their contribution to Yahwist spirituality as the patriarchs. In the time of the Israelite Judges, Deborah was a leader and 'judge' (that is, a warrior-defender) of the Israelites as much as any male leader. And in the Ten Commandments, Ex 20:12 tells us to honour our father and our mother, but then in Lev 19:3, it tells us to honour our mother and our father – it reverses the order of the two. In Jewish tradition, this tells us that mother and father have equal authority in the family.

Some will respond by saying that Yeshua` only had male apostles, but this argument doesn't cut it. Yeshua` was working in the culture he was born into, and it would have been difficult for him to go around with 6 women and 6 men. The fact is, he *did* have a lot of female followers who supported his ministry – several women with the name Mary (a very common female name) are named in the gospels, along with a number of others.

I recall seeing a series of programmes[a] in the 1990's about the Marranos[b] in Portugal. For centuries, while the Jewish faith was forbidden and hidden, it was the Jewish *women* who kept the faith alive, who passed the faith onto their children, and who were the caretakers of the customs and traditions of Israel. Without access to the mainstream rabbinic community, all they knew was what the Hebrew scriptures taught them. So in their hidden, secret communities, men and women were considered equal, and mixed gatherings were the norm. Then, only a couple of years after the programmes were made, they were pressured into conforming to the Orthodox tradition – in prayer services the

---

[a] 1992, *'Out of Spain: the Crypto-Jews of Portugal'*, episode 6-7, recounting the story of the Marrano community of Belmonte in northern Portugal.

[b] Jews who were forcibly converted to Christianity in Spain and Portugal, but who secretly practised the Jewish faith.

women, who were once prayer-leaders and the guardians of their community, were relegated to a back room, apart from the men, and all teaching authority was stripped from them. I felt so very sad for the women. This shows me what freedom men and women have under God, and what subjugation women suffer under man's rules.

In the Talmidi community, no religious positions are closed to women.[a] It is quite conceivable that, should our community be blessed with a Nasi once more – a leader in the tradition of Jacob the Pious and Shimon bar Qlofas – that such a Nasi might even be a woman.

Talmidaism is about mutual respect; a man should not oppress or ill-treat a woman, and a woman should not oppress or ill-treat a man. A healthy Yahwist society is one where all of its members are accorded equal dignity and respect.

A light for the world, and salt for the earth

When a good person sees others doing bad things, it is easy for the good person to become disheartened. It is easy to fall into a rut of thinking, 'What's the point when there are so many people around me doing bad things?'

People in Yeshua`'s day were faced with the same depressing thoughts. Ordinary, decent people could see the blatant wrongdoings around them – the corruption, the ill-treatment of good people, the weight of debt on the poor, the increase in crime and banditry, and the cruelty of the occupying Romans. They were faced with the same thought: 'What's the point?'

So Yeshua` told good people two things – he gave them two basic instructions: be a light for the world, and be as salt for the earth. You, as a good and decent person, are here with a mission. God sent you here to earth with a purpose – God didn't just send Yeshua` to earth, Yahveh sent **you** to earth too! Now, people cannot see God, but they can see you. They can see the good things you do, and they will gravitate towards that. Your goodness will help reach out to people around you, and the people you need to touch will be touched, and the wrongdoers around you – well, leave them to God. Your job is to be a light on God's behalf:

'No one lights a lamp and covers it with a basket, or puts it under a bed. Instead, they put it on a stand, so that it gives light to the whole house. And when someone enters the house, they'll see that light. In the same way, let your light shine before others, so that they may see that

---

[a] that is, apart from a priest, which Torah restricts to born male descendants of Aaron. *However*, outside of the Temple, any woman or man who is not an Aaronic Levite, can perform the same pastoral and ritual functions of a priest, by permanently taking on the Nazirite vow.

light, and glorify your heavenly Father.[a]

In the same vein, we are also exhorted to be as salt for the earth.[b] In modern secular usage, if you call someone 'the salt of the earth', it means that they are 'one of the people', someone who is an ordinary person, unpretentious, hardworking and reliable. I think we have Chaucer's *Summoner's Tale*, written in 1386, to thank (or blame) for this false application of the phrase. Even though he took the phrase from the *New Testament*, he used it in an entirely different way to the one Yeshua` intended. If we are to understand the metaphorical image that Yeshua` was trying to put across, we have to leave aside modern and non-Jewish references.

First, let's look at what salt was used for in *Jewish* culture. Its widest use is obviously universal – to bring out the flavour of food, as well as to preserve it. Other uses were to sanctify and purify sacrifices, and it was also a symbol of God's Covenant with Israel. It was even used in the tanning process of leather.

In the Jewish context, to 'act as salt' would be to bring out the best in others – to act as a kind of catalyst which draws out faithfulness to God and God's ways. It also implies someone who *encourages* others to be faithful to God's ways.

Yeshua`'s saying also talks about salt losing its flavour. So the next question is: how can salt possibly lose its saltiness or usefulness? In the tanning process, the salt becomes contaminated by the tanning agents, and therefore cannot be used again. You cannot reuse it for anything – neither for food, for sacrifices, or even for tanning. It cannot even be thrown on a compost heap, because if you used the salted compost, you would poison any fields you threw the compost onto.

It is possible that Yeshua` was warning his followers not to become contaminated by the ways of the world. He was exhorting us to maintain our outlook and behaviour in accordance with God's teachings, encouraging us not to allow the bad outlook, behaviour or habits of others to bring us down or make us disheartened.

Finally, how does this apply to our daily lives? Well, to be a light for the world, is to act in such a way as your positive outlook and decent behaviour draw others to God's light. So also acting as salt, brings out the best in others. In Yeshua`'s time, he expected his followers to live their lives in such a way that their words and actions would encourage others to lead better lives, and return to God's ways.

And if people around you don't seem to be taking any notice, don't become disheartened – you are doing your God-given job, and you may

---

[a] S.Yesh. 74:1-3 – cf Mt 5:14-16, Lk 8:16, 11:33, Mk 4:21
[b] Mg. Ms. 73:1-2 – cf Mt 5:13

be influencing people in ways you are entirely unaware of. You might even affect people you don't even know.

As Followers of the Way, we have a responsibility to be like salt and light. In the way we live our lives, in the words we say, in the things we do, we can tacitly influence others to act in a similar way. We should resist going along with the crowd, and behaving in the same way as others. And do not be disheartened. Going against the grain is often very difficult, and will bring taunts and criticism. But ultimately it makes people think. It challenges others to realise that there is another way, that there is a better way to doing things. This is how we sow the seeds of the Kingdom in others' hearts and minds.

So be as salt to the peoples of the earth, and as light for the nations of the world.

Wholeness and Perfection

Yeshua` also told us to be perfect like our heavenly Father.[a] Few people today are aware of what this means – it doesn't mean 'sinlessness' or never doing wrong. To understand what being 'perfect' means in Yahwist Israelite terms, you have to understand how the ancients understood the nature of the human soul.

Yahveh, our heavenly Father, knows we are not perfect (in the modern English sense of the word). Yahveh knows that we will trip up and make mistakes. We should not become terrified of ever making a mistake, or give up and conclude there is no use in trying to be perfect, just because we never will be. The important thing is that we keep *trying*.

In the ancient Israelite way of thinking, when a person sinned, or when they became ill, the wholeness of their being (their life-force or *néfesh*) was diminished. In the case of sin, repentance obtained forgiveness, but reparation and good works restored the soul to a healthy wholeness – to a state of 'perfection' or 'completeness' – that is what being perfect means in Aramaic and Hebrew – being healthy, complete and whole. One could maintain this state by following God's ethical laws – being merciful, just, compassionate, considerate, and so on. A complete or 'perfect' soul was not sinless, but maintained a dignified and peaceful bearing, and was a light to others.

In the case of illness diminishing one's wholeness, the healer was seen as the messenger of God. Ultimately God was the Great Healer, and worked through the human healer. The goal of our daily lives is to maintain this wholeness – that is, the health and wellbeing – of our souls, the healthy completeness of our being. In doing so, we will be imitating

---

[a] Mg.Ms. 10:1; cf Mt 5:48

our Heavenly Father, who is ever whole and complete. And when Yeshua` advised the rich young man[a] to follow the ethical commandments of God, he told him that in doing so he would be perfect – again, this is what was being referred to, the healthy wholeness of his being. A perfect soul is a whole and healthy soul. Being perfect therefore like our Heavenly Father, means working towards the healthy wholeness of our souls. When Yeshua` said, 'Be perfect, as your Heavenly Father is perfect,' this is what he meant. We are to maintain the wholeness – the health and wellbeing – of our soul, the healthy completeness of our being. In doing so, we will be imitating our Heavenly Father.

Creating an atmosphere of 'warmsomeness'

A whole, complete and healthy society functions in a certain way. This atmosphere of 'social wholeness' – social *shleimut* – is not achieved without hard work, however. It needs a commitment to get there, a belief that we can get there, and a constant vigilance against complacency once it has been achieved.

On the Sabbath, we create an atmosphere of *ne`imut* – pleasantness, geniality and cosiness. The Sabbath has to be set apart – different and special from any other day in the week. On the Sabbath therefore, you leave behind your problems, anything that upsets or annoys you, and you seek out those things that bring you comfort in the Presence of Yahveh. You also spend time with people who will help you create this sacred, warm and pleasant atmosphere of Shabbat.

Being human, there is a downside to this. Most people forget that our Yahveh is not a one-day-a-week God! Agreed, the Sabbath has to be holy and different to the other days of the week. However, this does not mean confining human warmth and spiritual goodness to that one day. Human society often gets into the conflictive, discontented and simmering mood that it is in, because we do not allow Yahveh to penetrate and permeate the rest of the days of our week.

There isn't really an English equivalent to *ne`imut*. In German they call it *Gemütlichkeit*; in Swedish it is translated as *Gemytlig*, and in Danish it is called *Hygge*. It is basically an atmosphere that is consciously created by behaving in a warm, friendly, convivial and genial manner. It is important, because it has wider implications. It is conducive to a mind-set of cooperativeness, helpfulness, modesty, living according to your means, mutual trust and respect – respect not only for those around you, but also for your resources and your land. This positive atmosphere is built in the absence of anything annoying, irritating or

---

[a] S.Yesh. 171; cf Mt 19:16-22, Lk 18:18-23, Mk 10:17b-22

emotionally overwhelming, but rather deliberately replete with comforting, calm and soothing things.

In the absence of an English word for this, I have created one: Warmsomeness. Creating a warmsome atmosphere – an atmosphere of *ne`imut* – for example in a school, creates an ethos of mutual respect, and is conducive to teenagers growing into balanced adults, rather than angry, confrontational sociopaths. *Ne`imut* in the workplace eliminates the 'us-and-them' attitude, and fosters an atmosphere of cooperation and purpose. *Ne`imut* in politics encourages politicians to realise that they serve not themselves or their financial or political interests, but rather the people who elected them. It encourages politicians to put the wellbeing of their society and their country above the ideals of their political party.

There is also some scientific indication that it is in the interests of a government to encourage economic and social *ne`imut*. When a government forces the mind-set of absolute competitiveness upon its population, causing unwanted stress to become an ingrained way of life, this has a knock-on genetic effect. The science of epigenetics[a] tells us that external factors, such as stress and pollution, can actually cause various genes to get switched on or off. Stress effects DNA to the extent that subsequent generations become more violent and aggressive, just to cope with genetically perceived threats to the survival of the individual and the species. A society can be economically competitive without forcing its citizens to struggle simply to survive, thereby making it easier for poorer people to be exploited. A stressed society inevitably becomes a *genetically* more violent society.

There will of course be some who say that human beings are not flawless, and that warmsomeness is a totally unreasonable ideal. However, if we have no ideals, what else is there to reach for, but selfishness, greed, conflict and violence?

The opposite mind-set to that of warmsomeness is that of the psychopath. I will talk about this in greater depth later on in this book. A psychopath isn't just someone who murders and commits heinous crimes; there is something called, 'psychopathic personality disorder' or PPD. These individuals constitute about 2% of any given human population. They are self-centred, narcissistic, uncaring, manipulative, greedy and materialistic. They also have a disproportionate influence on the values of human society, disturbingly greater than their small numbers warrant.

A psychopath will typically hold views such as: teaching your

---

[a] this is the scientific understanding that environmental factors actually cause certain of our genes to be turned on or off, which is then passed on to the next generation.

children to have ethical values is a danger to their success; that having concern for others or helping others is only for weaklings; that the needs of society are irrelevant; that it's OK to step over others and make their lives miserable in order to get what you want; that you have to be materially successful in order to be respected as a human being; that if you are not constantly striving to achieve or attain wealth, then you have no useful part to play in human society; that having free time to spend with your children or loved ones is a threat to the economic success of society; that you have to be aggressively competitive, otherwise you will never be successful or happy in life; and that the intrinsic usefulness of anything in life is judged by how much money it can generate.

If your society is based on these above values, then worry indeed! Not least because these values perpetuate themselves – they pass on psychopathic values to each successive generation. A society that holds psychopathic values should not be surprised if it has a high rate of poverty, violence or murder!

Such a society probably also has a high number of people with psychopathic personalities in positions of influence. To protect these ungodly values, they will manipulate their fellow citizens to ensure that their values and their high position in society remain unchallenged, without any care or concern for the cruel effects of their manipulation. They will typically end up leading by the nose that section of human society which does not like change.

Ne'imut – warmsomeness – is the best contribution that any individual can make towards creating a society in which such psychopathic personalities cannot function. A society that values warmsomeness is generally a happy, balanced and less violent society.[a]

Giving worship to God through the sacredness of life

The English word 'worship' comes from the Anglo-Saxon word *weorþscipe*, which means 'worthship' – that is, the act of giving worth or honour to a deity. That act can be expressed in many different ways. I would like to show you that worship is not just confined to being inside a synagogue, a church or a mosque.

In traditional religious congregations, worship is performed by praying and singing together. Some prefer well-established or classical tunes, some folk music. Some people value silent prayer, some the words of spoken and congregational prayers. However, most people understand

---

[a] Denmark, for whose people *Hygge* (warmsomeness) is a long-standing cultural value, is consistently ranked amongst the happiest countries in the world.

worship as something that is done in a building, which involves the obligation to be in that building regularly on a particular day of every week. For some people, this in itself becomes an empty exercise. For some people, it has become an exercise in parochial control on the part of ministers of religion over their congregants.

Some people prefer instead to meet and pray in each other's homes. Some prefer to have a space set apart in their home as a prayer-space, somewhere they can be alone with God in private prayer – Yeshua` himself envisioned this to be an option for prayer when he said, *'when you pray, go into your innermost room and shut the door, and pray to your Father who's in secret places; and your heavenly Father who sees what's done in secret will reward you.'*[a] In Middle Eastern Jewish homes, the prayer space was sometimes indicated by a simple, framed prayer in Hebrew, placed on the wall to signpost the direction of the Temple in Jerusalem – towards which all Jewish prayer was directed.

I would encourage each congregation and each person to work out for themselves what form of worship is most meaningful for them – and to be sensible in the endeavour; but I also want to show you that worship – giving honour to God – is not just confined to our times of communal or private prayer.

A group of people who have come together to provide food for the poor, or tend to the sick – whether people or animals; or to defend the rights of the least in society, or to find shelter for the homeless, or to rescue those who have suffered in natural disasters, or to educate those who otherwise would never receive education, or to make a barren part of God's creation come to life again, or to reconcile enemies who have been at war for generations – these are all worthy acts of worship for our living God. These real things in the real world also give honour to Yahveh, and magnify the souls of those who engage in them.

For religious people who cling to the old ways of looking at God – as a distant being up there, who can only be connected to in designated sacred places, and who only exists for us to ask and get things from – God becomes an unreachable mystery, and in the modern world, that God is an increasing irrelevance. To a Follower of the Way, whose faith is about the real world, and about a God who is interconnected with real life and present in the daily sacredness of life, Yahveh is here and now alongside us, to be experienced in the immersion of the human soul in the real task of living in the present moment.

Worship ultimately affirms that to which we ascribe worth. When we have engaged in acts in life which give worth to the values and precepts of Yahveh, such as those examples I have listed above, the act

---

[a] S.Yesh. 57:3-4, cf Mt 6:6

then of sanctifying those acts with prayer – with communion with God – becomes all the more meaningful. An act of worship affirms life and that which we love, celebrates the good, and brings us into the living presence of God; sometimes that presence can even be found in the faces of our brothers and sisters whom God has placed alongside us here on earth, to help one another in our journeys towards God's Kingdom.

The importance of not being fooled by religious charlatans

There is another aspect – another responsibility – involved in acknowledging Yahveh as our Father. In Deuteronomy chapter 13, we are told not to follow people who perform signs and miracles in order to entice us to fall for other gods or their religions. These signs and miracles may even be real, and their predictions may indeed come true; but if their intent is to encourage followers of Yahveh to follow a different god and a different religion instead, then we are to ignore these signs. The trueness of a sign does not validate the message it supports; if you follow a message because of signs, then your faith will be weak. A true message does not need signs to support or prove it; a true message proves itself.

Throughout Israelite and Jewish history, people have faked prophecy. Today, evangelicals think that prophecy is basically the first ecstatic thing that comes into their head. But fake prophecy defames the reputation of God's holiness; to claim that something is a prophecy from Yahveh when it actually isn't, comes with a very heavy price for the faker. Prophecy is meant to act as a warning from God, so that people change, and so that bad things don't happen. False prophets manipulate people by telling them that the natural disasters around them are God's judgment, so that they will become frightened, so that gullible people follow them. The intent of real prophecy is to get people to change and become better people; the intent of false prophecy is to get people to become frightened. God is even able to send deceptive prophecy Himself, if it will cause the vainglorious to fall and make fools of themselves.[a]

A community which gives false prophets free rein, lays itself open to charlatans who take pleasure from deception, and seek power over others who blindly follow them. A community with false prophets becomes a laughing stock when their prophecies are proved false; a community with false prophets blithely sleepwalks down a road that leads to spiritual ruin and ill-repute amongst the world community of faiths.

---

[a] 1Kgs 22:23

Yahveh says through the prophet Isaiah:[a]

"I will frustrate false prophets and their omens,
and make fools of diviners;
I will drive back their sages
and make their wisdom look stupid.
But I will confirm my servants' prophecies,
and make my messengers' plans succeed."

The false prophet loses all credibility, and they are cut off from the blessings of God. A false prophet therefore gains no wisdom, and his or her soul is not purified or cleansed by God's glory; they gain no understanding or discernment, and they never get the opportunity to walk with God in this life. Through the prophet Ezekiel,[b] Yahveh says:

"My hand will be against the prophets who have futile visions and produce false divinations; they will not be allowed into the council of my people, or be written in the book of the house of Israel, or enter the land of Israel. Then you will know that I am Yahveh God."

A community on the other hand that forbids prophets, cannot be warned by God when terrible religious or social catastrophes are about to happen to their people; without prophets, a people will be given fallible and misleading rules and interpretations. These mistakes will be compounded over the centuries and generations, until the only things such a community is left with are mistakes layered over errors, without any form of escape or liberation. And a people without prophets – genuine, God-centred prophets[c] that is – cannot be protected from unscrupulous individuals who lead their faith into violence and ruin; a violent religious community has no prophet to tell them that God disapproves *vehemently* of their actions.

In contrast, a religious community that is renewed in every generation by the knowledge and experience of the living God, will ensure that their collective faith is not contaminated by the errors and prejudices of human misjudgement.

King Solomon warns us[d] that deceptive people have the ability to

---

[a] Isa 44:25-26
[b] Ezekiel 13:9
[c] a man or woman who is genuinely called and guided by Yahveh, whose overriding concern is for the upholding of Yahwist values, without concern for their own welfare or their safety. They typically have no desire for influence, money or power.
[d] in Proverbs 26:24-26

say positive and pleasant things to us. Such people have the expertise to say things which are not from Yahveh, but which sound good and pleasing enough to the human heart. Throughout Israelite history, Middle Eastern pagan beliefs have enticed Israelites, and caused us to become attracted to beliefs and practises which were not from Yahveh. The best way to protect oneself from these traps is to 'know Yahveh'.[a]

There are many religious cults and sects around today. You can tell unhealthy sects from decent ones by the general ethos they project. Sects tend to project the personality of the person who founded them.[b] If the founder was an angry, tyrannical, unbalanced individual, intolerant of differences of opinion, then that will be what the faith builds itself upon, even generations after the leader is gone. However, if a sect is willing to seek God, to know God and find out what God is truly like, and base their faith on that, then instead for generations throughout all eternity, their sect will be a vehicle for the true values and teachings of God.

Beware therefore of any religious community which becomes violent when faced even with fair criticism; a wise and noble faith will be strong enough to stand up to fair criticism, and answer any critiques with grace and dignified composure. Beware any religion that forbids its followers and others to delve into its origins and foundation, or to cast a critical eye over its scriptures;[c] for a true faith has nothing to hide – Talmidaism, after all, is all about the honest and responsible interpretation of scripture.[d] And beware of any religion which threatens death against those who disagree with them; a true and strong faith will not be threatened by disagreement. If someone leaves Talmidaism as a simple result of no longer having the conviction of Talmidi beliefs and principles, then the godly response is to part amicably – not with hate, but with acceptance. Our God is not a tyrant.

Now, there are some people who say that God is unknowable. This is not true! A false god is unknowable, because such a god doesn't exist, but Yahveh is knowable – just not completely knowable. Yahveh has a

---

[a] cf Jer 31:34, 1Chron 22:19; in the Yahwist Israelite faith, Yahveh is a knowable God. Only a false god is unknowable.

[b] for example, the faith of someone who concentrates on the teachings of Yeshua` alone, will project quite a different aura to someone who concentrates on the teachings of Paul of Tarsus. The difference is between someone who sees the basic good in others, and shows compassion and humility towards all, and someone who sees the basic bad in others, and is spiritually belligerent and uncompromising.

[c] For example, the Quran forbids asking critical questions about scripture and the religion, Surah 5:101 – "O Believers, ask not about things which, if made plain to you, may cause you discomfort." Questioning Islam therefore becomes a sin.

[d] Sefer Ya`aqov 29:3

personality, qualities and traits which are discernible to those who love God and follow God. In this way, if someone approaches a follower of Yahveh, and claims something about Yahveh which he or she knows is not part of Yahveh's personality, then that follower will automatically know such a person is lying. If someone from another religion tells you that their god is the same as ours, examine the personality of that god – what that god claims and what that god 'says'. Would Yahveh say the same things as their god?

For example, during the Second Temple period, many Jewish people started believing in horoscopes. It was common at that time to even find mosaics of the Zodiac signs on the floors of synagogues. However, the Yahwist attitude to astrology is found in Lev 19:31 – *'Do not turn to mediums or seek out spiritists, for you will be defiled by them. I am Yahveh your God.'* Practises such as divination, fortune telling and consulting the dead were considered pagan practises, and not something that a follower of Yahveh was to get involved in.

In modern times, we have seen certain religious groups become troubled by astrological signs and portents. They have come to rely on various celestial alignments of planets and stars, and as a result, declare that 'The end-times are near!' But again, this is a pagan way of seeing and understanding such things, because through the prophet Jeremiah, Yahveh has told us, *"Do not learn to follow the ways of the Gentiles, nor be dismayed by signs in the heavens – let the Gentiles be dismayed by them instead!"* [a]

Even those who consider themselves above such things, still maintain a pagan attitude of needing to know the future. For example, the purpose of prophecy is not to know the future, but to warn people that terrible things will happen if the current bad state of affairs does not change. If people repent and change, then the terrible future will not happen – which is the end of the relevance of such a future on the present.

Unfortunately, some people search through prophecies as if they were horoscopes, and instead of concentrating on the core message in them – 'Repent, become better people and you can avoid terrible consequences,' – they scrutinise the parts about 'the terrible things that might happen if people don't repent', as if these possible events were the heart of the message. We are not supposed to try to figure out what might happen in the future from prophecies; that's not what they are for. [b]

Often the future frightens us. We cannot control the future, and it

---

[a] Jer 10:2

[b] How many times have religious people claimed to know when the end of the world will be, and gotten egg on their faces when it doesn't happen? The only person who knows when the end will be is Yahveh; not even his angels know (S.Yesh. 163:4 – cf Mt 24:26)

seems that knowing what might happen in the future gives some people the feeling that they do indeed have some control over it. That feeling is, unfortunately, a false feeling of security.

Someone who knows and follows Yahveh, their heavenly Father, will feel safe and secure in God's care. They will trust the embrace of God's love. Such people do not feel a need to know what lies in the future, because they are not afraid of it; they know that if they walk according to the advice and teachings of their heavenly Father – if they *'do justice, love mercy, and walk humbly with God'*[a] – they will always have the wise guidance of their Heavenly Father with them to lead them through the uncertainties of life.

In Yeshua`'s day, the Zealots sought to bring about the messianic kingdom with violence, not only by killing Romans, but also by killing our own people when they disagreed with their methods. The Zealots persuaded and deceived many into thinking that what they were doing was the right thing to do – that God Himself would want such a thing. But those who knew and trusted their Father in heaven would have known that their methods were not God's methods, and that it was wrong – evil even – to kill in God's Name.

God does not require the blood sacrifice of anyone

Here's another good example of the necessity of knowing the personality of our heavenly Father. In the 7th century BCE, there was an Ammonite god called Molekh. His followers claimed that if one sacrificed an only-begotten child, then the death of that child could bring about the permanent forgiveness of sin and redeem you. In other words, you would gain permanent salvation from your sins. This cult gained a foothold amongst the Israelites, and they began giving their children over to death through fire, so that they could be saved from their sins, and gain permanent salvation. These followers even began claiming that this Molekh was an incarnation of Yahveh.[b]

This way of thinking horrified and repulsed Yahveh to such a degree, that God instructed the prophet Jeremiah to tell this to the Israelites:

> *'The people of Judah have done evil in my eyes, declares Yahveh. . . . They have . . . burn[ed] their sons and daughters*

---

[a] Micah 6:8

[b] It was the common practice in ancient pagan religions, to find equivalents of their gods in other religions. So Zeus in the Greek religion, becomes Jupiter in the Roman religion. However, it is a fundamental assertion of the Israelite faith that Yahveh has no equal or incarnation.

*in the fire – something I did not command, nor did such a thing
even enter My mind.'*

A true follower of Yahveh would have known that Yahveh would
not invent anything that would require the death of anyone's son to bring
about salvation from sin. Such a concept would never have entered
Yahveh's mind. The Israelite followers of Molekh should have realised
that such a concept was alien and abhorrent to Yahveh. So when
Molekh's followers came telling them that Molekh was an incarnation
of Yahveh, they should have known that such a thing was a lie; they
should have remembered what Yahveh had taught them – that no one
can die for another person's sin.[a]

Around the world, you find cultures that degenerate into human
sacrifice when things get tough. In ancient Britain in the 7th century
BCE, when the climate started to change and crops failed, some ancient
Britons turned to human sacrifice in the hope that their crops might grow.
The ancient Minoans on Thera – a highly advanced civilisation – turned
to human sacrifice when earthquakes and volcanic eruptions became a
fearful constant in their lives. And after the arrival of the Spanish, when
faced with diseases they had not known before, the Chachapoya of Peru
turned to human sacrifice, falsely thinking that the death of an innocent
would bring them salvation.

It was common around the world in ancient times to think that the
shedding of innocent blood would appease the wrath of a god or obviate
some misfortune – it's a common, universal, but **pagan** way of thinking.
Such thinking might have given pagans a warm, fuzzy feeling to think
that an innocent had willingly given up his life for them, but to Yahveh,
such a way of thinking was abhorrent and repugnant – *and is always so,
and will always be.* Such a concept would never enter the mind of
Yahveh. Why? Because Yahveh is not appeased with blood or death, but
with a change of heart, a turning of the mind to choose life. A person
who knows Yahveh – the knowable God – would not be fooled by claims
to the contrary, no matter how persistent or forceful.

Even today, it is important to get to know Yahveh, so that if anyone
comes to tell you something about the God of Abraham that you have
previously known not to be true, even if they speak sweet words and
perform showy miracles, and claim that their god is our God, then you

---

[a] Ex 32:30-34 (where Moses tried to offer himself to be punished in place of
the Israelites); Dt 24:16 (the basic Israelite principle that no one can die for
another person's sin - everyone shall suffer for their own sin); the whole of
Ezek 18 (which includes the principle that sins are not passed on through the
generations – 18:14, 17); and Jer 31:29-30 (which emphasises that sin is not
passed on from parent to child; each is punished for their own sin).

will be familiar enough with your real Heavenly Father, to know that they do not tell the truth.

Lastly, knowing Yahveh as Father helps us to understand scripture. Yahveh is a living God, with a real personality, real idiosyncrasies and real character traits. There are many so-called religious people around today, who are simply unable to embark on the long journey towards getting to know their heavenly Father as a living Being, in a living relationship. Instead, they teach that the *only* way to know God is to read about God. That is like never speaking to or even looking at a friend or your spouse, only reading biographies, reports and letters about them!

I always advise people to take counsel from the words of King David,[a] to 'seek Yahveh'. Seek the living God who is Yahveh, and understand the Miqra in the light of what you experience of Yahveh, not the other way round. A lot of people filter God through the lens of the bible. Talmidaism stakes its foundation firmly in the compassionate mercy of a loving and powerful God of glory and majesty, a living God who can be experienced and felt emotionally and spiritually, in the very depth of one's soul. We then read the bible from that experience; to do it any other way is to say that Yahveh is not a real, living God. Seek to know Yahveh, and the message of the Miqra becomes clear.

Therefore, calling God 'Father' has a responsibility that goes along with it. We have the responsibility to be like our heavenly Father – to show this in our words, thoughts and actions; and to know our heavenly Father, by learning what Yahveh is like, and what Yahveh is *not* like. Know your heavenly Father, and then learn to be like your heavenly Father.

The deception of religious fundamentalism

When the dictator of a country tries to impose his cruel and unjust will on others, he is rightly condemned by the international community as a despot, and every effort is made to remove such a tyrant. But when a religious leader tries to impose his will on his community, and leads others into hatred and intolerance, he is praised for upholding 'traditional values', and for defending his faith. There exists this insidious double standard. In secular life, despotism is unacceptable; in religious life, it is perfectly acceptable, even encouraged in extreme conservative circles. My brothers and sisters of all faiths, this cannot be! Why do we put up with this? The control of minds through religion is just as evil as the control of minds through political and cultural means.

---

[a] 1Chron 22:19 – that is, get to know Yahveh, seek to intimately experience Yahveh as a Living Being.

Yahveh fully understands that certain people need the security of being sure where religious truth is concerned, and the need to have one's faith stand on unshakeable foundations. I do not criticise literalism or the need to have such an unambiguous faith. What I do criticise is the hypocrisy and hatred of the fundamentalists of any religion, and their lack of any kind of spiritual humility or godly compassion. At best, they lack the empathy and mercy required of those who call themselves 'people of God'. At worst, they lack respect for the lives of those who disagree with them. They claim they are doing God's will, but each tree is known by its fruit.[a] By speaking only hatred and violence, they speak from what is abundant and plentiful in their hearts[b] – which is dangerously empty of anything from God.

The Book of Proverbs says, *'There is a certain type of people who . . . are pure in their own eyes, yet have not been cleansed of their own filth; those whose eyes are haughty and whose glances are full of disdain. Their teeth are swords, and their jaws are set with knives.'*[c] Fundamentalists criticise the sins of other people, but not their own. They criticise others' lack of observance, but they do not see their own hatred and spiritual violence as a sin. They point out the splinter in their neighbours' eyes, but do not see the whopping great plank in their own eyes![d] That is what is so distasteful to God! Such people need to learn and realise that the only sure, unshakeable foundation they can rely on is the living God, Yahveh. They hold up their example as the only way to follow, but those who place themselves first, will end up last in the kingdom of God.[e] They do not realise that hoping in anything less than Yahveh, is hoping only that the best *might* be; but hoping in Yahveh alone, is trust in the assurance that the best *will* be.

When a Christian is faced with the unconscionable actions of right-wing Christians, or with the blood-drenched history of religious wars and persecutions, many Christians will say, "Oh, they were not true Christians – their actions were nothing to do with Christianity", and so brush the uncomfortable episodes under the carpet. When a moderate Muslim is presented with the violence of murderous jihadists, the response is often, "I am not responsible for the actions of my fellow Muslims; what they are doing has nothing to do with Islam." No further examination of the problem is countenanced.

Let me tell you this: if I am presented with the violent actions of an extremist Jew, *it has everything to do with me, and with the Jewish*

---

[a] S.Yesh. 52:2-5 – cf Mt 7:16-20, Lk 6:43-44 (see also Gosp. Thomas 45:1)
[b] S.Yesh. 53:2-3 – cf Mt 12:34-35, Lk 6:45 (see also Gosp. Thomas 45:2-4)
[c] Prov 30:12-14a
[d] S.Yesh. 17:2-4 – cf Mt 7:3-5, Lk 6:41-42
[e] S.Yesh. 76:2 – cf Mk 10:31

faith! If I am made aware of a sin, and I take no action – either to condemn it, or if it is in my power, to stop it – then my inaction or lack of condemnation is itself a sin. An extremist Jew, by his or her violence, curses God's Name. Such a person sullies the holy reputation of God, and the reputation of the Jewish people. *It therefore jolly well is my problem!* It is my duty to look at that part of my religion that has caused the extremist Jew to engage in violence, and ensure that such problems are dealt with in myself, and in those directly around me. Because if I don't, and if I am not alone in what I fail to do, then the Jewish people will be in big trouble with God further down the road.

During the widespread looters' riots in England in 2011, one religious man of humility stands out – Tariq Jahan, whose son and two others were killed by looters while protecting their property. With dignified calm, in spite of his grief, he called for peace – for his son's death not to have been in vain, or the cause of more violence. His widely publicised appeals ensured that the violence did not take on any religious or racial dimension.

I also have a great respect for the Amish. They stick to the literal words of the Bible and the New Testament, but what is different about them, is that they focus on the *right* things to be literal about, such as the commandment to love one's neighbour as oneself. Their emphasis is on a simple, unadorned and peaceful existence. This illustrates the difference between biblical literalism, and biblical fundamentalism.

I am equally moved by the personal faith of the Victorian writer, Charles Dickens. His faith concentrated on what is truly important in life, and as a result, his books did a lot to change Victorian attitudes to the poor in Britain. He criticised those who went to church on Sunday, but then upon leaving church, ignored the poor on their way home.

Fundamentalists are hypocrites in the English sense of the word – of saying one thing and doing another – because they demand that others take Scripture literally, but are actually unwilling to do so themselves. This is because they pick and choose what they will be literal about. They emphasise the smaller teachings about punishment, sin and death, and ignore the greater commandments about justice, compassion and mercy.[a] They strain to practise the commandments to love one's neighbour,[b] and not to hate one's brother in one's heart,[c] and yet with ease, they swallow whole the teachings on putting wrongdoers to death![d]

Not everyone who calls out 'Lord! Lord!' will find the Kingdom of

---

[a] see S.Yesh 59:4-5 – cf Mt 23:23
[b] Lev 19:18
[c] Lev 19:17a
[d] S.Yesh. 59:6 – cf Mt 23:24

God, but only those who do the will of their heavenly Father.[a] The only assurance that fundamentalists have, is that they will stand before their Heavenly Father when they leave this life, just like everyone else. Yahveh will say to them, 'What have you done for My children on earth? What have you done to further the cause of My Kingdom?'

And these fundamentalists will say to God, 'We cursed those we didn't agree with, we preached hatred against those who didn't believe in You, we condemned those who didn't follow our faith, and we hounded and threatened people until they converted.' And God will say to them, 'Did you not practise any kindness or compassion?[b] Did you not help the weak and the poor?[c] Did you not encourage the oppressed,[d] or give solace to the sick and the dying?' And the fundamentalists will say to God, 'All that's fine, but it means nothing if You don't accept Christ as Your lord and saviour!'[e]

And God will say to them, 'You will remain in the Outer Darkness[f] and you will experience for yourselves the very suffering that you have caused!' But then the fundamentalists will say, 'But did we not prophesy in Your Name? Did we not perform many great miracles in Your Name?' And God will tell them, 'Away from me, you evildoers! I had nothing to do with anything you said or did!'[g]

I remember back in the 1980's when HIV and AIDS was just starting to gain the public's attention. At that time it was confined to male homosexuals and intravenous drug users. The religious right were like those in Yeshua`'s parable of the good Samaritan, who walked by on the other side of the road and did nothing to help. Instead, because those affected by AIDS lived 'distasteful' lifestyles, those who fell sick were condemned and vilified with extraordinary venom.

Yahveh our God is merciful and compassionate to whomever God

---

[a] Mt 7:21 – cf S.Yesh. 107:2

[b] Micah 6:8 – *'And what does Yahveh require of you? To do justice, love mercy, and walk humbly with your God.'*

[c] Lev 25:35, Dt 15:7

[d] Zech 7:10

[e] Here I am not criticising a belief, but an attitude. I have personally found that those Christians who actively perform charitable works and help others of other faiths, are generally decent and pleasant people. However, I have found that those who insist beyond all reason that belief is more important than being a good person, in general have quite unpleasant and disturbing personalities.

[f] the dark place between heaven and earth where souls are purified of their sins before going on to heaven. For a fuller explanation, see chapter 7.

[g] S.Yesh. 108:2-3 – cf Mt 7:22-23; the Greek (and presumably the underlying Aramaic) literally says, 'I never knew you'. This is an idiomatic way of saying, 'I didn't have anything to do with what you said or did'.

pleases,[a] and no religious person can dictate to God to whom God should show God's compassion. Regardless of what a religious person feels towards homosexuals and drug users, it is not the place of a religious person to act in such a godless and hateful way towards the sick and the dying. The judgment of God against such people who lack even simple compassion towards God's children, will be like those to whom God will say, 'Get away from me, you wicked! Because I was hungry and you gave me nothing to eat, I was thirsty and you gave me nothing to drink, I was a stranger and you didn't invite me in, I was naked and you didn't clothe me, I was sick and in prison and you didn't come to visit me . . . *whatever you refused to do for the least of these – My children – you refused to do for Me.*'[b]

Religious fundamentalism is an anathema and an affront to God, not because they take things literally, but because they lack godly compassion and empathy for those who are not their own. It projects a form of religion which makes God appear hateful and tyrannical. Such behaviour in the guise of religion is a desecration of God's holiness.

The ultimate fate of those who do evil in God's Name

To do evil is one thing – and bad enough; but to do evil in the Name of God is a completely different level of wickedness. It is blasphemy, because it contravenes the 3rd commandment not to use God's Name or authority for false or evil purposes.[c] For a religious person to be hateful and cruel in God's Name is blasphemy; and to oppress others and cause them mental or physical suffering is blasphemy – a desecration of the holiness of God's good reputation. Those who abuse religion can dredge up as many excuses as they like; they may even consider what they are doing is a noble thing,[d] but in the end what they are doing is an abomination in the sight of God.[e] In the end it is not to me, nor to any other human being they should address their excuses, but to God – the Judge of all the earth – for it is God's good Name they have defamed. In the end, Yahveh will judge them for what they have done, for Yahveh knows what is in the heart.

God will not hold anyone guiltless who abuses God's good Name with hatred or violence.[f] Sins against human beings can be forgiven, but

---

[a] Ex 33:19
[b] S.Yesh. 134:8, 10 – cf Mt 25:41-43, 45
[c] The Hebrew word *shav* has the meaning of false, deceitful, evil.
[d] S.Yesh. 111:2; cf Lk 16:15
[e] S.Yesh. 111:3 – cf Lk 16:15
[f] Ex 20:7, Dt 5:11

sins against the holiness of God cannot be forgiven in this life.[a] To represent religion – and therefore God – as hateful and cruel, and to do evil things under the auspices of religion, are sins against God that cannot be forgiven in this life.

If someone has indeed desecrated and defamed God's good and holy reputation in this way, then the only way to lessen the punishment for this sin – because that is the only thing that can be done – is to do something extraordinarily positive for humanity, as well as doing all they can to restore the good and holy reputation of God that they have so wickedly desecrated.

This is because the only destination of the unrepentant soul who commits violence and murder in God's Name is not paradise, but eternal oblivion.[b] The prophet Yeshua` told us to store up treasures for ourselves in heaven;[c] therefore the one who murders in God's Name *has no treasure stored up in heaven*, and what little treasure they did have, even that will be taken away from them, because of the unforgiveable wickedness they committed in life.[d] So when they leave the Outer Darkness, their last sin and evil will be burned away by the glory of God as they approach heaven, like the fire of a smelter purifying silver.[e] However, because nothing good was instilled in their souls in life, then once the blemish of their sin has been burnt away by God's glory, there will be nothing left of their soul to enter heaven – hence the oblivion of the soul for those who kill and do violence in God's Name, and revel in it.

That is why my message to those who commit violence in God's Name is this: "Repent! Turn from the way which will lead to the eternal death and oblivion of your soul, and follow the way of life! Build up spiritual treasures for yourself now, while you still can." It needs to be pointed out to the religious men of violence that their fate is not eternal paradise, but eternal oblivion.

'They have said false things about Me'

Modern religion has debased itself to the extent that what is corrupt, obnoxious and unjust about religion has been transferred onto the

---

[a] S.Yesh. 166:2 – cf Mk 3:28-29. See also Isaiah 22:14, and 1Sam 2:25, *'If a man sins against another man, God may mediate for him; but if a man sins against Yahveh* (i.e. against the reputation of God's holiness) *who will intercede for him?'*
[b] cf Num 15:31, Ps 37:9, 37:38
[c] S.Yesh. 100:2; cf Mt 6:20
[d] S.Yesh. 81:1; cf Mt 25:29
[e] Mal 3:3

character of God. So much so, that the failings and injustices of human beings with regard to religion, have now become the failings and injustices of God.

Bible-thumping preachers, religious fundamentalists, religious extremists – all have offended God by misrepresenting God's reputation. They have made ordinary people think that what they say is from God. But they have said false things about God.[a]

They have said angry, hateful and evil things, things that would never enter the mind of God. They have portrayed God as a raging, vengeful tyrant who is more like a deranged despot than an enlightened, wise, compassionate and loving Father. They have tarnished the holiness of God, and darkened God's good Name.

To falsely represent God is to defame the holiness of God; bible bashers, God-botherers[b] and fundamentalists who have nothing to say but death and condemnation, who speak hatred and violence with their words – these people incense God deeply; they call out to God and claim to follow God, but they do nothing that God says.

If we, as Followers of the Way, were to put forward a faith that is angry, oppressive, bigoted, belligerent, hateful and judgmental, then we would not be representing God; we would only be representing our own human prejudices, hates, inadequacies and failings. But if we do something extraordinary and go beyond ourselves – show ourselves to be generous in our compassion, merciful in our understanding, reaching out to those who are on the edge of human society, caring for those who cannot care for themselves, and providing for those who have little or no means, then we truly do represent the wondrous and awesome Being who is Yahveh, the living God of Israel and of all nations!

Religious people who make God look stupid

Imagine someone who doesn't understand nuclear physics, and because they don't understand the science, they firmly believe that nuclear bombs are not possible, that the dropping of H-bombs on Hiroshima and Nagasaki therefore never happened, and that there has been a global conspiracy since 1945 to say that they did happen. Now imagine someone who, because they don't understand that air has molecules, believes that air is also a myth. Most people would think that

---

[a] "I am incensed with you [....], for you have not told the truth about Me." (Job 42:7)
[b] a northern English slang term, implying that bible-thumpers are so unpleasant and intrusive that they even bother God – that they are even a nuisance to God.

such people are veering towards the utterly ridiculous. Now imagine someone who, because they cannot understand gravity, or the movements of the planets and stars, they believe that the earth is flat. And now imagine someone who says that, because dogs can't evolve from cats, and elephants obviously can't evolve from ducks, that therefore evolution is false – just because the bible says that God created the earth and all life in six days.

To those of the same mind-set as these people, such individuals are standing up for a noble cause, but to those of us who actually understand how science works, they are foolish. And such foolish individuals who claim they are standing up for God, actually end up making God look dumb and stupid in the eyes of most of the world. We even have people now who believe that the Moon is a giant projection – also part of a global conspiracy!

Yahveh is a God of great wisdom, learning and knowledge. I will later on show you how Yahveh is 'the Message' – the essence of all the ethics and principles that God teaches. I will show you how God is not just the teacher of the Message, Yahveh *IS* the Message. So therefore Yahveh not only teaches us wisdom, Yahveh *IS* Wisdom. Knowledge, Learning and Wisdom are all inseparable aspects of what Yahveh is.

Religious people who argue against evolution, who are against the great age of the earth, or who say that the earth is flat, make God look stupid and foolish. They argue from a position of ignorance of science, bringing up illogical, ridiculous and groundless premises that only make sense to other people who also know nothing about science. Fundamentalist preachers have taken to teaching their followers to distrust all knowledge and learning, because that is the only way that they can maintain their grip over their gullible congregations. This results in some serious consequences, such as parents refusing vaccinations for their children against life-threatening diseases – such that the terrible scourge of polio[a] is in danger of returning. These preachers tell us that science is a danger to faith, but science is only a danger to religious faith *if your religious faith is false*.

If you want to know why some religious people claim that the earth is flat, well, it's because the Bible says so. Think about the firmament – that niggling little word in the first chapter of Genesis that no one quite knows what it means, but sort of means 'sky' – ever wondered what it *actually* means? Well, I'll tell you. The Hebrew word it translates is רקיע *raqia'* (pronounced raa-KEE-aa), which comes from a verbal root meaning 'to beat thin' (as with metal). The Hebrew word *raqia'* actually

---

[a] In the worst cases, individuals are paralysed from the waist down, and cannot breathe without assistance from a machine called 'an iron lung'.

means 'a thin metal dome' (some dictionaries give it as 'the *physical* vault of the sky'). Elsewhere, this vault of the sky is referred to as a *ḥūg*[a] (a sphere). So the way the earth is described in the first chapter of Genesis, makes us think that God created the earth to have a metal dome over it, into which are studded the Sun, the Moon and the stars. There is a permanent body of water above this metal dome, and there is a permanent body of water underneath the flat earth – the dry land basically floats in a giant tank or reservoir (*miqveh*).

If the first chapter of Genesis cannot be taken literally (because there actually is no sphere or metal dome above the earth, the earth revolves around the Sun, and doesn't float in giant basin of water), then a religious person can start to take science seriously. To a fundamentalist literalist, the purpose of the first chapter of Genesis is to tell us that God created the earth in six days – and that's it. To someone who actually thinks that God is the wise and sophisticated Author of the infinite Universe, it actually tells us:

- that Yahveh is the sole creator of all that exists
- that God created order out of chaos
- that behind most things that happen, we can find meaning and purpose
- that the heavenly bodies should be used to calculate the timing of the days and months, and the appointed festivals (*mo'edim*)
- that God set human beings as caretakers over God's creation
- that God created male and female as equal
- it tells us why we have a seven-day week, and
- why the Sabbath exists

I have no problem with evolution – and very few Talmidis do. The Bible does not tell us *how* God created the Universe, only that God *is* the Creator. My personal belief is that God put in place all the laws of the Universe – that Yahveh is the Author of all those laws – and that the universe and nature follow along with those laws. I am not a proponent of 'intelligent design', because that implies that God is a puppet-master, who was cruel and sadistic enough to create babies without brains, or babies with their spines open, or fused legs that look like dolphin flippers, or babies with one eye, and so on. To believe that God's

---

[a] such as in Isa 40:22, which describes the *ḥūg* as being like a tent which God has spread out like a tent over the earth. Prov 8:27 describes this ḥūg or sphere which God set upon the face of the deep at creation, and Job 22:14 describes this sphere or vault which is the sky.

intelligence designed these children to be the way they are, is to believe in a cruel, heartless and sadistic God. God is not a sadistic designer. God did not create these children to suffer.

I believe that Yahveh, our loving Creator, set in motion the laws of the universe, and created it to function in a particular way. I also believe that Yahveh created our physical souls. I believe that God guides and directs us, if we are willing to listen, but I do not believe that God pulls our strings. When a mutation or mistake happens, that is not God, but nature making mistakes. Sometimes Nature and the Universe make mistakes, but not God. No matter what our bodies or minds may be like, God created our souls perfectly in heaven, and as heavenly beings, God created all of us with the capacity for reason and compassion. We all have a part to play in God's creation, no matter what our ability or disability.

For me, the greater and more infinitely powerful Deity is the One who created everything over the course of *billions* of years, and used the most complicated of processes to do it, rather than the one who simply waved a magic wand and made everything we see around us in six days, just over 6,000 years ago. The God I believe in is so wise, so awesome and *so* creative, that my Creator used the complex laws of physics and nature to create the Universe and all life over billions and billions of years.

Or you can go back to taking the first chapter of Genesis literally, and believe that the earth is flat, with a metal dome over it. You choose.

The danger of missionisers

In most religions, there are certain people who engage in aggressive, persistent and traumatising evangelisation to convert others to their religion. These are the people I call 'missionisers'.

I have been the unfortunate victim of missionisers on several occasions. Several years ago, I was ostensibly invited to speak to a non-Jewish group on Jewish matters. I hoped that the talk would build bridges between our faiths. Unfortunately, that is not what happened. I was set upon as if by jackals and vultures, with my supposed 'hosts' trying to convert me. I can say without doubt, this was a very disturbing and traumatic experience. On another occasion, I was told that I would convert to their faith when God deemed it the right time, but one thing would be certain: I would convert.

That run of experiences actually made me *more* determined to learn about my own faith, and to find the truth behind their deceptive claims. I can honestly say that their distasteful and inhospitable behaviour was a turning point in my learning process, and I learnt many new things about the Israelite way of thinking, that I would otherwise never have encountered.

In researching my family tree, I discovered that some ancestors on the Portuguese side of the family were Marranos – or more properly, *anusim* – Jewish people who were forcibly converted to Christianity during the Portuguese Inquisition. At that time in the 16th century, Jewish people were herded like cattle into churches and aggressively preached to in order to convert them. Those who did convert but secretly practised the Jewish faith were persecuted, and many were even put to death in public spectacles, being burned at the stake. Although my own life was never in danger, I felt that I had come to understand the spiritual and physical violence that my ancestors were forced to suffer all those centuries ago, in these terrible *autos da fé*.

The majority of people do not comprehend the force behind the Yahwist principle that we should not serve any other god but Yahveh, and often get the wrong end of the stick. Most non-Jews take it to mean that the God of Israel is against all other religions, *but that is simply not the case.*

Yahveh says through Moses in Deuteronomy,[a] *'And take care, when you lift up your eyes to heaven and see the Sun and the Moon and the stars – all the host of heaven – not to be enticed to worship them and serve them – something which Yahveh your God has allotted to all the peoples under the whole sky.'*

In this verse, we Jews understand that other nations may follow *any* religion they may please, and Yahveh has given His blessing for them to do so. However, as the descendants of Jacob, we can never follow any other religion except the Israelite religion – the Way of Yahveh. We *alone* are expressly forbidden to serve other gods, or turn to other religions.

Our faith also advises us to respect the traditions of other religions, as long as they do not hinder or harm the traditions and ethos of the Israelite religion. For example, when a pagan woman was taken captive after her family were killed in battle, she was to be allowed to mourn the loss of her family in her native way.[b] Pagan mourning rites are forbidden to us[c] as followers of the Way of Yahveh, but they are not forbidden to pagans; we are actually commanded to permit them.

The most notable instance in the Bible, where God requires Gentiles to follow a way of righteousness, without requiring a change in religion, is when the prophet Jonah is sent to tell the pagan city of

---

[a] Dt 4:19
[b] Dt 21:10-14
[c] Lev 19:27-28, Dt 14:1-2

Nineveh to repent of their wrongdoing. If you notice, nowhere does God require of them to change their religion and become Israelites. Jonah was told to rebuke them for their wickedness,[a] and tell them if they didn't change, they would be overthrown.[b] The Ninevites trusted in God's message,[c] and God relented. There is no historical evidence that the Assyrians were converted to the Yahwist Israelite faith; what they changed was their way of behaviour, not their religion.

Because of what Yahveh teaches us, it is an intrinsic part of the Israelite faith that we are to respect the religions of others, while staying fast to our own. So when missionisers come to us to turn us away from the Jewish faith, they are setting themselves up against God and God's law. Deuteronomy[d] calls such people *bᵉney Beli'al* – the 'Sons of Destruction'. Simply because the Israelite religion was instituted to stand as an eternal witness for Yahveh, it will never become extinct, and no one will ever succeed in converting the entire Jewish people to another religion – Yahveh has already decreed it.

As long as non-Jews are just and ethical, the Israelite religion does not have any problem with the beliefs, customs, traditions or cultures of *any* other people or religion. It simply has to be noted that we, as followers of Yahveh, are forbidden to *take on* any of those beliefs and customs, or participate in any other traditions or cultures.

There are some who think that the only way to bring about God's kingdom of peace is for every human being on earth to belong to the same religion and culture, and to share the same belief system. Paullist Christianity teaches that everyone has to become a Christian,[e] and Islam teaches that everyone has to become a Muslim,[f] *but this is not the teaching of Yahveh.*

To insist that everyone should belong to the same faith (whatever that faith may be), is to share the mind-set of a sociopath, who loves only what is his or hers. By giving the whole human race over to just one religion, you then prepare the stage for the whole human race to be handed over to psychopaths on a platter, who will more easily be able to

---

[a] Jon 1:2

[b] Jon 3:4

[c] Jon 3:5 – *"va-ya'amīnu anšey nīnéveih beilohim"* – 'and the people of Nineveh put their trust in God' i.e. they believed in the message God was giving them through Jonah; this does not mean they converted *en masse* to Yahwism.

[d] Dt 13:13

[e] Acts 4:12 – "Salvation is found in no one else, for there is no other name under heaven given to humanity by which we must be saved".

[f] Islam teaches that everyone is born a Muslim, and human cultures then take us away from Islam. The goal of Islam is to restore everyone to the 'one true faith' i.e. Islam. (Sahih al Bukhari, Volume 2, Book 23, Number 441),

control the whole world with that one philosophy, after they have hijacked it. Making the whole world follow just one religion, just one culture and just one set of beliefs will deliver the world into the hands of power-hungry psychopaths, who will seek sovereignty over that one religion; it will not deliver the world into the hands of God.

Now, there are those who think that the mission of Yeshua` was to convert the entire human race into believing that he was a god, and that he had come down to earth to save humanity from their sins. The reality is that he didn't even come to found a new Jewish sect – he was called by God to reiterate the founding principles and moral values of the *original* Israelite faith. As such he wasn't calling the Jewish people to join a sect that he founded. He was calling people of *every* Jewish sect to amend their ways, and return to the original teachings of the Israelite faith. In so doing, they would avoid the calamity to come – or at least, be protected from it.

With a proper understanding of the Yahwist attitude to other religions, and of Yeshua`'s personal mission amongst his own people, you can understand that Yahveh does not expect everyone to become Jewish, or even to be of the same religion, but God *does* expect every human being to grow towards a certain way of thinking, speaking and behaving within their *existing* religion or private philosophy.[a]

'Every scribe who becomes a citizen of the kingdom of God, is like someone who is the owner of a house, who brings out of their storehouse treasures new as well as old.'[b]

Desecration of the Holy Name

I cannot emphasise enough how serious the desecration of God's holiness and reputation is, because it is one of the sins that brought about the Roman exile in Yeshua`'s time, and also threatens the modern state of Israel. If, by one's intolerance, hatred or hurtful words and deeds, a Jewish person causes another person (whether Jewish or Gentile) to hate the God of Israel, then this is a really serious desecration of God's

---

[a] According to the Yahwist way of thinking, no non-Jew is even expected to *belong* to any religion. People who are atheist out of conscience are actually not a problem for Jewish people. All that God requires of atheists is a certain decent standard of ethical and moral behaviour.

[b] S.Yesh. 156:2 – cf Mt 13:52. Our community takes this teaching to mean that someone who amends their behaviour to accord with the ways of God's kingdom, is able to draw not only on old things (their existing beliefs and traditions), but also on new things (what they have learned about thought and behaviour under God's care). We therefore deduce from this that Yeshua` did not expect anyone to convert to a new sect or religion, but simply change their ways within their present spiritual home (if that is where they are happiest).

reputation. We are meant to be a blessing and a benefit to others,[a] but if we become a curse to others, by being hateful and intolerant towards non-Jews, then this desecrates the holiness of God.[b]

Some people think that idol worship and rejection of Yahveh – or even just non-observance of religious ritual – are what warranted exile. However, we should always remember the main sins that resulted in the Roman exile of the 1st century – violence in religion, corruption of the High priesthood, and the gross inequality between rich and poor. Anything that shows to the world that Yahwism is not working – and by extension, that the God of Israel is ineffective – will result in the expulsion of the Jewish people from the Land.

In the Land of Israel, if by the unjust actions of the Jewish authorities, a non-Jew is ill-treated or delivered an unjust ruling in a court of law, and thereby that non-Jew is caused to hate the God of Israel, then the perpetrator of that ill-treatment or injustice has committed a desecration of God's reputation – a sin that cannot be atoned for or forgiven. Such an act undermines God's holiness that is supposed to be represented by the whole people of Israel, and puts us all in danger of retribution against such defamation. The future of the very existence of modern Israel is at stake if these actions are not corrected.

Israel's possession of the Land is always conditional; once we are back, it does not mean we will stay back – *we must always remember that*. The Jewish people dwelling in the Land of Israel will *always* be provisional. God brought us back once before (when the Jewish people returned after the Babylonian exile), and we were then re-exiled by the Romans. The Roman exile effectively ended in 1948, but that does not make our return this time permanent either. The Israeli government must never put God in such a position, whereby the only solution to rectifying God's sullied reputation and holiness is to expel the Jewish people from the Land yet again.

God knows the danger that Israel as a state faces every day from people and nations who hate her. God understands the need for her people to live in safety and security. However, in pursuit of that security,

---

[a] Gen 12:2

[b] The Talmud will define desecration of God's Name (*chillul ha-shem*) as 'anything which brings down the reputation of the Jewish community.' I would agree that the things the Talmud considers desecration of God's reputation are bad things, but if indeed the full range of sins covered in the rabbinic definition of desecration were true, then we would all eventually build up a backlog of sins that could never be forgiven, and that cannot be the case. For example, deliberately embarrassing someone or humiliating them, would in Rabbinic Judaism be classed as a desecration of God's Name. However, in Talmidaism, although it would still be considered a sin, it would not be an *unforgivable* sin, and therefore not a desecration of God's name.

God expects her citizens to act towards non-Jews with justice, equity and fairness. In the routine conduct of security enforcement, there is no need to be petty, rude, pushy, hateful, oppressive or unjust. If this injustice goes on, there will be a reckoning for it.

'Blessed are the humble in spirit ...'

The remedy to religious fundamentalism, is religious humility. Now, with religious fundamentalists, I can say (tongue in cheek) that I have witnessed something of a man-made miracle. I have met individuals, who before their conversion had no previous learning or interest in anything biblical or spiritual even. However, immediately after conversion, they are suddenly *expert* theologians and biblical scholars, giving their (often misguided and usually incorrect) interpretations of very difficult biblical texts.

They are unfortunately not the only ones who suffer from this form of self-deluded arrogance. Men and women who have studied for decades are also guilty of it. We, more than anyone else in this field, have to ask ourselves: Do we rely on the pride of our own knowledge and authority? Do we tell people, 'I've read and studied a lot, I have tons of academic qualifications, so you'd better listen to me, 'cos I know what I'm talking about!' Or are we willing to acknowledge that, before Yahveh, we actually don't know everything? Are we willing to sit still and listen when Yahveh is trying to teach *us*?

Are we willing to be corrected by what Yahveh teaches us? Or do we go through life with the arrogant, opinionated conceit of one who says, 'Everything I experience in life proves to me that I am right; I don't need to amend my worldview in any way.' Only someone who is humble before God is willing to be taught by God, and to learn from God. Only those who are humble in spirit can discern the handiwork of God in the experiences of their lives, and so 'hear' what God has to teach them.

I know that there are certain people – because I was once one of them – who think, 'I've studied for many years, I've read hundreds of insightful books, I've cast my net widely and learnt many new things, and I've gained an understanding of the message of God'. Unfortunately, until we are willing to admit that compared to God, we don't know anything; and until we are willing to sit before Yahveh, the living God, so that we may learn from the very mind of God, then we are not going to learn anything of any vital importance to God or humanity.

On the day I finally accepted that I wasn't in charge – that what Yahveh knew was far greater than what I could ever know, and that what Yahveh wanted was far more important than what I ever wanted or planned – I fell on my knees and touched my forehead to the ground.

With tears in my eyes I said, 'Heavenly Father, I have been such a fool! Compared to You, I know nothing! I am no one! Teach me what I should know, take me where I should go, and lead me along the path I should follow!'

There are occasionally certain assertive and self-opinionated people who try to enter our community. They start to 'rearrange the furniture' and try to change things to the way *they* want them to be, and they soon find they cannot. That is because our community, in all humility to God, strives to build its foundations on what *God* wants, not on what *we* want. These people enter on the assumption that they have studied the Miqra and religious history well, and they believe they know how things should be. They soon learn that there is One greater than they who knows far better how things should be!

To the ancient Israelite mind, between boastful egotism and total self-effacement stands spiritual humility. The Israelite mind does not equate humility with weakness, cowardice or wretchedness; a humble person is *not* a weak person. Indeed, it is perfectly acceptable to speak of one's good qualities, as long as one acknowledges that one's good qualities and successes ultimately come from Yahveh. Nor is a truly humble person the same kind of sickening, grovelling individual as the Charles Dickens character, Uriah Heep in *David Copperfield*. A humble person has a real, dignified uprightness, but is possessed of a kind and compassionate heart.

Through the prophet Jeremiah, Yahveh teaches us,

> *"Let not the wise man glorify himself in his wisdom, nor let the strong man glorify himself in his might; let not the rich man glorify himself in his riches: but rather let him that glorifies himself glorify in this instead: that he understands and knows Me, that I am God who exercises loving-kindness, justice, and righteousness on the earth."*[a]

The Israelite concept of humility is based on a realistic evaluation of the world and of the proper worth of human beings. Abraham, Moses (described as *'the humblest man on earth'*),[b] Gideon (who refused a crown), and David are all set up as model types of Israelite humility.

Humility is a virtuous estate to be achieved, where one realises and understands one's modest place in the infinite universe and in the overall scheme of time; and that everything is ultimately under the control, and under the loving care and guidance of Yahveh.

---

[a] Jer 9:22-23
[b] Num 12:3

A humble spirit does not judge others; they give humane help even to their enemies (a humble spirit is not vengeful or proud); and they try to do the most just and fairest thing, even though it is not advantageous for them. A humble spirit gives others a fair hearing, even if he or she disagrees with them; a humble spirit knows that it is not his or her job to triumph over everyone who holds a different viewpoint to themselves, but realises that all souls are brothers and sisters, and as such are all children of one heavenly Father, the Most High God.

Our ...

Notice here that Yeshua` says that God is *our* Father, and not just his. Yeshua` obviously saw all human beings as the sons and daughters of God, regardless of their station in life, or what they had done. Yahveh would never abandon anybody. Yahveh's Presence was ready to enfold and envelope anyone, at any time. Yeshua` saw God as a kind and loving parent, who was deeply concerned and involved with the needs of all God's sons and daughters. Yahveh is not a remote or a distant God, but One who would always be with us to care for us.

In addition, we debate and focus so much on Yeshua`'s mission, that we often forget that our heavenly Father sent *all of us* on a mission here too. We human beings are all of us here to work with each other to change the world, and to prepare the earth for the fulfilment of God's kingdom. If we just sit back and do nothing to advance God's kingdom, then we are failing in our own personal missions to work for our heavenly Father. All of us were sent here by *our* heavenly Father with a purpose, and the sooner we realise that, the closer comes the day when God's glory will shine on earth.[a]

... who ...

In Aramaic, the little word d^e- has a number of uses. It can mean 'who' as a simple conjunction, but it can also mean 'the one who'. Some have translated the line in English as 'Heavenly Father', and this is indeed the basic meaning of the phrase *abbun d^e-bishmáyya* in English. However, for poetical reasons, given what we now know about the seventh line ('Our bread, which is from the earth'), this word should be left as it is.

---

[a] Ch.Sh. 22:23; cf Book of Revelations 21:23; also *Clementine Recognitions*, Bk 2 Ch 68, Bk 3 Chs 27-29, and Bk 3 Ch 75.

... in heaven,

Even in modern times, there are still some of us who see heaven as being 'up there'. If heaven is 'up there', then how could God, who is in heaven, be right next to us? Yeshua` taught us that we could find and pray to God even in the innermost rooms of our homes. '[a]

If God is in the innermost room of a house, then heaven, where God is, must be there too. Heaven, although not visible, exists in the same space that we exist – like another dimension. Therefore, we do not need to call 'up' to heaven to God, because Yahveh our heavenly Father is right next to us.

'Our Father, who .... loves us'

In the first chapter of Genesis, we are told that as God created each thing, 'God saw that it was good'. From these words, we tend to get the impression that God created things in a cold, mechanical way, saw that what He had created was up to scratch, and then moved unflinchingly onto the next thing, without a second thought. However, I would like to suggest a new take on this. Just as a new mother or father is taken aback by the beauty of their new-born child, so too God was taken aback at the 'children' of His Creation. Metaphorically, God's breath was taken away by everything God had made, and God instantly fell in love with it. So too with the birth of every new human soul, our heavenly Father falls in love with each new child of His Creation.

I am sometimes asked, 'What relevance does God have today?' I don't see God as a 'magic wand' type of God, who is there give us anything we ask for; or a mafia boss type of God, who is there to frighten, threaten and punish us for every little thing we do that God doesn't like; God is not a dictator who must be flattered and appeased; God is not the puppet-master, who pulls our strings and directs every single thing we do, or is behind every little thing that happens to us; nor is God the controller of the weather, the cause of natural disasters, or the inflictor of diseases. This is not the type of God I follow.

The God I believe in – Yahveh, is the God who guides me in difficult times, who gives me strength and courage to get through when the going is rough, and who consoles me when my heart and mind are wounded; Yahveh is the God who teaches and inspires me, who gives me a hunger for knowledge and learning, and sometimes even challenges me; Yahveh is the God who renews me, and enables me to become more than what is already within me; and ultimately, Yahveh is the God who

---

[a] S.Yesh. 57:3-4; cf Mt 6:5-6

loves me, far more than any human being has ever done.

The relationship that Followers of the Way try to develop with God, is built around the love that our heavenly Father has for us. We plant our faith firmly in that love, and everything we learn about Yahveh is understood through the strength and power of that love. Have you ever wondered what God might say if God could express God's especial love for you, as a son or daughter of God?

"Do you know how so very special you are to me?
How precious in My sight?
You are my own, beautiful children,
The offspring of My own heart.
How can I not love you?
How can I not care for the infant I have borne?
Who knew when I created you,
When I first filled you with My breath,
that I would end up being so proud of you,
that My joy would be filled to overflowing?
What mortal could have told Me,
Or what human could report,
That I would gain so much out of holding you,
someone as small and precious as you
Close to my heart,
And near to My Being?
There are no human words to express how much I love you,
Nor any songster's lyrics to express My devotion.
I could never be away from you even for a moment,
Nor stray from your side for the length of a sigh,
because My heart would ache too much to be apart from you;
My Presence would be diminished.

My beautiful child, how I love to look into your precious eyes,
to gaze into your soul,
and see the goodness and purity that I created there,
the treasure I placed there before you were even born.

My child, you have only to breathe, and I love you;
You have only to open your eyes, and I am proud of you.
I accept you absolutely, and without condition.
My love for you is total, and without any terms.
I love you simply because you are My child;
that is the only truth I need to give My love to you.
You need never be afraid of the world,

Nor fear the deeds of mortals,
because I will always be here.
If you are sad or hurt, I will comfort you;
and if you stray and become lost,
then I will search high and low until I find you,
And I will bring you back to safety.

You need never be afraid,
Because I will come to you, and pick you up.
I will raise you up high, and carry you proudly.
Because you are my special child,
and I love you always, and forever." [a]

Line 2: Sanctified be Your Name!

Sanctified be...

To fully understand what this line means – to appreciate what an ancient Israelite would have understood by this, and not just how either a modern rabbi or a Christian theologian would understand it – you need to learn something about the ancient idea of God's holiness. If you thought as an ancient Israelite, then I could explain it quite easily in a few words, but I think there is no easy way to do this other than start from scratch.

In my first book, I began to explain what the Israelite idea of holiness was. When you mention holiness, most people think of goodness, kindness, sinlessness, purity, righteousness and so on. In the Pharisaic way of thinking, holiness means being separate from the ordinary and the physical. However, all of these aspects are secondary. To understand holiness in the Israelite way of thinking, you have to first learn something about the awesome and powerful nature of Yahveh, the God of Israel.

As I mentioned in my first book, the fire of God's glory and God's holiness is inextricably linked to God's physical unapproachableness. If we were to experience God the way that the angels in heaven experience God, then our physical bodies would all be burnt to a crisp.

Let me briefly go over the experience of Moses on Mount Sinai again to refresh your memory. In Exodus chapter 33, Moses asks God to show him God's glory – that is, God's *kavodh* or 'Divine Radiance'. God says that God will cause God's glory to pass by. God adds that Moses will need to be *protected* from God's glory, since, as God puts it, 'no one

---

[a] extracts from S. Kit. 1:4

can see My face and live.'

As God passes by, God has to shield Moses from God's glory. Moses is told that he may only see God's 'back'. We might ask, what is this about? What is so powerful about God that Moses has to be protected from God? And what is this talk of 'face' and 'back'?

There is also the episode of Aaron's sons who are killed because they were not properly prepared before entering the Tent of God's presence. Again, they died because they came into contact with the full force of God's glory. At many points in the story of the Israelites' wandering in the Sinai desert, the Israelites are warned not to approach the Tent of Meeting, 'lest they die'. Notice it does not say, 'or else I will kill them,' but rather God is saying that if they are not properly prepared, they will die as a direct consequence of coming into contact with the powerfully brilliant, fiery radiance of God's glory. At other points, God is described as coming in fire and smoke, such as when God comes down on Mount Sinai. In Exodus 24:17, God is described as a 'consuming fire'.

And in the vision of Ezekiel, again God is described as a vision of light and fire. I must emphasise that the light and the fire are not God; they are merely the effect that God's presence has on this world. In Exodus 24:10, when Moses, Aaron, and seventy elders 'see' the God of Israel, what they see is the 'back' of the glory, the same as Moses saw in Ex 33.

During the wanderings of the Israelites in the desert, they were given instructions on how to construct the Tabernacle (or in Hebrew, the *Mishkan*). This was built ostensibly to house God's presence. I want to tell you about the actual, primary purpose of the Mishkan.

What Moses actually experienced up on Mount Sinai was an opening between heaven and earth – a kind of doorway – one that allowed him to see heaven and the light of God's glory that suffuses all things there. What he saw was the 'face' (or front) and 'back' of this doorway. God would have been able to open this doorway anywhere, at any time. In this world, we can only really hear God's voice in visions and dreams, but with this doorway open, Moses was able to hear God's actual voice directly, and speak with God 'face to face'.[a]

The best way I can think of to describe this doorway is to compare it to the interface between two adjoining bubbles. If you have ever joined two bubbles together, you will have seen that the connection between them is circular and flat. Now imagine that the heavenly realm and the earthly realm as two 'time-space' bubbles interfacing. What is created between them is a portal between heaven and earth. Through it, the light of heaven and Yahveh's glory becomes visible on earth. This interface

---

[a] Ex 33:11, Dt 34:10

would be flat, and this flat disk of blinding light would need to pass by Moses so that Moses could see the back of it.

Once it had passed by Moses, he would have seen a diffused circle of light against the blue sky – rather like the corona of the Sun when it is completely blocked by the Moon during a full solar eclipse. However, instead of the dark shadow of the Moon and complete darkness, inside this corona of light would still be the blue sky, and outside, around the corona there would also be blue sky. This is the 'back' of the portal that Moses would have been able to see – and live. Seeing the 'face' or 'front of the portal would have been too much for any human to see and live. This power of Yahveh's glory, and understanding it, is central to understanding everything behind what the Israelite religion is for – it is **the** central revelation at Sinai – the zenith of the Exodus story. All Israelite theology is dependent on a proper understanding of the *kavodh Yahveh* – the divine radiance or 'glory' of Yahveh.

Now, Moses had asked God to travel with his people, but if God's glory opened up amongst the Israelites, they would have all been destroyed. So the Mishkan was built, to allow a doorway to God's glory in heaven to appear above the ark of the Covenant.[a] When this happened, the Mishkan would also protect the Israelites from being fried to a crisp. That was the main practical purpose of the Mishkan. Not only was the Mishkan to serve as a visible sign of God's presence among them, it was also there to protect the Israelites – as sentient beings capable of both good and evil – from God's glory by housing it in a thickly layered, inanimate tent.

If we, as the people of God, are to set ourselves on the right spiritual path, then we need to understand the power of this holiness, and gain knowledge of God's glory. When prophets such as Malachi speak against injustice and wickedness, their speech is full of metaphors about God's justice being like a consuming fire – that it would consume the wicked, but purify the good. Wickedness and injustice cannot endure before God's presence, because the fire of his holiness will destroy it.[b]

The symbolic purpose of the sin offering was to show what would happen to our bodies if we were to approach God's glory; the fire of the altar was a symbol of God's power and glory in heaven. It is the purity and power of the presence of God *alone* which cleanses us of our sin. No blood has to be shed, and no one needs to die for sin to be forgiven.[c]

---

[a] Ex 25:22
[b] Habbakuk 1:13
[c] Isa 43:25, 44:22

Sanctifying God's Name through our care of animals and the environment

Kindness to animals was one of those principles that were so ingrained in Israelite culture, that it was not considered necessary to have any direct commandment about it. This is in the same vein as for example, how there are no written laws on hospitality, because the rules of being a good host and guest were so ingrained in Israelite culture, that it was not considered necessary to write commandments about them. They are considered to be God's principles – *iqronot* – that are nevertheless to be followed.[a]

Similarly with the kind and humane treatment of animals. There are no direct references or commandments regarding the rights of animals, but you can see its ethos in several places, underneath the surface as part of Israelite culture.

For example, in Gen 24:14 & 19, because Rebecca had concern for her camels, Abraham's servant knew she was the right wife for Isaac. She offered to give the camels water to drink until they had all had their fill, which would have involved considerable labour (camels are able to drink an enormous amount of water). And the law forbidding eating an animal while it is still alive[b] presupposes a concern for the suffering of the animal. Also Moses and David were said to have been chosen as leaders of Israel, because of their experience as shepherds who showed concern for their animals.

The one explicit commandment that comes immediately to mind is the one that on the Sabbath, even the animals who serve us must rest.[c] If ancient Israelite society had had no concern for its animals, such a society would have gotten Gentiles to work their animals for them on the Sabbath. However, this commandment leaves no room for doubt; the right to rest on the Sabbath and refresh oneself extends *even to our animals*.

Torah does enjoin kindness to animals. "If you see the donkey of your enemy fallen under its burden, and your instinct is to refrain from raising it, you must nevertheless raise it with him."[d]

Prov 12:10 says, *"A righteous person has regard for the life of his animals, but the innermost feelings of the wicked are for cruelty."* Even though we are commanded to rest on the Sabbath, it is considered a

---

[a] Ps 119:4 – 'Your principles are to be fully obeyed', and Ps 103:18, where it says that God's love is with those who remember to obey God's principles/precepts.
[b] Gen 9:4
[c] Ex 20:10
[d] Ex. 23:5

kindness in Israelite tradition to feed animals even on this day of rest, or help them if they are in trouble on the Sabbath,[a] or carry tools and equipment to help save an animal on the Sabbath, or to milk a cow on the Sabbath if she is suffering from an over-production of milk. And before an owner could sit down to eat, it was considered a great virtue to feed one's animals *first*.

Furthermore, animals should not be subjected to psychological torture. For example, an ox must not be muzzled while treading grain,[b] but must be free to eat of the grain while working, exactly the same as a human worker is allowed to do.[c] It would be cruel to prevent an animal from eating the very food it is treading in plain sight. It is also forbidden to yoke animals of different species for ploughing,[d] because to do so would be a cruelty to the weaker animal.

Mother and young must not be slaughtered on the same day,[e] and it is forbidden to take both a wild bird and young from a nest. Once the mother has been set free, the eggs may be taken.[f] This law assumes a measure of conservation, since the mother can breed again and lay more eggs, but taking both would kill off the supply of eggs and young.

The only hunters recorded in the bible, Nimrod and Esau, are portrayed negatively. In Israelite culture, unlike the cultures of the surrounding peoples, Israelite kings did not engage in hunting for sport; it was not part of our culture, and in time it came to be considered entirely distasteful, even there are no explicit laws as such forbidding hunting for sport in Torah. Even when hunting for food, it was considered repugnant to hunt with dogs, as they were likely to torment the animal before its death. It is therefore against God's natural Torah – the laws of *Tsedeq* – to hunt for sport, or to enjoy the suffering or death of an animal.

The laws of kashrut do not apply to the *keeping* of live animals, only to the consumption and use of non-kosher animal products.[g] There

---

[a] S.Yesh. 60:3 – '... *if one of your colleagues has a donkey or a farm animal that's fallen into a pit, won't you help him immediately to lift it out, even on the Sabbath?*' cf Mt 12:11, Lk 14:5
[b] Deut 25:4
[c] Deut. 23:26 [23:25 Christian bibles]
[d] Deut 22:10
[e] Lev 22:28
[f] Deut 22:6
[g] Torah forbids us from using products derived from a non-kosher animal (Dt 14:8 '*nor touch their carcasses*' – see also Lev 11:8, 11, 24, 36), as it is considered *tamei* (ritually unfit), but Rabbinic law overrides this – for example, the Oral Law specifies the bodies of dead sea-snails to make blue techelet-dye (the written Torah does not specify what the dye is to be made from, but the plant *Isatis tinctoria* - Jerusalem Woad - would be acceptable); or interpreting the leather covering the Sinai Tabernacle to have been made from

would therefore not be any problem with keeping non-kosher animals as pets. However, as a proviso to this, God's natural laws of *Tsedeq* should deter us from taking wild animals from their natural environment to keep as pets – this should be considered a form of animal cruelty.[a]

One overlooked side to the killing of animals in modern times, is the ancient requirement that when any animal was killed, its blood was to be returned to God in payment for its death, by presenting it as an offering to God.[b] Its blood was either to be presented as an offering to God in the Temple, or returned to God by pouring it on the earth and covering it up.[c] This way the people of Israel do not incur blood-guilt for the death of animals. What this should mean for us in modern times, is that the arbitrary and cruel slaughter of animals incurs blood-guilt on the land; it pollutes the earth as much as the murder of human beings does.

As for the Jewish mode of slaughter of animals (*sh^echitah*), it is an underlying part of Hebrew culture that the slaughter should be as quick as possible, to cause the animal as little pain and the minimum of distress as possible. If the slaughter is carried out properly by a trained *shochet* (slaughterer), the animal does not feel the cut, and loss of consciousness is quick.[d] Problems arise with what the animal goes through *preceding* slaughter. This should be the focus of any reforms to the process.

By domesticating animals, we have effectively made them our slaves. We have bred dogs to the point that most breeds cannot survive without us, and so to abandon domestic dogs to their fate is a form of cruelty. In Torah's laws concerning the just and compassionate treatment of slaves, in many cases the just and righteous treatment of animals usually follows. For example, Leviticus allows the sabbatical produce of the Land for slaves, hired foreigners *and domestic animals*.[e] We must remember how, through an angel, God rebuked Balaam for striking his

---

dolphin-skins (the undecipherable Hebrew word תחש *tachash* likely meant a special type of suede made from the skins of goats or cattle; the ancients understood it to be hyacinth in colour, and that women's shoes were sometimes made of it – Ezek 16:10).

[a] It should be borne in mind, that in order to provide baby animals as pets, the mothers are **always** killed; and for every wild bird or reptile that ends up in someone's home, many more have died in cages or boxes in deplorable conditions along the way.

[b] Lev 17:4

[c] Lev 17:13

[d] With sheep the time averages at 10 seconds *(Newhook and Blackmore 1982, Gregory and Wotton 1984, Nangeroni and Kennett 1963, Schulz et al 1978, Blackmore 1984)*, and with cattle it can take up to 85 seconds *(Blackmore 1984, Blackmore et al 1983, Gregory and Wotton, 1984, Grandin 2010, Daly et al 1988, Gregory et al 2010)*

[e] Lev. 25:6–7

donkey.[a] We must remember how God told Jonah how much God had pity upon the animals of Nineveh, as much as God had compassion on the people within that city.[b]

Some of you may be aware that rattlesnake roundups take place in the southern US. Often, the collection of these animals goes beyond mere population control. Some events revel in the suffering of the animals before they are killed. I would hope that no Israelite ever participates in such events; God does *not* give us permission in Torah to ill-treat or abuse animals, or to enjoy their suffering.

Moreover, a righteous son or daughter of Yahveh does not treat their animals carelessly like objects, to be discarded like trash when they are no longer needed; our domestic animals have basic needs and are able to feel pain. Social animals feel depression, fear and loneliness, just as we do. Dogs especially feel loyalty, love and even courage in defence of their families, just as we do (in the story of the Exodus, one of the men who shows loyalty to God is even called Caleb / *Kélev*[c] – the Hebrew word for 'dog'). The mind-set of a tyrant is always unacceptable, and to exploit animals as if they were unfeeling machines is to become a tyrant. A person who abuses defenceless animals *is also likely to abuse defenceless human beings*. We are not free to ill-treat our charges as we wish.

Even though there are no direct commandments to show kindness or concern for animals, it is an ingrained part of Israelite culture. A person's compassion can be measured by how far they will go to show concern even for animals. The relationship between humans and animals, according to the Hebrew mind-set, is that of a benevolent king and his subjects, or of a caring and nurturing steward.

Psalms 104 and 148 speak of God's stewardship and care of creation. They describe God's stewardship with loving care. There is not even an inkling of heartless exploitation expressed in these psalms, and we are told to emulate God in His ways. Our position over animals and nature is that of a caring shepherd, not that of a cruel taskmaster. Let not any human being who abuses animals think that they have God's permission to do so!

I therefore want to close this section by asking of all religious people this question: In Gen 1:26, God says, *ve-yirdu ... be-khol ha-āretz* – 'let them have dominion ... over all the earth' or, 'let them rule ... over all the earth'. So let me ask you: what is the nature of that dominion or rule? Does your understanding of the nature of God, make you interpret

---

[a] Num. 22:32
[b] Jonah 4:11
[c] see Num 13:30

that as meaning that we can subjugate nature to our will? Does it mean that we can oppress, misuse, exploit and decimate nature in whatever fashion we like? Or does your understanding of God mean that you interpret this phrase to mean that we are to take wise stewardship over creation? Does it mean that we are to cause life to flourish and dwell in abundance upon the earth? Now let me ask you this: which of these two interpretations – subjugation or stewardship – will magnify the holiness of Yahveh's great reputation?

'Love your neighbour as yourself'

Yahveh teaches us to love our neighbour as ourselves.[a] The prophet Yeshua` was therefore asked, who are our neighbours?[b] The Hebrew word used in the verse from Torah does not mean 'someone who lives next door', but rather 'fellow human being', hence Yeshua`'s reply with the parable of the good Samaritan.

Yeshua` also taught us to 'love our enemies'.[c] If we have resolved the question of who are neighbours are, perhaps we should also resolve the question of who our enemies are.

When Yeshua` told us to love our enemies, he prefaced his statement with, *'You have heard it said, "Love your neighbour and hate your enemy."'* For almost 2,000 years, no one knew where this came from, since it is not found *anywhere* in Jewish literature. Until that is, the discovery of the Dead Sea Scrolls. In the *Community Rule* it advises Essenes to love one's neighbour, but hate one's enemies.[d]

If Yeshua` had been an Essene, he would have upheld this precept to hate one's enemies, but he actually spoke against it. I know that there are many who praise Essene teaching as a light to the world and a paragon of enlightenment, but as well as many positive things, it also contained some things which are pretty negative, and effectively *against* Yeshua`'s teaching – keeping wisdom secret, for example, whereas Yeshua` told his followers to proclaim his teaching from the rooftops. They also separated themselves from society; by the example of his way of life, Yeshua` did anything but.

If we look at the context to the Golden Rule, it is preceded by the statement, 'Do not seek revenge or bear a grudge against one of your people'.[e] The Essenes took this to mean that one was to love *only* those who shared one's views, and hate everyone else. Essenism was an

---

[a] Lev 19:17
[b] S.Yesh. 68:7 – cf Lk 10:29
[c] S.Yesh. 70:2 – cf Mt 5:44, Lk 6:27, 35
[d] 1QS 3:3-4, also 9:21
[e] Lev 19:18a

exclusive way of life even within Judaism.

So when Yeshua` told us, 'love your enemy', on the face of it his saying seems to be telling us that we are to love those who are engaged in open hostility towards us. However, this is not the whole picture.

The Aramaic words for 'enemy' – such as *be'el d'baba*, or *be'el d'sana*, all have a much wider meaning than just 'someone who is at war with us'. They can also cover anything from an adversary, a rival, to an opponent, or just someone who is not one of you – i.e. someone who holds a different theological, social or political view to yourself and your group.

When Yeshua` said, 'Love those who hate you,' he wasn't just talking about those who despise us, he was also referring to those who are not *one of us* – those outside our interest group. There are those who are not *us*, yet do not hate us, and in practical terms are not our 'enemies'. We are commanded to love them too.

Religious fundamentalists love only those who are of their faith, those who share their views and their beliefs, but they are arrogant, condescending and abrupt towards those who share a different viewpoint. They bully and harass those outside their faith into converting. This is not the way to love your neighbour *or* your enemy.

There is nothing wrong with disagreeing with someone. There is nothing wrong with holding very clear-cut views and beliefs. One does not even have to meet someone half-way to their opinions or even share their ways in order to love that person. You simply have to be at peace with yourself, and not be threatened by the fact that someone does not agree with you. The fact that someone believes something very different to you, does not automatically negate everything *you* believe.

If we look even earlier in Leviticus, we read, *'Do not hate your brother in your heart.'* [a] It is the heart (i.e. the mind) which is the most important thing to train and to nurture in the Israelite religion. If you are at peace with yourself, you can then prepare yourself to be at peace with others. We are to 'judge our neighbour fairly' [b] and treat them well, even if we disagree with them.

Leviticus could have used the Hebrew word *racham* – to have compassionate, unconditional love for someone, but it didn't. It used a much broader verb, *ahav*, and that is simply behaving in a way towards others which is not negative. By the use of the words 'as yourself' in the commandment, it implies that we also take a moment to consider our actions on others, as if our actions were being done to us. We need to ask ourselves, 'How would I feel if I were on the receiving end of what I am

---

[a] Lev 19:17
[b] Lev 19:15

doing to others?'

I strongly believe God causes the paths of different people to cross; for the people God wants us to meet, we should respect them, treat them fairly, and do them no harm. And of course, there are different ways of showing such love. When we encounter someone for a few short moments, someone we will never see again, it's expected that we will be courteous, respectful, not frown or pull a face that implies we are annoyed at someone communicating with us. 'Loving' such a person in that instance, does not mean getting involved in a full-blown emotional relationship with them! It's the very basic stuff – treating someone in the same way as we would wish others to treat us – no more, no less.

With someone who is not one of 'us', it may be more difficult, depending on the degree of difference from what is 'us', but in such a situation, it means 'not hating them in our heart' – not wishing them harm, not rejoicing over their misfortune, not putting obstacles in their way, not begrudging helping them, and so on.

We have a strong tendency to come at this with the associations that the English language has given to the word 'love'. The bottom line is that the English word 'love' is actually very limited, implying 'liking someone an awful lot', but in Hebrew, it isn't limited to that. It isn't restricted to the emotional level, but covers how you deal with other people as well. In English, when we hear the word 'love', we automatically think of things we *should* do to the object of our love, but in the Hebrew mind-set, you are *also* to consider the things you *shouldn't* do. When you love someone, there are just some things you simply *don't* do, and what you wouldn't do to a friend whom you love, likewise, don't do those things to an enemy, an adversary, or just someone who is different.

... Name ...

Having explained the power of God's holiness, let me tell you how to further sanctify God's Name. When we talk about sanctifying God's Name, in this phrase, 'name' actually means 'reputation' – the reputation of God.[a] Consider when someone slanders another person's good name, they say bad things to damage their reputation – it's the same kind of thing.

The Israelite religion is ultimately about living a way of life that will represent the holiness, distinctiveness and innate moral-ness of

---

[a] that's why proclaiming the Name of God doesn't simply mean calling out God's Holy Name; it also means recounting the great deeds of Yahveh throughout the ages.

Yahveh forever. It's about Yahveh, not us. Of course, we as human beings will benefit from this way of life, but ultimately it's about Yahveh.

Because God has no physical form,[a] he gave us a code of behaviour that would be representative of God throughout all time. The pinnacle of that code is righteousness, justice, concern for others, helpfulness, respect and dignity of life. Unfortunately Israelites, being made of the same stuff as all other human beings, are not perfect. Yahveh knew from the outset that this high standard would not always be adhered to, and if God only relied on us following a moral code perfectly, then God's holiness would inevitably be defamed.

So in addition to the moral laws, Yahveh gave Israel a set of customs and traditions that most Israelites *could* follow. Many of these laws have no logic or reason other than making us visibly different and distinctive from other nations. That differentness and distinctiveness was intended to be a fall-back or standby in case we didn't follow the moral laws properly; if we as human beings didn't manage to represent Yahveh in our moral character, then at least God would be represented in our customs and traditions. These customs are not dependent on belief, so they also give a nation of widely differing views and opinions a culture that would bring us together.

And these traditions were to be forever, because Yahveh is forever.

In an ideal world, it would be enough for our morality to be an eternal witness to our God. But even those who claim to believe in and follow God still commit adultery, still lie, still engage in malicious gossip, are still selfish, vain, unhelpful etc. If we relied on a religious community being morally perfect to represent God, then because we are only human, we are doomed to fail from the start. Hence God's choice of giving us a set of cultural traditions to represent God as well.

So bearing in mind that what we do as followers of Yahveh is meant to represent God, to sanctify God's Name means 'to do anything which augments God's reputation and brings honour and renown to God'. To sanctify God's Name means to live a life which causes others to love Yahveh, even those who are not of our faith. To Sanctify God's Name means to bring blessing to the peoples you live amongst through your faith, so that when they think of Yahveh's Name, it inspires awe and wonder in their hearts.

Now, an important question here, given that Yeshua` chose to include this issue in his prayer, is: Why is the sanctification of God's Name so important? Well, it's because the converse issue – the desecration of God's Name or reputation – was such an overwhelming

---

[a] Dt 4:12, 15

issue at the time.

Priests are supposed to be ambassadors for Yahveh on earth. They minister to Yahveh, and to God's people. When they do something badly wrong, it not only reflects on them as human beings, but on God as well. So in Yeshua`'s day, when the chief priests – mostly Sadducees – acted immorally and unjustly, they were impugning God's name or reputation; they brought ill-repute to God's Name.

The prophet Yeshua` prophesied the demise of the Sadducees. There is the parable of the steward who realises that his master's return is delayed, and so starts to treat the other servants in an abusive way; when the master finally does return, the parable relates that the steward will be severely punished.[a] Yeshua` also told the parable of the lazy and wicked servant, who buried his money and did nothing with it.[b] He also said, '... to everyone who has, more will be given, but from those who don't have, even what little they do have will be taken away.'[c]

Yahveh gave us Torah, not so that we would add to it (like the Pharisees), but so that we would profit by it. In the case of the Sadducees, not only did they not add to Torah, they did not grow, learn or profit by it either. Those who have, are those who use God's Teaching as their foundation, the root stock from which they grow spiritually. Those who had nothing, even what little they did have would be taken from them – their authority in the Temple, the lands they had stolen, and their widely despised sect.

Based on Isaiah 22:14, the ancient belief was that sins against human beings could be forgiven, but sins against the holiness of God could not be forgiven in this life.[d] The Essenes went to live in the desert, because they felt that the Sadducees had so corrupted the holiness of God's reputation, they believed that the Temple itself was no longer holy. Yeshua` obviously disagreed with this stance regarding the Temple, because he still prayed there.[e] He criticised the Saducean priests, but still believed in the holiness of the Temple.

However, what finally desecrated the Temple and removed its holiness occurred in the last days before its destruction. The Romans were closing in on Jerusalem, and had laid siege to it. Opposing factions

---

[a] S.Yesh. 110; I believe the wicked steward represents the Sadducees (cf Mt 24:45-51, Lk 12:41-46)

[b] S.Yesh. 80 – normally referred to as the 'Parable of the Talents'. a 'talent' was a measure of gold, not a personal forte. The lazy servant in the parable represents the Sadducees (cf Mt 25:14-28, Lk 19:12-27).

[c] S.Yesh. 81 – cf Mk 4:25

[d] see also S.Yesh. 166:2 – cf Mk 3:28-29

[e] this is yet another reason why Yeshua` could not have been an Essene; he would not have regularly visited the Temple if he had been an Essene.

of the Zealots had holed themselves up in the Temple compound. Not content with fighting the Romans, they also fought with each other. They brought weapons of war into the Temple – which in itself was a desecration (and may possibly have been the 'abomination of desolation' prophesied by Daniel and Yeshua`). They also shed human blood in the Temple by killing people during fights in the sacred precincts. You see, human blood is not kosher (for that matter, neither God nor humans are kosher;[a] therefore neither the blood of humans or gods would be acceptable as a sin offering). Having shed blood in the Temple, the Zealots thereby desecrated it – and sealed its fate. I believe that with the Temple's holiness now ruined, and the sacred reputation of God's house erased, God decided that the Temple could no longer remain standing – it had to fall.

As Jews, we lament the fall of the Temple – and rightly we should. But we should learn the lesson of the destruction of the Temple. If we try to rebuild it in the midst of hatred, war and bloodshed, then the task will never be completed; Yahveh will *ensure* that it is never rebuilt while negative conditions remain. It will only ever be rebuilt in peace.[b]

So how do we sanctify God's reputation, and increase the great renown Yahveh? If we as a community cause others to respect the God of Israel, to trust in Yahveh and seek Yahveh's wisdom, then we sanctify God's Name. If priests and ministers act in such a way that God, and not themselves, is praised, then God's Name is sanctified. If we, as religious people, act with humility and compassion before those who do not follow our faith, we will be respected, and in turn, God will be respected too. And if *as followers of Yahveh* we think, act and behave towards others with kindness, respect and understanding, then God's Name – God's reputation – is sanctified.

Those who are called by the Name of Yahveh

As I draw near the end of this chapter, I want to expand on an unusual phrase from the Miqra. In several places in the Torah & the Prophets, it refers to those who are 'called by Yahveh's Name.'[c]

---

[a] In the list of animals approved for eating (Lev 11 & Dt 14), notice that neither humans nor God can be included in the list; neither God nor humans have any of the signs that would classify them as kosher. Only kosher animals – and only very specific kosher animals – could be used as sin offerings. For this reason, neither humans nor even God can be classed as suitable kosher sin offerings.

[b] cf Micah 3:10, which criticises political and religious people who build Zion with bloodshed and injustice.

[c] e.g. Deut 28:10, 2Chron 7:14, Isaiah 43:7

In ancient times, you indicated which religion you belonged to by the name of the god you worshipped. An Israelite would have said, 'I am a son of Yahveh', or 'I am a daughter of Yahveh'. In this specific Hebrew phrase, the words 'son' (*ben*) or 'daughter' (*bat*) would also have the secondary meaning of 'follower'. Saying that you are a child of Yahveh means much more than indicating your religion. It says what your lifestyle is, what moral and ethical code you adhere to, and what kind of person you aspire to be.

Through the prophet Isaiah,[a] Yahveh our God has promised that there will come a day when God will pour out God's spirit on the earth, and the followers of Yahveh will spring up like grass after rain. Therefore in the future, Yahveh's followers will not only be those who follow God because their ancestors did; Yahveh will also call people scattered among the Gentile nations of the earth. Some individuals will identify themselves by proclaiming, *'I belong to Yahveh'*. Others will join the House of Israel and symbolically write on their hand, *'Yahveh's'*. God says that these non-Jews will attach *themselves*[b] to God – that is, they have not gone through any conversion process or been approved by a Beth Din., These people will show that they belong to Yahveh by their thoughts, words and actions – that they truly follow the Way of Yahveh.

As I have said, we show who our Heavenly Father is by the way in which we emulate God. Yahveh promised that the descendants of Abraham would be a blessing to the nations of the earth. Therefore, be a blessing to others by the dignity in which you conduct your life, the kindness you show others, the encouragement that you give to others, and in the helpfulness of your actions. In this way you can proclaim God's name (or 'reputation') throughout the earth.

On your mind, your heart and your soul, always wear a diadem of gold that says, 'I am a son of Yahveh', or 'I am a daughter of Yahveh', and even though that diadem will never be visible to the outside world, people will know that it is there – its light shining from Yahveh's Name – because through your words and deeds, people will know who your heavenly Father is – that Yahveh is your God:

'Then all the peoples of the earth will see that you are called by the Name of Yahveh, and they will have an awesome respect for you.'[c]

I want to end this section by telling you a Talmidi parable that demonstrates how the extent of what you do, can sanctify God's Name or reputation:

---

[a] Isaiah 44:1-5.
[b] this is what the term nilveh / nilvah in Isa 56:3 refers to – people who pledge allegiance to the God of Israel *themselves*, independent of any committee giving their approval to officially become a Jew.
[c] Deut 28:10

There was a rich Israelite who went to live in a foreign land. While he was there, he encountered another tribe of people who were also foreign to that land. However, he noticed how they lived in poverty and servitude, and the soul of their people was dying because they had forgotten their traditions and language.

Moved by their plight, he set up a place where food and clothing could be distributed to them, and paid for the education of their children. He also employed some of the elders of their people to teach the younger generation their customs and language, and even their pagan religion, so that they could regain their pride and self-worth as a people.

So moved were these people at the efforts of this rich Israelite, that they invited him to participate in one of their festivals to their gods. However, the Israelite man said, 'I am honoured that you would think of inviting me as a guest, but the laws of my God say that I can only witness to the ways of my God; I'm afraid I must decline your invitation.'

The elders of the people were offended, and said, 'But you have done so much for us; will you not join us so that we might thank you?'

But the Israelite man said, 'As I said, I can only witness to the ways of my God. I have done so by feeding and clothing your poor, educating your children, and giving you back the self-respect of your culture.'

The elders of the pagan people were astonished, and cried out, 'Blessed be your God, the God of Israel, who has compassion and love even for those who do not follow your God!'

A note on the pronunciation of God's Name

One major cultural difference between Rabbinic Jews on the one hand, and Karaite and Talmidi Israelites on the other, is that Karaites and Talmidis pronounce[a] the Holy Name. We are told by the mainstream that we are breaking the third commandment, which says:

'You shall not use the name of Yahveh your God for falsehood; for

---

[a] There is a difference in opinion over how the Holy Name is to be pronounced. Most Karaites pronounce it as 'Yehovah', and most Talmidis pronounce it as 'Yahveh'. however, it is not important *how* it is pronounced; what matters is that it *is* pronounced, and that you pronounce it in a reasoned way that is true for you.

Yahveh will not hold anyone guiltless who uses God's name for falsehood.'

The Hebrew word translated here as 'falsehood' is *shav*. This word implies that we should not use the holy name to lie and deceive, or for evil and destructive purposes, or use it in common, everyday conversation (i.e. as if it were worthless or of the same value as anyone else's name). The third commandment doesn't forbid the pronunciation of the Holy Name; it forbids the abuse and misuse of the Holy Name.

What we cannot do is use the Holy Name to curse others; we cannot use God's Name to swear that we will tell the truth, and then lie; we cannot use the Holy Name to deceive or mislead people; we cannot use God's authority to oppress or persecute others and make them suffer; we cannot use God's Name in bad language when we cuss and swear; and we cannot use the Holy Name in everyday conversation as if we were talking about a human being.

In the Talmidi community, we tend to be guided by the following counsel – that we can only use God's Name in private prayer, or in communal prayer when you know those present have great reverence for the Name of God; you can use the Name to bless others, and when speaking reverently of God to glorify God. We can never use God's Name in anger, or when engaged in a heated argument or debate with someone.

I can understand why Rabbinic Jews have such caution about pronouncing the Holy Name. If it were in common use, then there is a danger it could become a swear-word. I recall a joke about a small boy who asks his father, 'Why did Joseph and Mary name their son after a swear word?' In our tradition, if anyone is prone to using foul language – even someone who regularly says, 'Oh My God!' – then such a person should *never* pronounce the Holy Name, even in times of prayer; the danger of it being thoughtlessly used as a swear word is too great for such individuals.[a]

It is one thing to hold God's Name in reverence, and quite another to ban it, so that it is forgotten and blotted out. This fate is supposed to be reserved for the Amalekites and other enemies of Israel, not God. God said that God's name was to be remembered forever; in Ex 3:15 Yahveh says most emphatically, *'This is my Name forever, the Name by which I am to be remembered from generation to generation.'*

Blotting out someone's name is the worst curse you can wish on

---

[a] See Lev 24:10-23. In most English-language Jewish bibles, Lev 24:10 reads 'The son of the Israelite woman pronounced the Name' – making it look like the ensuing punishment was for merely pronouncing the Name. In fact, the half-Israelite half-Egyptian man used the Name of God as a swear word – something absolutely unthinkable and **unforgiveable** in the Israelite religion.

anyone in Israelite culture. In the Israelite religion, we are commanded not to use God's Name for false, evil or deceptive purposes. We are to maintain the holiness of God's Name – it cannot become commonplace, it cannot be used to make a false statement sound true, it cannot be used to curse or swear, and it cannot be used in anger. In the religion that follows the Oral Law, this has been interpreted as forbidding us to even speak God's Name – in effect, "You shall blot out God's Name entirely." Through the prophet Jeremiah, God warned us against those *"who intend to make My people forget My Name"*.[a]

What has our Holy and Living God done to deserve such a curse? To blot out God's Name is to curse God, and there are consequences. I cannot speak of the life-consequences, but the spiritual consequences remove you from the immediate Presence of God, so that God remains only a theological concept; only by acknowledging God's Holy Name can we truly acknowledge that Yahveh is a living God.

Writing God as 'G-d', and in Hebrew, writing *Elohim* ('God') as *eloqim* are but fanciful, pompous affectations which God has not commanded, and which God does not require. By blotting out God's Name, we have hidden the shining focus of our spiritual attention under a bushel, so that now we go after physical objects in religion, and follow adoringly after human leaders as if they shared God's authority. People can now only seek the symbols and accessories of their religion – the things that are not God, instead of seeking God.

By blotting out the Name of God, and by excising it from translations into other languages, we end up having no defence against those religions who claim that their god – one who once was visible and walked the earth – is an incarnation of our God – One who *cannot* be seen and who has – and will never have - *any* physical form.

In 2011, Pope Benedict XVI gave a directive to the Catholic Church that forbade the pronouncing of God's Name in Catholic churches. The ostensible reason for this cited 'longstanding Jewish and Church practice'. However, I suspect the real reason was to prevent people eventually realising that the 'Lord' mentioned throughout the books of the Hebrew Bible was not 'Jesus' but rather Yahveh. It is for this reason that the Miqra teaches us to speak the Holy Name, as Ps 83:19 (83:18 in Christian bibles) says, *"So people may know, that You alone – whose name is Yahveh – are the most High over all the earth"*.

Throughout history, various religions have claimed that their god and our God are the same, but if you read the original Hebrew, God proclaims 'I am Yahveh' 156 times i.e. I am not Molekh, nor Baal, nor Asherah, nor anyone else by any other name, whether god or human;

---

[a] Jer 23:27

only Yahveh is Yahveh. [a] In Jer 16:19-21, the prophet Jeremiah explains that one day, the Gentile nations will realise that they have manufactured gods for themselves, that they have inherited falsehoods from their forebears, and on that day, *God Himself* will make them know that God's Name is Yahveh, and not anything or anyone else – not 'Lord', not 'Jesus', not Molekh or Baal – but Yahveh.

In Num 6:24-26 we are given the words of the priestly blessing. [b] We are then told that this is how the priests will put God's Name on the Israelites, and whenever this is done, God will bless us. If we are blessed by the pronunciation of God's Name, then we will be truly blessed.

We can also call on the name of God to rescue us – the prophet Joel [c] says, *'And everyone who calls on the name of Yahveh will be saved.'* This implies that one actually has to say the Name – not 'Lord' or 'Jesus', but Yahveh.

The bottom line in this is that those who are blessed by the Holy Name will truly be blessed, and those who call for salvation by the Holy Name will truly be saved. Those who seek answers through the Holy Name will find *real* answers, and those who seek peace in the Holy Name will find true peace.

One last thing with regards to the Holy Name of Yahveh. I want to demonstrate to you the powerful effect of actually using the Holy Name – an effect that you can actually feel and experience yourself. Once you have finished reading this book, ask yourself, 'Do I now have a real sense of the personality of Yahveh? Do I now know who Yahveh is? Do I have a real sense of what Yahveh is about, why Yahveh does things, and what Yahveh *is* doing, right now among us?' Yahveh has a personality, and I assure you, by the end of this book, **you *will* know Yahveh!** That is the great and awesome power of Yahveh!!

The message of this couplet:

What we should now realise here, is that these words are actually a call to action. By acknowledging God as our heavenly Father, we are called to imitate God in our ways. And in calling for the sanctification of God's Name, we are calling for God's reputation to be bettered and upheld by the actions, thoughts and words of those who follow God.

---

[a] see Isa 43:11 – *'I, and I alone, am Yahveh, and besides Me there is no other saviour;'* also Isa 45:5 – *'I am Yahveh – there is no other* [i.e. there is no one else who is Yahveh]*; and besides Me there is no other god'.*

[b] 'May Yahveh bless you and watch over you; may Yahveh deal favourably with you and be gracious to you; may Yahveh turn good fortune towards you and grant you peace.'

[c] Joel 2:32

Show who your heavenly Father is, by the way that you think, speak and behave. As Jacob the Pious wrote, *'Become doers of the message, not just listeners.'*[a]

Illustrations from the words of the prophet Yeshua`

Yeshua` said:

'...when you pray, go into your innermost room and shut the door, and pray to your Father who's in secret places; and your heavenly Father who sees what's done in secret will reward you.'[b]

'...love your enemies, do good to those who hate you, bless those who curse you, and pray for those who abuse you, so that you may be called the children of the Most High.'[c]

'...be merciful, even as your heavenly Father is merciful.'[d]

'Be perfect therefore, just as your heavenly Father is perfect.'[e]

'Therefore, if you who are imperfect, know how to give good things to your children, how much more so will your Father in heaven, who is perfect, give you good things when God's children ask God.'[f]

'In the same way, let your light shine before others, so that they may see that light, and glorify your heavenly Father.'[g]

---

[a] Ig. Yq. 6:1 – cf Ep. James 1:22
[b] S.Yesh. 57:3-4; Mg. M. 34:3-4; cf Mt 6:6
[c] S.Yesh. 70:2, see also Mg. M. 4:1; cf Mt 5:44
[d] S.Yesh. 70:7; cf Lk 6:36
[e] Mg. M. 10:1; cf Mt 5:48
[f] S.Yesh. 37:3, Mg. M. 38:3-4; cf Mt 7:11, Lk 11:13
[g] S.Yesh. 74:3; cf Mt 5:16

CHAPTER THREE: Praying for the present and future Kingdom

תאתי מלכותך
תהי רעותך

titey malkhutakh,
tihey re`utakh,

May Your Kingdom be fulfilled!
May Your will be realised –

To understand this couplet, again it is important to know what was going on at the time. However, first there are some basic terms that we need to define and understand. For example, most non-Jews will not understand what the term 'kingdom' means with relation to God in an Israelite context. Nor will they be aware of ancient Jewish aspirations with regard to God's kingdom at that time either, so I will concentrate on these aspects for most of this chapter.

Yeshua`'s personal theology was very much centred on the Kingdom of God, and an examination of this couplet will throw light on what he meant. It is a good example of how knowing that in biblical poetry, the second line of a couplet often repeats the ideas of the first but expresses it in a slightly different way, actually helps us with the interpretation of *both* lines. So here, the line 'May Your will be realised' is like an explanation of the first: 'May Your Kingdom be fulfilled!'

Line 3: May Your Kingdom be fulfilled!

... Kingdom...

We have here in this one word a good example of how some things don't always translate fully from one culture to another. The most common misconception about God's Kingdom is that it is another way of saying 'heaven'. I think this stems from two things.

Firstly, from the evangelist Matthew's frequent use of the term, 'the kingdom of heaven,' and secondly, from some instances where such a kingdom is referred to as if it were in the future.

Anyone who is familiar with ancient Jewish culture would naturally be aware that in certain instances, the word 'heaven' was simply a common way of avoiding using the word 'God', or even the holy Name itself. Out of respect, Pharisaic Jewish culture used euphemisms to avoid explicitly referring to God,[a] and the word 'heaven' was a common euphemism for 'God'. Therefore, the phrase 'kingdom of heaven' means *exactly* the same as 'kingdom of God'.

Some people will think that the kingdom of God is a mystical place somewhere. Now, we have to be aware that ancient Jewish Aramaic and biblical Hebrew were somewhat limited in their range of vocabulary. Today, a child who has undergone a full education will be able to understand and use approximately 10-16,000 different words, an adult about twice that. In contrast, biblical Hebrew only had about 3,500 basic words to work with. As a result, many words had to serve many different purposes. As a consequence, most words were overworked, and given a wide range of meanings; to figure out which meaning is intended, you have to look at the *context* in which the word occurs – there are very few words indeed that mean the same thing in every context.[b] For example, the Aramaic and Hebrew word *malkhut* – normally translated as 'kingdom' was such a word. It was used not only to mean 'kingdom', but also 'kingship', 'royal authority', 'sovereignty' and 'reign'. In the *Book of Esther*,[c] it even meant 'royal apparel'!

In modern times, we might speak of the *reign* of a king or queen. For example, you might say, 'during the *reign* of Queen Victoria, many social changes took place'. However, in ancient Aramaic and biblical Hebrew you would have to say, 'during the *kingdom* of Queen Victoria', because there was no separate word for 'reign'.

So our next question would naturally be, *when is the reign of God?* Psalm 103:19 says, *'Yahveh has established God's throne in heaven, and God's kingdom rules over all.'* Psalm 145:13 furthermore says, *'Your kingdom is an eternal kingdom, and your dominion lasts from generation to generation.'* These two verses give us the understanding that God's reign – that is, God's kingdom – is now, and that it lasts forever.

So how does God's kingdom apply to us, and how are we to relate

---

[a] In my personal opinion though, I feel what this does to us psychologically, is put God at a distance, and turns Yahveh, a knowable God, into a nameless, unknowable entity.

[b] Even the simple word *vᵉ-* (and) can mean different things in different contexts: so, then, but, for the reason that, because, so that, etc.

[c] Esther 5:1

it as citizens of God's present kingdom? Let me put it this way. When we pick a new President or Prime Minister, each Presidency or Prime Ministership will be characterised by certain laws, policies and ways of thinking. Just as a presidency puts forward certain proposals, so also God's reign carries with it an implicit set of proposals. During God's reign, certain changes, policies and laws are meant to be enacted and followed.

Therefore, to live God's kingdom means to live in a just, compassionate, dignified and merciful way. The prophet Yeshua` said that 'the kingdom of God is within you.'[a] He also said that not everyone who called him 'Master' would find the kingdom of God, but only those who did the will of their heavenly Father.[b] Therefore to live God's kingdom means to treat the poor with dignity, to be aware of one's responsibilities to one's family and the society in which one lives; it means being considerate and respectful of the people we meet, both friends and strangers; it means not oppressing those who are not of our own people,[c] or those who are disadvantaged; it means families valuing their elderly,[d] and respecting their status and knowledge; it means not making fun of the less capable,[e] and living in a way that does not defame God's reputation or character.

The four aspects of the Kingdom of God

Whenever the prophet Yeshua` used the term 'kingdom of God', he talked about several different aspects of it. Because we are stuck with our modern, western view of what a 'kingdom' is, we don't quite get the full range of ideas Yeshua` was trying to put across. There are four main ideas conveyed in the phrase; to fully understand the faith and motivations of Yeshua`'s first Jewish followers, you have to make yourself familiar with all of them.

Firstly, he often used the phrase, 'The kingdom of God is at hand'.[f] This should more properly be translated as, 'the **kingship** of

---

[a] S.Yesh. 20:3; cf Lk 17:21
[b] S.Yesh. 107:2; cf Mt 7:21
[c] Ex 22:21
[d] Lev 19:32, Prov 16:31
[e] Lev 19:14, Dt 27:18
[f] The use of the words 'at hand' would here be similar to its use in the phrase, 'Help is *at hand*.' The Greek ἤγγικεν (engiken) implies 'drawing near', or 'approaching'. The Syriac translates this verse with a verb that has the same meaning. Another possible way of translating this verse to give its sense would be, 'God our Judge and King is about to act!' (see S.Yesh. 5:2, 63:12).

God is fast approaching'; you see, 'kingdom' and 'kingship' are both translated by the Aramaic *malkhut*, hence the confusion. In this sentence, he was referring to God's *royal authority* to act in human affairs as Judge and King – in effect, he was referring to the impending 'Day of Yahveh'.[a] This was the imminent event that Yeshua`'s first Jewish followers were fearfully awaiting and preparing for, as the age in which they were living drew to its close.[b]

With this meaning in mind, Yeshua` told a couple of parables that described God's imminent intervention under God's authority as Judge and King, in order to sort out the problems afflicting society at the time (such as the parable of the Ten Young Women,[c] and the Parable of the Large Dragnet).[d] God had seen how certain chief priests were corrupt,[e] and were thereby defaming the holiness of the Temple ministry; God had seen how rich people were ignoring their responsibility to the poor, thereby defaming God's Name as Provider; and how the Zealots were defaming God's Name by using God's authority to justify acts of violence. Yeshua` was saying that God Himself would intervene and act very soon, using God's authority as King to bring about justice, chastise wrongdoing, reward the righteous and punish the guilty – even in this life. Therefore, the only appropriate response by the unjust to such news was to repent.[f] On the other hand, such a declaration – that God would soon intervene in his authority as king to right wrongs – was indeed 'good news' for the long-suffering poor and innocent of the Land.

Secondly, he spoke about how difficult it was for the rich to enter the kingdom of God. Here he was talking about being able to change heart, and enter into a way of life that would be typical of God's *reign*; in such instances, 'kingdom of God' is more properly 'reign of God'. The rich were so centred on the accumulation of money, wealth and profit, that they ignored God's laws to forgive the debts of fellow

---

[a] This particular Day of Yahveh which Yeshua` called 'the coming of God's Kingship' was the destruction of Judea and Jerusalem, and the Roman Exile.

[b] The Greek of the NT (eg Mt 12:32) actually means 'at the completion of the present era/epoch'. The Aramaic equivalent for the Greek *aiōnos* (age/era) would have been *'iddana*. This is a span or portion of time – an era or epoch, not the end of time itself. All of time is divided into these epochs, and Yeshua` was referring to the end of the current era in which he was living (which ended in 70-135 CE). When one age ends, another age begins.

[c] S.Yesh. 168 – cf Mt 25:1-13

[d] S.Yesh. 169 – cf Mt 13:47-50

[e] for example, they seized tithes from the threshing floor before they were properly apportioned. As a result, many poorer priests' families starved (Josephus, *Antiquities of the Jews,* Bk 20, Ch 9, pt 2). The Sadducean priests also seized and owned land which they were not entitled as priests to own.

[f] S.Yesh. 5:2 – cf Mt 3:2, 4:17

Israelites every seven years (and thereby relieve the burden on the very poor). They were so enthralled by the lure of wealth, that they could not see that they were rich only because God gave them that wealth. If it was not used for good, then that wealth would one day be taken away from them (which it was when the Romans destroyed Jerusalem and exiled many of the Jewish population of Judea).

The third meaning of 'the kingdom of God' is the most vital to understand. It plays an *enormous* part in Yeshua`'s personal theology. To him, this aspect of the kingdom (or 'rule') of God was not a physical place, or necessarily a time in the future, or even heaven, but rather a present state of being *that had to live within us*.[a] God's rule was a way of justice and inclusion; Yeshua` saw it as a duty to be just and fair to one another in one's daily affairs, and to bring back into the fold those whom religious moralisers had cast aside as being permanently beyond redemption, thereby taking away their right to hope for anything better.

The fourth and last aspect of the kingdom was what it could become in the far distant future. It was not a time that would come about through war or conflict, but slowly, like yeast leavening a huge batch of flour,[b] or a tiny mustard seed that grows into a large bush.[c] In such instances, Yeshua` was speaking of the *fulfilment* of the Kingdom of God – what it had the potential to become in the far future, once God's full sovereignty was established over both heaven and earth.

To summarise, the term, 'the kingdom of God' doesn't have just one meaning; failure to understand this over the past two thousand years has blurred God's Message, and obscured God's plans. As Followers of the Way, we have an opportunity to put that right. We can make it clear to others that every mention of 'the kingdom' in Yeshua`'s parables and sayings can be categorised in one of these four aspects:

- God's imminent intervention as King and Judge (the coming 'kingship of God');
- God's set of external laws under which a just and stable society functions (the present 'reign of God');
- God's message and values that live within us (the eternal 'rule of God');

---

[a] S.Yesh. 20:3 – cf Lk 17:21
[b] S.Yesh. 25 – cf Mt 13:33, Lk 13:21
[c] S.Yesh. 24:3-6 – cf Mk 4:30-32

- and the future age of peace and light which has the potential to come about and be fulfilled in the future (the end-time 'full Sovereignty of God').

Whenever we read Yeshua`'s parables, it will help us to know which of these four aspects of the Kingdom he was referring to.

Yahveh as our true King

Every community in the ancient Middle East had kings. In the original Israelite religion, however, they alone had a king that no one could see. They alone had a king who would treat them justly, not take advantage of them, would not make extortionate demands on them, and who would protect them and care for them. This King was Yahveh.

In ancient times, kings were the leaders of armies. They were the ancient equivalents of generals. When ancient peoples sought someone to lead them and save them from their enemies, they turned to their human kings. It was not to be this way with Israel.

In times of conflict, Israel was supposed to turn to Yahveh, and Yahveh would appoint a temporary human leader. This 'deputy' would follow God's instructions and so save them from their enemies. Gideon was such a man during the time of the Judges (or 'warrior-defenders') of Israel. When Gideon gained victory over Israel's enemies, the Israelites sought to make him their king, but this was Gideon's answer: *'I will not rule over you, nor will my son rule over you. Yahveh alone will rule over you.'*[a]

This was the original Yahwist ideal. After generations of demanding a human king, God finally relented,[b] and gave them Saul. Unfortunately, Israel's experience of human kings was a disaster. Her kings were constantly unfaithful to Yahveh, and were sometimes cruel and unjust. They made ruinous decisions which put them into the hands of their enemies.

With such a history of bad kings, Israel and Judah began to long for an ideal king. Thus was born messianism – the idea of a king-saviour. Fuelled by contact with the Persian religion, Israelites began to long for a king who would rescue them from a world of darkness and deliver them into the world of light. What many Israelites just could not understand, was that instead of turning to a human king-saviour, they had only to turn to their original King-Saviour – Yahveh – and they would be delivered from their woes.

---

[a] Judges 8:23
[b] 1Sam 8:1-19

To those who advocate messianism – the idea of a human king-saviour – I say this: Why isn't Yahveh enough for you? Why isn't your heavenly Father sufficient – your living God, who loves you, who cares about you, who teaches and guides you, who comforts you in times of distress, who shows you the error of your ways and heals you, who understands every pain and sorrow that you endure, who knew you before you were born, and who has given you the promise of eternal life in the world to come, in the presence of God's radiant glory? Why isn't Yahveh enough for you?

Yahveh, through the purifying power of God's glory, is able to cleanse us of our sins, forgive us and make us whole – not through any blood or death. Yahveh is the love that does not have to be bought, and the happiness that does not have to be suffered for.

Yahveh is the father who guides you, the mother who loves you without condition, the best friend you can ever have, who loves you so much that God *lives* for you so that through God's *life*, you can have happiness here on earth, and eternal life in heaven; Yahveh is your defender who saves you on a daily basis, your advocate who fights your corner, the healer who cares for you in times of sickness, and the wise counsellor who provides every answer. Yahveh is the bread that comes without price, the drink that is completely free, the food that sates every hunger, and the wine that slakes every thirst.

To those awaiting a messiah-saviour I ask, why do you need more? What exactly is the 'more' that you need? You have a great and powerful King in Yahveh; why do you need another one? Why do you await another saviour? Search in your heart of hearts – is not Yahveh the true, living God that you know – the God whom you were created and born to know? The God whom you have always known? Why then seek someone else?

Modern Talmidaism holds to this original Israelite ideal of Yahveh alone as our King-Saviour. It has turned its back on messianism as the failed practice of putting trust and belief in imperfect human beings; and of hankering after the future, while forgetting the present. We don't have to wait for a king-saviour to arrive, because our true King-Saviour is already with us, *here and now.*

Becoming children for the sake of the Kingdom of God

The prophet Yeshua` said, *'Believe me I tell you, unless you*

82

accept the kingdom of God like a child, you shall never find it. '[a]

In Aramaic, the word for 'child' (*talya*) also means 'servant'. It's easy for us to imagine how becoming servant-like will help us find the kingdom of God. But Yeshua`'s play on words has this dual aspect to it – becoming servant-like, *and* becoming child-like. Most commentaries discuss our servanthood in the kingdom of God, but here I would like to touch upon becoming child-like for the kingdom of God.

I suppose for some, the question arises, how does one transform oneself into having a child-like nature, sufficiently that it allows us to find the kingdom of God? We want to retain our adult, mature personalities, but regain some positive child-like traits. We want to remain strong, yet give in to that inherent vulnerability that comes from trusting in God as our Father.

Over the course of my life, I have encountered a small number of sensible adults, who were well-liked, respected, wise, and kind-hearted. I would also say that these individuals also had a child-like innocence about them.

For example, they looked first for the good in others. They had no cunning or guile, and they were really bad at lying and being dishonest. They were calm and unaggressive souls, with a child-like enthusiasm for the things they were interested in. They took things and people at face value, and didn't read too much into things. They didn't try to put on a special face for the outside world, so what you saw on the outside was the same as what was in their hearts. I guess all these things gave them the appearance of having a child-like nature.

So from observing these types of individuals, what advice can I give on becoming more child-like? Here are a few things:

- trust in your heavenly Father
- say what you mean, and mean what you say
- don't play mind games with people
- try to see the best in people, rather than pick on their faults
- don't judge
- be constant
- don't say one thing to someone's face, and another behind their backs – don't be 'double-tongued'
- don't gossip – this will make you an untrustworthy person
- be honest; the truth is easier to remember than a lie
- don't read too much into people or things
- don't put on a special front for the world to see; be who you are

---

[a] S.Yesh. 147:4 – cf Mk 10:15

- don't seek vengeance for past wrongs; leave that up to God.

I'm sure that you could add more to this list, but they are principles I have tried to adhere to that have given me that child-like wonder and enthusiasm for the kingdom of God.

Innocent as doves, and cunning as serpents

Becoming children of God's Kingdom does not mean becoming naïve. Manipulative and self-seeking people will always be ready in the wings to take advantage of those who look for the best in others. That's why Yeshua` taught us, *'be as cunning as snakes, and as innocent as doves.'*[a]

When I visited Israel in 2004, one highlight of my trip was a visit to the Golan Heights. I was taken aback by the landscape of the area which, because of my familiarity with the wildlife of Africa, I noted was similar in appearance to the savannahs of that continent. As we travelled around, a number of abandoned homesteads were pointed out to us. Our guide told us that when European Jewish migration to Palestine began in the late 19th and early 20th centuries, new arrivals hoped they could live in peace with the Arabs already there. They were extremely optimistic and idealistic about Jewish-Arab co-existence. They learnt from local Arabs what life was like living in the Holy Land then, and in the Golan, there were small Jewish settlements that welcomed Arabs into their homes, as friends and neighbours.

Then came the nationalist Arab riots of the 1930's. Local people who had previously been considered friends, entered Jewish homes and murdered their inhabitants. Their homes stand abandoned in witness to those terrible events, and to the death of a dream.

In human society, there are unfortunately individuals who will prey on the innocent. They will take advantage of the kindness of others for their own gain. Becoming children for the sake of the Kingdom of God does not mean becoming naïve, and so remain oblivious to all dangers around you. Idealism about what life has the potential to become, does not mean ignoring what real life is actually like in the real world.

Yeshua` also taught us to be shrewd[b] in our dealings with this world. Pray therefore, my brothers and sisters, for wisdom from our Heavenly Father, to guide us in difficult times and places, so that we will not be blind to dangers when they arise.

---

[a] S.Yesh. 63:1; cf Mt 10:16, Gosp. Thomas 39:2
[b] S.Yesh. 78:13-14; cf Lk 16:8

... your...

Notice here that Yeshua` did not teach us to say, 'May Christ's kingdom come', nor 'May the kingdom of the Messiah come', but rather, 'May Your (i.e. our heavenly Father's) kingdom come.'

I have said before, that if we want to understand the motivation and mind-set behind the people who lived in those days, we need to be aware of what *they* believed. If Jewish people back then had believed that a messiah was someone who would die 'to save the human race from their sins', then their subsequent actions would have reflected such a belief. They don't. I can confidently say that before the preaching tours of Paul of Tarsus, with the possible exception of those who became influenced by Hellenist and Gnostic beliefs, there is no evidence that Jewish people held such a belief. We know that ancient pagan cultures – such as those of Mesopotamia, and of Neolithic northern Europe – believed in the ritual, sacrificial death of their kings, but the atoning death of a king is alien to Israelite belief.

In those days, because of the oppression of Roman rule, most Jewish people believed that a messiah was someone of the royal lineage of David, who would free the Jewish people of foreign oppression, re-establish the royal throne of David, and make Israel strong and secure again, protecting her from all her enemies. *That* was what a messiah meant to the vast majority of the Jewish people in those days; that is what the historical evidence of people's actions suggests.

In the gospels, we get the impression that Yeshua`'s main opponents were the Pharisees (and to a lesser extent, the Sadducees). However, there are some confrontations that would make more sense if his adversaries had been Zealots. Take, for example, the question of whether to pay taxes to Caesar or not.[a] This would not have been a huge problem for the Pharisees, who mostly took a cautious 'wait and see' approach to Roman occupation. However, it would have been a really big issue for the anti-Roman Zealots. So also would Yeshua`'s associating with tax-collectors (who collected taxes for the Romans), and prostitutes (most of whose customers were Roman soldiers); they were despised because, like tax collectors, they were seen as collaborators with the Roman occupiers.

Yeshua` may even have had a nickname for the Zealots: 'the Dead'. In his saying, "Leave the Dead to bury their own dead!"[b] he may have been referring to a man whose father had been a Zealot, and had been killed by the Romans because of his anti-Roman activity. The son

---

[a] S.Yesh. passage 82 – cf Mk 12:13-17
[b] S.Yesh. 7:7; cf Mt 8:22, Lk 9:60

obviously wanted to bury his father, but Yeshua''s advice was to leave his father's fellow Zealots ('the Dead') to bury their own dead (possibly because there was a danger that the son could be dragged into the same way of life). The son was to leave the other Zealots to bury his father, and instead, follow Yeshua'.

Why would he call the Zealots 'the Dead'? He may have been thinking of Dt 30:19. That verse referred to those who followed God's ways as 'the Living', having chosen the way of life; and those who went against God were 'the Dead', having chosen the way of death. Because the Zealots had chosen to act contrary to God's ways, they were 'the Dead [Ones]'.

At one point, Yeshua` refers to one of the signs of God's present kingdom as 'the dead being raised to life'.[a] There is no evidence that there were mass resurrections of the dead in that time period, so could it be that he was referring to the Zealots ('the Dead') being brought back to [the way of] life, referred to in Dt 30:19?

Whatever the case, the actions of the Zealots, and their potential influence on the ordinary people, would have caused big problems for Yeshua`. His ministry was focussed on calling people to repent, so that the coming destruction and tribulation would not take place – or at least if it did take place, it was hoped that good people and those who had repented would be sheltered from the tribulation, by avoiding violence and therefore direct confrontation with the Romans.

However, the violent actions of the Zealots were hastening the inevitable retribution from the Romans. Yeshua` had great difficulty making people see where their violent methods would lead; to any shrewd observer of current affairs at the time, it should have been obvious: *'How is it you know how to read the signs of the earth, yet you can't read the signs of our time?'*[b] He understood that the ways of the Zealots would lead, not to life, but destruction.[c]

Yeshua` alluded to his disdain of the violent actions of the Zealots when he said, *'the kingdom of God has been violently advancing, and violent men lay hold of it'*.[d] He criticised them and said, *'You justify what you're doing in the eyes of human beings, but God knows what's in your heart. What you do may be considered by some to be a noble thing, but it's an abomination in*

[a] see Mt 11:5, Lk 7:22; cf S.Yesh. 63:13
[b] S.Yesh. 6:3; cf S.Yesh. 5:4, also Mt 16:3 & Lk 12:56
[c] S.Yesh. 51:2-3 – cf Mt 7:13-14, Lk 13:23-24
[d] Mt 11:12; cf S.Yesh. 111:4

the sight of God.[a] Such a comment makes no sense in any context, except if it were directed against the violence of the Zealots.

Originally, the messiah was supposed to be a servant of God, who had to remain faithful to God if Israel was to prosper. But instead of acknowledging Yahveh as Saviour in the present here and now, messianism abandons that hope and places it in a superhuman king who would come in the future. Messianism is therefore the theology of despair in the present, and abandons hope in God's ability to intervene and act in our present affairs *right now*. It is the theology of doing nothing in the present, while waiting for something to happen in the future.

The Zealots sought to establish the kingdom of the messiah with violence. They knew what the people of the Galilee and Judea wanted in their promised messiah, and they were willing to make it happen at any cost. To them, and to most ordinary people, the kingdom everyone talked about was the messianic kingdom.

In complete contrast, the kingdom that Yeshua` taught was not the messianic kingdom expected by the ordinary people, nor was it the Davidic kingdom forcefully advanced through the violent actions of the Zealots, but rather the kingdom of *God*. I believe that the most pertinent reason why Yeshua` concentrated *so heavily* on the kingdom of God, was to place it in stark contrast to the messianic kingdom of the Zealots. Yeshua` prayed for the kingdom of *God* to come, not the *messianic* kingdom. And the message he preached about the kingdom of God was 'good news' for everyone.[b]

The cruelty of the Romans vs. the justice and compassion of Yahwism

The Romans, it must always be remembered, were a very cruel people. As an Empire, they killed to remind themselves of their power. Their way of life, their sports and their pastimes (such as fighting with animals, gladiatorial contests and throwing dissidents to the lions) were all designed to numb the population to blood and death. In this respect, the Roman Empire was run like a slaughterhouse. To be cruel was to be strong. In Rome, brutality was admired – you could not succeed unless you were cruel, and compassion was seen as a weakness.

That is why Roman culture looked down on Jewish culture. The Roman mind-set could not understand why the Jewish faith laid such emphasis on compassion, kindness, mercy and justice. Because the Jewish people held these concepts as high ideals, they saw Jewish culture

---

[a] S.Yesh. 111:2-3; cf Lk 16:15
[b] S.Yesh. 63:12; cf Lk 8:1

as inherently weak. For example, for a Roman to be a man was to be able to kill without remorse, to enjoy slaughter and battle, to control those around you with fear, and to seek one's goals ruthlessly. In Jewish culture, the concept of the ideal king[a] embodied the ideal man – someone who protected the weak, defended the cause of the oppressed, stood up for those who suffered violence, spoke out on behalf of those who have no voice in society, and someone who would be admired and respected for the goodness of his example to his family and neighbours.

... come / be fulfilled

In the vast majority of translations of the *Our Father*, the verb used here is 'come', for that is indeed the literal translation of the Aramaic and Hebrew words. Now, this has led many people to think wrongly that the kingdom of God is *not* here and now, but something that will only arrive in the future. In order to understand this problem, you have to make a distinction between what the kingdom is like *now*, and what it has the potential to become *in the future*. This is the fourth aspect of the Kingdom I mentioned earlier.

Yeshua` tells the parable of the small amount of yeast that leavens an incredibly large amount of dough.[b] He alludes to the process of change that we all have to work for, in order to achieve what the kingdom of God can become in the future. Similarly with the parable of the mustard seed, where the small seed becomes a large bush or tree.[c]

Whereas many religious people today view the future as a time of destruction and apocalypse, Yahwist Israelite views of the future are generally more positive.[d] It envisages a time when the glory of God fills the whole earth,[e] when there is no more war,[f] suffering, disease or death.[g] Everyone will dwell securely and without fear.[h]

Much of the ancient *Clementine Recognitions* is of Ebionite

---

[a] e.g. Ps 72:12-14
[b] S.Yesh. 25:2; cf Mt 13:33, Lk 13:21
[c] S.Yesh. 24; cf Mk 4:30-32, Mt 13:31-32, Lk 13:18-19
[d] cf Jer 29:11 – *"For I know the plans that I have for you," declares Yahveh, "plans for peace and not for disaster - to give you a future and hope."*
[e] Isaiah 4:5, Habakkuk 2:14; cf Book of Visions 2:11, also Rev 21:11
[f] Isaiah 2:4
[g] see Book of Visions 22:4; cf Revelation 21:4
[h] Micah 4:4

origin. It contains passages[a] which recount the ancient Ebionite view of what will happen in the far future:

> '... *there are two heavens, one of which is that visible firmament which shall pass away, but the other is eternal and invisible . . . this visible heaven is to be dissolved and pass away at the end of the world, in order that that heaven which is older and higher may appear after the judgment to the holy and the worthy .... it must of necessity be dissolved, so that that for which it seems to have been made may appear. .. it is necessary that* **the condition of this world pass away, so that the sublimer condition of the heavenly kingdom may shine forth.** *... when that sky shall be dissolved, and that superior condition of the heavenly kingdom shall shine forth, then those who are pure in heart shall see God....*'

Basically, as we have things now, there is this world and the next – two realms. However, in the future, the veil between the two will be dissolved, and heaven will exist on earth. As a result, the light of God's glory will shine on the earth,[b] and no one will be harmed by it. Perhaps this was the symbolic intent of the veil in the Tabernacle that the Israelites built in the desert. On one side were the symbols of heaven, and on the other were the symbols of earth. Between the two was only a veil; drawing it aside would imply the glory of God entering this world, cleansing it and making it new.

In this sense, the idea expressed in the verb 'come' means 'fulfil',[c] just as a prophecy comes to pass, or a promise is fulfilled.[d]

To summarise, the line *May Your kingdom be fulfilled* reminds us of a way of life that must be lived – God's ways which must be followed in the here and now, in order for their promises to be fulfilled in the future. If good people remain respectful, just, caring and merciful in spite of the misfortune they encounter, then each little thing they do will slowly build and accumulate – all the while building treasures for ourselves in heaven. The kingdom of God can be spread to people of all faiths and of none – not as a religion, but as a universal way of acting with justice, tolerance and peace towards one another. All humanity can be taught by the followers of Yahveh how to get along, how to create a just society, how leaders can govern to look after all their people, and how to look after and respect the resources of the earth.

---

[a] excerpts are from Clem Rec. Bk 2 Ch 68, Bk 3 Chs 27-29, and Bk 3 Ch 75.
[b] Isaiah 60:19-20. See also Rev 22:1-5 / Ch.Sh. 23:1-5
[c] see Prov 13:12
[d] cf Dt 13:2, 18:22

Eventually, when a sufficient majority of humanity learns to walk in these ways, then heaven will break through on earth. God's glory – God's brilliant light – will shine on earth. There will be no more night and day, there will be no more death, and there will be no more conflict. We will all be spiritual beings, and we will live in the radiant glory of our heavenly Father.

I will explain this in greater detail in the section on 'the Son of Man' in chapter four.

Line 4: May Your will be realised

This line gives us the meaning of – and expands on – the previous line (as is often the convention with couplets in Hebrew poetry). The desire for God's reign to be fulfilled, is synonymous with the desire for God's will to be realised.

Let's first turn to the question of why this particular petition should be included by Yeshua` in the prayer he was giving his followers. What was of such contemporary importance and concern that it was an emphasis worthy of being included?

It had to be something that was, in Yeshua`'s mind, *not* God's will – human will, human plans and human designs. In his time, the scribes,[a] elders and teachers of the Pharisees[b] had built up a tradition of legal decisions to explain and clarify the Torah. Unfortunately, their interpretations were often in direct opposition to what Torah actually said.

Furthermore, their vision of the future – of what God's plan is – was markedly different to the one portrayed in the Torah and the books of the Prophets. By ignoring God's plan or God's will, and by following human interpretations instead, it would – and indeed did – lead to catastrophe.

---

[a] A scribe or *sofeir* was someone who gave an interpretation of Torah. Most religious groups had them – they were not the exclusive preserve of the Pharisees. If an ordinary layperson wanted to know what Torah said on any particular issue, or how something was to be done according to Torah, then they would approach the scribe of a group they were comfortable with.

[b] For the record, I must make it clear that I am not 'anti-Pharisee'. Their legacy enabled the survival of the Jewish people through many centuries of persecution and hatred. Throughout this book, I am not criticising Pharisees *per se*, but rather attitudes and beliefs which were a hindrance to God's message to warn and protect His people.

... will ...

Here we have a line prayed by millions – the desire for God's will to be done. However, there are many who call on God, and to put it in Christians terms, 'call Jesus lord', yet they do nothing that he says, nor anything that God wills. There are those who maintain that being a good person is not enough; you also have to hold certain beliefs. This has led far too many people to the conclusion that as long as you believe certain things, everything will be all right. You don't actually have to *do* anything either, just believe. But Yeshuaˋ said, *'Not everyone who calls out to me, saying "Master! Master!" will find the kingdom of God; but rather those who do the will of their heavenly Father.'*[a] Notice that Yeshuaˋ himself stated that simply calling him 'Master' (or 'lord') was not enough; you also had to *do* the will of our heavenly Father.

I have actually met people who quite happily hold the required beliefs of their faith, and yet are still vulgar, inconsiderate, vengeful, hateful, and even vindictive and violent. At the lower end of the scale, I have met people who hold their faith's required beliefs, and are arrogant, condescending nuisances towards people of other faiths.

There are people today who start out being an unpleasant person, change their religion and take on new beliefs, and they are *still* unpleasant people. If your new faith has made no difference to your personality, outlook, thoughts, words or behaviour, then your new faith is a dead one. To all intents and purposes, your faith is utterly useless to both God and humanity. Faith without works is dead.[b] God's will is to transform society and the people in it, so that the weak are not oppressed by the strong, the disadvantaged are not trodden on, family members act according to their responsibilities within their households, as well as within society at large.

Dt 29:15-21 warns those who enter the Covenant without any intention of keeping it. It warns against those who think that they have peace of mind and soul simply for being Israelites – that the mere fact of them being Israelites will keep them from harm: *"I will be safe, even though I follow my own wilful heart"*.[c] This is also relevant for those Christians who think that simply by being Christian will keep them from harm – that they are 'saved' simply because of their faith, regardless of what they actually do in life. What these verses tell us, is that the intent of your heart is what will keep you close to Yahveh; the intent of your heart, the actions of your being and the words of your mouth will keep

---

[a] S.Yesh. 107:2; cf Mt 7:21
[b] Ig. Yq. 8:4 'In the same way, faith by itself, if it is not accompanied by good works, is dead.' cf Letter of James 2:17
[c] Dt 29:18 / 29:19 in Christian bibles

you close to Yahveh, not what you believe.

Someone who thinks that their faith alone will 'save' them, is like the root-stock of a tree that has been grafted with *"poison weed and wormwood"*,[a] because being grafted onto something without changing what you are will not in itself change the fruit you bear; **poisonous fruit grafted onto a tree bearing edible fruit, will not make the fruit of the grafted branch edible**.

Every so often I see so-called religious people act with disrespect towards others, engage in social bullying, and are unhelpful and selfish. This is the best way to ensure that God's kingdom is never brought to its fulfilment. It is the best way to ensure that we never live in a better world, with a better society, where young people respect others, where the elderly are valued for their knowledge and wisdom, and where people look to the future with hope; ignoring good works is the best way to ensure that God's kingdom is never fulfilled, and that God's will is never realised.

God's will for the individual is to transform that individual, so that he or she can become a better servant of God, playing his or her part towards the fulfilment of God's kingdom on earth. You cannot become a spiritual or religious person, and then remain the same person as you were before. You have to show who your heavenly Father is by your actions, by your words and your outlook. Your life has to become a source of light to those around you.

Some people will then say, 'But I'm not perfect! If I make a mistake, then I have sinned, and it'll just make things worse.' Let me tell you this: No, it won't; that's what you have been brainwashed to believe. Doing *nothing* will make things worse. People complain about evil in the world, and how evil constantly increases, but they themselves do nothing to add to the good in the world, or cause good to increase.

God is not displeased when you try and then fail. However, God *is* displeased when you do absolutely nothing. If you fail, then God will pick you up, dust you off, and let you try again. God does not punish those who try, but God *is* displeased with those who know the good they should do, and yet do not do it.[b]

How shall I describe the Kingdom of God? There were two exceedingly rich men. One of them would go out into the streets and seek out the poor. And he would wash and bind up their sores and wounds, giving them to eat

---

[a] Dt 29:17 / 29:18 in Christian bibles
[b] Ig. Yq. 15:4; cf Letter of James 4:17

and offering them fresh clothing. And at festival times he would make an invitation to the widowed and the fatherless – all those who were without – and asked them to join him at his table. And at harvest times, he would seek out the poor – even those who were not of his own people – and encourage them to take from the gleanings of his fields. And he would give of his wealth to help the sick and the dying.

And there was another man who was also very rich. He feasted on his best food and wine, inviting all his family and friends. And he ensured that he paid his tithes, prayed at the appointed times and said all the prescribed blessings. He would wash and immerse to ensure ritual cleanliness, and he would attend Temple services, and rise to read the Torah in synagogues.

Now, which one of these men truly did the will of his Heavenly Father, and lived the Kingdom of God? [a]

The Fence of the Mind

Most rabbis will tell you that one purpose of the Oral Law is to build a fence around the Torah – to forbid certain things so that it becomes impossible to break the commandments of Torah itself. For example, it is forbidden to buy and sell on the Sabbath, so to make that commandment impossible to break, the ancient rabbis invented the commandment that one must not even *carry* money on the Sabbath – if you don't have any money with you, you cannot spend it or take it in payment for something.

The prophet Yeshua` said a number of things which at first glance seem unreasonable. For example, he said,

'The commandment was given to our ancestors, "You shall not commit murder"; and whoever commits murder will be liable to judgement. But let me just say to you, that everyone who's angry with their neighbour shall be liable to judgement – whoever says to their neighbour, "Worthless moron!" shall be answerable to the Great Council, and whoever says, "Fool!" shall be cast into the Outer Darkness!' [b]

The prophet Yeshua` had the habit of emphasising a point by using extreme analogies. We in the modern world tend to see angry words spoken in the heat of the moment as pretty harmless. Ancient Talmidaism, on the other hand, saw them in quite a different way. This

---

[a] S.Kit. 3:3.1-6
[b] S.Yesh. 124:1-3 – cf Mt 5:21-22

becomes obvious when you read the *Teaching of the Emissaries:*[a]

> *"My child . . . . do not become prone to anger, for anger lies on the downward path to murder. Be neither jealous, nor quarrelsome, nor hot-headed, for out of all these things, murders are engendered."*[b]

In the *Teaching of the Emissaries*, the whole gamut of anger intensity, from quarrelsomeness, to hot-headedness, right through to murder is laid out. Yeshua` wanted to drive home a point, so he cut out the middle bits and equated anger directly to murder, saying that anger deserved bringing someone before the justice of the Great Sanhedrin; using extreme analogies was his way of teaching.

When approaching a complex ethical issue, many thinkers ask themselves, "Where do you draw the line?" With many hot moral topics and sticky ethical matters, there seems to be a gradation between what is acceptable and what is not. Between the two is a grey area within which it is difficult to give any kind of clear judgment.

In his teaching, Yeshua` was not making our thoughts sinful, but rather advocating *self-control* over one's thoughts. I believe that in this saying of Yeshua`, his solution was to build a mental fence before you even got to the grey area, so that moral uncertainty doesn't even become an issue.

Take a look at the example I quoted earlier from the Oral Law. Forbidding people from carrying money stops them breaking the biblical commandment, but some people will still wish they could buy and trade, wishing the Sabbath would hurry up and be over so that they could carry out their normal business again.[c] Yeshua` saw that a change of heart would be needed, not just a change in legislation. God's teaching needed to be implanted in people's minds,[d] so that in time it would become second nature (this is what 'writing something on one's heart' means).

Today in our society there is a stark lack of respect for the individual. You have people who see nothing morally wrong with watching someone being humiliated, and being made fun of; that leads to a lack of respect for the dignity of the individual; that in turn leads to an attitude where you do not consider it wrong to humiliate someone *yourself*; some will take it further, and take it to the point of physical humiliation, even bodily harm; a few will go

---

[a] also known as the *Didache*; it is the fifth book of *the Exhortations* (the Talmidi Israelite equivalent of the *New Testament*).
[b] T. Sh. 3:2 (the *Teaching of the Emissaries* is based on the *Didache*).
[c] Amos 8:5
[d] Jer 31:33

further, to the point of having no regard for life, to a point where they are willing to take a life.

I hear people every day decrying the fact that muggings and murders happen, but in the next breath they mention how much fun they get out of seeing other people's misfortune, or how laughable it is to play practical jokes on people that lead to real distress. Attitudes need to change in society.

I believe that part of Yeshua''s solution on changing society's attitudes was this fence of the mind – the rule of 'don't even go there!' Taking the example above, you build a mental fence at the point before you get to 'I enjoy seeing people being made fun of'. You build a fence before you get to the stage of, 'I am so angry I could imagine actually hurting someone'; you build a mental fence before you get to the state of mind where you could call someone '*raqa*' (worthless moron).

The fence of the mind means that there is no grey area, because our thoughts – and consequently our actions – don't even go there in the first place.

Reprogramming the mind

I want to tell you about a recent scientific discovery.[a] There are certain people who have ongoing problems with chronic pain. For example, some people experience pain long after the source of the pain has healed. It was recently found that the brain had actually reprogrammed itself to *expect* the pain, and thereafter, continued to experience the pain even though the original injury was long healed.

It has long been known by spiritual healers, that one can reprogram the mind to assist with healing. Psychiatrists have also learned that one can realign our thought processes so that they are more positive – so that what has hurt us in the past no longer hurts us.

If we are permanently scared or angry, or could conceivably consider hurting someone we don't like, then in the heat of the moment, that is what we will do. By being in a constant state of anger, we are in fact programming our mind to react in an angry and hateful way, and to naturally default to that in similar situations in the future. Neuronal pathways will be laid down in the brain to ensure that our reaction in difficult moments will not be pleasant.

Prayer and meditation, as well as engaging in positive and calming rituals, will help to reprogram the mind to think in a less aggressive or angry way. We can actually train our own minds to think in such a way, that when faced with a sudden and potentially volatile situation, we do

---

[a] reported on the BBC's *Horizon: The Secret World of Pain*, 31 Jan 2011

not explode with anger or violence ourselves. Our default reaction will have been reset to a more sensible and adult setting.

For example, if your nature is to constantly swear and use foul language, you are in great danger of abusing God's Holy Name. If you are someone who constantly says, 'Oh my God!' for no reason, then if you are considering becoming a Talmidi – part of a community which uses the Name of God with great respect and reverence – then you will have to train yourself not to swear, and not to call out to God for no reason.

In studying ancient documents that exhibit Talmidi influence, what became immediately obvious to me was how ancient Talmidaism concentrated on training the mind, putting aside those ways of thinking that hindered the kingdom of God, and retraining it in those ways of living that bring its promises nearer.

For example, both Yeshua` and Jacob the Pious spoke about the necessity of being careful about what we say. Yeshua` said, *'Beware your tongue, of what you say, because the day will come when you'll have to give an account for all the heartless words you've spoken; because as the saying goes, "By your words you shall be acquitted, and by your words you shall be convicted." '* [a]

We are answerable to God, not only for what we have done, but for what we have said too. What we have said to do others harm, whether directly by cruel speech, or indirectly by malicious rumour, are not unimportant things simply because they are fleeting, intangible things. The words we say have weight – they have currency with the human soul.

Jacob the Pious wrote, *'If anyone thinks himself to be religious and yet does not keep a tight rein on his tongue, he deceives his own heart and his religion is empty ... With the tongue we praise our Sovereign Father, and with it we curse men and women, who have been made in the image and likeness of God. Out of the same mouth come forth praise and cursing. It is not fitting, my brothers and sisters, that things should be this way. Can a spring produce fresh and salt water from the same vent? My brothers and sisters, can a fig tree bring forth olives, or a grapevine bring forth figs? Then neither can a salt spring bring forth fresh water.'* [b]

It is not a matter that they plucked out of nowhere; it was even a concern of no less than Solomon himself: *"From the fruit of a man's mouth his stomach is satisfied; he is satisfied by the yield of*

---

[a] S.Yesh. 154:2-3 – cf Mt 12:36-37
[b] Ig. Yq. 9:1, 11-14 – cf Letter of James, 1:26, 3:9-12

his lips. Death and life are in the power of the tongue, and those who love it will eat of its fruits."[a] *"Gracious words are like a honeycomb, sweetness to the soul and health to the body."*[b] And even King David prayed, *"Set a guard, O Yahveh, over my mouth; keep watch over the door of my lips!"*[c]

It is a curious fact, that what we say has an effect on the mind. If we allow our mouths to speak gossip, to cuss and swear, to hurl abuse at other people, or merely to be impolite, then our minds begin to think unconsciously, 'Oh, it's not only OK to speak like that – selfish, rude and uncaring things – it's also OK to *act* like that.'

Our ill-spoken words do harm, not only to our victims, but to ourselves as well. *"It is not what goes into the mouth that defiles a man, rather it is what comes out of his mouth – this is what defiles a man."*[d] The words we speak are an indication of the content of the storehouse of our hearts.

Just as a rudder directs the path of a ship, so too does the tongue direct the course of our relationships with others.[e] They can be directed into stormy waters, or they can take us into calm harbours.

Keeping a tight rein on the tongue is a discipline that takes time to master, but if we take the time and effort to vet what we say before it leaves our mouths, then in the end, it will pay dividends.

If anyone has difficulty controlling what they say, let them bring themselves before the glory of Yahveh, and submit reverently and with humility to God's cleansing fire. Let such a person allow God's fire to burn out all the impurities within them, until all that is left, is the precious gold that God created them to be.

If we can train the tongue, we can train the mind too. Training ourselves to curb our gossip, not to put people down or humiliate them, not to hurl insults at others – this will help the subconscious mind to realise that this is not the way to speak, and therefore not the way to behave.

God's Kingdom demands a transformation of the mind & soul

When you enter Talmidaism, you cannot remain the same person you were before; I know that I for one am not the same person as I once was. One cannot hang onto undesirable traits and say, 'This is how God made me!' because if you were right about that, then you would remain

---

[a] Prov 18:20-21
[b] Prov 16:24
[c] Ps 141:3
[d] SY 154:4; cf Mt 15:11
[e] Ig.Yq. 9:5-6; cf Ep.Jam. 3:3-4

a drooling, cooing mumbler all your life, crawling around on all fours, having to be fed, washed and clothed by others. Just as a baby grows into an adult, so also an unreformed human being is changed by the glory of Yahveh. The very nature of what a human being is, is that we grow and change.

Jacob the Pious wrote[a] how when we compare ourselves to what we see of ourselves in our reflections, there is little desire for change. We look into a mirror and see ourselves as we are, and whatever imperfections we find, we tend to overlook. But when we use Yahveh's perfect teaching as our mirror, we see what we are supposed to be, and we are moved to change.

Some parts of our personality are genetically inherited, some are controlled by our hormones, and yet others are moulded by our upbringing. However, we cannot make the excuse that we cannot change because of what we have been made to be. Maybe an animal, one of the lesser creations of God can put forward this excuse – that they are only acting according to their nature – but not a human being. We have the faculty of reason. We have the ability to override our inherent programming. We have free will. We have the choice to do right or wrong, the choice to go against what the inherited side of our natures tells us to do.

Through Torah, Yahveh teaches us to fight our baser natures. Torah often tells us to fight our instinct – our feelings, our genes and what we were born with.

For example, Yahveh teaches us, *"When you encounter the ox of one who hates you, or his donkey wandering about, you must take it back to him. When you see the donkey of your enemy collapsed under its burden, and your natural reaction is to refrain from raising it, you must nevertheless raise it with him."*[b]

We must never let our resentment or anger get in the way of doing what is just and right. We must never let our hatred hurt the innocent. Our instinct tells us to hurt anything that belongs to our enemy, but we have to fight such an instinct in order to do our heavenly Father's will. We have to fight the instinct to be vindictive against those who hate us – doing an unjust thing in order to spite our enemy. We may not like who or what our enemy is, but we should not let an innocent suffer for it – in this case, the animals that belong to our enemy. And if we should show this kindness to animals, how much more so should we show this kindness to human beings.

---

[a] Ig. Yq. 6:2-4 – cf Letter of James, 1:23-25
[b] Ex 23:4-5

Proverbs 25:21 says, *'If your enemy is hungry, give him bread to eat; if he is thirsty, give him water to drink.'* This compassion is not just the teaching of Yeshua`; he was calling us back to the Way of Yahveh, whose compassion and mercy is boundless.

Now, there are quite a few science-fiction stories of androids – artificial life-forms – that gain sentience, or something near to what we would call a soul. They do this in most cases because they break or exceed their programming. We too must break our programming. We must exceed what we were genetically programmed by millions of years of evolution to be. There are some atheists who say that all we can do – all we can ever be – is to follow our gene-encoded natures, but surely, isn't being human to go beyond what our genes tell us to be or do! Responsible religious faith tells us that we have to go *beyond* our natures, and be *more* than what we are. In effect, rediscover the heavenly side of our natures, and become what God wants us to become.

When you become a Follower of the Way of Yahveh, the arrogant person has to learn how practise humility; the angry person has to learn to embrace peace, forgiveness and reconciliation; and the selfish or inconsiderate person has to learn charity and concern for others. We have to be willing to allow the power and presence of God to take hold of us, and transform us, so that we become a people who will better serve the cause of God and God's kingdom on earth.

'the eye is the lamp of the body'

Yeshua` taught us, *'The lamp of the body is the eye. So if you've got a good eye, your whole body's full of light, and your good eye becomes a source of light to everyone around you. But if you've got a bad eye, your whole body's full of darkness, and your bad eye spreads only darkness around you. So therefore, if the lamp within you is darkness, how great is that darkness!'*[a]

These verses prove a complete enigma to most people. To understand them in their proper context – and therefore, to be able to apply them to our own lives – we need to know a little bit of Aramaic.

Have you ever heard people speak whose native language is not English – especially those who don't speak English very well? You'll notice they sometimes get the order of their words wrong, or some phrases where everything is grammatically correct, but as sentences they make no literal sense at all? That is because they are using the word order of their native language, or idioms from their mother tongue.

These verses of Yeshua` are a good example of this phenomenon,

---

[a] S.Yesh. 73:1-2; cf Mt 6:22-23a, Lk 11:34, Gosp.Th. 24.3

but the other way round. Yeshua` used some idioms in his original Aramaic, which the gospel writers didn't know about (which suggests that *their* mother tongue was not Aramaic but Greek; if any of the gospel writers had actually been Jews living in the Holy Land, they should have picked up on things like this, but they didn't, so *none* of the gospel writers could have been immediate followers of Yeshua`). They translated the text of their sources into Greek, according to what they thought the words meant.

In Aramaic, the phrase 'that man has a good eye' becomes גברא ההוא אית ליה עין טב *gabra hahu it leyh `ayn tab* (literally, 'man that there-is to-him eye good'). If you didn't know any Aramaic, you might think that this saying is about the health of the man's eye. It is with this very understanding that the Greek editors of the gospels of Matthew and Luke used the word 'healthy'[a] to describe the condition of the eye. The subsequent phrases about the body being full of light or darkness only lend confusion to the matter.

In Aramaic, 'to have a good eye' actually means 'to be generous'. Conversely, 'to have a bad eye' means 'to be selfish'. The equivalent verse in the Gospel of Thomas adds that a person with a good eye lights up the world around them. We can surmise that a person with a bad eye i.e. someone who is selfish, brings only darkness to those around them.

So now, let's take a look at the verses in modern English:

> *'The lamp of the body is the eye. So if you're generous, your whole body's full of light, and your generosity becomes a source of light to everyone around you. But if you're selfish, your whole body's full of darkness, and your selfishness spreads only darkness around you. So therefore, if the lamp within you is darkness, how great is that darkness!'*

Do you see how understanding this one Aramaic idiom has effectively brought the whole passage into clearer focus? The play on the word 'eye' is unfortunately lost in the new translation, but now you can appreciate the full intent of Yeshua`'s words. Yeshua`'s opening words, עינא היא נהורת גושמא *`ayna hi nehorat gushma* ('the eye is the lamp of the body') make sense if you understand that for an Aramaic speaker, the eye was the mirror of

---

[a] Matthew and Luke both use the Greek word ἁπλοῦς *haplous* (sound, perfect).

both generosity and selfishness in one's soul.

God's will for society

God's will for society in general is to transform it too. Society has a responsibility to its members, but its members also have a responsibility to society. We must contribute to build the society that we want to live in; we cannot sit back and expect someone else to do it for us. No one expects us to change the world by ourselves, but there are small things that we can do which will add to the sum of change. We can refuse to go along with the crowd when they do wrong; we can disagree with someone when they express a view or comment which is manifestly unjust, hateful or evil; and we can show kindness to those who are put upon by others through no fault of their own, other than they are different.

As I write this article, I am watching the UK television news. There are looting riots going on in many cities in England.[a] The vast majority of the people are young people. They are not protesting about social or civil issues; they have simply lost all respect for persons and property, and see nothing wrong in what they are doing.

There are many issues that have contributed to this. The generations are losing touch with one another, and becoming isolated from each other. Young people tend only to mix with other young people, and have little contact with their parents or grandparents who could have a better influence over them. I recently read a report[b] that said ancient humans made a big leap forward when grandparents lived long enough to pass on their knowledge and wisdom to their grandchildren. Nowadays, children do not learn how to behave from their parents or grandparents, but rather *from each other.*

Another problem is that parents spend so much time trying to earn enough to support their families, that they do not have enough time to actually interact with their children – they do not have enough time to give their children adequate guidance. For example, I have always felt that an important part of a child's psychological formation and development, is to be read to at night. They learn valuable life lessons from the allegorical tales written specifically for children. The morals of these stories also have more chance of sticking when they are told last thing at night.[c] Nowadays, few parents read to their children, and so their

---

[a] week commencing 7th Aug 2011; the looters' riots went on for several days.
[b] *Scientific American*, Jul 2011
[c] I can say with conviction that many of my early life-lessons were learnt from my bedtime stories; they had a profound influence on my own life. I firmly

children do not have the opportunity to take in these valuable lessons.

Modern technology is also breaking up family life. Teenagers are increasingly turning to cyber communication instead of face to face communication. The danger in this, is that youngsters become removed from the social contact necessary for humans to develop a healthy, balanced psyche. Some young men are increasingly spending more and more time playing violent computer games. The danger in this, is that such people become so entrapped in this violent world, that they remain angry and aggressive in the *real* world, and behave in the real world in the same way that they allow themselves to become in the cyber world. I read a while back[a] that Koreans are becoming so worried about this phenomenon, that they are instituting programs to get their children into the countryside away from technology, where they can re-bond with their families and make friends in the real world.

I also heard recently that there are some children starting out in British primary schools, and at the age of five they don't even know their own names.[b] It was also claimed that some children had never seen a book; they didn't even know what one was or what to do with it when given one at school. This points to a severe neglect and lack of communication between parent and child. A recent study[c] found that a third of children in the UK don't have any books of their own at home.

There is also the issue of absent fathers. Sometimes, through no fault of their own, a family has no father – such as when the father dies; the children are fatherless, and the mother is widowed. What *should* happen in such circumstances – and indeed, in *any* circumstance where there is no way a father can be present – is that someone else who is blood-related takes over the psychological position of the male rôle model. For teenage boys especially, they need the guidance and example of a male mentor-figure to live up to.[d] In ancient Israelite society, being a widow or being fatherless

---

believe that reading as a child improves the quality of one's mind, and makes you a better person.

[a] BBC News, 3 Jan 2008; NY Times, 18 Nov 2007

[b] Frank Field, Labour MP for Birkenhead, in a debate in the House of Commons, 3rd March 2011 (after a report on the BBC New website).

[c] in research published by the National Literacy Trust, 5 Dec 2011

[d] In Pilanesberg Game Reserve in South Africa, it was found that young male elephants were becoming aggressive, behaving violently and killing rhinos just for the sake of killing, simply because they had had no older adult males who could have taught them discipline. They had become the elephant equivalents of juvenile delinquents. I believe something similar happens to

also meant that one had no means of income. In such a case, it was normally the deceased husband's family who helped out.

In Yeshua''s case, tradition leads us to believe that his natural father, Joseph, died while he was still quite young. It is logical to assume that his father's brother, Qlofas, took on the responsibility to look after Yeshua` and his mother Miriam ('Mary') financially. Qlofas did not marry his dead brother's wife, because he was already married to 'Mary, the mother of James and Joses'.[a]

Given the abundance of problems we now have in western society, with the breakdown of the natural bonds and structures of human society, and the pressures we face to balance working enough hours to feed the family, and actually spending enough time with one's family, surely this is not how God intended our families to be? From a purely scientific viewpoint, this is not how nature evolved families to behave or interact either. We shouldn't have to struggle with these types of problems, in what seems to be a losing battle. There has to be a better way.

Mishpachah – the extended family

Around the world there are basically two views of what family means. In most of Western Europe and North America, if you mention 'family', people will automatically think of 'mother, father and their children' – and that's it. However, for the rest of the world – in Asia, Africa, Latin America, the Middle East, Aboriginal Australia, and for Native Americans – when you say the word 'family', people automatically call to mind a *much* bigger picture. Family is anyone related by blood or marriage – including children's spouses, aunts, uncles, cousins, grandparents, second/third cousins, great aunts and uncles, etc. People who in the West would be considered distant relatives, in these societies are considered integral members of the close family.

In most non-westernised countries, it is the *extended* family (and not the nuclear family) which is the basic unit of their society. In India (where it is called the 'joint family'), this natural structure is enshrined in law, to the extent that any attempt to fracture Indian society and break it up into *nuclear* families, has been decried as 'an attack on traditional family values'!

The ancient Israelites had no concept of the 'nuclear family' either (a term apparently coined in 1947). The Hebrew word '*mishpachah*',

---

some young men when they have no male role models upon whom to base their adult behaviour.
[a] KJV - see Mk 15:40, Mt 27:56; cf Lk 24:10

usually translated as 'family', is actually the *extended* family. In ancient Hebrew, there is no word for 'cousin'; all your cousins were seen as your brothers and sisters, and you referred to them as such. The only practical equivalent of the western, nuclear family would have been the 'household' (Hebrew: *bayit*), but it's still not the same, as that would include anyone and anything living under the same roof – including servants and animals.

Therefore the basic unit of Israelite society was the *mishpachah* – the extended family. The *mishpachah* generally functioned in the same way that it does around the world, where the extended family is society's basic unit.

Many of the practical stresses of family life are alleviated to a greater or lesser extent within the extended family. The upbringing of a child is still the responsibility of its natural mother and father, but other close relatives take up the slack in things like babysitting, childminding etc. Children are never left with friends or strangers, they always have someone related looking after them, and the added bonus is that they get to play with their cousins – instant friends. Childless people are not left out of the extended family, because they too contribute to the social wellbeing, cohesion and care of their clan.

Having several adults look after a child apparently does not confuse small children in any way. Studies[a] were done into separation anxiety in children brought up in *kibbutzim*. In a *kibbutz*, the care of children is a shared task between all the adults, but the children still had a greater attachment to their natural parents – their separation anxiety was greater with their natural parents than it was with other caregivers.

Children will also have a wide number of older relatives as rôle models in extended families. If any parent is lacking in parenting skills, it has less of a negative impact on the children's wellbeing, if the child can see how his or her grandparents, aunts and uncles behave. If an extended family functions properly, you actually learn parenting skills from being able to witness several sets of parents – to whom you are related – and experience their abilities as parents. If things go very badly wrong within a 'nuclear family' (such as with abuse or neglect), then in societies based on

---

[a] Bettelheim, Bruno. *The Children of the Dream*, Simon & Schuster, 2001, p. 15. also Scher A.; Hershkovitz R.; Harel J. *"Maternal Separation Anxiety in Infancy: Precursors and Outcomes"*, from *Child Psychiatry and Human Development*, 1998, vol. 29, no. 2, pp. 103–111(9).

the extended family, in extreme circumstances close relatives have the right to perform an intervention for the sake of the lives of the children. For example, in Sri Lankan society, this is most often done by the grandparents.

Hanging out with your cousins is common in extended families. It is through them that children gain their earliest introduction to social interaction in a safe environment. Through your cousins you meet other people who are not related, and begin to form a circle of friends of your own.

Children have a greater respect for the frailties and vulnerabilities of life if they have a good relationship with their grandparents. In extended families, even young children participate in taking care of their grandparents, doing what they can, from whom they learn about the complexities of life. Growing up does not mean a severance with one's family – either with parents or grandparents; there is constant contact. There is a permanent stream of life-lessons from one's older relatives; membership of the school of life called *mishpachah* is life-long.

In extended families, the elderly are not carted away to be forgotten in Old People's Homes; the responsibility of their care is shared, and the task is not placed on the shoulders of any one nuclear family. Jewish society has an enormous respect for its elderly – in Orthodox communities, very elderly rabbis are still valued highly for their wisdom and experience, when in western societies their great age would mean that they are retired and well past it.

If a marriage is faltering, rather than having to turn to friends who have no interest in the welfare of your extended family, you turn to your close relatives – especially ones who have been married a very long time – who actively help mediate, and have a vested interest in doing so.

In extended families, one's heritage and culture is actively passed down. This has implications for the rest of society; studies have shown that those who have a strong yet balanced sense of identity and of who they are, are happier than those who have no awareness of cultural identity. Such individuals are less likely to hold other cultures in disdain because they are comfortable with their own.[a]

Some religious communities in the West seem to take some sadistic delight in demonising those households which do not conform to their idea of what a 'family' is supposed to be – such as single-parent families,

---

[a] Iceland has a strong tradition of telling and retelling family sagas. Having an awareness of who you are, that you also have both heroes and villains in your past, gives a person a balanced sense of their identity – no better and no worse than anyone else. As a result, although they are an island, they have little enmity or fear of outsiders – they don't have an 'island mentality' like Britain does.

long-term single people, or couples who have made the decision to remain childless. In many western countries, this condescending view ends up cutting off more than *half* of the population – not a good thing for the welfare and cohesion of society. However, in extended families, *no one* is excluded – the childless, the widowed, the fatherless, even gay relatives – they would all be part of one extended family or another. Even these individuals have a part to play in the collective welfare and wellbeing of their extended families.

Among the religious right-wing in the West, there is the unpleasant (and if you ask me, offensive) opinion that unless you are married and have children, you are morally debased and have no place in human society – that you are of no use to it. In societies based on the extended family, *every* single human being has their part to play – even childless and unmarried ones. To an evangelical fundamentalist, 'family values' means being legally married and having children; to someone in an extended family, family values means being there for your extended family in both good and bad times, looking after one another, passing on one's culture and traditions from generation to generation, making sure that children are brought up with good discipline and moral values, and *that no one is left out.*

Yahveh said, *'Let not any childless person complain. "I am only a dry tree."*[a] In the Talmidi home Shabbat service, it forms part of a reading which emphasises the *whole* community, and that *everyone* in that community matters; **it is God's way.** A properly functioning extended family ensures that those who live alone are actually not alone or lonely.

The key to the good and effective functioning of extended families is the maintenance of good relationships. It is vitally important, because without them, the extended family, and ultimately society at large, begins to fall apart. Minor disputes are often diffused by the women in the extended family, major ones being mediated and resolved by the oldest members of the family. Regular contact with family members is vital in enabling good relationships. The diplomatic lessons you learn from maintaining good relationships within your extended family, bear fruit in the wider world when dealing with other groups, peoples and nations.

All these examples are from various cultures around the world, but I have to say that not all of them are upstanding examples of the extended family. There are downsides to extended families.

---

[a] Isaiah 56:3

Certain societies based on the extended family tend to be collectivistic ones, where the good of the family completely overrides the good of the individual. Taken to extremes, the individual has no rights. In South Asia for example, breaking the family's code can lead to honour killings.

I firmly believe that the ideal society – the one where God's ways function best, and where *everyone* is included – is one based on the extended family, but the rights of the individual have to be respected and protected too. In Israelite society, for example, no one – man or woman – could be forced to marry anyone they did not wish to marry, even though arranged marriages were the norm.

There are societies in the West that have a positive outlook towards the extended family. Amongst the democratic western nations, the lands around the Mediterranean tend more towards the extended family – such as Greece, Spain and Italy. In Italy, for example, most Italians remain close to the place where they were brought up, so are able to reap the benefits of staying near their relatives. The social welfare system there is not like in the UK; people tend to turn to their families for support rather than the state – an important fact to take note of.

Now the question arises, what if you are not part of an extended family? In England, many of whose communities were broken up during the Second World War, an interesting phenomenon has developed. People not part of any extended family have, without prompting or design, begun to create their own extended families from amongst their network of friends and neighbours. These networks become so dependent on each other, that they function almost exactly like extended families – the children are looked after, they have role models, there is less pressure on parents, the elderly are taken care of, and so on. A fully functioning religious community can also bring people together like this, and enable such artificial networks to function like an extended family.

In Jewish society, the *extended* family is the basic unit. On the whole, it is the one that works best with human nature. As long as the rights of the individual are respected, then this is the model that, in my humble opinion, I think we should support and work towards. I think that it is God's view of family, and how God intended human society to function, since in such a society, no one is abandoned, and no household would be vilified or excluded.

The importance of culture and traditions

In England where I was brought up, culture has tended to be something that is passed on haphazardly – unfortunately so much so nowadays, that most English people alas only have a vague idea of their heritage and of what constitutes traditional English culture. On the whole it is something you watch rich people and royalty do on TV, not something you participate in yourself as an integral part of your daily life. However, in other European countries like Greece and Italy, it is a deliberate and active effort of the family to ensure that cultural values are passed on. Culture is not just a set of customs, but a set of values too.

A good example of useful, traditional British culture that is not being passed on, is what one is supposed to do when a hearse or funeral cortège passes by.[a] The older generation will show deference and respect. Pedestrians will stop, take off their headgear and stand silently while the cortège passes. They will, for example, wait and allow the hearse to pass by through a pedestrian crossing. Older drivers will patiently drive along behind the slow-moving hearse. Many younger people, never having been taught these customs, will cross the road and get in the way of a hearse; drivers will sound their horns, and generally obstruct the passage of the cortège.

Over the centuries, English culture has lost many helpful and meaningful traditions, customs that helped bind society together, gave it meaning and purpose, engendered an atmosphere of respect, and kept up its spirits in troubled times. There was once a healthy integration of pre-Christian Anglo-Saxon culture with English Christianity. The Venerable Bede, in his major work *An Ecclesiastical History of the English People*, portrayed a culture that had successfully and meaningfully integrated Anglo-Saxon culture with Roman Christianity. Unfortunately, by the era of the Puritan movement in the 16th century CE, many cherished ancient customs were derided and discarded as being 'pagan'. The Industrial Revolution in the 19th century, with its need for long working hours and low pay, further weakened the ability of English society to maintain and pass on these traditions, traditions that enabled the structure of society to function in a healthy, respectful and cohesive manner.

And why am I saying all this? How is this relevant to the Israelite faith? Well, it is not Yahveh's will that everyone should belong to the same religion, but it is the gift of Yahveh to other peoples that they should learn how to live at peace with themselves and with other nations. The law of Israel extends only over the people of Israel, but the law of God extends over the whole earth, and over all peoples. Yahveh is the God of all Nations, and gives

---

[a] from research conducted by the Co-Operative Funeralcare organisation; reported in *The Independent* (18 Oct 2011) in an article by Kevin Rawlinson.

to all of us a way of living at peace in whichever society we were born into.

The four levels of a healthy society and nation

Ancient Israelite society was built on four levels: the nation (*ha-'am*), the tribe (*ha-shévet*), the clan or extended family (*ha-mishpachah*), and finally the household (*ha-báyit*). All these levels have to be present in the nurture and upbringing of an individual, in order to create a whole and mature human being who is psychologically balanced.

If I wanted to transfer these levels onto British or American society, the place of the tribe would be taken over by local or regional culture (or in the case of ethnic or religious groups, by the culture of one's ethnic or religious background). If you were to remove the bonds of any of these levels, you have the potential makings not only of a psychologically ailing individual, but also of an ailing society.

The lowest level of this structure is the household. In ancient Israel, this was anyone living under the same roof, and did not necessarily mean that you were biologically related. Still, the basic learning unit was the parent-child one. The parent helps the child learn how to love, how to be loved, and how to relate to others. Ideally, within the parent-child relationship the child learns self-respect, and how to respect others.

The parent has to put aside the hang-ups that have plagued his or her own childhood, and ensure that these negative passions are not passed on to the next generation. In a religious household, this is achieved by adhering to cultural standards which have not been affected negatively by the past experiences of individuals. The parent also has a duty to pass on his or her family's cultural values. This will enable the child to form its identity within its society, and participate in that society. In Jewish society, it is the family that begins the process of teaching Jewish culture, not the rabbi, scribe or sage – *'Train a child in the path he should follow, and when he is old he will not turn away from it.'*[a]

Then comes the extended family. There are two aspects to this: relationships and history. It is vital for a child to build relationships with the members of his or her extended family. The most important of these is the one with the grandparents. Such a bond gives a child an awareness of the value of the wisdom of age, as well as a respect for and love of one's elders. As Proverbs[b] says, *'Grandchildren are a crown for the elderly, and parents are the pride of their children.'*

The second benefit of bonding with one's extended family is

---

[a] Prov 22:6
[b] Prov 17:6

learning about one's ancestors. I cannot stress enough how psychologically important it is to know who you are, where you come from, and what kind of a person you might become, simply by being taught your family history from a young age. Learning about your ancestors helps you understand your own potential. Being aware of your family's successes will give you pride and self-worth, and knowing of your family's failures will give you humility – you cannot have one without the other; the mistakes of your ancestors humble you. If you are only told of their achievements, you will become arrogant and conceited. You will look down on other cultures and think them inferior. Similarly, knowing only their failures will take away your hopes and dreams. You will also become jealous and envious of those families or peoples with 'better' stories, eventually growing to hate them.

Israelite history is a lengthy saga of both heroes and villains. Our ancestors were not perfect beings – even our heroes had faults and failings. The Miqra teaches us about their good deeds as well as of their sins. Other ancient cultures told stories of how they were descended from gods and perfect heavenly beings; Hebrew culture was possibly unique in the ancient world in that it did no such thing. This has made us, as a people, realise that we are not perfect, that we are not conquerors whose culture is founded on boast of conquest and empire; we do not base our culture reminiscing on a glorious past, but on a quest to do better, with the intent of learning from our mistakes.

It is therefore important that any religious community which considers itself holy before God, should never hide the sins of its collective past, or make excuses for them. Take pride in one's accomplishments, but never hide or excuse the wrongdoings of one's religion – if you do, no one will respect you or believe you, God's face will be turned away from you, and you will share in the punishment due to the sins you are defending and hiding.[a] The sins of one's religious community will come back to haunt you, and weigh you down like a millstone around your neck. Sins defended or hidden can never be atoned for as long as they are denied, and will actually prevent such a community approaching God in holiness.

The next level is the tribe – either one's local heritage, or one's ethnic or religious culture. The good thing about *local* culture is that everyone of any background can participate in it. Having an

---

[a] Prov 17:15 – "He who justifies the wicked, and he who condemns the righteous, both of them are an abomination to Yahveh".

awareness and an appreciation of one's local county or regional culture[a] and history, and actively participating in it on a regular basis, will give you an interest in where you live. This is the basis of civic pride; it will give you an enthusiasm for looking after your home-town or region – an invested interest, because it *matters* to you. Having local traditions give people something to do together with other people, something more than simply going out every night and getting drunk.

The top-most level is the nation (*ha-'am*). In order for you to understand what a nation meant in the ancient world, you have to rid yourself of any modern understanding of the word. The idea of a nation based on ethnicity is a relatively modern concept, beginning with the political struggles of the peoples of Europe after the First World War. Ethnicity is effectively the tribe; 'nation' is actually something else.[b]

In ancient times nationhood was based, not on ethnicity, but on a shared, inter-tribal culture. For example, you were Egyptian because you shared Egyptian culture, not because you were ethnically Hamitic Egyptian. You were Roman, not because you were descended from the Latin tribes of the Seven Hills, but because you held allegiance to Roman principles and values. You were Greek, because you held to Greek ideals and culture. Similarly with the Phoenicians, Babylonians and others.

The Israelite idea of nationhood was slightly different. Great importance was placed on shared ancestry – that all Israelites were descended from Jacob, son of Isaac. However, this was never intended to be a racial distinctiveness, rather it was meant to give the diverse Israelite tribes the bond of a common origin story, an unbreakable link to their homeland, as well as a shared sense of destiny. In the ancient world, one's homeland was where one's ancestors were buried. Therefore the emphasis on ancestors was an awareness of homeland and identity, not genetic ethnicity in the modern sense of the word. Over the centuries, many people *not* descended from Jacob have been admitted into the congregation of Israel;[c] for the convert, our ancestors become

---

[a] such as local music, local food and produce, dialect poetry, local folk tales, practising local customs in daily life, or occasionally participating in local cultural events.

[b] In a study published by the journal *Nature* (19 Mar 2015 – *'The fine-scale genetic structure of the British population'*), it was discovered that neither the Scots, the Welsh nor the English were any of them one single, homogeneous people; each was a mixture of many different ancient tribes, residing within defined areas that still reflected ancient tribal divisions even after several millennia.

[c] For example Uriah the Hittite (2Sam 11:3-21), Ruth the Moabitess (direct ancestor of King David), Caleb ben Jephunneh the Kenizzite (Num 32:12), Ebed-Melekh the Ethiopian (Jer 39:16-18), and the Canaanitess Rahab of

your ancestors, and therefore our homeland becomes your homeland.

A nation was a group of people founded on a common set of values, who shared a common culture and used a common language.[a] In the modern world, within any given nation there are now many diverse cultures. If we wish to engage in nation-building in such an environment, rather than chasing the elusive and mythical concept of racial purity, we have to bring the diverse 'tribes' of our nation together in common purpose, by encouraging shared values and shared ideals.

Modern nations consist of peoples who each value their own unique identity and heritage. A wise government will build and strengthen their country first by recognising this immutable fact. Such a government will seek rather to encourage in its citizens a common set of values and ideals. Such a tactic will give newcomers access to local culture, and foster within them a willingness to participate in it. A country that holds even its legally resident 'foreigners' at arms' length will ensure that they *never* integrate into it. However, a country that is welcoming to foreigners legally resident there, will encourage such people to participate and integrate, eventually to become valuable members of that nation who appreciate and help the cultural life of their adopted country.

If we have a realistic idea of nationhood, we can justifiably have pride in our nation, rather than a baseless vainglory. It is perfectly acceptable to value your country's history, traditions and heritage; it is perfectly acceptable to hold up the contributions your country has made to the commonwealth of humanity; there is nothing wrong with teaching your country's values to each successive generation – these things we can comfortably do without accusations of racism. However, it is something else entirely to say that your country is superior to all others, that your language and heritage is better than anyone else's, to look down your nose at the poor estate of other peoples, to glory in your country's conquests over other peoples, and to exclude outsiders from participating in cultural events and gatherings on the basis of their ethnicity.

Through the prophet Jeremiah, Yahveh told us, *"Seek the peace and security of the city to which I have exiled you, and there*

Jericho (Josh 2). Also the Rekhavites (Jer 35:5-7), the Kenites (1Chron 2:55), and the mixed multitude who left Egypt with the Israelites.

[a] local dialect and group slang make for a living language, but I think one it is important *also* to be fluent in the standard form of one's native language; restricting oneself to dialect or slang severely restricts one's economic and social options.

pray to Yahveh on its behalf. For in its peace and security, there shall be peace and security for you. "[a] There are many anti-Semitic bigots who claim that we Jews work against the countries and cultures where we live, but to do this is actually against our faith – against what God has told us to do. Yahveh tells us to work for the prosperity of the lands and peoples where we have been sent by God, because if they prosper, we prosper. Any religion that works to deliberately subvert the countries to which they have been sent, is not from God, and is in fact working against God.

The distinctiveness of Israelite culture

There can be few people in the world who will disagree with the statement that Jewish culture is very distinctive and different. I have earlier mentioned that one reason for this is so that other peoples would sit up and take notice, and thereby become aware of the distinctive nature of the God of Israel.

There is another purpose behind the very concept of culture itself that many people ignore today. It brings people together; it gives people a valid excuse to share time together. In Israel today, there are many different Jewish sects, and many different beliefs. However, when a religious festival comes round – such as Passover or *Sukkot* – all those sects can come together and share community together, regardless of their theological differences.

I think this may have been one of the many reasons why God decided there would only be one national place of worship. With many different places of worship, the nation would become fractured as denominations and sects arose. However, with only one national place of worship, Israelites of widely differing views are forced to get on with each other, in order to maintain their cultural and religious way of life.

One part of religious tradition that is often criticised is ritual. I think this is partly because it has exceeded its boundaries, and become more than it was originally intended to be.

Scientists have recently found that there is a hormone that is released when we do things together.[b] It is called oxytocin, and is sometimes called, 'the hug hormone'. It is the chemical that is released by the brain when someone hugs you, and gives you a nice, warm feeling inside. Apparently, the same hormone is released when a group of people engage in a shared activity together – whether it is formation dancing,

---

[a] Jer 29:7
[b] in the report: *'Oxytocin: the Great Facilitator of Life'*, Heon-Jin Lee, Abbe H. Macbeth, Jerome Pagani, and W. Scott Young.

group singing, or ritualised religious activity.

There is another purpose to religious ritual that becomes evident when it is practised alone. Let me first tell you about Pavlov's dogs (in case you don't already know the story).

In the 1890's, the Russian scientist Ivan Pavlov conducted certain experiments on dogs. The dogs were fed by assistants in white overalls. He noticed that the dogs would begin salivating immediately when they saw the men in white. He wanted to investigate whether there was a psychological link between an external stimulus and salivating. So he began using the sound of a metronome whenever the dogs were fed. After a while, sure enough, the dogs would salivate every time they heard a metronome, since they began to associate the sound with being fed.

This cognitive association also occurs in human beings, and can be very powerful; the positive emotional association with actions or things helps us through the ups and downs of life. For example, I found that whenever I ate half-boiled eggs with white pepper, I would feel a sense of peace. I wondered why, and then I remembered that it was one of things that my grandma would give me for breakfast when I was little. In an exceedingly unhappy childhood, being at my grandma's house gave me a sense of security, safety and peace. In time, my subconscious mind began to associate the special activities, foods, and objects that I experienced only at my grandma's house with this sense of security and calm.

This is the most powerful aspect of the distinctiveness of Israelite culture. Sometimes, there is no reason for the strangeness and oddness of our customs and traditions, other than to remind us of the good, holy and compassionate character of our God. We can't see or touch our God, but we can do things, eat things, and possess things which cement the emotional link that our religion creates within us *to* our God, so that these strange and unusual things give us this sense of peace and calm. That's why it's so important that these psychological links be laid down in our psyche with love and a sense of safeness.

The same effect can be seen with ritual. I used to have a prayer-room in my old house in Surrey, England. I made sure that I would leave my problems outside that room, and try to regain an inner sense of calm whenever I entered it. In time, merely entering that room immediately gave me a sense of inner peace.

Similarly, when you start associating the Holy Name of God with peace, calm and happiness, in time whenever you speak or whisper the Holy Name, it will calm you down. In fact, any ritual action or word that you train your mind to associate with tranquillity and inner peace, will in time enable your mind to quickly reach that state merely by performing the ritual, or speaking the word or words.

In most mainstream synagogues, the synagogue is a place for socialising and nattering. There is no place for what I would call 'reverent centring' – to prayerfully calm one's spirit before the service. I would therefore encourage Talmidi synagogues to have the main area for reverent prayer, and a separate area for socialising.

I think the earliest humans realised this psychological effect that ritual had on the human mind, and the benefits that it could confer. Unfortunately, as time passed, I think that people started abusing the real effects of ritual actions and words, so that they lost all benefit and meaning.

It is not the ritual that matters, but the heart that you put into it. Because of this, if you start doing things in a sloppy or half-hearted manner, you actually diminish the positive and beneficial effect that it can have on your psyche. Participating with your whole heart, will lay down great strength in your heart and soul for later, so that when you fall on difficult emotional times, you can draw on the strength you have already laid down. But if you did everything in a careless, slipshod fashion, your spirit will not be strong enough to get you through hard times.

When the perfection and exactitude of a ritual matters more than the heartfelt participation in it, then the original purpose of that ritual is lost. But when ritual is used to serve human needs – to bring people together, to give them a common sense of identity and purpose, a sense of belonging and an inner sense of peace – then ritual fulfils the objective and service to the human mind for which it was originally created.

God's will for Israel

The nation and people of Israel – and by Israel, I am not talking about the modern state of Israel, but rather all the Jewish people around the world – Israel is expected by God to *be* something distinctive in the world, to change itself so that the world will change. If Israel becomes Yahveh's light, then the rest of humanity will change. But if Israel does not stand out, if it does nothing positive – if we seek to be just the same as other peoples and nations, then we should not be surprised when we are scorned, criticised and held in low esteem.

I am proud of the modern state of Israel – of what it has achieved in the decades since its recreation, of its democracy in an undemocratic region of the world, of its insistence on the equality of women, and of its recognition of the rights of all religions in the country. I am also proud of the nature of the Jewish society of Israel. I was in Israel in November 2004 when Yasser Arafat died, and I was impressed that there were no scenes of jubilation from Jewish crowds – because you do not rejoice at the misfortune of your enemy; when there are social protests by Jewish groups against the Israeli government, there is no looting or burning of homes or businesses, because as Rabbi David Wolpe put it, 'being a good Jew means being a good citizen'.[a] I am proud of what the Jewish faith can achieve when it remains close to the ideals that Yahveh gave us.

We as a people are meant to be representatives of Yahveh's moral and ethical standards on earth. We have to be seen as a fair and a just people. We cannot let ourselves slide; we have to be vigilant in every generation. We cannot look at what others have done to us, and then go and do the same thing to them – because then we will lose God's support. God intended us to become such an example to the nations, that we would become respected by the world, a nation who would be admired so much that it would be copied, and whose standards would be aspired to by others.

If Israel as a dispersed people has obligations, the modern state of Israel has obligations too. The state of Israel will always be judged to a higher standard than any other country in the world – by Yahveh, not just by other people. That is why its government has such a responsibility to behave in an ethical manner towards all non-Jews within its borders. It must ensure that foreign workers are treated with fairness and not taken advantage of, and it must ensure that non-Jewish citizens within its borders are treated with dignity. It cannot oppress another people simply because of their ethnicity or religion. If an individual or organisation has committed a criminal or terrorist act, then the due process of law must be seen to prevail. But if an innocent individual is trying to go about their daily life, they must not be mistreated, harassed, or abused simply because of who they are; God will have something to say (and do) about it.

If the oppression goes on for too long, then the consequences will be dire for the state of Israel – and God will be behind it, and we will have no recourse to God for help,[b] for God will not hear

---

[a] podcast 12th Aug 2011
[b] Ex 22:22-24; although this refers to 'widows and the fatherless', the principle is the same; that if we oppress *anyone* who is disadvantaged in our society – including those who are not of our own people – then God will defend them: 'If ... they cry out to me, I will certainly hear their cry.'

our cries.[a] We have to remember that those who bless us will be blessed, and those who curse us curse only themselves.[b] We should work towards increasing the number of those who have cause to bless us as a people; those who curse us are agents of their own destruction.

More recently, the current, right wing Israeli government has resumed its removal of Bedouin from their nomadic life in the Negev, and dumped them in poor, crime-ridden townships. Now, the Bedouin of the Negev are for the most part loyal citizens of Israel. They serve in the armed forces, and in skirmishes with Palestinians, Bedouin men have died alongside Jewish Israelis.

The Negev Bedouin are descended from the Idumeans of the region. According to ancient tradition, Jacob's older brother was 'Eisav (*Esau* in English), and 'Eisav's nickname was Edom.[c] The Israelites are descended from Jacob, and the Idumeans (or Edomites) were descended from 'Eisav. The ancient history of Israel and the Edomites has not always been good; for much of the time, the Edomites were at war with Israel. The prophets often condemn the belligerent actions of the Edomites.

In spite of all this, Torah tells us: *'Do not despise the Edomites, for they are your brothers.'*[d] In other words, do not despise or ill-treat the Bedouins of the Negev, for they are our brothers. We are further told by God, 'Do not provoke them to war, for ***I will not give you any of their land***, not even enough to put your foot on. ***I have given 'Eisav the hill country of Seir*** (the eastern Negev) ***as his own.***'[e] The southern border of the land that Israel had a permanent right to was the northern border of Edom.[f]

In my humble opinion, through 'Eisav the Negev Bedouin are the Idumean brothers and sisters of the Jewish people. The current Israeli government should not treat them with such disdain because, again, Yahveh our God will exact justice for it. If we ill-treat the Negev Bedouin, they will eventually side with the Palestinians, and one of our valuable allies in Israel will be lost.

It also disturbs me how authoritarian and restrictive the present government in Israel is becoming, little by little removing the rights of

---

[a] Dt 31:14 – turning away from God's principles will close off God's help and protection from us.
[b] Gen 12:3
[c] Gen 25:30
[d] Deut 23:7
[e] Deut 2:5
[f] Num 34:3

its citizens to criticise its actions.ᵃ If the actions of the present government of Israel do not change – if it does not end its erosion of democracy, or if it does not cease treating its non-Jewish citizens with disrespect– then Israel's enemies will take advantage of such godless behaviour, and the consequences will not be pleasant for anyone.

We can be a treasured people, a respected people, and a people admired and copied throughout the world, but we have to follow God's teachings on how to treat others with fairness and justice:

*'Yahveh has declared this day that you are God's people, God's treasured possession as God promised, but that you have to keep all God's commands. God has declared that God will set you in praise, fame and honour high above all the nations God has made, and that you will be a people holy to Yahveh your God, as God promised.'*ᵇ

*'Yahveh will establish you as God's holy people, as God promised you on oath, **as long as** you keep the commands of Yahveh your God, and walk in God's ways. Then all the peoples of the earth will see that you are called by the name of Yahveh, **and they will have an awesome respect for you.**'*ᶜ

When we live amongst a people who are not our own, that society should benefit from our Jewish presence among them. Before the creation of modern Israel, when Jewish communities lived in disadvantaged regions around Europe, did we become hotbeds of crime and vandalism? Did our communities harbour delinquents who went out at night, beating up innocents and mugging people? No, we did not. Jewish communities did not do harm to or undermine the societies in which they lived, *because we lived in those societies too.*

Throughout the generations, Yahveh has moulded the Jewish soul, the Jewish consciousness. Human society can learn from the Jewish experience. Doing God's will means allowing yourself to change for the better. It is only by changing ourselves, that the process of changing our societies for the better can begin. Doing God's will does not allow us to sit back and do nothing. Doing nothing will mean that society stagnates and eventually degenerates into a feral rabble of people with no self-dignity, and no respect for

---

ᵃ e.g. the NGO Law, which will allow or deny funding to organisations relying on government funding, based on their political affiliation – in effect, denying funding if a group disagrees with the government.
ᵇ Dt 26:18-19
ᶜ Dt 28:9-10

others.[a]

Following God's will is crucial for Israel

When the Jewish people of Judea were taken into exile by the Babylonians in 586 BCE, they struggled to understand why this had happened to them. The conclusion from the final editor of the *Book of Joshua*, was that they and their leaders had failed to obey God's teaching and guidance. The *Book of Joshua* therefore portrays a leader – Joshua[b] – who perfectly obeys God, and when he does, Israel is successful. She is able to defeat her enemies, and succeed against overwhelming odds. However, when she goes against God's law and values, then Israel becomes vulnerable, and suffers defeat.

Right-wing Israelis can react to fair criticism and concern in as angry, unreasonable and bigoted a manner as they wish, but if the Israeli government reacts in ways which go far beyond what is reasonable for defence and security, then God will take action (and directing vile, ugly comments towards people like me will not deter God; it is futile to think that it will). As long as security and defence measures are within what is necessary to protect Israel and her citizens, then God will defend and protect us.

Right-wing Islamists like Hamas know how to manipulate and incite a right-wing Israeli government. They know it can be provoked into harsh and unjust measures against the Arab population, *which is precisely what the Islamists want them to do*. Islamists know that the Israeli right-wing will react in a way that makes them do cruel and unjust things to ordinary people; the Islamists know that this will sully Israel's reputation abroad, and they don't really care about the effect it has on their own people.

I say all this because Israel's possession of the Land is *always* conditional; once we are back, it does not mean we will stay back – *we must always remember that*. The Jewish people's continued habitation in the Land of Israel will always be provisional. God brought us back once before (when the Jewish people returned after the Babylonian exile), and we were then re-exiled by the Romans. The Roman exile ended in 1948, but that does not make our return permanent even this time. The Israeli government must never put God in such a position, whereby the only solution to rectifying God's sullied reputation and holiness, is to expel

---

[a] as witnessed in the looters' riots around England, Aug 2011

[b] Joshua is depicted almost as a royal figure, even though he wasn't a king. According to the Davidic covenant, as long as the kings (=messiahs) of Israel were obedient to God, then Israel would have peace, and would dwell safe and secure in the Land.

the Jewish people from the Land *yet again*.

It is vital to understand this point. Obedience to God's will is crucial in order to protect and guide Israel, and to secure her permanence in the Land. The advice of the Psalms[a] is that trust in Yahveh will assure salvation from Israel's enemies. That means trust in Yahveh's teachings, values and principles. We have to be willing to admit that God is in charge; that we do not have all the answers ourselves, but that if we trust in Yahveh our Heavenly Father, we will prosper and succeed in most of what we do. This view reflects the Yahwist belief that putting our complete and total trust in *anyone* and *anything* else, will cause our endeavours to end in failure.

Just as a child believes with his or her whole mind and soul that as long as their parents are with them, they will be all right, so also a child of Yahveh has to come to know that as long as Yahveh, their heavenly Father, is in charge, everything is going to be all right.

Today in Israel, we desperately want to see peace. I believe that we will have peace when we trust in Yahveh alone, and not in human leaders, allies or teachings. Ps 9:10 says, *"Those who know Your name will trust in You, for You, O Yahveh, have never forsaken those who seek You."* We speak too much of what *we* want to see happen, what *we* want people to do. But things will only begin to change when we seek what Yahveh wants, because we, the Jewish people, are what we are and where we are *only* because of Yahveh; and through seeking what God's will is, will Israel and all the nations have peace.

... *your* ...

The difficulties posed by the Oral Law[b]

As I have previously mentioned, I think this line of the prayer *('May Your will be realised')* was included because of the issues surrounding the Oral Law.[c] Most people who have no background knowledge of the Israelite religion, think that when Yeshua` is criticising practises from 'the Law', he is criticising the very basis of the Israelite legal code – Torah, the first five books of the

---

[a] e.g. Ps 20:7, 22:8, 37:3
[b] for a longer treatment of this topic, see 'The Hebrew Yeshua vs the Greek Jesus', by Nehemia Gordon, chapter 3
[c] The Oral Law is made up of the decisions of the ancient Pharisaic rabbis. In Orthodox communities it has greater authority than the Hebrew Bible.

Hebrew bible. What most people *don't* realise is that what he is actually criticising are Pharisaic practises contained only in their Oral Law.

In certain cases the Oral Law actually forbids the observance of Torah. Examples are the observance of the New Moon holiday, the wearing of blue cords (*techelet*) on the corner fringes of our garments, the observance of the Nazirite vow,[a] not pronouncing God's Name under *any* circumstances, and many more. They may seem like trivial and unimportant *mitzvot* (commandments), but they are part of a heritage which was designed to mould the Israelite soul, and give us a sense of the greatness and holiness of God. Leaving them out is like leaving bricks out of the very wall that was meant to protect us.

The Oral Law can also be manifestly unjust. We only have to look at how it looks upon patrilineal Jews,[b] widows whose dead husbands cannot be traced,[c] and divorcées whose husbands refuse to grant a divorce,[d] to name but a few. However, Modern Orthodox rabbis are not willing to lift the burden and return to God's Torah, because it would mean admitting the Oral law is unjust. Yeshua` criticised their Pharisaic antecedents for the same inflexibility: '*You tie up heavy loads, hard to carry, and lay them on people's shoulders, but you're not willing to lift a finger to help!*'[e]

The Oral Law teaches the absolute authority of the rabbis, even

---

[a] Without the Temple, the Nazirite vow cannot be ended. However, there is no requirement to have a Temple in order to *start* the Nazirite vow. It simply means that for the time being, the Nazirite vow is for life. The vow enables any man or woman to attain the same ritual state of holiness as a priest. Whereas a priest has to be a male, and a descendant of Aaron, a Nazirite can be any lay man or woman who is an Israelite (native born or convert).

[b] Individuals whose father is Jewish, but whose mother is not, are not viewed as Jewish according to the Rabbinic Oral Law. However, if your mother is Jewish, and your father is not, then you *are* Jewish. In contrast, the Talmidi community accept both patrilineal and matrilineal Jews as Jewish (and therefore don't need to convert, just re-acquaint themselves with the Jewish faith).

[c] If the body of a woman's dead husband cannot be traced, then she cannot be declared a widow, and consequently cannot remarry. There is no provision in the Oral Law to remedy this.

[d] According to the Oral Law, only a man can initiate and agree to a divorce. If a man refuses a divorce, then even if the woman is suffering violence or hardship, then she cannot get a divorce or remarry. The just way to get round this would be to resort to ancient Israelite tradition, and use the *shidduq* (betrothal agreement). One could insert stipulations in the *shidduq* which is like a prenuptial agreement. If the man refuses a divorce, or if a woman is widowed and her husband's body is not found within a certain time, then it could be stipulated in the *shidduq* that the divorce or widowhood could be declared by a Beth Din, and the divorce or widowhood granted.

[e] S.Yesh. 115:3 ; cf Mt 23:4, Lk 11:46

when they say something that is illogical, contradictory, or against Torah. For example, it says in the Oral Law:

"Even if before your eyes they [the rabbis] show you that right is left, or left is right, you must obey them. "[a]

This is in contrast to what the Prophets declare: *"Woe to those who call evil good, and good evil; who call darkness light, and light darkness; who call sweet bitter, and bitter sweet. "*[b]

According to the Oral Law, what is decided by rabbinic authority in matters of religion cannot be questioned, even if it is known otherwise to be blatantly incorrect. Even if Torah says one thing, and the Oral Law says another, people must go according to the Oral Law:

'If there are one thousand prophets, all of them of the same standing as Elijah and Elisha, giving a particular interpretation, and another one thousand and one rabbis giving the contrary interpretation, you shall incline after the majority, and the law will be according to the one thousand and one rabbis, not according to the one thousand revered prophets. "[c]

This is despite what it says in Torah:

"You shall NOT follow the majority when they do wrong, " [d]

The Oral Law decrees that if God declares something through one of God's prophets, we are still not to obey God:

"By God, if we heard the matter directly from the mouth of Joshua son of Nun, we would not obey him, nor would we listen to him. " [e]

And:

"God did not permit us to learn from the Prophets, only from the rabbis who are men of logic and reason. " [f]

Yeshua` felt that the opinions and decisions of the Pharisaic rabbis were actually a hindrance to the Kingdom of God: *'... you shut the door of God's kingdom in people's faces and throw away the key. And you neither enter yourselves, nor allow those who wish to enter to go in!* '[g] In the Gospel of Thomas, there is a saying which further clarifies Yeshua`'s view: *'You're like a dog sleeping in the feeding-trough of an ox; because neither does the dog eat the hay,*

---

[a] Sifrey Deuteronomy S154 on Deut 17:11
[b] Isaiah 5:20
[c] Maimonides, Introduction to the Mishnah
[d] Exodus 23:2
[e] Maimonides, Introduction to the Mishnah
[f] Maimonides, Introduction to the Mishnah
[g] S.Yesh. 116:1b-2; cf Mt 23:13, Lk 11:52

nor does he let the oxen do so either. '[a]

The obstacle of the Oral Law in Yeshua`'s ministry

There are a number of cultural norms and spiritual beliefs that existed in Yeshua`'s day, which actually became a hindrance to his ministry and teaching. Jewish contact with Greek, Hellenistic philosophy had caused some Jewish beliefs to become deformed, like in personifying Wisdom and the Divine Logos (which I shall discuss in Chapter seven, in the sections on Wisdom Mysticism and *Ha-Davar* – 'the Word'). This transmogrification of Yahwist beliefs into something they were never intended to be, is why I do not take Jewish philosophy at the point of its condition in the First Century CE, but rather that of pre-rabbinic, pre-Exile Yahwism – the noble and holy form of the Israelite faith I believe that Yeshua` was trying to restore us to.

Likewise, another major issue with the teachings of the Pharisaic rabbis, was that their view of the future and God's ultimate plan, was actually contrary to what was written in Torah, and spoken of by the biblical Prophets.

In the *New Testament*, we are deliberately given the false impression that the reason why the Pharisees hated Yeshua` so much, was that he supposedly claimed to be the messiah. Now, in those days, messianic claimants were two a penny; they were regularly popping up all over the place. In reality however, the only people these 'messiahs' actually bothered were the Romans. As for the Pharisees, they generally took a 'wait and see' approach to them all. They would not have persecuted or sought the death of such claimants, and they would not have sought out the death of Yeshua` – they would have had no reason to. If you were familiar with their historically attested beliefs, you would realise that the part of Yeshua`'s message that the Pharisees would logically have had a problem with, is the part where he claimed he was a prophet.[b]

The biggest obstacle to Yeshua`'s own ministry, was the fact that the Pharisees had declared there were no more prophets. So when two prophets came along, both proclaiming that the unjust had to repent, or else there would be dire consequences, the Pharisees' beliefs were a major hindrance. Yochanan the Immerser ('John the Baptist') and Yeshua` both called for repentance, otherwise Jerusalem would be destroyed, and the Jewish people would be exiled. However, because of the rabbinic stance on prophets, the Pharisees would not believe them or

---

[a] Gosp. Th. 102:1; cf S.Yesh. 117:1b-2
[b] see Mk 6:4, Mt 10:41, 13:57, 21:11, 21:46, Lk 1:76

even listen to them. Yahveh told us through the prophet Amos[a] that forbidding genuine prophets to prophesy was a sin.

The Pharisaic position on prophets was not held by everyone. When Yeshua` visited a village in the Galilee, the inhabitants there heard that a man of God was coming to visit them, and so got their children ready for Yeshua` to bless them.[b] This had been a normal Jewish practice even in the days of the Israelite prophets – to have a prophet bless your family on behalf of God.

The only person the Pharisees would listen to was 'the messiah'. Now, a messiah or 'anointed one' is a title given to *any* king of Israel.[c] *All* kings of Israel were 'messiahs', even the bad ones.[d] This logically implies that there would be *many* messiahs in history. Some would be great, others would be disobedient to God. The positive prophecies in the Miqra refer to those kings in Israel's history who will be great, and be obedient to God's law. Unfortunately, the Pharisees had lumped together all the prophecies about Israel's good kings, and created an image of a 'super-messiah' – one who was so impossibly fantastic, that no such person could ever be born. I think there was some pre-planned human purpose in this; living in the assurance that no such person could ever realistically exist, ordinary people would *have* to turn to the Pharisaic rabbis for guidance.

Can you now see the impossible situation that Yeshua` was in? If the Pharisees accepted the existence of prophets, then Yeshua` could declare himself as such, and ordinary people would listen to his warnings, repent and return to God's ways, and so avoid the destructive tribulation. But the Pharisees had effectively banned prophets. The only person they would listen to was this impossible 'super-messiah' that they had created. Since Yeshua` was not in any way this super-messiah, they would not listen to him.

I suspect that as the day of reckoning in 70 CE fast approached – as it became blatantly obvious that the time of which both Yochanan and Yeshua` spoke was drawing near – some of

---

[a] Amos 2:12

[b] S.Yesh. 147; cf Mk 10:13-16

[c] For a brief period after Yeshua`'s death, Herod Agrippa (41-44 CE) reigned as messiah (that is, 'anointed king') over the whole of Israel (or Judea as it was then called). However by this time, the term 'messiah' had come to be so identified with the liberation and redemption of Israel, that he was probably not accorded this title himself.

[d] The phrase 'The Messiah' (*ha-mashiach*) does not appear anywhere in the Hebrew Bible, only 'a messiah', implying that there will be a succession of many messiahs or kings.

Yeshua`'s followers, in a desperate attempt to get people to listen, may have made the unfortunate decision to claim that Yeshua` *was* the promised messiah. Simply to get people to listen, and heed the warnings that Jerusalem and the Temple would be destroyed if there was no repentance, they *might* have made a decision that would have far-reaching consequences for everyone for the next two thousand years. If the Pharisees had not created this super-messiah, and instead accepted the existence of prophets, then Yeshua` *would never have become a messiah* – there would have been no need.

The Pharisees also believed that a prophet like Elijah would *precede* the messiah. Unfortunately, this belief comes from Pharisaic teaching, and *not* from the Hebrew bible. Mainstream Christians eventually took over this belief from the Pharisees. Whereas most modern Jewish people look forward to the day when Elijah comes, thinking that he will presage the 'messianic era', the Prophets tell us that a prophet like Elijah will actually precede a calamitous day of judgment:

'Behold, I will send you the prophet Elijah before that great and terrible day of Yahveh comes.'[a]

Yochanan's ministry was to call the guilty parties to repentance in order to avoid this Day of Yahveh – the corrupt priests, the murderous Zealots, and the unjust or unobservant[b] among the rich and powerful. The ministry of Yeshua`, in addition, was to gather together the good and the righteous, and add to their number, so that they would be sheltered on the day of God's anger:

'Seek Yahveh, all you humble of the land, you who do what he commands. Seek righteousness, seek humility; perhaps you will be sheltered on the day of Yahveh's anger.'[c]

In short, Pharisaic beliefs hindered God's message from being promulgated and acted upon. They didn't believe in Malachi's Elijah, or any kind of prophet after Malachi. They only believed in this super-messiah of their own creation, who would be preceded by what they defined as the prophet like Elijah. They would only listen to this messiah they had made; everyone else would be ignored. As a result, when Yochanan and Yeshua` were called by God, calling for repentance so that the Day of Yahveh could be averted, they ignored them both. Yochanan the Immerser was not the kind of Elijah they believed in, so they didn't listen to him. Yeshua` was a prophet, not a messiah, so they didn't listen to him either – because they didn't believe in prophets.

What would have happened if the Pharisees had never declared that

---

[a] Malachi 3:23 (4:5 in Christian bibles)
[b] particularly those rich and powerful who ignored the laws on social justice, and forgiveness of debt
[c] Zeph 2:3

Elijah would precede the messiah? What if they had not created this 'super-messiah', and instead accepted that God would continue to speak through prophets in every age? Perhaps they would have listened to both Yochanan and Yeshua`. Perhaps they would have joined in the call for national repentance. Perhaps the priests would have repented, the Zealots would have desisted from their violent campaign, and perhaps the rich and powerful would have paid attention to their responsibilities to the poor. Perhaps as a result, Jerusalem and the Temple would never have been destroyed, the Jewish people would never have been exiled, and 2,000 years of misery and suffering could have been avoided.

Or perhaps the guilty parties would still have refused to repent. But at least, Yeshua` and Yochanan would have had the largest Jewish religious party behind them, and we would have known that everyone did everything they possibly could have to prevent the tribulation, destruction and exile. But the Pharisees are guilty of the sin of omission. Their policy was to wait and see. They did nothing – they did not do the good that they could have done. The will of human beings thereby became an obstacle to the will of God.

... be realised / be done

The Greek word for this is very revealing and suggestive. In 1998 when I worked on my translation of the *Our Father* into Jewish Aramaic, I decided to translate it into Aramaic as *tihey* – from the basic verb 'to be', instead of 'to do' – because of what the Greek verb implied.

In the Greek *Our Father*, in the phrase 'Thy will be done', the verb used for 'be done' (*genethēto*) is *ginomai*. So I searched the Septuagint[a] version of the Torah for instances of the Greek verb *ginomai* to see what Hebrew verb it was normally used to translate. I didn't have to look far.

In Gen 1:6, it says, *'and God said, "Let there be an expanse in the midst of the waters."'* In Greek, for the words 'let there be' the Septuagint has *genethēto*. This word is exactly the same word as the *Our Father* has in Greek for 'be done' (as in 'May your will

---

[a] In my view, the Septuagint is the best ancient Greek translation of the Torah in existence. The Torah translation is a very precise one – so much so, that we can even recreate the Hebrew that the translators were translating from. However, the Septuagint's translation of the *other* books of the Hebrew bible is not so precise – they are more like 'free' translations, and so are not reliable, in my view.

be *done*'). This means that the original translator of the prayer understood the line as suggesting that God's Will will 'come into being' – that it 'come about', 'become', 'be carried out' or 'be done'. The original verb in Aramaic therefore would have been *tihey*, and in the subsequent Hebrew translation by the editor of the *Q-Gospel,* it would have been *y'hi* (יְהִי come about), and not *ye'aśeh* (יֵעָשֶׂה be done).

The Greek verb *ginomai* suggests that something come into existence that has not existed before. It has the idea of something new. In Genesis, light, the dome of the sky, and the lights in the dome all come into being at God's command. God's will is realised – it comes to fruition.

I think this is what is meant here. This petitionary line is asking for God's will or plan to come to fruition. It is therefore a perfect accompanying line for the petition, 'May Your kingdom be fulfilled'.

Now, the mere fact of including this petition – asking for the will of God to be realised – suggests that in Yeshua`'s opinion, in his day it was *not* being done or realised. There was some obstacle to God's plan being fulfilled evident in what was going on in the events around him at the time.

In heaven, whatever God wills comes into being. God's plans are carried out and are realised there. But on earth, God's plan of action was and is not being followed.

The one ubiquitous and overriding problem in Yeshua`'s time was the Roman occupation. Even though the Romans are portrayed in the *New Testament* as beneficent overseers, in reality they were little better than Nazis. They were cruel and oppressive. Pontius Pilate, for example, is well known from other sources (such as Josephus's writings) for being a figure who enjoyed embarking upon religiously provocative projects[a] simply to aggravate Jewish sensibilities. Later governors would enact laws that made the fragile religious and political situation amongst Jewish factions even worse.

God would have had a plan to deal with this terrible situation. Human beings have a tendency to see the problem of evil as a battlefield, a war to be fought and won with might and strong-arm tactics. But God approaches the matter in a very different way. God's way is that of a farmer or a gardener. You see, just as no amount of darkness can extinguish a source of light, and just as no amount of cold can extinguish a fire, so also no amount of evil can extinguish good. But the sources of light, of fire and of good all need to be tended, nurtured and fed to keep

---

[a] The episode of the Roman standards (which bore the imperial image), erected on Pilate's orders near the Temple is a well-known one; see *Wars of the Jews*, Bk II, Ch 9, pss 2-3; also *Antiquities* Bk 18, Ch 3, ps 1

going.

Yeshua` often spoke of growing crops, and tending to them until harvest when the grain was taken into the barn, the stubble burnt, or the chaff thrown onto the fire. This was God's plan to deal with the Roman occupation. No matter how cruel and oppressive the Romans were, they were not a threat to the Israelite religion. In time, God would deal with them in God's own way.

In Jeremiah's day, the Babylonians were a threat to the kingdom of Judah. However, they were a political, not a religious threat. God's plan then was not to resist the Babylonians,[a] and eventually, by remaining faithful to God's ways, the Jewish people would be set free. Even if they were sent into exile, as long as they followed God's laws and values, and sought the prosperity of the places they were exiled to,[b] then one day they would be able to return to Judah.

The message that Yeshua` was given by God to deliver to the Jewish people was a similar one. Those who lived by the sword would die by the sword, and one day not one stone in Jerusalem would be left standing on another. But if the Jewish people stood firm, and lived their faith, the time of harvest would come, and the injustice of Rome would blow away like chaff, and be burnt off like stubble.

Two major obstacles stood in the way. As I have said before, the Pharisees had forbidden God's continued guidance to be delivered through the mouths of human prophets. The second obstacle was that the Zealots reacted to the Roman oppression with violence. Violent opposition to Roman might and rule only had one possible outcome: annihilation.

It was a known practice of the Romans that they gave two options to nations that defied them: capitulate, or be annihilated. Carthage suffered this fate, as did the Dacian city of Sarmitsegethusa. If the Jewish people wanted their chief city to avoid the notorious Roman punishment of annihilation, they had to follow the instructions given to them by God's prophets – Yochanan and Yeshua` – and not resist the Romans with arms.

If God's will or plan was to come to fruition, then it was not a battle that was to be fought with armies and weapons, but rather a metaphorical field of grain that was to be sown, tended and then harvested.

Even today, there are religious people who hold to a

---

a Jer 27:11-17
b Jer 29:5-7

belligerent, militaristic way of approaching the problems in society. They see them as problems that have to be fought, conquered and overcome with might – with anger, intolerance, intransigence and stubbornness.

But God's way is to plant a garden. God sends his workers to sow seed far and wide. If this seed is tended, nurtured, watered and fed, then it will become a great paradise, a place of unsurpassable beauty. But if we do nothing, plant no seeds, nurture no virtues and uphold no ideals in our society, then that garden of paradise will never come into being.

If we give in, and do not endure in our persistence, then the ideals of the kingdom will wither on the vine, and the suffering of good people through the ages will have been for nothing. But if we spread God's kingdom by exercising our faith with humility and compassion, by teaching our children and grandchildren how to respect themselves and one another, how to take responsibility within society and be tolerant of our differences, then God's kingdom will one day be fulfilled, and God's Will will be realised.

Illustrations from the words of the prophet Yeshua`

Yeshua` said:

'The kingdom of God won't come by watching and waiting for it. Nor will people say, "Here it is!" or "There it is!" Because the kingdom of God is within you.'[a]

'Blessed are the humble in spirit, because theirs is the kingdom of God.[b]

'Not everyone who calls out to me, saying "Master! Master!" will find the kingdom of God; but rather those who do the will of their heavenly Father.'[c]

'... whoever does the will of our heavenly Father, they are my mother, and my brother, and my sister.'[d]

---

[a] S.Yesh. 20:2-3; cf Lk 17:20-21
[b] S.Yesh. 3:2; Mt 5:3, Lk 6:20
[c] S.Yesh. 107:2; cf Mt 7:21
[d] S.Yesh. 151:20; cf Mt 12:50, Mk 3:35, Lk 8:21

CHAPTER FOUR: As it is in heaven, so also on earth

הי כמא דבשמייא
כי ן אף בארעא

heykhma de-bishmáyya,
keyn af be-ar`a

Just as it is in heaven,
So also upon the earth.

It is odd that the two parts of the sentence should be in this order, even though they make perfect grammatical sense as they are. The traditional English version reverses them, although many other languages leave them in the same order as they appear in the Greek version available to them. Perhaps the reason why the lines are this way round, is to reflect the traditional Israelite understanding of how heavenly things come first, and earthly things second. For example, in the list of the Ten Commandments, the laws of piety (the human relationship with God) come *before* the laws of justice (concerning human relationships with each other).

To gain an understanding of this couplet, we need to enter the realm of ancient Israelite mysticism. We will look at some of the mystical beliefs that existed in Yeshua`'s day, and even at some of his possible personal beliefs.

Natural & Supernatural - Yahwism as the defeat of superstition [a]

Before we step into an exploration of Israelite views of heaven and the afterlife, you need to understand a fundamental aspect of

---

[a] For a greater in-depth study of this topic, see *Hebrew Religion and Development*, by W Oesterley & TH Robinson

the nature of Yahwism. Now, there are many features of the ancient Israelite religion that we just don't understand today in the modern world. A lot of Israelite ritual and custom seems to be just one whole lot of mumbo-jumbo, utterly pointless and of no relevance to us today. When you examine some of the customs of the Israelite religion, enshrined as they are in the *mitzvot* of Torah, we have a tendency to think that Moses – or even God – just made these things up out of thin air and told Israelites to blithely follow them. But they must have come from *somewhere*.

Some atheists point out that many biblical customs actually originate from pre-Yahwist pagan Semitic religion, and that this apparently proves that the Israelite religion is as pagan as any other religion. However, this oversimplifies the story, and completely misses the point. It is true that a number of traditions and rituals have indeed passed from Canaanite to Israelite religion (such as dwelling in booths during the autumn harvest), but what *has* changed are the symbolism and meaning *behind* those traditions. Moses gave existing, familiar customs new meaning – a Yahwist meaning. Animal sacrifice for example, was tolerated but given new symbolism. As so often happens, it is nigh impossible to completely replace something with a totally new 'other'; it is easier to modify, adapt and give new meaning to older traditions, otherwise people simply return to the previous way of life after a while out of nostalgia.

If you are able to read the sub-text of biblical books such as the *Book of Kings* or *Chronicles*, you will see that there is a barely concealed tension between those Israelites who followed Yahveh exclusively, and those Israelites who followed pagan gods and their Canaanite customs. There was a centuries-long struggle for Yahwism before it could claim that it had gained ascendancy over pagan Semitic belief.

After the time of David, the main struggle was between worship of Yahveh and the worship of Canaanite Els and Baals. Before this however, the struggle was with Animist beliefs. Animism is the oldest, universal human religion. Animism is the belief that everything around us – such as trees, rocks and rivers – contains a spirit or a god. The distant ancestors of the ancient Israelites practised a form of Semitic Animism. Even though most of the editing of the Torah took place after the Babylonian exile, the mere fact that the Book of Genesis describes Animist customs that died out centuries before, suggests to me that they weren't making up the stories; they were using material that had been passed down through the generations from a much earlier time.

Semitic Animism was still active around the time of Abraham,

Isaac and Jacob. When Abraham arrives in Shekhem,[a] he stops at the sacred Oak of the divine Teacher (*'Elon Moreh*). There God 'appears'[b] to him and tells him the whole country shall be given to his descendants. He builds an altar to Yahveh by the tree. He similarly goes to the other sacred places of the Land (such as the sanctuary at Beth-El, and the sacred terebinth of Mamre in Hebron), and builds altars there. Abraham's actions do not show that he is honouring the pagan sacredness of those places, but rather that Yahveh supersedes and overrides the gods of those places.

Dt 29:16 (29:17 in Christian bibles) speaks against those who put faith in *"fetishes of wood and stone, silver and gold"*. The Hebrew word is *gillulim*, and refers to any object one wears or uses as a charm, thinking that it, in and of itself, will ward off evil and keep one safe. If you wear something as a reminder of your faith, then that is not what is being spoken of – there's nothing wrong with that and is perfectly acceptable. What is detestable to God is wearing an object thinking that the object *itself* will keep you safe and protect you. The word used for 'fetish' is deliberately similarly to the Hebrew word for 'excrement' (*gelalim*), implying that you might as well be wearing pieces of excrement for all the good they will do you! So also for example, using mezuzahs as a reminder of God's laws and the Covenant is good (indeed commanded), but thinking that only a perfect mezuzah will keep you safe, and that a badly written one will bring you misfortune, is using the mezuzah like a pagan fetish. For the Israelite who holds to such superstition, the reward is the very ill-fortune he was trying to avoid.[c] Superstition and irrational belief was and is not part of the Israelite religion.

As I study more and more about the Israelite religion, I am amazed at how far ahead of its time it was in many areas of religious life. At a time when all other religions worshipped the spirits or gods of rivers, hills, pillars, trees, standing stones, or springs, and held objects to be sacred, and believed that incantations could affect the course of natural events, here was a revolutionary religion that was *against* superstition and all forms of magic. God was not to be

---

[a] Gen 12:6-8

[b] When the Hebrew bible says that 'God appears', this is a euphemism for 'an angel of Yahveh appeared'. The reason why the angel is not mentioned, is because if it were, human readers being what we are, our attention would be diverted from Yahveh and onto the angel; the angel would take on more importance than it warrants. In Yahwist tradition, the angel says and does exactly what Yahveh wants it to.

[c] Dt 29:21

found inside anything, and was not limited to one place; God had no form, no body, and did not live or dwell inside any spring, tree, well, statue, man or beast.

Yahwism could not do away with the primitive Animist traditions, but it could overlay them with new meaning. If Yahveh had instead forbidden *all* pagan customs, the Israelites would simply have gone off and practised them anyway. The tactic that followers of Yahveh used – most notably Moses – was to take existing pagan Canaanite customs, and give them a new, Yahwist meaning.

For example, ancient Semitic religion worshipped trees and planted sacred groves – and I'm talking here long before they were just seen as symbols of pagan gods. I'm referring to a time when the trees were seen as the abode of the gods, or as gods themselves. The rustling of leaves and branches supposedly gave oracles. Pagan Semitic peoples used to decorate evergreen trees and hang ornaments on them, gather round them, and sing prayers and songs especially at festival times to their pagan gods.

The Yahwist response to this was to show Israelites that the tree was not special and had no power. You pull off its branches, and use them instead to adorn a completely ordinary, everyday agricultural object such as a *sukkah* (a field shelter or booth). You would pull off the tree's fruits, and hang them on the *sukkah*, showing that it was not the tree that was the provider, but rather Yahveh. The myrtle and the date palm were symbols of pagan gods (such as Astarte), so to break off their branches and leaves and use them to build something for Yahveh, was a symbolic defiance of these gods, showing that Yahveh was the more powerful.

Realising the pagan significance of trees, the burning bush that Moses witnessed also takes on possibly new aspects of meaning. Most films portray it as a tiny little thing, but it was probably quite a large bush like a broom-bush. The fire of Yahveh's angel envelops the bush – it is no longer the bush that is sacred, but rather the more powerful God whose angel surrounds it in flame.

Wells and springs were seen as the dwelling places of spirits in Semitic Animism. Springs produced living water, and were often the destination of pilgrims seeking oracles. To show that there were no spirits in the water, 'living water' (that is, fresh flowing water) was given a new Yahwist meaning – it was merely the instrument that Yahveh used to purify God's followers and mark transition. The water had no power of salvation or cleansing in and of itself. Whereas the wells of pagan settlements could only be built around the springs of water-spirits, a *miqveh* (immersion pool) could be built anywhere, showing Yahveh to be the more powerful.

Worship and reverence of ancestors was common in primitive religion. Excavations in Çatalhöyük in southern Turkey show that 9,500 years ago, people considered their ancestors to be so important that they actually buried them in their homes. In contrast, Israelite religion taught that the dead ritually defiled a home, and so the dead were buried away from homes and holy places. In time, many ancient peoples came to believe that they were descended from a sacred animal or god. To combat this, the Yahwist history of Israel is replete with heroes who have faults, who make mistakes, and who are ultimately subject to Yahveh.

And sometimes the believers of pagan baals (or 'lords') would offer up their shorn hair as a sacrifice to their illustrious ancestors. This would be given a new Yahwist meaning in the Nazirite vow – to merely signal the end of the vow, the hair being a symbol of the Nazirite's holiness to Yahveh. Whereas in pagan terms the hair was an offering to the dead, in Yahwist terms the dead actually *contaminated* the hair – a psychological device employed to wrench Hebrew spirituality away from the reverence of one's dead.

What I am trying to get at here, is basically that Yahwism is not a continuation of superstitious hocus pocus – it was supposed to be the defeat and end of superstition. The Israelite religion maintained these customs (in an albeit altered form) to show to the nations around them that sprites, demons, water-spirits, tree-gods, sacred ancestors or hill-goblins had no power. Mediums, witches, wizards and necromancers ultimately had no power to control or affect the forces of nature. Yahwism deliberately turned the ancient Canaanite customs on their head, in deliberate defiance of pagan superstition.

In a sense, our Yahwist traditions are an eternal witness to this ancient defiance of pagan superstition and magic. The customs of our pre-Yahwist Israelite ancestors have been remoulded by Moses and the prophets to show that Yahveh is supreme, Yahveh is Sovereign over all, that Yahveh is more powerful and more wondrous than any pagan god or spirit could ever be. We continue the traditions and customs of our heritage to remind ourselves that superstition has no power over us, and to demonstrate to the nations that Yahveh is a just, reasoning and rational God who is supreme and Sovereign over all.

Tapping into the Divine Presence

It is often the case in the Miqra that theology and beliefs are rarely explained. This is because it is assumed that the reader is already familiar with the religious reasoning and logic that underpins the whole Hebrew Bible. Unfortunately over the millennia, as numerous events disrupted the national awareness and familiarity with Yahwist theology, the glue that held disparate passages of the Miqra together, and bound them into a vast, wondrous landscape has been dissolved. The colossal and inspiring architecture of Yahwist theology was intended to be one manifestation of the rich splendour of God's personality, and of the awesome wonder of the great reputation of Yahveh. Over the centuries, the map to that theological landscape has frayed and faded, until all we have left are fragmented scraps that modern interpreters struggle to put together and make cohesive sense of.

Fortunately, our God is a living God! Our God is an eternal God, bridging distant generations! Yahveh instructs us and teaches us, restoring knowledge that was lost, and passing it on to new and eager minds. Yahveh's wisdom still guides those who are willing to stop and listen to it. What is lost, Yahveh will return to us. What is broken, Yahveh will mend. And what has collapsed and fallen into ruin, Yahveh will rebuild, renovate and fill with new life.

However, we must be on our guard not to mistake our own thoughts for God's message. I have often been the victim of overly confident evangelicals, who mistake their own oppressive opinions for God's message. You know a message is from Yahveh, because it is something you could not possibly have known yourself. Sometimes God will give you new knowledge. Sometimes God will actually disagree with you, and encourage you to understand God's own point of view from a new perspective that you had not considered before.

Now, there are doorways to heaven, and pathways to the holiness of Yahveh's living Presence. These can be opened in any place where we come together in reverence to commune with God, so that our souls can be restored and refreshed by God's indwelling Presence. Through prayer and meditation, links can be set up between our minds and the heavenly kingdom – a kind of phone-line to the home of God's voice.

Many religious people make the mistake that a place itself can be intrinsically holy – that its stones, soil, buildings and mortar all contain God's essence, and if we are near to those things, then we can touch them and take away some of those good vibes. However, in Yahwist Israelite theology, it is not the physical things we can see and touch that are holy, but rather *God's Presence in that place that makes them holy*. Our reverence of God, our adherence to sacred ethics in daily life, our honourable behaviour and the sanctity of our considerate example can actually open doorways – portals – to Yahveh's heavenly realm. And as long as we work on the health of our spiritual lives in order to keep these doorways open – as long as we nurture our thought, speech and behaviour so that they are worthy of God's reputation – then these portals and communication lines to heaven remain; these 'phone lines' to Yahveh stay open, and God's glory flows through to sanctify and strengthen everything it touches.

However, if we fall into modes of thought, speech or behaviour which harm the reputation of God, then it is we ourselves who close off these vital arteries to the heavenly realm; the stream of life-giving blood flowing through those arteries is cut off, and we shut the door on the divine Presence. The holiness of Yahveh withdraws, and a place is no longer holy. And in a mind that is no longer open to the goodness of Yahveh – the sacred lines of communication are disrupted by our own behaviour.

That link cannot be regained simply by touching once sacred rocks or soil, because the sanctifying *Shekhinah* (the In-dwelling Presence) of Yahveh is no longer there; the holiness was never in the rocks, but in the Presence of God that dwelt there. If we walk away from the reverential witness of God in our daily words and actions, then we ourselves close off the roads to God's knowledge, wisdom and blessing. No special formula of words or prayers will instantly restore that link – not without a change of heart, a return to the mind-set and way of life that enabled us to forge that link in the first place.

The evolution of belief in heaven

Now that you understand something of the proper place of the supernatural in Israelite thinking, I now want to examine Israelite views on the afterlife. The Hebrew for 'heaven' literally means, 'skies'. If you want to understand 'heaven' in its historical context, you have to engage in some 'theological archaeology'. You have to realise that originally, the Israelites did not have any concept of heaven as we understand it today.

The first chapter[a] of the *Book of Genesis* is heavily abused by literalists, who have little or no understanding of the world that wrote it. Putting 'theological archaeology' into practice, we come

---

[a] Christian fundamentalists believe that the first chapter of Genesis tells us how the universe was created. However, for Jews, that is not the message. For us, it says that Yahveh is the sole creator of all that exists; that He created order out of chaos; that behind everything that happens, there is meaning and purpose; that the heavenly bodies should be used to calculate the times, festivals and seasons; that God set human beings as caretakers over His creation; and that God created male and female as equal. It also explains why we have a seven day week, and why the Sabbath exists.

to understand that the early chapters of Genesis are from a time when Israelites had not yet evolved the concept of heaven. The first chapter is therefore not speaking of the creation of heaven but rather of 'the sky'. The sky was believed to be a metal dome ('firmament'), into which the Sun, the Moon and the stars were studded like gemstones.

At this time, no belief in the soul had yet evolved. It was believed that when we died, we went to dwell in a dark underworld called *She'ol*.[a] It was a place of unknowingness. Nothing happened there; at that stage it was believed to be a place of eternal sleep, not punishment. In time, this evolved into what became known as 'the Outer Darkness'.[b]

What this view of the afterlife did, was to concentrate one's efforts on what one did in this life. Salvation (how God rescued us from difficult or impossible situations) was very much what God did for us in *this* life; and the fact that both the good and the wicked returned to the same dust, was a source of consolation to those who saw the wicked prosper and the good remain destitute.

Once the early Hebrews made contact with the Babylonian, Persian and Assyrian religions, with their views in a life after death, it was not enough that a person should exist in a dark shadow-world of unknowingness. It was felt that there had to be something more, so the idea of the resurrection of the body developed – the belief that at a certain time in the future, all the dead would rise from their graves to be judged; the wicked would go back to the grave, but the righteous would dwell forever as immortals in some kind of paradise on earth. However, resurrection still assumes no belief in a soul or in heaven (after all, if being alive meant possession of a soul, then where is one's soul while you are in the ground)?

As I explained in greater detail in my first book, the main difficulty was to figure out what the resurrection actually implied. Questions began to arise: In what state was the resurrected body – whole and healthy, or as it was when it died? If a woman was wife to several men during her lifetime, whose wife would she be upon resurrection? Was resurrection universal, or only of the Jewish people, or only of the righteous. And when did this resurrection happen? Was it to form part of the 'messianic redemption' of Israel, or was it to usher in the final judgment?

Many scholars contend that a belief in heaven arose only after contact with other religions, but the embryonic potential for a more developed theology about heaven was already there – for example, where did people like Elijah, Enoch and the other pious dead go – they were taken up alive, but where were they taken alive *to*? Where did the angels

---

[a] This should not be confused with the Christian concept of Hell.
[b] see chapter 7

that Jacob saw abide?

Once Israelites had developed a theology with regard to the soul being distinct from the body, it was inevitable that a belief in heaven should also evolve. Once a belief in the soul became part of Israelite theology, spurred on by the teaching that ultra-holy people avoided *She'ol* and resurrection altogether, to go and dwell **alive** with God, curiosity naturally evolved on where the pious actually went. There was by that stage a common belief in the pre-existence of the souls of all human beings; therefore there had to be somewhere where the souls existed before life, and after death.

Now think about it: if one believes in the unknowingness of *She'ol* and in the resurrection of the physical body to dwell in an earthly paradise, logically any belief in a soul and heaven becomes redundant. Conversely, belief in a soul and heaven makes resurrection redundant. Good examples in our own time of this division are the Jehovah's Witnesses and Liberal Jews. Jehovah's Witnesses only believe in resurrection and an earthly paradise, and reject any notion of the soul and heaven. Liberal Jews, on the other hand, reject resurrection, and instead believe in the continued existence of the soul after death in heaven.

In Yeshua`'s time, the Pharisees made it an article of their sect's fundamental teachings that they would believe in all three – resurrection, the soul *and* heaven. The fact that Yeshua`, as a practitioner of Common Judaism, held to all three is evidence that the Pharisees were not the only people who tried to reconcile all three. In Yeshua`'s time, different sects believed different things about the afterlife, reflecting the history and evolution of Jewish thought. Modern Talmidaism leaves what one believes about the afterlife up to the individual.[a]

Belief in heaven gave people a sense that there was something more than this life, a purpose greater than what we could see and understand. More than the other two views, it seemed to accord better with what ordinary people experienced in their personal spiritual lives.

A balance between this life and the next

In observing the many different religions and cults of this world, I have noticed how a person's views on the afterlife (or lack

---

[a] My personal belief is that I have left ideas of resurrection behind, as being logically incompatible with ideas of the soul and heaven. I therefore simply believe in the continued existence of the soul after death in heaven.

thereof) have a very direct influence on how one behaves in *this* world, and on how one treats other people. How you understand the way in which the heavenly realm connects to this one – what your place in this world is, how the natural relates to the supernatural, and how God acts in your life – dramatically affects the quality and conduct of your spiritual life.

The mind-set of Israelite culture is focussed on *this* life, on the here and now. Living this life as the only one you will ever have, encourages the individual to make the most out of it.[a] When you focus *too* much on the afterlife, you are in danger of becoming so discontented with your life here on earth, that you cannot wait for it to be over!

The mistake that many seekers of the mystical make, is to think that the emphasis of our spiritual journeys is on the other realm, and on what we can gain for ourselves in the afterlife. It becomes almost an escape from this world. However, that is why Israelite mysticism is different. Heaven is our natural home, and we were all sent here to do a job for God (i.e. Yeshua` was not the only person who was sent to earth). We can gain strength from our meditation on the nature of the other realm, as well as wisdom from the time our souls spend in the spirit in the immediate presence of Yahveh. But ultimately, the emphasis of Israelite mysticism is on our mission here in this world, not the next.

The pre-eminent question we should be asking ourselves in our spiritual quest therefore is not, 'How do I get to heaven?' (even though such a question is important), but rather, 'What am I supposed to do while I am on earth? What manner of life do I have to lead while I am here, so that I play my full part in helping God to fulfil God's Great Plan?' It must also be said, that since one of our rewards in heaven will be access to limitless knowledge, our purpose here on earth is not necessarily to acquire all the knowledge of the Universe, only sufficient knowledge to be able to live rightly and healthily, so that we fulfil the mission God has sent us here to accomplish.

A proper and healthy balance is maintained when you come to realise that you are here for a purpose – that like prophets and holy people, every single human being was sent to earth for a reason. When we have finished doing what we came here to do, God will call us back home.[b]

---

[a] Belief in reincarnation is therefore foreign to the Israelite religion, even though Kabbalists accept it and claim it is Jewish – it's not.

[b] Some modern Talmidis believe that our natural home is actually heaven; earth is merely a temporary, one-off assignment.

The Sadducean and Pharisaic stances on the afterlife

Now, it is vital to understand that the various Jewish groups in Yeshua''s day all had different beliefs where the afterlife was concerned. The Sadducees, for example, did not believe in the soul, in heaven, or in an afterlife. Most important to realise of all, they did not believe in *any* kind of reward or punishment after death. As a result, they concentrated *so much* on this life, without any concern for why God created them, that they lived to material excess. They were aristocratic, they sought out the best things in life, and were the social elite. They ignored the commandments in Torah that were meant to limit the excesses of priests. They believed that if they were wealthy and successful, then no ill-fortune could possibly touch them – no matter how bad their wrongdoing was. They were accused of being morally and spiritually corrupt, of taking advantage of the poor, of amassing illegal wealth for themselves, and of abusing the judicial system. They were often self-centred, and used others for their own ends. For them, their material success was their reward and justification.

The *Book of Ecclesiastes* was written, not by Solomon,[a] but by someone who was the *Qohéleth* or 'Convener' of the Jewish Assembly of elders in Jerusalem. This Convener seems to espouse proto-Sadducean beliefs.[b] The writer therefore does not have any belief in the afterlife, and as a result, cannot see any higher purpose to life other than what he can see before his own eyes. As to his view on the purpose of life (which is a very Sadducean one), he says *'I therefore commend the enjoyment of life, for there is nothing better for a person under the sun than eating, drinking and enjoying oneself.'*[c]

In contrast, the Pharisees believed not only in the soul, but in heaven, resurrection of the physical body, angels, and judgment after death – in fact, they believed in the opposite of everything that the Sadducees did. The Pharisees believed fully in the glory and majesty of God in heaven, but they did not seem to have acted as though that glory and majesty extended *here* – and that was their biggest problem. For the Pharisees, God's will ruled in heaven, but *their* will unquestionably ruled here on earth.

---

[a] The opening verse only says that he is *a* son of David i.e. a descendant of David.

[b] The author of Ecclesiastes may or may not have been a Sadducee, but he writes from a perspective that may have later become Sadduceanism.

[c] Ecc 8:15

Making God's will matter

In order for God's will to rule on earth, you have to live your life as a demonstration that God's will *matters* – that it already affects the conduct of your life on earth. You have to live in a way that shows that Yahveh is a *living* God, who is as powerful on earth as God is in heaven.

How do we do this? Well, by behaving in a way that openly suggests to others that the One, True, Living God is in direct communication with your soul, and guides your daily life. You do this by not simply relying on religious figures, priests, ministers, prophets, Torah or sacred scripture *alone* for your guidance, but on the direct instruction that God gives your soul through your times of prayer and meditation, as well as through the learning experiences of your life.

This, more than anything else, was the major difference between the way the Pharisees lived their lives, and the way the followers of the prophet Yeshua` lived theirs. The Pharisees saw *themselves* as the arbiters, interpreters, dispensers and keepers of God's will on earth. They had elevated themselves[a] to the state where ordinary people had to come to *them* in order to learn and understand God's will. They themselves sought God's will, not from God or even from Torah, but from each other's fallible human opinions. These opinions are now recorded in the Talmud, and are referred to as 'the Oral Law'. In Rabbinic Judaism, the Oral Law has greater authority than the Hebrew Bible; modern Rabbinic Judaism is, in effect, the religion of the Talmud, not the Hebrew Bible.

Modern biblical fundamentalists are guilty of the same disrespect for the holiness of the will of our Living God. Like Pharisees, they do not seek God's will directly; fundamentalists seek God's will *only* from scripture. Nor do they do *that* faithfully, interpreting scripture only according to their personal biases, hatreds and prejudices, or through the blinkered understanding of their particular religious community's beliefs. Instead of seeking the Living God, and the living will of Yahveh, they read a book, and elevate that book above God.

This is bibliolatry[b] – turning the Bible itself into an idol to be

---

[a] They even annulled the commandment to 'honour your father and mother'; according to the Talmud, if your father and your rabbi were drowning and you could only save one person, then you had to abandon your father and save your rabbi.

[b] This is no different to the sin of the Golden Calf. The Israelites did not ask, 'Make a god for us' but rather 'Make God for us'. They were not asking for *another* god to be made, but for a visible representation of Yahveh. They worshipped the Golden Calf *as if it were* Yahveh. Biblical fundamentalists revere the Bible as if it were a physical representation of God – infallible, perfect and incapable of error.

praised, adored, venerated and worshipped over and above God. It's a bit like having a garden, and a book about gardening; it's like paying more attention to the book, while ignoring what's growing in the garden. Similarly, what the Pharisees did was Talmudolatry – setting their own opinions above those of God.

Torah is not just commandments, but principles and values too. You cannot say that just because a good thing or positive principle is not directly commanded in Torah, then it is not to be done *at all*; or because a bad thing or negative value is not forbidden in Torah, then it is allowed. One cannot say, "There is a good thing that common sense says I should do in this circumstance, but I will not do it because Torah does not tell me to", or, "There is something I want to do that common sense says is a *really* bad thing, and because Torah does not forbid it, that means I can go ahead and do it".

For example, in the case of returning lost animals to their owners: Dt 22:2 tells us to take in a lost animal if you don't know who it belongs to, and look after it until the owner turns up. Now, Torah does not forbid us to conceal the animal, nor does it command us to actively look for the owner, but concealing the animal and not looking for the owner would be against the *values* of Torah. Also, it is not overtly commanded that 'a parent shall not instruct their child to do evil', but the values and principles of Torah say that such a thing is wrong. So when a child is commanded that they should honour and obey their parents, there is no written proviso saying '*except* when you are told by your parents to do evil', *but the whole ethos of Torah tells us that this is inherently wrong*. Torah is not only commandments, but the principles and values that Yahveh has placed in our hearts, and written on our conscience.

Similarly, Torah tells us not to make fun of or put obstacles before the blind or the deaf,[a] but it is silent on putting obstacles in the way of other disabled people, or making fun of them. It is obvious to anyone who listens to the divine laws that God has written on our hearts, that such a thing would be wrong,[b] but a right-wing fundamentalist would say that, because no such commandment is written, we therefore have no such obligations to have a concern for the needs of other disabled people.

Yeshua` spoke against such literalists. In his parable of the

---

[a] Lev 19:14

[b] These are all good examples of where the unwritten laws of *Tsedeq* come into play.

man who buried his one talent of gold in the ground, he was challenging people who only follow the words of the bible, *and nothing more.* He was challenging those who know the good they should do, but because they are not commanded by scripture to do that good thing, they do not do it. And he was challenging those who know that an evil is wrong, but because that evil is not forbidden in scripture, they see no reason not to refrain from that wrongdoing.

When you reject Yahveh's values, you reject Yahveh. Simply doing and following commands is not enough – you have to seek the wisdom of God's values. Before the northern kingdom was exiled, the tribes of Ephraim rejected Yahveh's social and spiritual values.[a] By turning to the *values* of other gods, they effectively turned to follow those other gods. In rejecting God's ethics and values, we reject Yahveh. Can you see how the Israelite religion is concerned with very real things in the real world?

For example, if a right-wing government is content to let a large section of its people fall by the wayside, denying it no means by which to better itself, taxing it and working it to the point where it cannot complain or stand up for itself, then such a government has rejected God – even if it claims to be built upon 'the Word of the Bible'. In turning to other values and other principles – by practising values that are not God's – such a government turns to other gods. When we ignore God's values and principles, we are in fact ignoring God.

Faith in the active, living Presence of God

The followers of the prophet Yeshua` lived their lives with the knowledge that their heavenly Father was alive and present in this world, dwelling among us and interacting directly with humanity. They respected scripture, referred to it and used it as their legal and spiritual authority. *However*, they also took to heart God's unwritten values and principles. They lived their lives in a way that demonstrated their faith in a living, sovereign Yahveh, whose Will guided their lives each and every day. Knowing therefore the personality of God, one could ask, 'What would God wish me to do in such and such a situation?' 'How would God want me to behave and speak in a way that sanctifies God's good Name?'[b]

Thinking this way shows that one has faith in the active Presence of God in this world, and in the ability of God to directly intervene in

---

[a] see Amos 5:7-11

[b] Remember, sanctifying the Name means doing good things which will enhance the good reputation of Yahveh, and so raise His standing in the eyes of humanity.

human history. Seeking God's will in heaven, means putting our own will on earth in second place. It means acknowledging that it is God, and not we humans, who has supreme sovereignty over the ultimate plan. It means living in a way that shows how God daily guides us, teaches, advises, consoles, comforts and supports us every hour of every day.

Ancient 'Common Judaism' and fringe movements

Now, the Sadducees and the Pharisees were by no means the only religious groups around. If someone had no belief in the soul, resurrection or heaven, that did not automatically mean that they were Sadducees; similarly if someone *did* believe in these things, that did not automatically mean that they were Pharisees. Indeed, the majority of Jewish people during the Second Temple Period did not formally belong to *any* official religious party. Faith and opinion was not so rigidly fixed along denominational lines as it is today. There was a great deal of individual freedom to listen to others, and come to one's own personal conclusion about many matters. Some writers[a] have called this type of Judaism 'Common Judaism'.[b] It would not have been a type listed by Josephus in his list of the four philosophies of Judaism, simply because it was not an officially organised grouping. It is this form of non-sectarian Judaism that Karaite Judaism is descended from.[c] I would also venture to suggest that it is this form of non-denominational, popular Judaism that the prophet Yeshua' grew up with.[d] In my

---

[a] such as E P Sanders (*Judaism: Practice and Belief 63BCE-66CE*), and Wayne McCready & Adele Reinhartz (*Common Judaism: Explorations in Second Temple Judaism*).

[b] Writers such as EP Sanders, Wayne McCready and Adele Reinhartz restrict this term to only mean 'that which is common to all sects of Judaism'. In my book, I use it to refer to the 'non-denominational and non-sectarian Judaism of ordinary people during the Second Temple period, which is not governed solely by the doctrines of one particular sect'.

[c] Most Karaites are not aware of the historical concept of Common Judaism, and so some look for their origins in the Sadducees. However, on examining the diverse nature of Common Judaism, which relied on the individual listening to various opinions and making up his or her own mind, it makes more sense to seek Karaite origins in non-sectarian Common Judaism, rather than with the Sadducees.

[d] Yeshua''s personal emphases seem to be an eclectic mixture of John the Baptist's teaching, Essene ideals, Pharisaic ethics and fringe beliefs. This would suggest that he followed the custom of Common Judaism, grounded as it was in the custom of taking what was meaningful from each and every sect around you, to form one's own personal belief.

humble opinion, ancient Talmidaism was therefore that form of 'Common Judaism' that accepted Yeshua` as a prophet; Karaism and Talmidaism are remarkably similar in practice and outlook.

There were also many smaller fringe groups that held various mystical beliefs. One such belief was the 'Son of Man', which I shall go into more detail later in this chapter.

The various forms of Jewish mysticism

At this point, I think it is important to state that mysticism is not for everyone. I have no idea what type of personality or even genetic make-up is required, but if you find mystical meditation difficult or impossible, don't worry about it. I'm sure God has a reason why some people are adept at it, and why some people just aren't interested. If you *are* interested in Jewish mysticism, then I hope that what follows will help in your understanding of the mystical, and in your practice of meditation and prayer. If you are not, then I pray that what I have written will increase your knowledge of the Israelite perception of the universe.

In the mainstream Jewish tradition, the studying of mystical knowledge is generally discouraged, because of the danger of it being misinterpreted, and the peril of spiritual devotions being misplaced and manipulated by unscrupulous individuals. I would agree to an extent with this trepidation, but hiding knowledge itself causes problems too.

The danger of withholding mystical knowledge is that human beings, being the curious and inquisitive creatures that we are, are not dissuaded simply by being told we cannot look into something. We will start speculating, and speculation only ends up getting our ideas disastrously wrong, veering off into directions they were not meant to travel down.

The prophet Yeshua` said, *'Nothing's so covered up that it won't be revealed, or so hidden that it won't be made known.'*[a] I think his personal conviction was that religious teachers and instructors are not meant to keep things secret or hidden forever. However, there is an implicit proviso in this. In the *Book of Writings*[b] there is a maxim which says, *'The truth is not hidden to be kept secret; it is hidden in order to be revealed.'*[c] This implies that if we are given the answers to problems straight away, we will not learn, or grow or profit by them. If you are

---

[a] S.Yesh. 66:1 – cf Mt 10:26, Lk 12:02; also Gospel of Thomas 5:2, 6:5-6

[b] the 12th and final book of *The Exhortations* (the Talmidi equivalent of the New Testament). It is a collection of modern Talmidi wisdom sayings, parables and thoughts. It is intended for inspirational use only, and does not have any authoritative status.

[c] S. Kit 5:44

taught an academic subject, and you always look at the answers at the back of the book, you will learn nothing because the answers mean nothing to you. The lessons that inform us most in life are those that require time and effort to absorb them properly; what we learn along the way is just as important as the ultimate answers themselves.

Therefore, what I am presenting to you here is sufficient knowledge to understand the basic concepts of Israelite mysticism, but the rest of the journey is up to you. I will show you the pitfalls to avoid, and how to recognise the more fruitful paths.

Most people today have heard of Kabbalah, but in ancient times there was also *Merkabah*[a] and *Kavodh*[b] mysticism. Although there have been many attempts to reform Kabbalah, at its heart Kabbalah is an early medieval[c] attempt to understand the ethereal, heavenly realm using the structural images of pagan spirituality. By imposing a logical, rational, Greco-Roman overlay onto what lies beyond the earthly realm, Kabbalah seeks to understand spiritual forces ultimately in order to control them.[d] Kabbalist cosmology also leads to dualism – that there is an evil and equal counterpart to God, a concept totally alien to Israelite Yahwism.

Merkabah mysticism is based upon the study of the first chapter of the *Book of Ezekiel*. It is far older than Kabbalah, dating from around the 1st century CE or even earlier. At its core, the practitioner of *Merkabah* mysticism studies and meditates on the *merkavah* or 'war-chariot' of God; also on the symbolic meanings of the four *chayyot* or 'living creatures' carrying God's chariot, on the nature of the angels surrounding the chariot, and so on.

Ultimately however, both Kabbalah and *Merkabah* mysticism seek to study God by studying God's surroundings – heaven, the throne of God, the angels and so on; they assume that it is not possible to meditate on God directly. Few people are aware that underlying the prophetic experiences of holy men and women –

---

[a] literally, 'chariot'. This form of mysticism is centred on meditating on the chariot of God mentioned in the 1st chapter of the Book of Ezekiel, and on the nature of the four living creatures supporting that chariot.

[b] literally, 'glory' or 'Divine Radiance'. This form of mysticism is centred on examining the nature and power of God's glory mentioned throughout Exodus and Leviticus.

[c] Although Kabbalists claim an ancient Jewish origin for their beliefs, inventing various myths and legends to 'prove' an ancient origin, there is no evidence of Kabbalism before the 11th century CE.

[d] For example, Kabbalah teaches the power of words, in and of themselves, to effect our fate; also in charms, incantations and numerology. These are common practices of pagan mysticism, but are alien to Yahwist spirituality.

including Moses – there is an understanding of the true nature of a living, sentient Being – Yahveh, and that Yahveh is knowable. This form of mysticism does not have a name in the Miqra, but it has an obvious label – *Kavodh* mysticism. As I mentioned in my first book of this series, *kavodh* means 'glory' – the fire of God's 'Divine Radiance' – and the powerful effect of that radiant Presence on earth. *Kavodh* mysticism is based on the direct, human experience of the power and presence of God. The doorway to *Kavodh* mysticism is the passage[a] where Moses asks to see the glory of God, and then God tells him, 'No one can see my face and live'.

As I explained in my first book, the effect of God's presence is purifying, cleansing and justice-seeking; it wipes clean human souls, blots out our transgressions, restores and renews our inner being. Before the fire of the glory of Yahveh, evil, sin and wickedness cannot endure. And a holy people, who seek to imitate God in God's ways, immerse themselves in God's sacred *kavodh*, in order to become a people before whom evil and injustice cannot endure.

Line 5: Just as it is in heaven,

... heaven

When we read the vision of God in Ezekiel chapter 1, we are given an insight into the majesty and glory of Yahveh. There and in the Ebionite portions of the *Book of Revelation*,[b] the tranquillity, blessedness and awesome spectacle of heaven is subsequently contrasted with the chaos, suffering and cruelty prevalent on earth.

In both the first chapter of the *Book of Ezekiel*, and in the fourth chapter of *Revelation*, we are given a glimpse into the 'throne room' of God. God's Presence is represented by a being of light, who is the centre of worship and praise. In the immediate presence of God are the *serafim*. In Hebrew tradition, they are like fiery winged serpents, the colour of burnished copper. Also present are the seven archangels who, by tradition, are the only angels allowed into the immediate presence of God, and are therefore privy to God's will.

---

[a] Ex 33:18-23

[b] The Christian Book of Revelation seems to a composite of Ebionite Jewish and Paullist Christian prophecies. The Ebionite portions are probably chapters 4, 7-14, 17-19, and 21-22. The purpose of the Ebionite prophecies were to warn the ancient Jerusalem community that the destruction of the city was imminent, and that they were to flee the city; that many Jews would suffer and die, but the righteous would go straight to God, and that Rome would one day be punished for its crimes.

The nature of angels in the Israelite tradition

In the book of Psalms[a] it says, *'Bless Yahveh, God's angels –
mighty warriors who do God's bidding, who obey God's
commanding voice. Bless Yahveh, all God's heavenly battalions,
God's ministering servants who do God's will.'*

According to Yahwist Israelite belief, angels cannot act apart
from or independent of God; they therefore cannot disobey God or
rebel from God.[b] The sole reason for the existence of angels is to
do God's will. Apart from the angels, there also exist 'the holy
ones',[c] a type of heavenly being when sent to earth becomes human
(see the later section in this chapter on the 'Son of Man'). In
Yahwist thought, no angel can 'fall from grace' or disobey God.[d]
Humans and angels are not the same – they exist as separate beings
in heaven, and we do not become angels when we die. Humans
have free will; angels do not. Humans can only come to earth once,[e]
whereas angels can go back and forth between heaven and earth
many, many times.[f]

Free will is not the same as freedom of choice. Free will is
specifically the freedom to either obey or disobey God's will or
instruction. Lack of free will does not mean lack of choice, because
there are other choices apart from moral ones. On earth, you can
choose to eat or not, whether to drink or not, whether to wear a
black suit or a grey one, whether to go to the shops, or to a film,
whether to go by car or walk, and so on. A being who lacked free
will would not be an automaton, simply a being who was incapable
of doing anything against God. So for example, the angels who

---

[a] Ps 103:20-21

[b] The apocryphal *Book of Enoch* contains references to fallen angels; just
because the book contains many spiritual truths, does not automatically mean
that everything in it is true. A belief in fallen angels was gaining ascendency
at the time the book was written, and such a belief must be seen in that
context.

[c] See Dt 33:2 – it says that when Yahveh appeared on Mt Sinai, Yahveh
appeared from amidst 'myriads of holy ones' – these are the souls of human
beings before we come to earth.

[d] The original concept of Satan in Hebrew thought was as a kind of 'counsel
for the prosecution', who merely laid bare a person's sins before God.
However, when Judaism came into contact with the Persian religion of
Zoroastrianism (which believes in a good and a bad god), it took on the idea
of an angel that disobeyed God and fell from grace. However, such a concept
is foreign to the true ideals of Yahwism.

[e] implied by Prov 30:4

[f] in Jacob's vision, the angels go back and forth between heaven and earth,
up and down the stairway (Gen 28:12)

visited Lot initially decided to sleep in the square, but after persuasion from Lot, they decided to sleep at his house. This was nothing to do with God; the choice was neither for or against God. It was purely a matter of free choice, so they chose to stay at Lot's house.

If God tells an angel to do or not to do something, then they are compelled to obey. However, if God were to give them a choice, then they have the freedom to choose.

A good example of how angels are messengers for God, and speak on God's behalf, is the episode of when the three angels visit Abraham.[a] For most mainstream Christian theologians, it is often claimed that the three messengers are in fact the three persons or incarnations of the Christian trinity. However, if you read the passage in Hebrew, the Person of Yahveh and the persons of the three messengers are most distinct and separate.

For example, verse 22 clearly states that, "the men went on from there to Sodom, but Abraham remained standing in the presence of Yahveh". When God speaks in the presence of the three messengers, God's voice is not one of the messengers' voices, but an independent fourth voice. They start the conversation, but God almost finishes their sentences for them.

We should always remember that in the Yahwist Israelite tradition, angels have no will of their own. They are the mouthpieces of God, the instruments God uses in order to speak audibly to human beings. What they say comes direct from God, so when you speak to an angel, you are speaking to God, albeit second-hand. And when an angel speaks to you, what they say are God's direct words, verbatim.

Prohibition on speaking to the dead

God's law and Israelite tradition prohibits consulting the dead. In all matters, Yahwism lays emphasis on consulting Yahveh, and Yahveh alone. When we need to be reassured about anything, we are to rely only on Yahveh for that reassurance.

Yahveh is the great Comforter and Healer, who comes and sits with those who mourn. Yahveh understands the loss we feel for a loved one. The pain that gnaws away inside our chests when we lose someone is unbearable, and sometimes it seems like it will never go away. Often we are inconsolable. It hurts so much that we desperately want to be able to see or simply hear our loved ones again.

Some of us turn to mediums and spiritualists for comfort. It may even be possible for a small minority of people to actually be able to

---

[a] Gen 18:1-33

speak to the dead – it may be a real phenomenon.

On the eve of the battle of Gilboa, King Saul wanted assurance that he would triumph against the Philistines. Instead of consulting God, he went to a medium and consulted his dead friend, the prophet Samuel.[a] Now, the Israelite religion absolutely forbids consulting the dead.[b] This is because it causes us to turn our reliance away from Yahveh, whose knowledge and wisdom is sure, reliable and true, to reliance on the spirits of the departed.[c]

If we wish reassurance about the future, or that the afterlife will be all right and that we will go to a better place, what better 'person' to reassure us than our Heavenly Father, who will not lie or deceive us! Who better to let us know that we have lived with purpose, that what we did mattered, and that we will find our ultimate and blessed rest in Yahveh!

Do not worry. You do not need assurance from your loved ones who have passed on that everything will be all right in the afterlife, *because Yahveh gives you that assurance Himself.*

Line 6: so also upon the earth

The tseva'ot: God's Battalions in heaven and on earth

When you read the Miqra, you sometimes come across this seemingly innocuous word in English, 'Hosts', as in 'Lord of Hosts' (the NIV unhelpfully translates the latter phrase as 'Lord Almighty'). It usually refers to the heavenly beings or angels. The Hebrew word behind this is *ts^{e}va'ot*, and in Hebrew, this word literally means 'armies' or 'battalions'.

Now in Ex 12:51 it says, *"And it came to pass on that very same day, Yahveh brought the Israelites out of the land of Egypt by their battalions."* The word that is used to describe the *ts^{e}va'ot* – the battalions – of heaven, is the same one that is used to describe the departing Israelites. This means there are both heavenly and earthly battalions of God.

---

[a] 1Sam 28:1-25. King Saul was punished for consulting the dead, by being defeated and killed in the battle.

[b] Lev 19:31, 20:6, Dt 18:10-11. Consulting the dead is considered idolatrous in the Israelite religion.

[c] It may be that there are some things about the afterlife that we are not meant to know while we are here in this life. It is possible that knowledge of the afterlife will cause a chain of events in our lives that is not meant to happen. Only God has the wisdom to give us the right information and knowledge at the right time.

Now, the vast majority of these Israelites were not military – they did not all leave Egypt kitted up in their army gear with swords and shields and bows and arrows. Yahveh's 'battalions' are here for another purpose, and I hope to show you that we – every human being alive and who has ever lived – are all part of those battalions.

If Yahveh's battalions do not fight military campaigns and battles, then what do they do? Ps 148:2 says, *"Praise him, all his angels, praise him, all his heavenly battalions."* And Isaiah 6:3 says, *"And [the serafim] were calling to one another: 'Holier than the holiest holiness[a] is Yahveh of the Heavenly Battalions; the whole earth is full of God's glory."* It seems that the job of Yahveh's battalions in heaven is to praise God.

But what of God's earthly battalions – us, humanity? Ps 103:21 says, *"Praise Yahveh, all his heavenly battalions; you his ministers who do his will."* God's battalions in heaven do God's will; it is often said that we on earth are here to do God's will too; God sent us here to do God's work. Therefore we, God's battalions on earth, do the same as God's battalions in heaven – carry out God's will.

This mystical concept is related to the enigmatic 'Son of Man' figure, which I shall go into shortly – not the Christian one, but the Israelite one.

I was once given a pearl of wisdom by my great grandmother, that the reason why we are not made perfect, is so that we would need each other. Now, you have probably heard it said that our inherent weaknesses and disabilities are given to test us; I disagree. I would say that our human imperfections are there to test the compassion of *other* people. Some might then say that it is not very nice of God to use us this way.

Imagine a race of beings who, like us, are morally imperfect, but who are physically perfect in health and stature. They cannot die, they cannot become ill, experience accidents, suffer pain, or feel sadness or grief; furthermore, they cannot fall into disadvantage or suffer any kind of misfortune. Such a race would eventually grow tired of one another. They would lose all sense of caring about one another, and since they cannot hurt or feel pain, they would live out their lives seeking to engage in mischief or humiliation of one another – much like the race of Q in Gene Roddenberry's Star Trek.

For some, the task of doing God's will may seem too great, but part of this way of life, of living on earth in the Kingdom of God now, is to help and support one another in the here and now. The reason we are not made perfect, is so that we would need one another and help one another.

---

[a] lit 'holy holy holy'. The scholar David Stern believes this is a supreme superlative, and I personally agree with his interpretation.

God set up this thing called conscience within us, so that our God-given conscience would feel drawn to reach out and help, because yes, we go through pain and unhappiness, but God never intended us to have to bear any of it alone. The individual members of Yahveh's battalions on earth are meant to have each other's backs – to watch out for one another.

As men and women who serve in Yahveh's battalions, we come here, we do a job for Yahveh, and then we return to our heavenly home – to Yahveh, hopefully with mission accomplished – *im yirtseh elohim* ('God willing').

The mystical 'son of man'

In mainstream Christianity, the term 'son of man' has messianic connotations. It has in fact become a title of the Paullist Christian 'Jesus'. Now, I have read a lot over the years about what the Hebrew / Aramaic idiom 'son of man' means. Much of the confusion over its meaning has arisen because of the heavenly 'Son of Man' figure that appears in Daniel 7:13. For this reason I shall deal with that example last. First, I'd like to go through the commoner meanings of the idiom.

As I have said before, you first have to understand that ancient languages, including biblical Hebrew and ancient Jewish Aramaic, had a very limited vocabulary. Individual words had to be stretched to cover a wide range of different uses and meanings; many were overworked in a way that we would not tolerate today. We all speak modern languages with many, many thousands of words, so enabling us to convey the exact shade of meaning intended. Ancient languages did not have this luxury; the Semitic idiom 'son of man' was a prime example of such an overworked term.[a]

The most common use of the term was to mean, 'human being'. In both ancient and modern Hebrew, the idiom 'son of man' (*'ben adam'* or *'ben enosh'*) is the **normal**, everyday way of saying 'human being'. It is as simple as that – there is no mystery about it, no hidden messianic connotations, just that: 'human being'. It is the basic root meaning of the term, and the first thing that a Hebrew

---

[a] I must stress at this point that although ancient Hebrew words often had many, many meanings, they don't have every single meaning all at once! The meaning that comes to mind is the one that is demanded by context; any further meanings would have to be deliberately and consciously brought to mind. For example, in English, you would not immediately associate the word 'heavily' with the word 'cat', until someone uses the phrase 'it's raining cats and dogs'.

speaker thinks of when they hear the phrase, 'son of man'. When we are considering other meanings, this is what we should always hark back to. In biblical Hebrew, there are several examples from the Miqra:

> *'God is not a man, that God should be fickle, nor a son of man* (= human being), *that God should change His mind; for doesn't God speak, and then not act? Or promise, and then not fulfil?'* [a]

> *'Even the stars are not pure in God's sight; how much less so man, who is a worm? And son of man (*= human beings*), who is a maggot?'* [b]

> *What is man, that you are mindful of him? Son of Man* (= human beings), *that you care for him* (= them)*?* [c]

As these examples show, the basic meaning of 'son of man' is 'human being'.

Yeshua`'s use of the term, 'son of man'

In Jewish Aramaic, the term *bar nasha* is identical in meaning to the Hebrew *ben adam*. In Matt 12:8 it says,

> *'For the son of man is lord of the Sabbath'*,

or more properly, using our knowledge of Jewish Aramaic,

> *'For human beings are masters of the Sabbath'* (here, note the singular 'son of man' stands for the plural 'human beings'; this will become relevant as we go on.

And similarly in Matt 12:32,

> *'Anyone who speaks a word against the Son of Man will be forgiven, but anyone who speaks against the Holy Spirit will not be forgiven, either in this age or in the age to come.'* (NIV)

---

[a] Num 23:19
[b] Job 25:5-6
[c] Ps 8:4, similarly Ps 144:3. A better, free translation would give: 'What are men, that you are mindful of them, or human beings, that you care for them?' It is not unusual for a singular noun in Hebrew to be better rendered by a plural one in English.

which, given our knowledge of Israelite theology, we can read as:

> *'Anyone who speaks evil against **human beings** will be forgiven, but anyone who speaks evil against **the holiness of God** will never be forgiven – either in this world, or in the world to come.'*[a]

There is yet another meaning that can be ascribed to the idiom, 'son of man'. In Daniel 8:17, and throughout the Book of Ezekiel, God and the archangels address these two prophets as 'son of man', emphasising their mortality, in contrast to the eternity and superiority of those who are addressing them. In these instances, 'son of man' can be translated as 'mortal man', as if it were a humbling term used by a greater being when addressing a lesser one:

> *'He* (the angel Gabriel) *came near to where I was standing, and as he came, I was terrified, and fell prostrate. It said to me, "Understand, O son of man* (= O mortal man)*, that the vision refers to the time of the end".*[b]

Similarly in Ezekiel:

> *'And* [God] *said to me, "Stand up on your feet, O son of man* (= O mortal man)*, and I will speak to you.'* [c]

The Aramaic *bar nasha* has a couple of additional uses that are absent from Hebrew. In Jewish Aramaic, it can also mean, 'person', 'fellow', or 'guy'. For example, it can be used to refer obliquely to another person (that is, an unnamed, indeterminate person). In modern slang, I guess we would use the word, 'guy'. For example, in the phrases, 'There was this guy', or, 'See that guy over there?' in both instances, 'guy' (or in older English, 'fellow') would be translated as *bar nasha* = son of man.

A second use unique to Aramaic would be as an oblique or

---

[a] This is not a new belief of Yeshua`, but an existing Yahwist principal – see Isaiah 22:14, and 1Sam 2:25. Things such as violence in God's Name, cursing using God's Name, or deceiving in God's Name, are covered by this.
[b] Dan 8:17
[c] Ezek 2:1

humble way of referring to oneself[a] – as a replacement for the pronoun 'I'. Yeshua` makes fine usage of this other meaning in Aramaic, which is a humble avoidance of the personal pronoun. When you are explaining claims about what you will do, in order not to sound grandiose or boastful, you substitute 'I' with 'son of man'.

For example, in Matt 17:12

> *'But I tell you, Elijah has already come, and they did not recognise him, but have done to him everything they wished. In the same way, the son of man is* (= I am) *going to suffer at their hands'.* (NIV)

And in Lk 6:22

> *'Blessed are you when men hate you, when they exclude you and insult you and slander your reputation, because of the son of man'* (= because of me).

This particular use of the Jewish Aramaic *bar nasha* is essentially a humble avoidance of the first person pronoun 'I'.

The use of 'the son of man' in the Book of Daniel

Now we come to the most important use of all. I would like to deal with the mystical 'son of man' spoken of by Daniel in Dan 7:13-14. Let's read that first:

> *'As I looked on, in the night vision, one like a son of man* (= one like a human being) *came with the clouds of heaven; he reached the Ancient of Days (= God), to whom he was presented. Dominion, glory, and kingship were given to him; all peoples and nations of every language shall serve him. His dominion is an everlasting dominion that shall not pass away; and his reign will never be destroyed.'*

Later writers, such as the author of the *Parables of Enoch*, interpreted this 'son of man' as a messianic figure, and that interpretation subsequently passed on to other writers in the late Second Temple period. However, this is not the meaning intended by the author of Daniel. We have to remember that this is a vision, and as such, what is

---

[a] see Matthew Black, *'An Aramaic Approach to the Gospels and Acts'*, Appendix E, page 310 (written by Geza Vermes).

in it *represents* something else. Often the meaning – what something represents – is given later on. So if we actually do read on, in Dan 7:18 it actually gives us the meaning; it says that the son of man represents 'the holy ones' (note here the plural) who will possess the kingdom forever after a time of great trial.[a] Verses 7:22, and 7:27 say the same:

> *'Then the Holy Ones* (notice the plural) *of the Most High will receive the kingdom, and will possess the kingdom forever and ever'.* [b]

> *'... for the time had come, and the Holy Ones* (again, notice the plural) *took possession of the kingdom'.* [c]

> *'Authority,*[d] *dominion and grandeur belonging to all the realms under heaven will be given to the people*[e] *of the Holy Ones* (plural again) *of the Most High. Their reign*[f] *will be an everlasting reign, and all realms shall serve and obey them.'* [g]

There are certain people who insist that 'Jesus Christ' is this particular 'Son of Man' – that it is singular, and therefore only refers to one person. However, after reading the passages in Daniel that explain who or what this 'son of man' – this human – actually is, this interpretation cannot possibly be correct, because Daniel *himself* says that the 'son of man' (= the one in heaven like a human being) represents a group of people: *qadisháyya* – 'the Holy Ones'.

Now, such people still insist that 'son of man' cannot possibly stand for a plural; "It is quite plainly a singular noun!" they proclaim. But in Semitic languages, a singular noun can quite often stand for a plural entity, and vice versa. For example, when listing the animals and people that belong to him,[h] the patriarch Jacob

---

[a] the prophecies were written during the time of the Syrian persecutions of the Jewish faith and the Maccabean revolt; the trials and redemptions should be seen against this backdrop.

[b] Dan 7:18

[c] Dan 7:22

[d] that is, royal authority; lit: kingdom

[e] That is, the earthly counterparts or mortal incarnations of the heavenly holy ones.

[f] lit: kingdom. The word in Aramaic can mean reign, kingship, royal authority etc

[g] Dan 7:27

[h] Gen 32:5

says, *"I have an ox, and a donkey, a sheep, a manservant and a maidservant"* – this is what it literally says in Hebrew; all the nouns are quite plainly in the singular. But Jacob was not complaining about a paucity of possessions – quite the opposite in fact. What he meant was, *"I have* [a great number of] *oxen, donkeys, sheep, menservants and maidservants.*" Similarly in Job 25:5-6, Ps 8:4, and also in Ps 144:3, both 'man' and 'son of man' are in the singular, but they are obviously referring to collective plurals i.e. singular *man* = plural *people*,[a] and son of man = human beings.

In summary therefore, the mystical 'Son of Man' figure represents a particular group of people – the 'Holy Ones'. So who or what are these 'Holy Ones'? Let's find out!

The Holy Ones

The Book of Deuteronomy tells us that during the theophany on Mount Horeb, Yahveh appeared from amidst 'myriads of holy ones'.[b] At that moment in time, the glory of God was breaking through from heaven to earth, and so logically, these 'holy ones' are some kind of entities or beings in heaven. When this verse was written, it was assumed that the reader already knew who these 'holy ones' were, and so we are never told *anywhere* in the Miqra who these 'holy ones' are.

Consequently, for the answer as to who these 'Holy Ones' are, we have to look outside of the Hebrew Bible, to the writings of ancient Jewish mysticism. The non-canonical *Book of Enoch* also mentions a 'son of man' figure. Enoch seems to suggest that angels can take on human form (like the angels who visited Abraham), and that humans could in turn become angels – or more correctly, 'heavenly beings' (which is what the Hebrew word *elohim* means when it is not referring to God).

My personal opinion is this: We humans exist as heavenly beings before we come to earth. These heavenly beings – our 'pre-earth' selves – are being referred to as 'holy ones', when distinguishing them from the angels.[c] In heaven, these 'holy ones' perfectly do God's will. On earth, if we grow, learn and develop into people who naturally behave in the

---

[a] We even do this in English. We use the singular 'man' sometimes to refer to our species as a collective plural e.g. 'Man has overrun the planet and dominated it.' In this sentence the word 'man' does not refer to one single person, but our species as a collective whole.
[b] Dt 33:2-3.
[c] When referring to all the inhabitants of heaven, the word *elohim* can be used. In this instance, *elohim* does not mean 'God' or 'gods' but rather 'heavenly beings'.

same way as our souls did in heaven, then we too become 'holy ones' on earth, because we are then behaving as we did when we were in heaven. This way, God's will is carried out and obeyed by us on earth, just as it was when we were in heaven. Perhaps this petition – this line of the *Our Father* – is asking God to help us become people who will perfectly carry out God's will on earth, to the same degree as our souls did as 'holy ones' when we were in heaven.

In the New Testament, members of the community of Yeshua''s followers are called 'saints'. This would be a Greek rendering of the Aramaic *qadisháyya* – holy ones. I am theorising that this might have been like a nickname for the community of Followers, referring back to the nature of their heavenly selves. By calling them 'saints' or more correctly, 'holy ones', I think the community is being complimented and encouraged in its behaviour, implying that their souls have become closer in nature to how they would have acted when they were in heaven.

The 'son of man' in Daniel therefore represents 'heavenly humanity'. In relation to their earthly counterparts, we can further construe the figure as being representative of 'perfected humanity'.

Now, the particular Holy Ones mentioned in Daniel's prophecy undergo a time of great trial and persecution. But at the end of that tribulation, they would be perfected and vindicated by God. The *Book of Daniel* was written at the time of the Syrian persecutions of the Jewish faith in the 2nd century BCE, before the Maccabean revolt. In my humble opinion, it is even possible that they also double up as prophecies of the tribulations in 70 CE and again in 135 CE. The immediate relevance of the prophecies of Daniel, was to give comfort and consolation to the Jewish people who faced death at that time. It reassured them that the kingdom of the fourth beast (Antiochus Epiphanes, and maybe also later Rome) will be judged by God[a] and brought to an end. Those who suffered or lost their lives would be perfected by God and held in high honour. In Daniel therefore, the specific holy ones being persecuted are the Jewish people facing trials under Antiochus Epiphanes.

However, there are also wider theological implications of these Holy Ones, relevant for people of all eras. Those who live in such a way that they become whole, complete, perfected beings who live on earth according to God's ways, who endure through their trials and rise above them, will one day be given respect and dominion throughout the earth. In time, these people will be looked

---

[a] In the vision, Dan 7:11, and in its interpretation, Dan 7:26

up to as the standard of how to be truly human. This perfected humanity will be given authority, dominion and sovereign power, and every nation will respect such people and aspire to be like them. When these people die, they will go straight to God, and sit 'at God's right hand' i.e. they will dwell throughout eternity in the immediate presence of God.

In short, it isn't just Yeshua` who will gain this kingship (= dominion) and authority, but *all* human beings who aspire to be perfected in God's ways, by doing God's will on earth. When we come to realise that this 'son of man' represents the eternal 'heavenly human' that resides within *each and every one of us* – when we understand what we truly are – then one day, humanity will collectively come closer to God's Presence, even while we are here on earth; we will realise the power and magnificence of what God has in store for us. As a result of this realisation, this heavenly part of us will 'rule' the earth – forever. The Kingdom of God will have been fulfilled, and perfected heavenly humanity will collectively 'come on the clouds of heaven', and have eternal dominion over the earth.

Daniel's 'Son of Man' is not a messianic title, even though that is how some ancients understood it; its primary meaning is 'human being'. Extrapolated from that, it is the mystical 'perfected heavenly humanity' of Jewish mystics, whose potential resides within all of us. One day we will all release this power in order to bring God's Holy and Eternal Kingdom to its fulfilment.

To summarise: in heaven, our souls are known as 'holy ones'. These holy ones, together with the angels, form Yahveh's *tseva'ot* or 'battalions' in heaven. These battalions do God's will in heaven, and praise God there. Some holy ones are sent to earth, and here they become human – us. On earth, we are meant to do the same job as we did in heaven – carry out God's will. In time, certain individuals will perfect themselves to the extent that they become respected and emulated by others. One day in the future, all humanity will be perfected by following God's ways, and God's heaven will reign on earth.

Yeshua`'s possible personal beliefs about the Son of Man

I personally feel that *this* is the son of man that Yeshua` hoped for – perfected humanity which would arise at the end of time, just as God's kingdom was approaching its fulfilment. However, I suspect that Yeshua` *assumed* that this kind of end-time was coming very soon, even though he himself admitted he didn't know when the end would be.[a] He

---

[a] S.Yesh. 163:4 'But concerning that day or hour, no one knows, not the angels in heaven, **nor this son of man**; only our Father in heaven.' – cf Mk

did not seem to think there was a distinction between 'the end of the Age' in the prophetic messages given to *him* by God, and the end of time spoken of by Daniel. This was a very human mistake – just because he was a prophet, it does not mean that he did not hold his own personal beliefs; he was human, and so his human wisdom and knowledge were not infallible.

Because of Pharisaic ideas about Zech 14:4, it was a common belief in Jewish tradition that the promised messiah would first appear on the Mount of Olives. However, if you actually read the verses surrounding it, it doesn't say that the messiah would arise on the Mount of Olives, but rather that *Yahveh* would appear (or rather, the power of God's glory – verses 14:3-5).

I think that Yeshua` probably connected the two passages in Daniel and Zechariah himself. He probably thought that his own era was the time when Yahveh would come in glory to save God's people, *and* that the end of all time was near. Whenever he was in Jerusalem, perhaps he thought that *this* kind of end was imminent. Perhaps he wanted to be there when our heavenly Father came in glory, and – knowing that one day the Romans might arrest him and put him to death – he went there frequently towards the end of his life, in the hope that this end would come soon, so that he wouldn't have to die at Roman hands.

Unhappily, this personal belief in the end that would bring 'the son of man on the clouds of heaven' was not to be – at least, not in his life-time. Even at his trial,[a] he still clung to the forlorn hope that this final chapter of human history would come very soon, and sadly it didn't. He was mistaken. However, he was correct in his prophecies about a coming tribulation, and his ministry contributed to the survival of the Jewish people in the Galilee.

The true gifts of God's spirit and Presence

In rabbinic parlance, the term 'Holy Spirit' simply means 'the spirit of God'; the use of the word 'holy' is simply a further example of an avoidance of the word 'God'. In Yahwist terms, this refers to the observable influence and action of Yahveh's Presence in this world. Unfortunately, the 2nd century inheritors of Paullist theology eventually came to believe that 'the Holy Spirit' was actually a separate entity, a third person within one God.

13:32

[a] Mt 26:64

This is like saying that the strength of force that is displayed by the roaring waters of a raging river, is in fact a separate entity or element of the water, rather than being an inseparable quality of what the water does; or that the wetness of the water is a separate and distinct element of the water, instead of being an intrinsic quality of the water itself. Yahveh's spirit is the observable power of God in this world, not an entity possessed of a separate consciousness or will. Similarly, the 'Davar' or 'Word' of God is not a separate person from God, but an integral part of what Yahveh is (I'll go more into this in chapter seven).

Some religious communities have a skewed idea of what effect the Presence of God has on a person. Such communities think that God's Presence makes you ecstatically happy, causing you to sing and clap uncontrollably. While God is certainly true happiness, this is not a sign that God is with a congregation; it's just a sign that they are happy about God.

There are others who think that inspiration under God's spirit means saying the first thing that comes into your head. I have heard such people tell me, "God wants me to tell you that . . .etc etc". The words that subsequently come out of their mouths show little evidence of the inspiration of God, but rather the prejudices and false beliefs of their own human hearts.

Isaiah 11:2[a] tells us that one of the gifts of God's Presence in a person's life is fortitude (Hebrew *gevurah*). Indeed, the truest sign of the gift of God's Presence in a person's life, is that they are able to achieve things that they would not normally be capable of doing, or have the strength to do. When you achieve goals that are beyond your normal range, and display wisdom and understanding beyond your natural capability, *that* is proof that Yahveh is with you.

The same verse in Isaiah goes on to say that four other major gifts of God's Presence are wisdom, understanding, counsel, and knowledge. Ex 31:3 also lists three of these gifts – wisdom, understanding and knowledge. For example, the Prophet Amos was an ordinary man who tended orchards, so when he started voicing things that could not have come from him, people knew that God was with him. Simply being 'happy-clappy people', or talking in a loud, angry voice does not mean that God is working through you; when you speak with great wisdom, discernment and understanding beyond your normal capabilities to do so, *that* is a sign that the spirit of God is with you.

---

[a] This verse is part of a group that lists the gifts of God's spirit that will rest on any anointed king of Israel that has God's favour. It lists the 6 gifts of God's spirit as: wisdom, understanding, counsel (that is, the ability to accept God's purpose), fortitude (to do more than what one would normally be able to do), knowledge and reverent awe of Yahveh.

Conversely, if what you say displays no wisdom, no knowledge and no understanding, then what you have said *cannot possibly be from God.*

When God's spirit – that is, the living power of God's Presence comes upon a person – they speak knowledge that they could not have known. With their disabilities and handicaps, they achieve things that they could not otherwise have achieved. With the imperfections of their personalities and characters, they realise acts of mercy and compassion that they could not have otherwise undertaken, given their own limitations. You know that the spirit of Yahveh is with a person, because they say, do and teach things, with such an understanding that they could not otherwise have had.

The gift of counsel (Hebrew `eitsah*) is double-edged. It can mean 'advice' – that one is able to give advice. However, it also refers to advice *received* i.e. from God.[a] In this respect, it can also mean 'plans' or 'purpose'. For example, Isaiah 46:11 literally says, *"a man of my purpose"* – that is, a man whom God uses as an instrument to bring about and realise God's plans. For this reason, the spirit of counsel is not just the ability to *give* advice, but also the ability to *accept* God's advice, and become an instrument of God's Divine purpose. Any man or woman upon whom God's spirit rests, displays a profound and intense desire to seek the living will of Yahveh and God's purpose, putting aside his or her own desires, opinions and beliefs. Such a person yearns to believe what God believes, to understand as God understands, and does not allow their own weaknesses, hopes or theories to overrule God's plans or stand in the way of God's teaching. This comes from a profound realisation of the power and might of God, and of the true importance of bringing God's will to its full realisation.

The final gift of God's Presence in a person's life is the reverent awe of God (Hebrew *yir'ah*, often translated as 'fear'). A person who has a reverent awe of Yahveh, realises the tremendous living power of Yahveh. The gut-punching impact of this realisation causes a person to fully recognise that there is nothing you can do to alter God's purpose or will to your own. There are many religious people who think to themselves, 'This is how I want the world and humanity to be. I will therefore create a god and a belief system in my own image, who will justify what I want.' It is more important to such people that *they* are right, rather than be trustful in the rightness of *God*. Such people are nothing more than idolaters, who have created a god in their own image – even if they

---

[a] see Job 38:2

claim to worship only one God, they are still idolaters.

However, the person who reveres Yahveh in awe, realises that he or she can never claim something that God has in fact never said or taught, or hide anything from God. Many religious people commit wrongs against God, deceiving humanity for their own purpose, without fully realising that God is *completely* aware of what they are doing, and will judge them for it. Someone who has a reverent awe of Yahveh will not use or abuse religion for their own benefit, but will fear and respect the power of God.

When people come to realise that having the spirit of God upon them is far more than simply being ecstatically happy, jumping up and down, clapping wildly and singing in a loud voice, some people will then be disturbed by the fact that the spirit of God does not in fact rest on everyone. Their religion has told them that the power of God's spirit falls on everyone who believes their religion's beliefs, accepts their religion's saviour, and belongs to their faith. When they come to realise that *this is not true*, there develops an empty feeling within them. They begin to ask, what more must I do to experience the living spirit of God?

The answer is, that the Presence of God lives with those who do the will of their heavenly Father. Remember, perfection (*shleimut*) refers to the healthy wholeness of your being – keeping your heart, mind and soul healthy, keeping them working as they were designed by God to work. God's spirit rests only on those who can be trusted to fulfil God's purpose. A heart closed to God's Will, cannot be filled with the glory of God, but a heart open to God's Will, will be filled by God's glory to overflowing!

What is important therefore is the intent of your heart. If your heart is inclined towards doing good, if your mind and soul are directed towards the effort of fulfilling God's will, then even if you stumble and fail, it is enough that you keep trying; God's blessing and favour is with you simply because you are doing your best. When we fail, we repent, and we make good on any mistakes we have made. God will not bestow eternal punishment on anyone for trying their best and failing. God loves you, no matter what – even because of your imperfections.

There are some who would fool us into thinking that the mere human propensity for stumbling and failing, means that our souls have been irrevocably poisoned by sin – such that only the death of a god-man can cure this ailment. In contrast, the Israelite religion gave us a way of healing after our mistakes, by turning to Yahveh in a spirit of repentance and of striving to do better – of approaching the healing power of Yahveh, so that God's glory can wipe our souls clean of the wrong we have done – completely.[a]

The power and effectiveness of a community to work for good and stand against evil, is not dependent on the perfection of the human spirit, but on the perfection of the spirit of Yahveh – remember, we are holy because it is Yahveh who sanctifies us and makes us holy. We are to do the best that we can do, and Yahveh's holiness will magnify a genuine and sincere heart beyond its natural self.

A human soul will be filled with God's spirit when it is ready to be directed by God's will, rather than by our own will and desires.

Our heavenly selves should be reflected in our earthly selves

And finally . . .

It seems to me that the early Jewish followers of Yeshua` were very much of the mind that our heavenly lives should be reflected in how we live our lives on earth. For example, in *The Teaching of the Emissaries,*[b] it says, *'For if you are going to hold in common immortal things in the world to come, how much more so should you hold in common the things of this world!'*[c] The followers of the Emissaries (Apostles) believed that in heaven, there was no such thing as personal wealth or belongings; therefore, in this life, they were bidden to share what they had as a reflection of life in heaven.

In this section I want to share with you some thoughts on a passage from the words of Yeshua` that are rarely looked at. This is the version as it appears in Mt 22.23-30:

The Sadducees, who believe there is no resurrection, came to Jesus with a question. 'Teacher', they said, 'Moses told us that if a man dies without having children, his brother must marry the widow in order to bear children for him. Now there were seven brothers among us. The first one married and died, and since he had no children, he left his wife to his brother. The same thing happened to the second and third brother, right on down to the seventh. Finally, the woman herself died. Now then, in the world to come, whose wife will she be of the seven, since all of them were married to her?'

Jesus replied, 'You ask these things because you do not

---

[a] Isa 43:25, 44:22, Ps 51:1-2
[b] the fifth book of *the Exhortations*, the Talmidi Israelite equivalent of the New Testament.
[c] T. Sh. 4:11 – cf Didache 4:8

*know the Scriptures or the power of God. At the resurrection **people will***
neither marry nor be given in marriage; they will be like the angels in
heaven.'

In the *New Testament*, the emphasis is on the strength of argument for resurrection, but I want to look at a different aspect of it, because I think there is more to it than that. In the *Book of Writings*,[a] there is the following passage which puts forward the same idea as the passage from Matthew:

'In heaven, there is no romantic love,
*   only love.*
In heaven, there is no marriage,
*   or being given in marriage;*
there is no husband or wife,
*   no man or woman.*
In heaven there is no parent or child,
*   no partner or companion.*
There are only heavenly beings who have great love for one
another,
*   just as our heavenly Father has one great love for them*
all.[b]

In this life, there are many conventions that we take for granted. What we never stop to think about is the purpose of those conventions. What we have on earth is precisely that – for our life on earth. They exist to guide us, protect us, and enable us to have a strong foundation and framework to work within, given the nature of earthly life and earthly human nature. We just never stop to consider whether they exist in heaven as well.

In heaven, there is no male or female, and the nature of our human bonds of connection to one another does not exist either. We are no longer husband and wife, parent and child, friend or caregiver. In heaven, we are more than that. In heaven, we are no longer defined by our human relationships, but by the love that we have for one another. In heaven, we are heavenly beings who have no gender – just as God and the angels have no gender. In heaven, there is no male or female.

In heaven, you will once again see and live forever with those whom you loved on earth. You will love each other with a love greater

---

[a] a book of Talmidi prose and poetry written as a source of spiritual encouragement and consolation.
[b] S. Kit. 2:13

than you had for those people on earth, and it will be a love that is perfect, full of trust and acceptance, without guilt or apprehension. There will be no judgment in that love, nor any lack of understanding of each other's needs, nor any fear or hurt or sorrow – no ups and downs, no suspicion, no mistrust; only love.

In this life, so much is bound to our social identities – whether we are male or female, what our sexuality is, our rank and social status, whom we are related to, our wealth or lack of it, and so on. Some earthly relationships, and the attitudes that stem from them, are healthy. If those social conventions and attitudes induce within us peace, love and compassion for others, then they are good. But if those social conventions and beliefs bring us hate, and encourage us to oppress others, deny them justice and the right to pursue happiness, then we have to question our attitudes to those social conventions, *because such negative and destructive attitudes are not from God.*

I am not going to tell you what to think, but it is important for you to meditate on what you once were *before* this life, and what you will be again one day in heaven, and how *that* should inform your behaviour towards others in this life here and now. If in heaven you were neither male nor female; if rank, status and the hierarchical nature of the bonds you have in this life are not carried over into heaven; if we gave no substance to the possession of wealth; if we did not hate others simply for who and what they were – if you, like the angels, were purely heavenly beings who had a great love for one another – then how should that inform and modify your behaviour towards one another here on earth?

Think about it.

Illustrations from the words of the prophet Yeshua`

Yeshua` said:

'Don't build up storehouses, nor put away treasures for yourselves on earth, where moth and maggot eat away, and thieves dig through and steal. Rather, build up storehouses and put away treasures for yourselves in heaven, where neither moth nor maggot can eat away, nor thieves dig through and steal.'[a]

---

[a] S.Yesh. 100:1-2 – cf Mt 6:19-20, Lk 12:33

CHAPTER FIVE: Interlude – The Lessons Of The Prayer So Far

Overview

The fifth commandment starts off with, 'Honour your father and your mother'. Our western culture gives us two aspects of this commandment, but it doesn't allow us an understanding of what the commandment goes on to promise: *'so that you may endure a long time in the land Yahveh your God is giving to you.'*

When we think of this proclamation of God, we think of respecting our parents, and of obeying them. These are two vital and important components of how to fulfil this commandment. However, there is a third aspect to honouring your parents that is now absent in modern western culture – that of acting in such a way that you do not bring dishonour to your parents' reputation, but rather that you behave with dignity, grace, justice and kindness in this world, such that your parents will have no reason to regret calling you their son or daughter. When a child acts with righteousness in the world, the reputation of the parents will increase.

If the reputation of enough parents and families is upheld, collectively the honour and dignity of your people will spread far and wide. If you are widely respected and held in high esteem by other nations, then naturally *'you will endure long in the land Yahveh your God is giving to you'* – in peace, without fear of attack or exile.

Because this is Israel we are talking about here, if Israel is held in high esteem, then it naturally follows on that Yahveh, the God of Israel, will be held in high esteem – the 'Name' or reputation of God will be increased, and the kingdom of God will spread. The benefit to Israel, is that she will be respected by her neighbours, and not live with the constant fear of war.

If this is how we are to behave towards our earthly parents, how much more so are we to behave like this towards our Heavenly Parent. We honour our Heavenly Parent by acting, thinking and speaking in a way that brings renown to our Heavenly Father. We honour God, who is our father and our mother, by living honourably in this present world that God created, daily increasing the renown of God.

Every relationship has two sides to it. For example, where hospitality is concerned, there were unwritten obligations both on the host, as well as the guest. The host was not to be abusive to his or her guests, or ill-treat them in any way.[a] However, at the same time, the guest was not to take advantage of the kindness or generosity of the host. Even though the host traditionally told the guest, 'My home is your home; eat and drink your fill', the guest was not to trash the place, consume everything or bring the host to ruin. A similar code existed with gleaning rights.[b] You were not meant to set off on a journey thinking, 'Oh, I don't need to take any food with me, because I can take from other people's fields'. This would have been an abuse of the gleaning laws. The gleaning laws aided you if you were very poor and didn't have enough for the whole journey, or if you unexpectedly ran out of food.

So again with the relationship between parent and child. Just as a child was to be obedient and respectful towards its parents, so also a parent had a responsibility not to give their child an evil or immoral command to follow. In such a case, the child has no obligation to obey a harmful or evil command. A parent was also not to abuse or treat the child in such a way that would mentally scar them for life.

We need not fear such a situation with God. However, the same obligation to our heavenly Father remains. If we wish to call God 'Father', then we have to imitate God in our ways and bring honour to God's reputation through what we do. In this way, we sanctify the name of God by causing God's reputation to spread positively among humanity – instead of the current situation, where many religious people generally give God a negative reputation with their intolerance, narrowmindedness and bothersomeness.

In short, our relationship with God has to show that we call God 'Father' in what we do. We have a responsibility towards God in how we behave. It is not enough merely to believe in God; belief in itself does nothing to further God's cause on earth.

All through these chapters, I have tried to explain the meaning of the words of the *Our Father*, and the relevance of these petitions to Yeshua`'s own world. As a reader you must have seen by now that every single petition so far is a call to action. Each petition signals that we cannot just sit back and hope for someone else to

---

[a] In the Christian tradition, the sin of Sodom was homosexuality. However, in the Israelite tradition, the sin of Sodom was the abusive and heinous ill-treatment of guests – the worst sin you could possibly commit in the ancient Middle East. With this in mind, the saying of Yeshua`, where he declares that those cities which did not welcome him would fair worse than the people of Sodom, makes much more sense (S.Yesh. 63:17 – cf Mt 10:15, Lk 10:12).
[b] Deut 23:24-25

act on our behalf, because we ourselves are instrumental in assisting God's kingdom to be fulfilled, for humanity to be perfected, and for God's glory to shine on earth. If we do nothing, then this wondrous fulfilment will never come.

Hypocrites and religious phonies

Yeshua` often criticises 'hypocrites' in his sayings. Now, to English-speakers, this means someone who says one thing, but does another. From the context of Yeshua`'s sayings, it's obvious that he is talking about something much bigger.

He speaks of people who make a show of being religious simply to get the praise of others, but *inside* they are no better than anyone else. He speaks of people who are merely observant – those who simply observe the external customs of religion, but inside are morally or spiritually empty or even corrupt.

The word used in the New Testament in Greek is *hupokritos*, which does mean 'hypocrite' in the modern English sense, but it also means 'pretender' or 'actor'. I think the evangelists chose this Greek word, because it contained the idea of putting on a fake show for others to see. The most suitable equivalent in English I can think of would be 'religious phoney' or 'faker'.

I think the Aramaic equivalent would have been *bar chanpin* – literally 'a son of flatteries' or 'son of deceptions'. This idiom comes from the practice of flattering a conqueror to please him, so that one will not be killed. Hence the idea of saying one thing with one's mouth, and feeling another with one's heart (this meaning would explain Mt 22:18, where Yeshua` describes those who are trying to trick him as 'hypocrites').

So the basic idea of a *bar chanpin* is someone who makes a show of being one thing – a devoted religious person who is loyal to God – but whose inner heart is something else. Yeshua` was criticising those who made a fake display of following the externals of their religion, even of giving the outward appearance of being supposedly good people, but in their hearts they ignored the higher moral requirements of justice, compassion and mercy. He criticised those who made a phoney show of religious piety towards others, but inside were just cold and empty.

The prophet Yeshua` criticised those who *'clean the outside of the cup and the dish'*, but who are inside *'full of greed and wickedness'*.[a] In other words, those who maintain an external show of respectability, but are internally morally corrupt, greedy and unkind. The same criticism

---

[a] S.Yesh. 59:8 – cf Mt 23:25, Lk 11:39

was intended by the words, *'You are like whitewashed tombs, which look beautiful on the outside, but on the inside are full of dead men's bones.'*[a] I would apply this saying to the religious fundamentalists of the modern world too.

Today we have religious people who attend church or synagogue every week, who speak fine words about family values and criticise society's ills, but inside they are full of materialistic greed, hatred for those who disagree with them, and vicious judgment for those who don't live up to their standards.

In Yeshua''s teaching, he encouraged his followers to change the inner heart and mind. It is the metamorphosis of the heart and mind which is the most important thing to God. One can observe all the customs and traditions of the Israelite faith in witness to God, but if they are not accompanied by an inner moral, spiritual and ethical transformation, then merely observing customs and traditions (or in terms relevant for us today, merely adhering to certain beliefs) is worthless.

Yeshua' said that unless our righteousness exceeds that of the Pharisees, we will never find the kingdom of God. If we are merely observant of the external requirements of our religion as the Pharisees were, and ignore the inner change of the heart, then the kingdom of God will remain a mystery to us. The same applies to those who stubbornly continue to think that beliefs are more important than what we do or the way we think.[b] Yeshua' calls for an inner transformation of the soul. The kingdom of God demands a change of heart. Without that change, we are merely hypocrites.

So to summarise: a hypocrite, in Aramaic, is not someone who says one thing and does another, but rather someone whose external behaviour displays one set of values, but whose inner heart is really home to a different set of values – of dark, negative ones. The heart has to match the deeds. In other words, mean what you do. Don't be a faker – make sure your heart changes, as well as your actions.

The aura of the pious

If you have ever had the good fortune to meet a saintly and holy person, someone of great piety and devotion to God – regardless of their religion – you will be moved by the strange combination of their simple humility on the one hand, and yet also

---

[a] S. Yoch. 4:2 – cf Mt 23:27
[b] Consider Yeshua''s parable at Mt 25:32-46 (S.Yesh. 134), where those who do God's will are those who inherit the Kingdom of God.

of the powerful aura you experience from being in their presence on the other. Even their words have the same effect. Most religions will construe that power as emanating directly from the holy person him- or herself. However, amongst the ancient Israelites, there was something that people who showed true humility towards God would often say: "I am who I am only because of Yahveh." An Israelite who came across such a holy person, and understood this concept, would not heap praise on the holy person, but rather on God. They would witness the simple yet powerful words and deeds of the pious person, and then give praise to Yahveh.

A pious and holy person strives to live God's ways, to experience the power of God's Presence and be changed by it. In so doing they move closer to the state of the heavenly human – the mystical 'Son of Man' – that is, how they were when their souls were in heaven, like all of us before we came here.

They reach a stage when they become a living channel for God's glory and holiness, willing servants who do God's will on earth, just as they did in heaven. When we meet such people or read their words, we should not mistake the powerful aura of those people as something that comes from *them*; rather, we are experiencing nothing short of God's own power *through* them. They are what they are – or rather, have become what they have become – only because of God.

Perhaps this power is what was mistakenly identified by others in the Prophet Yeshua` for divinity. Perhaps this is what happened – indeed, what happens even now – when some people read Yeshua`'s words. Perhaps he was so in tune with God's will for him, that our Heavenly Father's power was plainly evident in his life. Even now, the living power of God shines through his words, because he submitted so completely to God's will, and allowed God to speak through him – which is the job of any prophet in the Israelite religion.

In our movement, we do not believe that Yeshua` was a god. However, there are still people who come to us, who still put the prophet higher than anyone else in the whole of human history. Such people naturally say to us, 'But if he was just a man, where did all his wisdom come from? Where did all his insight and discernment, compassion and loving-kindness come from?' For such enquiries, the simple answer from someone who thinks like an Israelite – like a servant of Yahveh – is this: they came from Yahveh, and Yahveh alone.

Yeshua` said, "Whoever hears you, hears me."[a] There was the principle that, if you faithfully reproduced your spiritual Master's words (without subtracting or adding anything of your own), then it would be

---

[a] S.Yesh. 90:1; cf Mt 10:40a, Lk 10:16a

as if you were hearing the Master himself. It is the same with God. If you strive towards living a way of life that is in accordance with God's will – for example, by being considerate, kind, forgiving, helpful and compassionate – then people who meet you will gain an insight into God; people who witness your actions will be witnessing God's actions and personality *through* you, because you will be living your Master's teachings (i.e. God's teachings), just as Yeshua` did.

Having once held Christian beliefs myself, I can now fully appreciate that by ascribing divinity to Yeshua`, I was missing out on experiencing the full impact of the glory and majesty which properly belongs to Yahveh alone. Yeshua`, like any holy man or woman of God, was only a channel for God's wisdom and power; he, like any person who shows humility and willing service towards God, was only who he was because of Yahveh. The astounding revelation that comes from understanding that – that Yeshua` was just a man – is that *we all have the potential to become that kind of person too.*

The living Ark of the Covenant

What comes across most powerfully from understanding the first half of this prayer from a completely Israelite point of view, is that it is really important that we strive to change ourselves, and live a way of life that will reflect God's personality and will. In the Book of Jeremiah,[a] Yahveh says,

> *"In those days, when your numbers have increased greatly in the land, declares Yahveh, people will no longer say, 'The Ark of the Covenant of Yahveh.' It will never enter their minds or be remembered; it will not be missed, nor will another one be made."*

This prophecy of Jeremiah implies that we will never find the Ark, nor will another be crafted to replace it. Most important of all, we will not miss it, nor should we miss it. The question begs to be asked: But why? Why should we not long to see this sacred object again, which still has such a hold on our hearts and imagination?

Well, Jeremiah goes on to explain why in the next verse:

> *"At that time they will call Jerusalem 'The Throne*

---

[a] Jer 3:16

of Yahveh', and all nations will gather in Jerusalem to honour the name of Yahveh." [a]

The Ark was meant to be a tangible, physical metaphor for God's throne, and Jerusalem itself would one day become a replacement for the Ark as God's throne on earth. But that would not happen until a crucial change took place. The same verse concludes with:

> *"No longer will they follow the stubbornness of their evil hearts."*

Do you see the implications of this? Jerusalem will not become the Ark of the Covenant – the throne of God – until the people of Jerusalem change. In other words, the status of the City of Jerusalem as God's throne is inextricably linked to the behaviour and mind-set of those who live within it.

The Ark itself had no power. It was only a doorway for Yahveh's Divine Radiance, and as long as Yahveh was present, the Ark was holy. When Moses saw the burning bush, the ground on which he walked was holy *only* because Yahveh was present; the ground itself had no innate holiness. God also told *us* to be holy, as Yahveh is holy; the effective power of our holiness on the world will come *from the presence of Yahveh among us*. If we do our best to live a life of holiness, *we become a living ark for God.* **We** become God's throne, the portal through which God's glory enters the world.

Because God is holy – because God's glory is so powerful – no evil can stand against God. If we become God's Ark, then we carry the light before which no evil can stand. "Be holy because I, Yahveh your God, am holy".[b] In other words, *become a people before whom evil cannot stand or endure.* Remember – the power of our holiness depends on the presence of Yahveh among us; we become holy because it is the Living Presence of Yahveh among us which sanctifies us.[c] Our power to stand against evil, corruption and wickedness comes from Yahveh.

But then we will say, 'I am not a perfect person!' The response to that is: That is not what is important; that is not what is being asked of you. What is important is the intent of your heart. If your heart is inclined towards doing good, if your mind and soul are directed towards the effort of fulfilling God's will, then even if you stumble and fail, it is enough that you keep *trying* – God is present with you simply because you are

---

[a] Jer 3:17
[b] Lev 11:44-45, 19:2
[c] Ex 31:13, Lev 20:8, 22:32

doing your best. God will never punish anyone for trying and failing. The power and effectiveness of a community to work for good and stand against evil, is not dependent on the perfection of the human spirit, but on the perfection of the holiness of Yahveh – remember, we are holy because it is Yahveh who sanctifies us. We are to do the best that we can do, and Yahveh's holiness will magnify that.

If we accept that we are not perfect, and don't fret over it, then we are able to divert more energy into the effort of working towards God's will in our individual lives. And God accepts that we are trying, and looks with kindness and a deep affection upon us. You just have to let Yahveh take charge, and let God do the rest. In time, Yahveh's light will transform your heart, and God's glory will live within you.

Imagine a whole group of people who are aware of 'the knowledge of the glory of Yahveh',[a] and are inspired to live God's will. Imagine what effect that carrying the glory of God within us can do!

Even if just one person follows the way of Yahveh with their whole heart, Yahveh is so powerful that God's light can penetrate into this world through the doorway that one person holds open for God. Imagine what great power then can enter this world, if *many* people follow God's way with their whole heart! What great things can happen if many people act to become one great, living Ark for Yahveh – a living throne, a living portal for God's glory to enter this world!

In the ancient Sinai, right in the centre of the camp of Israel, the Mishkan[b] was a tent for the living, active Presence of God – the *Sh^ekhinah*.[c] It was a physical symbol of God's Presence among the Israelites. Within the Mishkan sat the Ark – a symbol of God's throne, above which the light of God – Yahveh's glory – would break through into our world[d] and appear.

If Israelites around the world – not just Israelites, but indeed *all* those who follow Yahveh – do our jobs right, all of us become a living Mishkan for Yahveh's Presence among the nations. And if those of us who set our hearts and minds on following God's ways

---

[a] Hab 2:14

[b] or Tabernacle. On the one hand, the Mishkan was intended to act as a physical symbol of God's presence among the Israelites. However, it also had a practical purpose – to protect the Israelites from the powerful effects of the living glory of Yahveh.

[c] pronounced shuh-khee-NAAH (i.e. with the emphasis on the final syllable).

[d] Ex 25:22

of justice, mercy, tolerance and peace do our jobs, then we become a living Ark of the Covenant – a living throne for God's glory, a living doorway for God's light to shine through into the world.

The old Ark of the Covenant will not be found, remembered or rebuilt – just as Jeremiah said – because if we do what we are supposed to do, then we ourselves become the living Ark of the Covenant, just as Jeremiah prophesied.

.

CHAPTER SIX: Prayer for food and daily material needs

לחמן דמארעא
הב לן יומא דין ומחרא

lachman de-mei-ar`a
hab lan yoma deyn u-machra

Our bread, which is from the earth,
Give us day by day.

Introduction

The second half of the prayer begins with a petition to God as our provider. It is an important principle in the Israelite religion to acknowledge Yahveh as the source of everything that we have. We have what we have, because Yahveh has provided it and given it to us. Even when it comes to the things that we create ourselves, in the Israelite mind-set, we are only able to create them because Yahveh has provided us with the raw materials with which to manufacture goods. Even artistic[a] and writing prowess is considered to be from God, because all knowledge, skill and wisdom ultimately come from Yahveh.[b]

In the time of Moses, the people of Israel came to know and experience Yahveh as Saviour and Redeemer, but in the time of Abraham, Isaac and Jacob, they knew God as the Creator and the Provider. These are the basic, fundamental qualities of God that we should never forget. For example, when we have eaten we bless God. This is because the Book of Deuteronomy[c] tells us,

---

[a] Ex 21:3-6 – the artisans who built the Tabernacle were considered to have been given their skill directly by God - cf Ex 31:3, where God says, *"I have endowed [them] with a divine spirit [i.e. of skill] in wisdom, understanding and all kinds of craftsmanship".*
[b] *'For Yahveh gives wisdom, and from His mouth come knowledge and understanding.'* (Prov 2:6).
[c] Dt 6:10-12

*"When Yahveh your God brings you into the land God swore to your ancestors, to give you – a land with large, flourishing cities you did not build, houses filled with all kinds of good things you did not provide, wells you did not dig, and vineyards and olive groves you did not plant - then **when you eat and are satisfied**, be careful that you do not forget Yahveh, who brought you out of Egypt, out of the land of slavery."*

In other words, when we are sated and have had our fill, we should never forget that it was Yahveh, and not us, who ultimately provided what we have put on the table. This is why in the Jewish tradition, we say grace *after* meals. [a]

Line 7: Our bread, which is from the earth

... bread,

Psalm 104:14 says, *'[God] makes grass to grow for the cattle, and plants for humanity to cultivate – bringing forth food* (literally 'bread') *from the earth'*. Job[b] also looked upon the earth as the place from which food (again, literally 'bread') came. Through the prophet Isaiah,[c] Yahveh promised us that the food ('bread') God gave from the earth would be plentiful. This is the basis of Yeshua''s confidence in our heavenly Father as our Provider.

In traditional Hebrew imagery, bread was what strengthened human beings,[d] and gave us sustenance and comfort. It therefore became a symbol for plenty; cutting off the supply of bread was a metaphor for famine.[e]

Bread was the staple of every diet; meat and vegetables were seen as the accompaniment to bread, not the other way round. It was eaten as part of every meal, just as rice forms the main part of most Asian meals, or as pasta forms the greater part of many Italian meals. In this context therefore, bread means food in general.

Many people bought their wheat and barley, and ground it themselves to make flour for bread. Since barley was not as expensive as wheat, the poor of the Galilee ate barley bread more often than bread

---

[a] although the Orthodox also say blessings before each individual mouthful they eat and drink as well.
[b] Job 28:5
[c] Isaiah 30:23
[d] Ps 104:15
[e] e.g. Isa 3:1, Ezek 4:16

made from wheat (and they probably didn't do too badly out of this; barley is more nutritious and higher in protein than wheat)! The Galilee was a very poor region in those days, and few people could afford the expense of ready ground flour, or to buy the bread ready baked.

People would go to market virtually every day; they earned so little and paid so much in taxes and debts, that they could not afford to save anything. Men were paid at the end of every day (a right guaranteed by Yahveh in Torah),[a] at the rate of just one denarius[b] a day. You can therefore understand how serious it would be for someone to lose this coin, knowing the value of the coin in real terms; you can appreciate what stress one would be under while sweeping the house looking for it, and what a joy it would be to find it again.[c]

Women went to market every day to buy food with the earnings of their husband's previous day's work. With the money they bought enough grain to feed the family, and a little over a litre of barley cost 30 prutan[d] (about 25% of one day's wages). Wheat would cost about one denarius – remember, this was a whole day's earnings.

The buyer would purchase a full container of grain. Women would often take their own containers to market with which to have grain measured (hence the saying, 'The measure you give will be the measure you get).[e] The custom for the seller was that each container or measure had to run over. When it was full, it was shaken, pressed down, and then more grain was put on top, until it ran over again. Then the seller would make a small hollow or depression in the middle, and build up a heap of grain until the measure could not hold any more. The grain was then poured into the woman's lap (or rather, her outer skirt or apron). This was what Yeshua` alluded to in his saying, when he talked about not judging others:

'give, and the same will be given to you – a good measure, pressed down, shaken together and running over will be poured into your lap.' [f]

Whether we judged and condemned, or gave generously, whatever

---

[a] Lev 19:13b
[b] This was the silver coin mentioned by Yeshua` in some of his parables (see next note).
[c] the parable of the lost coin, S.Yesh. 29; cf Lk 15:8-10.
[d] There were 120 prutan (Aramaic plural of prutah) in 1 denarius (zuz in Aramaic).
[e] S.Yesh. 98:2; cf Mk 4:24b, Mt 7:2b
[f] S.Yesh. 99:2; cf Lk 6:37b-38a

we did would be returned to us in full measure.[a] Whatever we do to others, God will make sure the same returns to us, whether what we have done is good or bad.

In ancient Israelite culture, bread was more than just what you ate; it was *anything* that was needed to sustain us. It could be any food, as well as clothing and shelter. Yeshua` said,

> *'Why worry about clothes? See the wild flowers, how they clothe the grass. The grass neither cards nor spins, yet I tell you, not even Solomon in all his splendour was dressed like that! So if that's how God clothes the wild grass, which is here today and tomorrow is thrown into the fire, how much more so will God clothe you!'*[b]

This teaching is not as unrealistic an ideal as it first sounds. If you took care of the land, God could realistically provide for all your needs from that land. The teaching is an expression of Yeshua`'s rock solid faith in God as our Provider, and that it was through the earth that God provided for us.

It is also acknowledging that our daily sustenance comes from the earth, and is therefore a gift from God. It is through the earth that God provides for us (and therefore we have a pressing duty to look after it). The ancients didn't really know or understand how grain germinated, grew, spread its pollen and seeded grain; they didn't understand how fish stocks were replenished, or how wild herds were sustained. All of it was provided by Yahveh; as long as the earth was cared for, looked after and nurtured, then Yahveh would continue to provide.

... which is from the earth

In ancient Jewish culture, there were three main things that were referred to as 'bread': food and general sustenance, money, and God's teaching. Just as the first line of the prayer clarifies which father we are talking about (*'the one in heaven'*), so also this line clarifies which kind of bread we are talking about (*'the one from the earth'*).

---

[a] cf Isaiah 65:6, where God speaks about paying people's deeds back into their laps; this is in accordance with the Yahwist principle that whatever we do to others, God will pay back the same in full measure; see also Ezek 16:59 – 'I will deal with you just as you have done.'
[b] S.Yesh. 44:1-3; cf Mt 6:28-30, Lk 12:27-28

Wealth and the rich

From analysing Yeshua`'s sayings and lifestyle, it would seem that money was not a major spiritual or practical concern for him and his followers. Though a necessity of material life, there were far greater goals and higher ideals in his world. It is possible that he considered praying for the acquisition of money was like praying for temptation.[a] In the *Our Father*, by specifying 'bread which was from the earth', it would seem that he wanted us to make a distinction between money (bread from human beings) and other kinds of sustenance, like food and shelter (bread from the earth), and teaching from God (which is bread from heaven).[b] If one considers Prov 30:8,[c] there is a distinction made there between wealth and the daily sustenance necessary for life.

If we look at wealth first, in Aramaic, the word for 'bread' is also slang for 'money'. For example, *itgar lechem*, which literally means 'to earn bread' is slang for 'to earn money'. Even though money was created by human beings, money was ultimately seen as a gift of God. Therefore, rich people had to realise that they were rich, not because of their own merit or skill, but because it had been given to them by God. And according to the Israelite way of thinking, if God gave it, God could just as easily take it away.

Being unaware of the ancient Yahwist attitude to money, many people think that the proper religious attitude to money should be that it is in itself evil. This is not the case. There was nothing wrong with money *per se*, but there was a general feeling in the Israelite religion that opulent and luxurious displays of wealth were distasteful, and that the excessive accumulation of wealth for its own sake was offensive. For example, God said, *'He* (the king) *must not accumulate large quantities of silver and gold.'*[d] Instead, the ideal state is expressed in the *Book of Proverbs*: *'Give me neither poverty nor riches; feed me only with my allotted portion of food.'*[e]

In the modern world, there is an unfortunate tendency to admire the enormous wealth and success of people who act with cold ruthlessness in matters of business. This is the opposite of God's will; through the prophet Isaiah,[f] Yahveh commands us, *"Cease to do evil, learn to do*

---

[a] see Prov 30:9 – 'Otherwise I [i.e. as a rich person] might have too much wealth, and then disown you and say, "Who is this Yahveh?"
[b] see Isaiah 55:1-3, Prov 9:5
[c] 'Keep falsehood and lies far from me; give me neither poverty nor riches, but provide for me bread sufficient for my needs'.
[d] Deut 17:17b
[e] Prov 30:8
[f] Isaiah 1:16b-17a

*good, seek justice, and **reprove the ruthless** ".* It has recently been found[a] that there is a brain pattern that indicates a natural tendency towards being psychopathic – a person who can be quite charming and convincing, but who can also be ruthless and unfeeling, unable to empathise with the needs of others. It was also found that the frequency of this psychopathic brain-patterning amongst company executives and CEO's was *four* times greater than in the general population. In another study,[b] it was found that disagreeable and unpleasant people on the whole tend to earn more than pleasant people. It seems to me that people today are more willing to strive to emulate the cold heartlessness of psychopathic individuals in order to be mega-successful, rather than behave with the just fairness of normal, healthy individuals.

It is not the wealth that God dislikes, but rather the attitude and personality necessary to obtain that great wealth – the greed, the ruthlessness, the lack of consideration of one's actions on other people's lives, and the thinking that 'I alone did this', when the mind-set of the Israelite religion is that all wealth is from Yahveh, and ultimately belongs to God:

'You may say to yourself, "My power and the strength of my hands have produced this wealth for me." But remember Yahveh your God, for it is God who gives you the ability to produce wealth' [c]

Many people have a tendency to think that Yeshua`'s attitude to wealth was that it always had to be divested and given away, in every circumstance. In my humble opinion, I think rather his insight was greater than that; that a rich person only has to give away their wealth if it is what is causing them to sin – if it is the very thing that makes them a bad person. If profit is the only god in their lives, and is what causes their ruthlessness and greed, then it is the limb that needs to be removed,[d] the cancer that needs to be cut out from their soul. Love of money is the origin of this kind of evil, not money itself. For if a rich person *helps* others with their wealth, and is bountiful in their giving, then their wealth does not need to be divested, because it is obvious that their wealth is not their god.

Let me finish with a parable:

---

[a] Horizon, 'Are You Good or Evil?' BBC TV, 7 Sept 2011 (the programme examined the question of whether humans were naturally inclined towards good or evil)

[b] *Journal of Personality and Social Psychology*, Dec 2011, by Beth A. Livingston (Cornell University), Timothy A. Judge (University of Notre Dame), Charlice Hurst (University of Western Ontario).

[c] Deut 8:17-18a

[d] S.Yesh. 157:5-7 – 'if it's your hand that's caused you to sin, cut it off, because it is better to enter the kingdom of God maimed, than with two hands be cast into the outer darkness!' cf Mt 18:8-9

There was a very rich man who had great wealth. And at the festival of Unleavened Bread, the rich man would take the best lamb – a male one year old without blemish – and invite all his neighbours to feast on it, according to the law of Moses, for he made sure that there was more than enough, so that he could invite all his neighbours to his house to see his wealth.

And there was a poor man, a beggar, who would simply wander around the Temple courts until he found a soul who was willing to allow him to join them, and give him a small portion of their Passover lamb.

And at the Festival of First-Fruits, the rich man would love to have everyone see the abundance of all his offerings, how he would bring the first and best of his wheat harvest, the first-born of his sheep, his cattle and his goats, as well as the money he had gained from the first of his flax, his figs, his grapes, and his olives.

The beggar had nothing that he had sown, nor grown, nor harvested, but he had kept the first little prutah coin given to him after the first day of the year in the month of Nisan, and this he put into one of the donation trumpets in the Temple, for he loved God and revered Him.

And at the time of the Festival, the rich man would build a large booth, and decorate it with the most luxuriant of branches, the most beautiful of all fronds, the finest of scented boughs, and the most succulent of fruits. It was taller and broader than anyone else's, so that none in Jerusalem could avoid the sight of it. And he would make sure that the offerings he made at this time were the best of all his harvests. He would give a tenth of all his produce to the Temple, but not one grain more.

But the beggar would raise just four sticks and cover them with but a few palm branches to dwell under. And he shared his bread with those who had less than he.

And when they died they both came into the Presence of God, and God said to the rich man, "What have you done to keep my Covenant, to follow my decrees, and to observe my statutes?"

And the rich man said, "Three times a year I appeared before you. I have built your booths, exactly as you commanded; I have sacrificed the best unblemished lambs for the Passover sacrifice, as you instructed; I have offered the first of all my crops and livestock at First-Fruits; and I have given tithes of all my produce. I have done everything that you commanded, exactly as you asked of me – no more, no less."

And then God turned to the beggar and said, "And you, did you keep my Covenant, and follow my decrees, and observe my statutes?"

And the beggar said, "Heavenly Father, I am not worthy of your blessing; I was poor in life; I did not have enough to build booths; I was never able to afford a lamb for the Passover sacrifice; I never owned anything to give at First-Fruits. I never had anything to offer You but the devotion of my heart."

So God said to them, "You who were rich displayed your piety before others so that they would praise you, yet your heart was cold and empty. Your intentions were towards vanity, and the direction of your soul towards your own self-importance.

But you who were poor have kept my Covenant; you have excelled in every commandment, and fulfilled every statute, because the aspiration of your heart was towards reverence, and righteousness was the intent of your soul.

Therefore you, O man of little means, I knew you because in humility you have walked with Me. Yours was the kingdom, and you never knew it!

But you, O man of wealth, since you had no love except for your own vanity, I tell you this: I never knew you, because in all the days of your life, you never once walked with Me, and never once did you set foot in My kingdom while you dwelt on earth."[a]

The ba`aley shav - the masters of deception

Is your society plagued with massive and gross social inequalities? Is your country apparently governed by the rule of law, but is nevertheless beset with a high crime rate and murder rate? Is your nation seemingly controlled by a wealthy and covert elite, one that ordinary people cannot seem to bring under democratic oversight? Is your civilisation heavily polarised in political and social terms? Then the 'masters of deception' have probably taken over your society, and you were too busy slaving away, day in and day out, trying to earn enough to support your family, to have ever noticed; you were more than likely even manipulated emotionally and psychologically into acquiescing to this state of affairs.

I'm going to introduce to you a new term. I have spoken already of people with a psychopathic personality – not simply the criminal type,

---

[a] S.Kit. 3:2.1-22

but those who are innately ruthless, greedy, manipulative, self-centred and uncaring. I call these people *ba`aley shav*, the lords and masters of deceptive, evil and destructive falsehood. Having suffered terribly myself as a victim of someone with Psychopathic Personality Disorder (PPD), and had my life completely ruined by one, it prompted me to look into the phenomenon of PPD.

There are many books and websites out there about an alleged group of people that have come to be known among conspiracy-theorists as the Illuminati. This seems to be a catch-all term to cover a seemingly organised group of people who want to control society and manipulate it. The thing about *ba`aley shav* however, is that they are not actually organised – there's no actual planned conspiracy among them; it's more organic than that.

They are innately, genetically predisposed to prey on their own species – us, the human race. They are genetically inclined to be on top, and use others for their own profit and benefit. They are inherently driven to be in control, to manipulate the opinions and values of society to ensure that they *stay* in control. They pander to our prejudices and fears for their own ends. I personally doubt there is actually a group of people *per se* called the Illuminati, but there **is** a high-level stratum of intra-species predator that is a hindrance and scourge to the majority of humanity, preventing us from becoming what God intended our species overall to become.

These masters of deception are easily able to recognise dangers to their power too. In any balanced, egalitarian and cooperative society, these *ba`aley shav* would not be able to function – there would be checks and balances on their influence and power inbuilt into our spiritual and legal systems. However, any society where *ba`aley shav* have managed to gain a foothold will have democratic moves against them suppressed; after all, they have the money to do it.

An oligarchic society – one dominated or ruled by a wealthy few – will be dangerously open to the power of *ba`aley shav*. Any *ba`al shav* will be threatened by democratic processes, and will inject covert propaganda and rumour into the media and social organisations in order to demonise all dangers to their power. One group of people whose godly values are a real and present danger to any *ba`al shav* are us Jews; throughout history, the Jewish people have therefore been demonised and persecuted by most civilisations where *ba`aley shav* have gained a foothold. When any society operates on Yahwist values, *ba`aley shav* cannot function; our Yahwist values are therefore a very real and present danger to them.[a]

So how do you recognise one of these *ba`aley shav*? Psychopaths are predatory. They like being on top of the pyramid; they like being always right and taking risks; they can turn on the charm when needed, but can turn it off completely when required to – after all, they managed to convince the world that greed is good, and how not to care about the problems of others. They routinely show little emotion – they record the same emotion whether they are seeing something pleasant or violent. They are accomplished con artists and liars – "you cannot trust a word that comes out of their mouths";[b] they have an inflated degree of self-worth, they are aggressive competitors, they are manipulative and do not see anything as their fault; and they have an incorrigible belief that it is worth hurting *everyone* as long as they get what they want.

The percentage of people with a psychopathic personality in the general population varies from 2% to 4%. They usually end up being the wealthiest and most influential people on the planet. It seems that the profession with the **highest** percentage of psychopathic personalities – 5 times the normal average at 6.25% – is financiers, people working in the banking world. Not surprisingly, such financial psychopaths had no conscience or remorse about bringing down the world economy in 2008, nor over the hardship it caused.

In a television survey[c] for the TV channel TCM, it was found that, when asked if they knew the difference between right and wrong, and could choose the morally correct course of action, one in eight people in Britain said, 'No'. In London (home of the UK's financial markets), the 'No' response was 1 in 5.

Personality types who are susceptible to psychopaths

Other studies[d] have found that there is an actual, physical difference in the brains of those who hold rigid, uncompromising and inflexible views, compared to those with moderate or liberal views. These people end up being willing accomplices to people with PPD, and swell the reach of their influence. Their brains, these studies postulate, were designed to give an immediate, negative reaction to anything new

---

[a] see Prov 10:29 – *'The Way of Yahveh* [i.e. the Israelite religion] *is a stronghold to those with integrity, but a ruin to the workers of iniquity'*.
[b] A quote from 'Psychopath Night', Channel 4 (UK), Dec 2013
[c] Reported in the *Daily Mail*, 24th May 2012
[d] *Differences in Negativity Bias Underlie Variations in Political Ideology*, by John R. Hibbing, Kevin B. Smith, John R. Alford in *Behavioural & Brain Sciences report 2014*

or unfamiliar, and that this stems back from a period[a] in human history when we were primitive hunter-gatherers, before anyone began living in settled communities.

There is also a phenomenon called atavism. This is 'reversion to original type'. Fundamentalists of all religions tend to revert to the basics of their origins, thinking that by hatefully and uncompromisingly affirming their original founding beliefs (which must be perfect, right?) they will achieve stability. This attitude fails to understand that religions evolve. They go through trials and events in history, which make them realise that certain beliefs are bad and even destructive, and that others serve them well. Over time, a wise religion throws out their imperfect beliefs and views, while similarly honing the better parts of their faith.

It may also explain why the rationale-seeking sides of these atavistic personalities go for the easiest and simplest solution, and stick to it in the face of all reason and human decency, even if their view is blatantly wrong or harmful. These individuals do well in a cut-throat, kill or be killed, dog-eat-dog environment, where one needs to be selfish and only look after oneself. They don't do so well in a communal setting, where you need to look out for the needs of others. Rigid atavistic personalities only do well in small, competitive communities; they don't do so well where the welfare of billions of human beings is involved.

A related psychological phenomenon is pareidolia. This is where the human mind seeks out patterns in otherwise random features – like sounds, shapes, words or events. It explains why we see faces in natural formations; why we find conspiracies in what are, in reality, unconnected events; it explains the need to find hidden, secret messages in random words and letters; and it explains the need to see Satan in every accident and misfortune. The primitive side of our human minds needs to make sense of what isn't meant to make sense, because it is more comforting to think that we are the victims of a government or global conspiracy, or that we are the innocent prey of satanic forces. If we need to believe in something, and take refuge in something comforting, isn't it better to take refuge in the shelter of Yahveh's warmth and wise, guiding Presence, rather than in satanic forces?

People with atavistic personalities, or personalities susceptible to pareidolia, are easier for psychopaths to control and influence, because they are more open to having their fears manipulated by psychopaths. If we happen to be one of these people prone to atavism or pareidolia, then we need to strengthen our belief in the power of Yahveh to guide us and give us courage.

---

[a] Before 12,000 years ago

Dealing with psychopathic and sociopathic values in society

Atavism and pareidolia are golden gifts to religious psychopaths. I now realise that, if you study the overall effect of Yahveh's teaching – God's principles, affirmations and laws – they actually make it difficult for someone with PPD to gain a foothold. At the top end of the scale, in the Israelite religion a king (the warrior-defender of a people) must never be High Priest – or any kind of priest for that matter; and a priest can never be king. Imagine what it would be like if a psychopath were a king *and* a priest! And in the Israelite religion, a priest should never own land, or seek political power – which is unfortunately what happened with the Sadducees. But where are they now? God dealt with them; God has good and wise reasons for giving us the rules and laws we have.

Here's another example: In the Israelite faith, charity is not a choice; debt has to be forgiven every 7 years; you have to leave some of your crop for the poor; and so on. Many people might see these rules as oppressive and difficult to follow in hard economic times, but they are there, in my humble opinion, for our protection as much as anything else. And if people with PPD do gain some ascendency in society, then God will deal with them. God has given us laws for our protection!

A lot of 'normal' people unfortunately seem to be fascinated by these individuals at the same time as being unsettled by them. Most normal people appreciate rules, but also like the freedom to break them occasionally. There is therefore a kind of subconscious envy for psychopaths, because they care nothing about rules.

This subconscious envy for rule-breaking has caused not a few people to admire psychopathic risk-takers, even though they are controlling and aggressive. This admiration has enabled people with PPD to mislead and manipulate the rest of us. Society in general has been led by the nose by psychopaths and they can't see it. Society has given them permission to be in charge; we have been fooled into legally giving them power over us to the point where, for example, there is nothing we can do to stop a world financial crisis.

We have to stop giving them that permission. We have to stop admiring the rich and powerful, stop trying to emulate them, stop trying to solve problems *their* way. If we stop yearning for what they crave, then they can have no hold over us.

A *ba'al shav* – someone with psychopathic personality disorder – loves to argue; they will argue even when they are blatantly wrong. Arguments are an excellent opportunity for them to take influence your thoughts and emotions, so the only way to counter this is to walk away and not argue. Reasonable people can be swayed by reasonable argument; people with PPD cannot be swayed. They cannot be made to see reason, they cannot be reformed, or redeemed. Don't try to make a connection or rapport with a psychopath either, because it won't mean anything to them, and will be utterly pointless.

In advise you not to follow their rules, because they like to be in charge. Don't argue with them, because they enjoy the fight. Don't flatter them, because they think they are the centre of the Universe *anyway*. Don't fall for their flatteries or charms, because there is always a hidden agenda, and you will be the loser. And I have realised now that there is no point in threatening them or reprimanding them, because it has no effect. It may help *us* to let off steam, but don't expect any result from *them*.

The only way to beat these values is to reject them, wholesale. The spiritual betterment of humanity is being held back by these *ba'aley shav* and their atavistic sympathisers, whose uncompromising and oppressive views are much better suited to a more primitive, unenlightened era in human history.

There is a petitionary call in Israelite culture that sums up the ultimate solution: "May Yahveh judge between you and me".[a] We assert God's ways, remind people of them, follow them and encourage others to do so as well, but in the end, it is Yahveh who is Judge.

In my humble opinion, I think that people like Yochanan the Immerser, Yeshua` and Jacob the Pious all understood this problem without knowing why. Since the impending catastrophe was so immediate time-wise, Yeshua`'s first followers had to opt out of the money-focussed economy of their day (which in effect, denied those with PPD any power over them). Instead, they followed a parallel path of operating under God's rules. Eventually, God dealt with the psychopathic personalities of that time – Jacob the Pious warned them that their money would be taken away from them, their land and property would be seized, and they would lose everything.[b]

At that time, the Galilee and Judea were controlled by a wealthy elite, often referred to as the Herodians. They and people like them eschewed Yahwist values, ignoring charity and debt remission. Instead they embraced values which in psychological terms can only be described as psychopathic – greed, lack of compassion or concern for others, lack of remorse for the harm they did to the poor, hunger for power, and so on. Yeshua`'s community therefore embraced values which were the only way to deny power to the psychopathic personalities that were leading them to ruin and destruction. In effect, the solution was to live a parallel way of life that denied *ba'aley shav* their power. In this

---

[a] Gen 16:5, 1Sam 24:12-15
[b] Ig. Yq. 4:7-12, Letter of James 5:1-6

respect, two important values we can apply today are: buy only what you need, and live according to your means. Don't be afraid; trust Yahveh's ways and teachings to bring results, because I say this to you: there will come a day when not only humanity, but also God will not be able to tolerate this cruel oppression any longer.

How sociopathic values endanger Religion

Having read the last three articles, you might be wondering, 'How is this all relevant to the teaching of Yeshua`? How is this pertinent to the Israelite faith?'

Yeshua`'s ministry began as a ministry of Yahveh's peace, compassion, justice and love. It began as a separation from the values of the greedy, oppressive, manipulative and heartless elite. However, after three or four centuries, it had *become* the elite – to the point where religious leaders in late Medieval times had more power than secular or temporal leaders. All the psychopathic values I have tried to speak about in the last three articles brought about that situation.

Yeshua`'s ministry called to the outcast, the poor, the dejected and the despairing; it gave them a place outside of the values of those whose only desire was for money and power – values which had oppressed many in Yeshua`'s audience. When set apart from the corruption which wealth and power brings, the human soul is freed to live a way of holiness of spirit – one that allows humanity's spirit to immerse itself in the purifying fire of Yahveh's glory.

However, when a religion tries to include the *ba`aley shav* and make an accommodation with their sociopathic values, they create an entry point for these individuals to manipulate that religion into serving their needs; some will eventually try to take over that religion, and then turn it into a vehicle for making money and gaining power over others.

I have met sociopathic individuals who claim to have been saved by faith in 'Jesus Christ', but on further questioning them, their values and attitude has not changed – they are still sociopaths. The only things that have changed are their priorities and allegiances, otherwise they are till sociopaths.

If one allows the unclean of heart into a religious community on faith alone, without any real change in values or outlook, then inviting in those individuals whose very nature is to manipulate others for their own ends, is like bringing an unclean animal into the Holy of Holies.

There are those who equate saving everyone with making everyone belong to the same religion, but this is like insisting that everyone become a bus driver or a doctor; it is not God's will that every human being on earth belong to the same religion – it is not God's will that everyone become a Jew, or a Muslim, or Christian.

The Assembly of Israel is to be a kingdom of priests and a holy nation, enabling the Presence of God to dwell among us, and thereby with humanity. By allowing psychopathic values to proliferate among us, God has no option but to withdraw God's sanctifying Presence, lest we are harmed.

Psychopathic and sociopathic values ultimately corrupt that which was meant to be a vehicle for God's holiness to enter and bless the world; I therefore urge our communities to be careful over who they admit for conversion.

Poverty and the poor

Concern for the poor even in modern society is a vital test instituted by God to expose the 'lords of deception'. There are those who think that because Yeshua` spoke up for the poor, and spoke out against the injustices of the rich, that these concerns were therefore something that he himself instituted – that *he* was the originator of religious concern for the poor, and was introducing something totally new to the Jewish religion. However, the real truth is that the reason why he spoke as he did, was because his concerns were the ethics and concerns of the original Israelite faith (and ultimately, of Yahveh).

Whenever he spoke against the excesses of the rich, it was because of the standards that Yahveh and the Israelite religion demanded – standards that were being ignored in his day. Whenever the needs of the poor were being ignored, or when the poor were being treated unfairly, it was the job of prophets to speak out about them. Concern for the poor and social justice originated, not with Yeshua`, but with Yahveh; they were not invented in the first century, but rather given to Israel as vital principles at Sinai, a full one and a half thousand years *before* he was born.

Yahveh is the Sovereign Ruler of the Universe; therefore, all life and all land belongs to God, and we humans are merely tenants. As a result God claims rent – the ten per cent tax or 'tithe' – on the land. Whereas a human ruler would then tend to misuse and squander this income, instead God uses it for the benefit of the poor. God claims a portion from God's gifts to humanity – that is, from the produce of the earth – as a share for the poor. Because God is the actual owner of the land, Yahveh claims certain portions of the produce for the fatherless and the widow, the Levite and the resident foreigner:

> *"Give generously to [the poor] and do not hold any grudge in your heart when you give to [the poor]; then because*

> *of this, Yahveh your God will bless you in all your work and in*
> *everything you put your hand to. For there will never cease to*
> *be poor people in the Land.*[a] *Because of this, I command you*
> *and I say, Open your hands wide towards your brothers, and*
> *towards the poor and needy in your land."*[b]
>
> *"If there is a poor person amongst you in any of the towns*
> *of the land that Yahveh your God is giving you, do not be hard-*
> *hearted or tight-fisted toward your poor. Rather be open-*
> *handed and freely lend them whatever they need."*[c]

Even the poor were expected to give a small part of what they received from God. Now, ten per cent of a poor person's income may not seem much to most people, but it is a lot to someone with next to nothing (remember the tale of the Widow's mite)?[d] However, if the charity system functioned properly, one could console oneself with the assurance that what a poor person would receive back in return for *their* 10 per cent, should far outweigh what they originally gave.

That is why even the poor considered it a sacred duty to give back to God a portion of what they received from God from the earth, because they expected their just and compassionate God to take care of them.

For this reason, a poor person should not feel embarrassed to receive charity, nor refuse to accept charity. If one refuses charity, one is putting an obstacle in the way of another person fulfilling their duty to God. One is also in effect turning away from God's generous hand, because charity is a sacred gift directly from God. In the West, we have also been conditioned by the *ba'aley shav* to think that charity is an insult, because that means that *they* then do not have to be charitable or generous.

An important concept to realise within the Israelite religion is that the poor and destitute are under the especial protection of God, who is *"Father of the fatherless and judge* (= warrior-defender) *of the widows."*[e]

The cry of the poor must be answered, in case God, who *'executes judgment on behalf of the fatherless and the widow,'*[f] hears it and punishes those who remain deaf to the call,[g] because *'When he* [i.e. the

---

[a] because of the failings and unfortunate nature of human society
[b] Deut. 15:10-11
[c] Deut 15:7-8
[d] S.Yesh 142 – cf Mk 12:41-44, Lk 21:1-4
[e] Deut. 10:18; Ps. 68:6, 15
[f] Deut. 10:18
[g] Ex. 22:20-25, Christian bibles 22:21-26

poor] *cries out to Me, I will hear, for I am compassionate.*[a] This is because the poor are *"My people,"* says Yahveh.[b] Furthermore, Yahveh says, *'If your brother becomes poor . . . you shall relieve him that he may live among you.'*[c] They are *"of your own flesh,"* and when you see them naked you should cover them, and give them food when they are hungry, and shelter them when they have been cast out.[d] The rich and powerful who refuse to listen to the cry of the poor and the weak, will in turn have their prayers ignored by God.[e]

The responsible men and women of wealth

As I go forward from here, it is vital for you as my readers to understand that neither I, nor Yahwist theology – or even God for that matter – is against rich people *per se*, or even against wealth.

The wealthy person who is responsible does not go out of their way to destroy or humiliate others. They are a source of good, of positive social influence, of reform, of example and of benefit to human society. They give of their wealth to help others, and their society is visibly a better one for their standing within it. These charitable philanthropists are admired and respected by others, and they are blessed by God. Such men and women realise the true value of money – as the means by which truly great things can be achieved for the betterment of their society.

There was an old concept known as '*la noblesse oblige*'. This was a phrase for the principle that, with high social standing comes a responsibility for those under you. I think what the nobility who coined that phrase understood and realised long ago, but what the wealthy elite today ignore at their peril, is its implication for society as a whole.

The prophet Yeshua` taught the biblical concept that the leader was the servant of all. He said, *'You know that the rulers of the Gentiles lord their authority over them, and those in positions of leadership arrogantly hold their authority over them. But it shall not be so among you. Rather, whoever would be great among you must be your servant, and whoever would be first among you must be slave to all.'*[f]

With high social rank come obligations. In a Yahwist society, the nobility have a duty to protect the least in their society. There are some obstacles that the poor alone cannot move. If the poor and destitute have good reason to respect and stand beside those of higher social rank, **then**

[a] Ex 22:27
[b] Isa 3:15
[c] Lev. 25:35
[d] see Isa. 58:7
[e] Prov 21:13
[f] S.Yesh. 149:1-2 – cf Mk 10:42-44

there is nothing that such a society cannot achieve. Greater still, there is no enemy who can stand against them, no foe they cannot defeat.

This was the foundational principle underpinning Yahveh's ideal of a king. You have to realise that in those days 3,000 years ago, the kings of the earth had no interest in anything but their own aggrandisement, power and wealth. The only things they cared about were the accumulation of more gold, land, herds, slaves, finery and influence than anyone else.

Yahveh forbade Israelite kings from behaving like this. Yahveh knew that a king who cared for and looked after his people – regardless of their station in life – would have a people behind him whom he could count on to defend their nation and their way of life *no matter what.* Such a nation would be a formidable one.

Israel was originally a remarkably egalitarian society. When King Ahab of Israel wanted Naboth's land, Naboth basically told him 'No way.'[a] Ahab, who had been brought up within Israelite culture, accepted this chastisement, because he knew he had no right to take the ancestral land of one of his people. His Gentile wife Jezebel, on the other hand, could not understand how an ordinary person like Naboth could rebuke his own king; one of her own people would never speak to their king in such a manner and say 'no' to him.

As time went on, the kings of Israel and Judah forgot Yahveh, and started to behave more and more like the kings of other nations. They abandoned the ideal that Yahveh had set for them, and in the end, the story of Israel's relationship with her kings became a long list of woes and miseries. It ended up just as Yahveh had warned centuries earlier through the prophet Samuel:[b]

> *'He (the king) will take the best of your fields and your vineyards and your olive groves and give them to his servants. He will take a tenth of your grain and of your vineyards and give it all to his officers and to his servants. He will also take your menservants and your maidservants and your best young men and your donkeys and press them into his own service. He will take a tenth of your flocks, and you yourselves will become his servants. Then you will cry out on that day because of your king whom you have chosen for yourselves.'*

After such a sorry royal history, I guess it was little wonder that the

---

[a] 1Kgs 21:3
[b] 1Sam 8:14-18. Before that, Israel was alone among all the nations of the earth in having no human king; Yahveh alone was her king.

Jewish people longed for a just and fair king – a messiah who would defend and save us. If we had but realised and remembered that we already had one – Yahveh, who could always be relied upon to be just and fair, and who was more than able to defend and save us.

The bottom line is that those of high rank, and those who have wealth, have a responsibility to their society. They cannot tell the less well-off that they have to contribute to society, *if they do not do the same themselves* (employing people on less than minimum wage is not 'contributing to society'). If each level of society does not play an equal part, then the lowest levels of society will reach a stage where they feel they have no investment or interest in that society. Countries where the gap between the rich and the poor are greatest, are also the most unstable and most crime-ridden.

There is one final thought for governments to consider when imposing bad fiscal policies which create unstable social conditions. Teenage minds are very adaptable, constantly seeking out the new and the different.[a] More than any other age group, they are better able to acclimatise themselves to adverse circumstances. If adults create negative and unstable social conditions through neglectful fiscal and political policies, teenagers will be the first to react and adapt to those negative conditions – and not in a good way.

You see, society changes most rapidly when negative conditions are encountered by the teenage generation, simply because they have no good reason to accept what has gone before them. Social and cultural stability will only occur when adults create the right conditions. That means not enacting policies that destroy the ability of parents to devote time, money and guidance to their children. If teenagers lack proper guidance from their parents (and to a lesser extent, their grandparents), and lack the fall-back of a healthy, stable society, they will revert to base human instinct and become feral.

The problem of the rich who are irresponsible

Let me tell you a parable:

> *There was a very rich man who would not listen to the*

---

[a] *National Geographic Magazine*, Oct 2011 'The Science of Teenage Brains', by David Dobbs. Between the ages of 12 and 25, the brain undergoes a massive reorganisation and rewiring process; whatever happens to us during this period, will affect the outcome of our personalities for the rest of our lives. However, 'Studies show that when parents engage and guide their teens with a light but steady hand, staying connected but allowing independence, their kids generally do much better in life.'

cries of the poor around him. Each day he would hear the pleas of those who worked in his fields and orchards for him to pay them a more reasonable wage, but he would merely tell them that he needed all his wealth for himself.

Then his country was engulfed in famine and terrible hardship, and people came to him for relief, but he would simply tell them, 'Be grateful for what I pay you; if it wasn't for me, none of you would have any jobs.'

Then his country was invaded and engulfed in war, and the rich man lost everything – all his family, his land and property. In desperation he went to his former labourers and asked them for help, but none of them had anything to give him. They said to him, 'When you were rich, you should have shared your wealth, so that when hardship befell our country, we could have helped you and each other, but now we have nothing, and you have nothing either.'

Of what use was his wealth to him then – the riches that he had hoarded for himself in the last days before the war?

It is an unfortunate truth that human beings look after their own; we are naturally tribal. The rich take care of the rich, and the working class look after the working class. The rich resent having to help those less well-off, and the less well-off resent the successes of the rich. This way of thinking is an immature and psychologically child-like way of thinking. God's way of thinking, by contrast, is emotionally mature and adult.

Human society is one family, albeit a very big one. You cannot favour one child over another – one section of society over another – otherwise you will breed resentment, which festers over time and eventually fragments that society. Governments fail in their social responsibility by favouring one social class over another. The Yahwist ideal is to give no particular social class any preference.[a]

In the Israelite way of thinking, the rich get their wealth through God's providence,[b] and the poor receive their lifeline when people better off than them follow God's poor laws. Both owed God.

The functioning of a just and fair Israelite society, living according to God's laws, meant that it was vital that everyone played their part, from the very richest to the very poorest. Otherwise it simply didn't work. If you wished to be a part of a fully functioning Yahwist society and enjoy its benefits – if you wished to be able to take both wealth and

---

[a] Lev 19:15 'Show neither partiality to the poor nor favouritism to the great...'
[b] see e.g. Ecc 5:19

charity from it – you had the responsibility to give back to that society too. This principle applied to the rich and influential, as well as the poor and destitute.

Unfortunately, as time went on, the rich and powerful, and also many ordinary people who just couldn't be bothered, ignored the righteousness of God's laws, and the poor went without. As a result, whenever God chose and sent out God's prophets to speak, through them Yahveh often reminded people that they were ignoring the poor at their peril:

> *'Listen to this, you who devour the destitute, and annihilate the poor, . . . you who buy the poor for silver, and sell the destitute for a pair of sandals . . . I will never forget any of your wrongdoing . . . I will turn your festivals into mourning, and your songs into funeral dirges.* [a]
>
> *"Learn to do right! Seek justice, encourage the oppressed! Defend the cause of the fatherless, and plead the case of the widow! Your rulers are rebels, companions of thieves; they all love bribes and chase after gifts. They do not defend the cause of the fatherless; the widow's case does not come before them."* [b]

Yahveh put forward the prophets to rail against those who *"issue oppressive decrees, to deprive the poor of their rights, and withhold justice from the oppressed of My people, making widows their prey and robbing the fatherless."* [c]

These are the teachings of Yahveh! The Book of Proverbs [d] says, *'He who oppresses the weak and needy is a poor man; because he is like a driving rain that leaves behind no crops.'* Many rich people, then as now, believed that the poor were poor because it was their own fault. Therefore they did not deserve to be helped. In those days, the poor were therefore seen as a resource from which taxes could be extorted, and the means by which a comfortable living could be made.

Today, rich people moan that if only the poor worked harder and were more enterprising, they could be as wealthy as the rich elite. But if everyone had a million pounds/dollars/shekels, then surely resources would be priced accordingly. Bread would be something ridiculous like £100 a loaf, and other basic items would not be far off something similar. If *everyone* was rich, who then would work for them? Whom would they

---

[a] Amos 8:4, 6-7, 10
[b] Isa 1:17, 23
[c] Isa 10:1b-2
[d] Prov 28:3

pay to clean their homes, grow and gather in the crops that feed them, make the latest fashions for them to wear, or manufacture their iPods, iPhones and plasma TVs? Most people who are excessively rich cannot see that in order for them to be rich, the majority have to be less fortunate than them.

It seems unjust that in a world where the poor struggle to survive, that they suffer the most in public spending cuts and tax rises, and the rich get off fairly lightly; or else they can afford to pay tax accountants who can arrange for them to pay as little tax as possible. The wealthy argue that the rich need to keep their money, so that the economy can be kick-started, and wealth created. But the truth is, that if the rich are given wealth, more often than not *it stays with them*; in such situations, wealth *is* created, but only for the rich – there is no such thing as 'trickle-down economics'. Rich business people might be able to provide more jobs, but surely if ordinary people – the majority of the population – have no leeway between what they earn and what they have available to spend just to survive, then the economy stagnates.

The irresponsible among the rich complain that the poor are lazy and workshy, and not playing their part in society. While this may be true of a small minority, some rich people do not play their part either – they do not give back to society in proportion to what they have taken from it.

In Israel, there is a particular way of looking at how the Sea of Galilee and the Dead Sea function. The Sea of Galilee has an inlet and an outlet – water flows into it, and water flows out of it. As a result, it is a living lake, full of life, sustaining everyone who depends on it. By contrast, the Dead Sea has an inlet, but no outlet – water flows in, but never leaves. As a result, it is a dead lake; nothing can live in it. Wealth and charity are like the two seas. A charitable person is like the Sea of Galilee – money comes in, and money goes out, and as a result, that person is spiritually alive – a source of blessing to everyone around. But a person who hoards wealth – who gathers in wealth for themselves, but never gives anything back to society – is like the Dead Sea. As a result, that person is spiritually dead, and nothing of any worth can ever grow within them.

I can see our economic situation getting worse if these injustices are not dealt with. I can see the day is coming, when the economic hardship experienced by society will be worse than anything in living memory. If the irresponsible among the rich do not play their part in society, then God will ensure that their wealth is taken from them – and it will be as a result of what they have done themselves.

As I have previously mentioned, in countries where the wealth divide is greatest, there is a frightening degree of crime and social instability. So to the rich who pay themselves vast fortunes, while fighting against decent wages for their employees; and to those who treat the international financial system with reckless avarice, I say this: **Do you despise your country so much, that you are willing to see your country fall into ruin?** Do you have so little respect for your nation, that your greed is more important to you than the pride you have in your country?

The other extreme – poverty for all

There are some who advocate that we take all Yeshua`'s words at their most literal, face value. They say that *no one* should own anything at all, no one should buy anything, no one should have a house, buy food or clothing or plan for the future (because these will come to you if you have faith and don't worry about anything); no one should work or pay taxes, save money or have any responsibilities; that we should all abandon our children and parents (because you should hate your family and love God instead).

If absolutely *no one* worked or cared where their next meal was coming from – I mean, *absolutely* no one – then with 8 billion people on the planet, nothing would get done, and millions of people would starve (because no one would be working to grow crops or distribute food). There would be no sanitation, no health professionals (because they would all have given up their jobs, and no one would be making medicines), and human society would devolve back to the Stone Age. No one would learn anything, children would live like wild animals, and … well, you get the picture.

Such people are focussing on a tiny few of Yeshua`'s sayings, and are not taking his overall ethos into account, or looking at the dire situation he was working with. They are also ignoring Yahveh's provisions for the greater society overall.

There was no word in Hebrew or Aramaic for 'to prefer', so to express a preference for one thing over another, you had to say you hated one thing, but loved another. Taking this literally shows an ignorance of Aramaic idioms. Yeshua` *never* intended for us to literally hate our parents – he would have been going against God's commandment to honour one's parents, and Yeshua` made a point of not going against God's Torah.

If *absolutely everyone* gave up their possessions, and bought nothing, the economy would collapse, and no one – especially those in cities – would be able to obtain even the most basic necessities to live: food, clothing, or shelter.

Yeshua`'s community of voluntary poverty was a radical and

necessary response to the terrible conditions of the time – people were taxed heavily, innocent people were put in prison for the most minor offence, and people literally starved, because they had nothing – and the system of charity that Yahveh our God had put in place to make sure no one went without, was just not working because the wealthy were not playing their part in God's plan. The object of giving tithes to the religious community, was so that the poor could be supported and fed. The religious community was the social security of the Bible.

In Yeshua's day, if you owned nothing, then you could not have anything taken away from you by debt collectors. If you earned nothing, you could not be taxed. The community relied on donors with means to support them – a rich person would be asked to give up everything they had, if their wealth had become their god.

A person seeking their place in God's plan might give up everything they owned. They might get rid of everything that meant anything to them, because they wanted to focus on what mattered in life. Such a person would follow this path of voluntary poverty in order to get their spiritual priorities right.

To be a Follower of Yahveh is to be sensible and practical. God expects us to be responsible and look after one another. Taking Yeshua out of his Jewish context and culture, leads people to both extremes – extreme greed or extreme irresponsibleness and stupidity. A Follower of the Way learns wisdom from Yahveh, and understands that there is a balance to everything – that congregations should not idolise their leaders, or lavish ridiculous amounts of money on their buildings; but rather everyone should contribute their skills to the life of the community, in whatever capacity they are able to; and that the organisation of the congregation should use their income wisely, spend it on what is needed, and support those in need.

Yahwist economics and modern Capitalism

I am not an economist. I just wanted to make that clear from the outset. I write what I write here from the gut feeling of my Yahwist soul. Although I mostly comment on what is happening in the UK, one could also look at any economic and social injustices around the world, and you can be sure that God is displeased with them too.

The current economic crisis[a] highlights some pretty unfair business practices. Bosses fight tiny pay increases for their employees tooth and nail, yet award themselves massive pay rises and bonuses beyond all

---

[a] This article was written around the time of the global financial collapse of 2008.

reason. Tax and price rises nullify the effective spending power of most pay increases. As a result, gross pay grows over time, while real disposable income stays the same.

Laws are sometimes passed in national parliaments based on the demands of those who are wealthy enough to pay for lobbyists, and not on the real and fair needs of their country. Financiers cannot see that it is their excesses, and not their jobs or social status, which anger ordinary people, who are then driven to protest against them. Banks are bailed out with public money, and then the top management pay themselves bonuses out of that money.

Recently in Britain, it was reported that wealthy businessmen often avoid paying council tax.[a] Large companies, who owe millions in back taxes, are regularly treated with leniency[b] – some even being let off paying – while smaller companies and private individuals are hounded until they pay back every last penny. All these injustices accumulate over time, giving ordinary people the impression that the rich can get whatever they desire, even if it is morally unfair or against the law.

It seems to me that for the most part, the world's economy is run by, and for the benefit of, the exceedingly rich. Banks and financial centres take unwise risks with trillions, and wreck the economies of countries all over the world. There doesn't seem to be *anything* that any ordinary man or woman in the street can do to stop the economy of their country from collapsing – we did nothing wrong, yet we suffer for it. We never wanted to play the markets or engage in hostile takeovers; we just wanted a roof over our heads, to feed our children and pay our bills.

Frightening economic catastrophes materialise around us, and there doesn't seem to be anything we can do about it. They happen beyond our control. There is nothing we can do to stop big men from letting their greed run away with them, selling money that doesn't exist (e.g. 'short selling' – selling something before you actually have it), or putting out vicious and entirely false rumours that ruin the economies of whole nations in order to make a few fast bucks.

The idea of striving for more and more profit confuses me, especially when it is in businesses that do not produce goods that we actually need, or to compete with rapidly expanding economies like China and India. I can understand the need for profit in order to grow and invest in companies that produce the useful things or necessities of life, but profit for profit's sake in products that are not vital for the healthy functioning of society, or to outdo mega-economies that we

---

[a] Miles Brignall, *The Guardian*, 9 March 2012
[b] Report by the Public Accounts Committee, reported in the Daily Mail, 20th Dec 2011

cannot hope to overtake, seems pointless to me.

In our western economic system, a company is judged to be successful purely on the profit it makes. In order to make more profit, you need to sell more; in order to sell more, your customers need to earn more so they can buy what you're selling; in order to earn more, their employers need to make more profit. It seems to be a pointless circle. It seems futile to persuade us to buy things we don't actually need, or *more* than we need – how often do goods once bought with enthusiasm sit unused and unloved in a closet or garage somewhere? How often do we throw stuff away when we realise we have bought too much? How often do we buy food in 'two for one' offers, and then end up throwing the extra food we don't need away? It is all money wasted.

There has to be a way ordinary people can create wealth among ourselves without it getting into the hands of the exceedingly rich, AND without putting impossible strains on the planet. With the present system, all we are doing is making money for *them*, not for us, and grinding the Earth to a standstill.

Communism, as an economic and political system, has shown itself a failure. We might be tempted to look at our own western system, and claim it is preferable. However, looking at the incredible amount of debt that such a large percentage of us find ourselves in, makes me think that our present system is not so perfect either. Our consumerist economy covertly uses psychological pressure to convince us that we want things we don't actually need. Consumerism pressures us into thinking that we can become better and happier people simply by buying and possessing more.

I'm not suggesting in any way that we get rid of our capitalist system; what I am saying is that we need to put safeguards in place that control its *excesses,* or figure out some way to protect ourselves from the excesses of the greedy. When I began research for this article, I soon learned there are hundreds of economic systems out there. For example, in the Incan Empire, they had no money, and no tax. Public works were paid for by getting individuals to work part of their labour year for the state.

In Britain and Canada, small groups of people participate in a system called L.E.T.S. ('Local Exchange Trading System'). Wealth is created by the work available to be done, and by one's ability to work, *not* by the money available to pay someone for it. It is like a bartering system, but with LETS, you give the guy who mowed your lawn a barter note for an agreed amount of 'local exchange units', and he can put that into a special account. When he finds someone with something he actually wants, he can then pay an agreed number of units for it. With our current economic system, you have to have money to pay for things.

But with a LETS system, if you have work to be done, or if you are able to do work, or if you simply have something that can be exchanged for something else, then you can create wealth.

Of course, that's just one system. We *need* a free, market economy. But the way that market economy works has to change. In order to function successfully in the present system you need to be aggressive, ruthless, greedy, brutal and pitiless – completely insensitive to the effects of your actions on ordinary people. For the majority of us who do not share these undesirable, psychopathic qualities, real wealth remains for the present out of reach. There needs to be a way in which you and I can become comfortable, obtaining our basic needs and have a little extra to enjoy time with our families, and give them occasional treats. It seems to me that 'the pursuit of happiness' has a lot more going for it than the unbridled pursuit of wealth.

Biblical Yahwist economics envisaged that people would buy and trade mostly in what they *needed*; the land belonged to God and was viewed as the root source of all provision; tax was 10%, and no interest was to be charged on loans. And every Jubilee Year,[a] land lost through debt would be returned to its original owners.

The foundation of a Yahwist society was to be social justice, compassion, the dignity of the individual and the sanctity of human life. Strangely enough, this was meant to drive biblical economics too. Remember, all this was 3,500 years ago;[b] while all the societies around her were driven by the principle of 'everything belongs to the king/priests/elite, and the economy serves them', Israel was to be driven by a more egalitarian ideal that was unique for her time. Perhaps even today, when most economies have wealth concentrated in the hands of the few, and when consumerism blinds ordinary people to common sense, Yahwist economics is still centuries ahead of her time. There would still be rich and poor, but no one would be obscenely rich, and no one would have to struggle for the basic necessities of life.

The Yahwist ideal was the spiritual well-being and happiness of the individual, as well as the justice, stability and cohesion of society. Unfortunately that didn't always happen. 'Greed was good' even in those days. People made the mistake then even as now, that 'The more we have, the happier we will become.' This is a dangerous fallacy, and we desperately need to realise it. The dream of 'having everything we could

---

[a] the year following every seventh Sabbatical year (i.e. the year after the 49th year of every cycle – that is, the 1st year of the next cycle) was a Jubilee year.
[b] perhaps the Israelites actually had an awareness that their system was unique in the Middle East and Mediterranean - so different from anything else around them, that it gave them an awesome realisation that it could only have come from God.

ever want' is only an attainable goal for the few, at the cost of the many who have to slave away to produce what the rich want, and ultimately at the cost of the planet.

Our attitudes need to change from 'I will buy everything I want' to 'I will try to obtain what I need'. There is too much peer pressure to buy what our friends and neighbours have, instead of what our families actually need. I think the well-being of the individual and the happiness of our families and households needs to become the driving force of our society, rather than the accumulation of wealth – what you need should come first.

I wonder if part of Yeshua`'s call to voluntary poverty was partly an attempt to exit the economic system that the rich controlled, and of which the poor were the powerless victims. By exiting such a system, they would deny the rich a vital section of their income; he and his followers could then start again and live by the Yahwist rules of economics, running almost in parallel to the existing system. I also think that part of Yeshua`'s ministry of healing, was to enable his followers to be well enough to earn a living; if the breadwinner was sick, there was no other income for a family.

I think that the practice within Yeshua`'s community of holding everything in common, was specifically to tackle the contemporary problem of the extorted wealth of the rich; like the Dead Sea, where life-giving water flows in but not out, so too with the rich in those days – life-giving wealth flowed only one way. By obtaining and using only what you need to live, and by giving to someone else things you no longer need, was an emergency solution to create a parallel economy, one that didn't funnel money into the black hole of the pockets of the rich.

By owning and earning nothing they could not be taxed, and by having no debts they could not be beholden to rich moneylenders.[a] Yeshua` never went to the wealthy capital of Galilee – Sepphoris – nor did he go to the affluent Gentile-dominated cities of the coast, like Joppa or Caesarea.[b] Instead, he remained only in the small towns and villages around Galilee and Judea. Jerusalem was the only big city he frequented – no doubt because of the future that he was given by God to see.

Yeshua`, it seems, was not interested in changing society from the top down. His actions suggest that he worked from the bottom upwards. If laws are imposed from the top, with no corresponding change in the

---

[a] Prov 13:8 'A person's wealth may hold their life to ransom, but the poor do not need to respond to such threats'.

[b] The gospels have Yeshua` travelling all over the Middle East, but this is highly unlikely to have ever happened, given the urgency of his mission to the Jewish people.

attitudes of society, then nothing will improve. Long term change needs a core change in the mind-set and values of those who make up a society.

Each generation also needs to be vigilant with regards to guarding those values once they are gained. I would make an analogy with how we treat naughty children. We would be fooling ourselves if we ever thought that making naughty children into well-behaved children in one generation, solved the problem once and for all – that there would never be naughty children again. The irresponsible among the rich are like naughty children, who have to be carefully reigned in with each successive generation, not by imposing laws, but by a sea-change in the attitudes and values of the common members of society itself.

God's reputation was desecrated by the greed of the rich in Yeshua`'s day

God promised the poor that God would help them – that when they cried out in their poverty, God would hear their cry. The reputation of God depended on God's ability to fulfil God's promise to come to the aid of the poor. God therefore instituted religious laws designed to ensure that the poorest in society would not be abjectly poor, and become the forgotten cast-offs of society. God's laws were designed to ensure that the rich were not obscenely rich, and that the poor were not miserably poor; God's laws envisaged a society which would not allow the two extremes to come about.

For example, when an Israelite lent money to a fellow Israelite, they were not meant to charge interest. You were also not allowed to demand conditions on a loan that would impose hardship on the borrower.[a] The prophet Yeshua` was following in the footsteps of the Israelite prophets of past generations when he said:

'Give to anyone who asks you for something on loan; don't turn away someone who wishes to borrow from you.'[b]

"Better still, give it to someone from whom you won't get anything back at all."[c]

Another example are the Sabbatical Year laws. These were designed to ensure that no one became slaves to debt. Every seventh year, all debts were forgiven – cancelled.[d] However, many rich people – including many in the ruling elite – ignored these laws, because their wealth depended on the continuance of indentured debt.

---

[a] This was how the prophets understood the sum of laws like Ex 22:25, and Dt 24:6, 24:10-13, 24:17, see also Micah 2:10

[b] S.Yesh. 33:1; cf Mt 5:42, Lk 6:30

[c] S.Yesh. 32:2; cf Lk 6:35c

[d] Deut 15:1-3

So when the rich ignored these laws, this of course meant that Yahveh could not keep God's promise to be the champion of the poor. God's reputation was therefore at stake. And to put the reputation of God's name at stake was a desecration of God's name. After the violence of the Zealots, and the corruption of the Sadducees, the greed of the rich was the third grievous sin that invited the calamitous judgment of the Day of Yahveh. That is why a prophet of God would be called to speak to the rich and demand that they repent.

Yeshua' said that such people were too busy for the kingdom of God.[a] The demands and priorities of wealth were in direct opposition to the demands of God.[b]

Ultimately, the irresponsible and greedy among the rich should not address their protests and excuses to me or anyone else on this earth; the only one who really matters when it comes to addressing ones excuses is Yahveh, the defender of the poor, and the eternal Judge of all the earth, who deals justice not only in the next life, but in *this* life too. What is dealt out by those who oppress and abuse the poor, will be returned to them in full measure by God.

The fate of the rich of Galilee and Judea during the Roman War

So what happened to the rich in Galilee and Judea when the Romans ravaged the Land during the Jewish-Roman war? Well, most of the biblical prophets spoke against the greedy rich. They knew that it was the normal practice of their enemies to first deport the rich and the elite, so that the lower classes would be more compliant.

In the time of the prophet Micah,[c] the rich devised schemes to encourage people into debt, and when they defaulted, the rich would seize their property and land. In effect, this was removing the wellspring of God's method of providing for each and every one of God's people. Because of this cruelty, through the prophet Micah, Yahveh our God warned the rich that there would be a calamitous disaster that they could not save themselves from.[d]

So what happened to the rich that the prophet Yeshua' spoke against? These were the rich whom Jacob the Pious warned would fade away to nothing,[e] and whose money would eat their flesh like fire.[f] These

---

[a] S.Yesh. 2:12 – cf Gospel of Thomas 64:12
[b] S.Yesh. 48:2 – Mt 6:24, Lk 16:13
[c] see Micah chapter 2
[d] Micah 2:3
[e] Ig. Yq. 4:6b – cf Letter of James 1:11b
[f] Ig. Yq. 4:9b – cf Letter of James 5:3b

were the rich who only fattened themselves for the day of slaughter.[a]

When the Romans destroyed Jerusalem and laid waste to Judea, the rich lost their properties, their businesses, their lands and their workforce. Some rich tried to flee with their riches, to get away from Jerusalem as it was being besieged. They took to swallowing their gold and silver coins. Some Roman soldiers and Syrians, however, realised that the rich were doing this, so they captured and eviscerated those who fled Jerusalem,[b] to get their hands on the gold and silver inside them.

This then was the known, recorded, historical fate of the rich who ignored the laws of God with regard to the poor.

The earth as the source of God's provision

The modern western economy is based on the concept that it is human work that earns money, and that money is then spent. In the world of finance, you can even invent the concept of money that doesn't even yet exist, and then speculate on it. Fortunes can be made from the confidence that people have in this imaginary finance, or lost when people lose confidence in it. However, God's economy is based on what the earth can provide, rather than what humans can create for themselves.

I have already mentioned that it is through the earth that God provides for us. The psalmist said:

> *The earth belongs to Yahveh*
> *and everything in it –*
> *the world,*
> *and all who live in it.*[c]

We have a duty to look after the land, because if we do not follow God's commandments concerning the land, the land will not provide. There is a saying in Israel: 'More than the Jewish people need the Land, the Land needs the Jewish people.' Inherent in this is the belief that the Land needs the Jewish people – ostensibly people who know how to look after it – to take care of it properly.[d]

The Book of Leviticus[e] tells us, *'If you follow My decrees and are*

---

[a] Ig. Yq. 4:11b – cf Letter of James 5:5b
[b] Jospehus, *Wars of the Jews*, Bk 5, Ch 13, passages 4-5
[c] Ps 24:1; cf Deut 10:14
[d] When the first waves of Jewish immigrants returned to Palestine in the modern era, before the foundation of the modern state of Israel, the entire Ottoman province of Palestine was a treeless, desert wasteland, no longer the 'land flowing with milk and honey' as it was in biblical times.
[e] Lev 26:3-4

careful to obey my commands, I will send you rain in its season, and the soil will yield its crops and the trees of the field their fruit.' Now, what appears in the chapter preceding this verse are the Sabbatical and Jubilee laws. They speak of letting the land lie fallow and uncultivated every seven years. Additionally, the year after every seventh Sabbatical year is a Jubilee year, and during that year, every plot of land lost through debt returns to its original owner.

Connected to these laws about the land, are laws concerning finances and the poor. We are to look after the land, as well as the poor of that land.[a] All this gives us the sense that living in a society that takes care of its land, and looks after its poor, will be a land that God will cause to be abundant and fruitful.

There has been an unfortunate tendency in modern times to believe that the earth was given over by God into the power of human beings, and that we are here to subdue and own it, using it for our own ends. Coupled with that has been a longstanding reaction against the pagan worship of nature; people have sought to control nature to show that it had no supernatural power.

The origins of this control over nature come from an unfortunate misinterpretation of the first chapter of Genesis. According to the NIV version, verse 28 says, *'God blessed them* [human beings] *and said to them, "Be fruitful and increase in number; fill the earth and* **subdue** *it.* **Rule** *over the fish of the sea and the birds of the air and over every living creature that moves on the ground."'*

From this verse, we have derived an apparent understanding that we are supposed to *a)* increase in population and spread out over the earth, and *b)* 'subdue' the earth and everything on it. Furthermore, we are to control and rule over all life on earth. All this has led to the unfortunate mind-set that the earth and all life on it belong to *us*, and are *ours* to do with as we please; that human beings are the pinnacle of life, and life on earth exists for *our* benefit.

This way of thinking has led to the extinction of hundreds of species of plants and animals, and the human manipulation of land and water[b] has had disastrous consequences.

The human subjugation of the earth seems to be justified by an earlier verse:[c] *'Then God said, "Let us make man in our image, in our*

---

[a] e.g. Lev 25:35-38

[b] Such as canalising or straightening rivers, so that in the rainy season, water has nowhere to go except to flood over its artificial banks; building on floodplains, so that people living there are at risk of flood; or diverting rivers to feed heavy industry or agriculture, so that lakes dry up (good example of which is the Aral Sea).

[c] Gen 1:26, NIV version

likeness, and let them rule over the fish of the sea and the birds of the air, over the livestock, over all the earth, and over all the creatures that move along the ground." '

I think I can improve on the translations of both these verses. However, first I'm going to work with them to show you that our understanding of our relationship with the earth and all life on it, as derived from these two verses, is flawed.

Verse 26 seems to contain two unconnected clauses:

- 'let us make man in our image'
- 'let them rule over all living things'.

Traditionally, religious groups have asked, 'How are we like God's image and likeness, since God is invisible?' The most common answer has been, 'We are like God spiritually, in our souls.' Now, let me say that I personally believe in the soul; such a belief is very important to my own personal spirituality. However, at the time this was written, the ancient Hebrews had not yet evolved any belief in the soul. So what was the editor of this verse referring to when he wrote it? What was his conscious understanding of our likeness to God, if he did not believe in a soul?

Well, the two clauses are connected by the Hebrew word *ve-* (literally: 'and'). As I have mentioned before, ancient Hebrew was limited in its vocabulary, and individual words were often overworked, and given many different meanings according to their context. This is such a word. The Hebrew *ve-* not only means 'and', but can also mean 'then', 'even', 'especially', 'namely', 'that is', 'but', 'because', and quite a few other things.

One use of v^e- is called the *vav conclusive*. This means that the second clause is an explanation – a conclusion – of the first. In English, this means that we would translate the word as 'and so', or 'and therefore'. This implies that the way that we are like God, is in how we are to rule the earth: 'Let us make man in our image, *and so* let them rule over all living things.'

If this is the case – if we are to be like God in the way we rule over the earth – the real question we have to ask ourselves is: how does God rule over the earth? How does Yahveh look after the earth? Does God subdue and oppress the earth? Does God abuse the earth for God's own benefit? Does God make the earth bend and break according to God's whim? Does God waste and squander the resources of the earth? Let's take a look at what the Miqra says:[a]

"God makes springs pour forth water into the rivers, and

---

[a] Ps 104:10-18

the rivers to flow between mountains.

They give water to all the wild animals; even the wild asses quench their thirst.

The birds of the sky dwell beside them; from amongst branches they put forth their voice.

God waters the mountains from his lofty heights; the earth is sated from the result of God's work.

God makes grass grow for the cattle, and vegetation for human beings to cultivate, bringing forth food from the earth

– wine that gladdens the human heart, oil to make our faces shine, and bread that sustains the human heart.

The trees of Yahveh are well looked after, and the cedars of Lebanon that he planted

– there, where the birds make their nests; where the stork makes its home in the pine trees.

The high mountains God made for the wild goats; the crags as a refuge for hyraxes.

From this we can see that Yahveh looks after the earth with great care, with concern for the welfare not only of human beings, but also of wild animals, wild plants and the natural structure of the very Earth itself. Take a look at those two verses from Genesis again, retranslated this time with the care of God as its primary image:

*And God said, "Let us make human beings in our image, according to our likeness; **and so** let them have dominion over the fish of the sea, and over the birds of the sky, and over the domestic beasts, and over every reptile and insect that crawls upon the ground. ... Then God blessed them, and said to them, "Be fruitful and multiply; replenish the earth, and make it abundantly fruitful;*[a] *and take guardianship over the fish of the sea, and over the birds of the sky, and over all life that crawls upon the ground."*

What this new view of Gen 1:26-28 implies, is that we are to be like God and **look after** the earth, making it abundantly fruitful – replenishing the earth, and making it more fruitful and more full of life than it would have been if left to its own devices.

Yahveh promises that if we look after the earth, and follow God's teaching, then God will *'send rain in its season, and the ground will yield its crops and the trees of the field their fruit. Our threshing will continue*

---

[a] this is based on the assumption that the Hebrew verb is written with the letters kaf-beyt-**sin**, 'to force to be fruitful', and not kaf-beyt-**shin**, 'to subdue' or 'oppress'. I am aware that there are no longer any examples of this root being used as an independent verb, but what if it once was, and this is the only example of it in the Miqra?

until grape harvest and the grape harvest will continue until planting, and we will eat all the food we want and live in safety in our land. '[a]

God also warns us of the consequences of not following God's laws and not looking after the earth:

'I will take away everything they have, declares Yahveh. There will be no grapes on the vine. There will be no figs on the fig-tree, and all the leaves will be withered. What I have given them will be gone. '[b]

Yahveh is our great Provider, but only if we look after the very earth we were created to care for.

Line 8: Give us day by day

Give us ...

Bread – or more specifically, grain – is considered the fruit of the earth, and therefore from God, as I have said. The traditional Jewish blessing over bread is, "Blessed are you, O Adonai our God, King of the Universe, who brings forth bread from the earth". All *natural* things were seen as coming from God, for example: *'... doesn't God, who made the sun, cause it to rise on both the evil and the good? Doesn't God send the rain, which God has made, to fall upon the righteous and the unrighteous?* '[c]

... day by day

The Aramaic for 'day by day' is *yoma deyn u-maḥra* – literally, 'today and tomorrow'. The Hebrew equivalent of this is *yom bᵉyomo* – literally, 'a day in its day'. This expression occurs 14 times in the Miqra.

Most Galileans were so poor that they could not see beyond the needs of today and tomorrow, which is probably the origin of the Galilean Aramaic idiom meaning 'day by day'. For this reason, mentioning doing something on the third day was therefore probably a way of expressing optimism. For example, in the *New Testament*, Jesus says,[d] *'I will drive out demons and heal people today and tomorrow, and on the third day I will reach my goal.'* A free translation of this, giving the sense of the original Aramaic underlying the Greek would be, *'I will drive out demons and heal people **day by day**, but **eventually** I will reach my goal.'* In next verse[e] he says, *'In any case, I must keep going today*

---

[a] adapted from Lev 26:4-5
[b] Jer 8:13
[c] S.Yesh. 34:2-3 – cf Mt 5:45, Lk 6:35b-36
[d] Lk 13:32
[e] Lk 13:33

and tomorrow and the next day— for surely no prophet can die outside Jerusalem!' Again assuming an Aramaic original behind this, a free translation would give, *'In any case, I must keep going day by day and on and on – for surely no prophet can die outside Jerusalem!'*

A good example of the idiomatic use of 'third day' from the Miqra occurs in Hosea,[a] when the prophet says, *'In two days God will revive us; on the third day God will raise us up.'* In modern English this would give us a free translation of, 'Soon God will restore our wholeness; eventually God will restore our fortunes.'

Summary

The basic image evoked by this line acknowledges our heavenly Father as provider. It petitions God to provide our basic sustenance – the food which God provides for us from the earth – each and every day.

Illustrations from the words of the prophet Yeshua`:

Yeshua` said,

'Don't worry about tomorrow, because tomorrow will worry about itself. Let each day's trouble be enough for that day.'[b]

'Who of you by worrying can add a single cubit to the length of their days? If you aren't able to do as small a thing as that, why be anxious about greater things?'[c]

'... therefore I tell you, don't worry about your life, about what you'll eat or drink, or about your body, about what you'll wear. Because life's more than just food and drink, and the body more than just clothes.'[d]

'Look at the birds of the sky; they neither sow nor reap, nor gather their grain into granaries, and yet our heavenly Father feeds them. How much more so will God feed you!'[e]

---

[a] Hos 6:2
[b] S.Yesh 47:1-2 – cf Mt 6:34
[c] S.Yesh 43:1-2 – cf Mt 6:27, Lk 12:25-2
[d] S.Yesh. 41:2-3 – cf Mt 6:25, Lk 12:22-23
[e] S.Yesh.42:1-2 – cf Mt 6:26, Lk 12:24

'Aren't five sparrows sold for just two *assaria*?[a] And yet not one of them will fall to the ground without God knowing about it! Why, even the hairs of your head are all numbered. So don't be afraid – you're worth more than many sparrows!'[b]

---

[a] singular 'as', a Roman coin in use throughout the Roman empire. It was the smallest Roman coin available The daily wage was 1 denarius, which was made up of 10 assaria, so two assaria is a fifth of one's daily wage.
[b] S.Yesh. 46:1-4 – cf Mt 10:29-31, Lk 12:6-7

CHAPTER SEVEN: Prayer about our sins and debts

ושבק לן חובין
היכמא דאף שבקנן לחייבין

u-shbaq lan chobayn
heykhma de'af shebaqnan le-chayyabayn

And forgive us our sins,
Just as we should forgive our debtors.

The Yahwist Israelite meaning of salvation and redemption

The first people ever to hear Yeshua`'s message were Jewish. When Yeshua` spoke to his Jewish audience and talked about forgiveness, sin and being 'saved', he never had to explain to them what he meant by those terms, because as Jews, his first followers already knew what they meant. And it therefore goes without saying that *their* understanding of things like sin, salvation, redemption and atonement was a *Jewish* understanding. In this book – which attempts to convey to you, my readers, the outlook of Yeshua`'s first Jewish Followers – it would therefore be remiss of me if I did not try to explain salvation and atonement to you from a fully Jewish point of view. In this chapter therefore, I will be concentrating heavily on these topics.

Early on in my spiritual journey, discussing matters of faith with my Christian friends, I quickly learned that what I, as a Jew, meant by the words 'salvation' and 'redemption', was something entirely different to what my Christian friends meant by those same words. On more than one occasion, I would be talking about the subject, but my Christian friends would be utterly confused, because they had been brought up on an entirely different understanding of salvation – they were coming at the subject from a different premise. The positive human images I was trying to convey just weren't getting across, because they had a completely different frame of reference.

To a Christian, I guess salvation is an esoteric concept that you just have to believe in – 'You are saved by faith in Jesus Christ' is a common refrain for evangelicals. It's a theological principle that you have to grasp on an emotional and spiritual level. It's the same with forgiveness, atonement, redemption, even the Kingdom of God – they are all other-worldly, spiritual and mystical concepts that you just have to accept as matters of faith, even if you don't understand them. To be 'saved', to a Christian, means being saved from the consequences of your sins in the afterlife – a cast-iron guarantee that you will go to heaven.

Not so for a Yahwist, Hebrew Israelite. As well as being emotionally spiritual concepts, all these ideas are also very much *this*-worldly, physical things that one is able to live and experience on a tangible level, here and now.

The mainstream Christian view of salvation is that, through belief in 'Jesus Christ', you are permanently 'saved' from your sins. This seems to mean that you are cleansed of the blemish of original sin through belief alone, and you are healed from the sins that you have actually committed in your life, all guaranteeing you entry into heaven, regardless of what sins you commit *after* becoming a Christian. However, in the Yahwist Israelite mind-set, this is not salvation but more like a type of atonement, because in the Israelite understanding, atonement means being cleansed of the blemish of sin, and being renewed and made whole again – restored to spiritual health by the glory of Yahveh. The most basic process of what Christians call 'salvation' – that is, being cleansed and healed – Yahwists would call 'atonement'.

In Yahwist theology, we must always remember that it is the glory of God (the fire of the Divine Radiance) which cleanses you of your sin. The glory of God cleanses your soul whiter than snow, whiter than a fuller can ever wash them.[a] When God's glory cleanses you, and makes you whole and renews you, it is as if you had never sinned. Your sins are thereby forgotten and done away with – your burden is no more! As Yahveh says through the prophet Isaiah, *"I – and I alone – am the One who blots out your transgressions for My own sake, and no longer remembers your sins".*[b]

So the use of the word 'salvation', is a prime example of us using the same words, but assigning them different meanings.[c] A Christian is

---

[a] Malachi 3:2
[b] Isaiah 43:25
[c] There is just one quote that appears to equate healing with salvation – Jer 17:14. However, I rather think that this is saying that by healing his soul, God has *as a consequence* saved him; I do not think Jeremiah was saying they are the same thing.

'saved' by the blood and death of 'Jesus Christ', but to a Yahwist Israelite, one's soul is atoned by God through our willingness to approach the Divine Radiance ('glory') of Yahveh in a spirit of repentance and prayer. God's glory cleanses and purifies us from sin. God's glory makes of us a new person; it is God's glory that makes us whole again, not blood or death.

So what does the Yahwist understanding of the term 'salvation' refer to? When the enslaved Israelites in Egypt cried out to God, *'hoshia' na!'* ('Please save us!') they were not asking God to permanently cancel out the effects of their sins! They were asking God to *rescue* them from their impossible plight – to deliver them from oppression and slavery. When David cried out to God for salvation, he was not asking for his sins to be forgiven, he was asking God to *rescue* him from his enemies. Salvation, for the Yahwist, is when God rescues you from a situation – be it material or spiritual – that you would otherwise not have been able to escape from yourself.

For those Christians who *don't* lay emphasis on salvation through faith alone, there is a lot of angst laid up in questions like, 'What can I do to be 'saved'? What can I do towards my ultimate 'salvation'?' I guess this is another way of saying, 'What can I do in this life to ensure I get into heaven?' It is very much worrying about the future to come, rather than focussing on the present that is already here.

However, for the ancient Israelite, the biggest questions were, 'How can I live a life which is righteous in God's eyes, *so that* our enemies will not attack us, our land will prove bountiful and plentiful, the rains will come, my children will be clothed and fed, and my family will prosper?' On a spiritual level, one can ask, 'How can I live a life which is righteous before God, *so that* I will have personal inner peace, so that I will not be weighed down by the burden of my past wrongdoings, and so that I can stay on a righteous path?' You see how enormous is this difference? The Israelite concerns are very much about *this* life. And if we take care of this life, the next life will take care of itself. Salvation, in its Yahwist sense, is very much about being saved by God – *rescued* by God – from this-worldly difficulties.

There is no such thing as 'permanent salvation'

Before I go into a fuller Israelite understanding of what salvation is, let me begin with a few simple statements about how an Israelite would see salvation:

- salvation is not a state of being
- salvation is not permanent

- salvation is not earned (i.e. there's no points system)

Now, if you had a Paullist[a] understanding of salvation, those statements would not make any sense whatsoever. They might even raise a few hackles! For evangelical missionisers, 'being saved' is about 'turning to Christ' and becoming a Christian. To them, being Christian means being in a state of 'permanent salvation'. Now, in chapter 2, I told you about the pagan god Molekh. Just in case you don't remember, let me recap. Round about the 8th century BCE, belief in the Ammonite god Molekh had started reaching the Israelites. The followers of this pagan god also taught that one could attain a state of permanent salvation. One could be permanently forgiven of all one's sins, but at a terrible price: the death of a firstborn – better still, an only-begotten child. Through the death of an only-begotten child, one could be 'saved'. If yours was an only child, you had to give him up to death by passing him through fire, and you would be 'saved' permanently from your sins.

To any decent person, this would be a horrendous thought – to send one's own child to his death, simply to be forgiven of one's sins. What is more, God said so too:

*"They have built the high places of Tofeth in the Valley of Ben Hinnom to burn their sons and daughters in the fire - something I did not command, **nor did it even enter my mind**."*[b]

Inspired by Yahveh, the prophet Micah[c] makes the point with a rhetorical question: *"Shall I offer my eldest son for my wrong-doing, the child of my own flesh for my sin?"* The obvious answer is 'No!' Yahveh is a holy God, and therefore not like the pagan gods. Yahveh did not like the idea of someone dying in payment for other people's sins back then; there is no reason to think that God would change His mind later.[d]

---

[a] relating to the philosophy, attitude and theology of St Paul of Tarsus. Modern Talmidis feel that the theology and outlook of mainstream Christianity come not from Yeshua`, but from Paul (this was, as I mentioned before, the opinion of the earliest Jewish followers of Yeshua` too).

[b] Jer 7:31, cf Jer 32:35

[c] Micah 6:7b

[d] Paullist theology claims that the death of Yeshua` on the cross was the perfect sacrifice for sin, and that it is in complete accordance with Jewish law. However, according to the Hebrew bible, the only perfect sin offerings are of kosher animals. Last time I checked with the bible's definition of what is kosher and what isn't (Lev 11:1-31), neither humans nor God are kosher. Sin offerings not only have to be without blemish, they also have to be kosher.

After all, just think about that for a moment. Would you even consider giving your own firstborn over to death in order to obtain permanent salvation from your sins – even if such a thing were possible? Would you kill your own child if it would save someone from their sins? No, of course not! Such a thing rightly horrifies us. And if it horrifies *us*, as mere mortals, would such a concept not horrify Yahveh to an even greater degree? We ultimately have to wonder, if it horrifies us to even think of such a terrible thing, then why did Israelites at that time debase themselves to expect such a thing of God? As Yahwists, we *have* to fix this in our minds permanently – that the sacrificial death of anyone in payment for someone else's sin is abhorrent to Yahveh, something that would **never** enter Yahveh's mind.[a]

In complete contrast, the authentically Yahwist belief was that each action was judged on its own merit – you **cannot** be permanently 'saved' from sin, because that would mean you would be free to commit the most heinous sins without any consequence. In Yahwism, if you do wrong, then any good you may have done in the past does not count in your favour – when you are guilty of really grievous wrongdoing and are unrepentant about it, you cannot escape judgment or 'be saved' from judgment. Likewise, if a bad person repents of their wrongdoing and does right, then their previous wrongdoing does not count against them. As God says through the prophet Ezekiel:

> *"The righteousness of the righteous man will not save him* [i.e. from judgment] *when he disobeys, and the wickedness of the wicked man will not cause him to fall when he turns from it. The righteous man, if he sins, will not be allowed to live*[b] *simply because of his former righteousness."*[c]

The fundamental premise of Ezekiel and other prophets, is that no one can die or suffer the punishment for someone else's sin; it is a basic principle of the Israelite religion that no one can be made to suffer for someone else's mistakes or wrongdoings.[d]

Furthermore, one cannot cry, 'I am saved!' and then go on to lie,

---

[a] Deut 24:16 – "each shall die *(a euphemism for: 'each shall be judged and suffer punishment for')* his own sin." Also Jer 31:30, Ezek 18:20

[b] here, a Hebrew euphemism for 'to escape judgment and go unpunished'. In other instances, 'he shall live' means 'he shall be judged and be acquitted – and live a life under God's blessing' - see Ezek 18:22, 33:19

[c] Ezek 33:12

[d] Deut 24:16 – 'Parents shall not be put to death for their children, nor children be put to death for their parents; each one is to die (i.e. be judged and punished) for their own sin.'

cheat and steal – there is no permanent state of salvation; believing that there is has resulted in a group of people seeing nothing wrong with immoral behaviour, because they believe they have been saved through faith. Such behaviour would mean that one's supposed 'state of being saved' is worthless and means nothing. I have actually encountered such individuals, who believe fervently that their faith has 'saved' them, and then they have gone and done the most sinful things. You are only 'saved' (in the Christian sense) for as long as you don't commit any sins; in Yahwist theology, the next time you do wrong, your life-force becomes unwell, is diminished, and needs to be healed, cleansed and atoned again.

Bottom line: there is no such thing as 'permanent salvation'. Each action is judged on its own merit. The daily spiritual aim of the Yahwist is to look after the health of one's soul. When your soul is burdened, injured and blemished by sin and wrongdoing, you repent and approach the glory of Yahveh in prayer. For serious wrongdoing, a radical change in one's life would be required – some kind of reparation to the ones you have wronged. It is one's daily nearness to the fire of God's glory, that enables one to be 'saved' – that is, atoned and healed each day.

The Israelite meaning of Salvation

To an Israelite mind, the phrase, 'I am saved' is an odd one, considering what it actually means within a Hebrew context. You can say, 'I *was* saved by God yesterday', or, 'I feel that I am being saved by God in my current situation'; or one can say, "I was living a very bad life, and something happened to me yesterday that saved me (that is, where God intervened and changed me, healed me and set me on a new path). This is all because salvation is very much something that God *does* for us in *specific* situations, in this life.

For example, if you are in heavy debt, with no way out of your misery, and then out of the blue, someone gives you a large amount of money, God has saved you. If you are depressed and unhappy about your life, and cannot see any way out – on the point of suicide even, and then quite unexpectedly, you are given a way out, then God has saved you. If you are surrounded by your enemies, and you face certain death, and suddenly you are given a way of escape, then God has saved you. Or in the spiritual sense, you have done wrong in the past, and it weighs you down terribly – even if you have repented – and God does something, causes you to experience something, which heals and separates you from that burden of guilt, so that you can move forward – then God has saved you.

These then, are the Yahwist definitions of salvation: in the physical sense, when God rescues you unexpectedly from an impossible situation. You escape a situation you would otherwise have no other way of escaping from. And in the spiritual sense, when God's glory cleanses and heals you from the injury and blemish of your sins, which enables you to move forward with your life. A good example of the spiritual sense of salvation is when the prophet Jeremiah says, *"Heal me, O Yahveh, and I will [truly] be healed; save me and I will [truly] be saved."*[a]

Now, with such a definition, you can then understand that you do not *earn* this 'salvation' – you do not earn being rescued by God from difficult situations. It is an act of merciful blessing on God's part. You may have asked and prayed for it – for a release, a rescue, to be 'saved' from your present misfortune – but that 'salvation', that rescue, that healing, doesn't come because you are better than anyone else. Conversely, when it doesn't come, it doesn't mean that you are worse than anyone else either. Sometimes God does it 'for the sake of God's name' (that is, for the sake of God's reputation).

For example, God will save/rescue/heal someone who has done bad things, in the hope that such a miraculous event will jolt them to their senses.[b] In such a case, the saving event has a purificatory and cleansing effect – especially if the person acts on what has been done for them. Sometimes God restores a sinner to spiritual wholeness in order for their lives to turn around, and become better servants of God and more useful to their fellow human beings.

Perhaps you can now understand that things like the Covenant are absolutely nothing to do with 'salvation from sin'; nor for that matter, is circumcision. What Christians call 'Salvation from sin' is just plain forgiveness and then being atoned – a restoration of the wholeness of one's soul by the cleansing fire of God's glory – plain and simple.

I hope you can now see that the Israelite understanding of 'salvation' is very specific. In the material sense it is 'divine rescue from an impossible situation', and in a spiritual sense it is 'healing from the injury and blemish of sin so that one can move forward'. It's not an esoteric, theological concept that the heart cannot feel; you know you have had a 'salvation event', because it's *real*, tangible, and recordable in scientific terms. It's not a concept that you have to struggle with on an intellectual or even spiritual level. It's real. Yahveh's salvation of any human soul is a real-time, *this*-worldly event that you can see with your own eyes. What Christians call 'being saved' is actually being cleansed and restored by the cleansing fire of God's glory (what we call 'atonement'). Understanding salvation from a Yahwist perspective

---

[a] Jeremiah 17:14
[b] Job 33:26-28

therefore means having to completely alter your definitions of salvation and atonement entirely.

Salvation in the Hebrew Bible

Now take a look at biblical phrases where the word *yeshu'ah*[a] ('salvation') appears. In the majority of cases, you need several English words to translate the one Hebrew word.

In most instances, it means 'God's power to save/rescue us' (such as when it refers to 'God's salvation', or 'Your salvation'). When it says, 'You have become my salvation', it means, 'You have become the agent of my salvation/rescue'. When it says, 'the horn of my salvation', it means, 'the *powerful* agent of my salvation/rescue'. When it talks about being 'clothed in salvation', it means 'being clothed in the purifying effects of salvation'.

Once you understand the Hebrew meaning of salvation, you realise that the Paullist Christian use of the term has brought in more than the Israelite one was ever meant to cover. For example, it has made it synonymous with forgiveness of sin – if you are saved, in Christian terms that means being forgiven of your sin – salvation, forgiveness and atonement are all a one-step process in Paullist theology. However, in the Israelite understanding, God can 'save' a bad person, in the hope that they will then repent and *thereby* be forgiven – and they can then bring themselves into the presence of God's glory to have God atone their souls and cleanse them. In the Christian understanding, you believe, you're forgiven and thereby saved; in the Israelite understanding, you can be saved, hopefully you will then repent and God will forgive you of your sins.

Another example would be the phrase, 'the salvation of one's soul'. I guess to a Christian this would mean, 'the ultimate cleansing of one's soul and acceptance of one's soul into heaven.' In an Israelite environment, this type of salvation is spiritual healing, since sin is anything that causes a sickness of the soul. It needs to be done on a regular basis – it is not a one-time event. That's the quintessential difference between the Israelite and Christian idea of salvation.

I hope this has given you an insight into how Christianity and the Israelite religion both use the word 'salvation' differently, and its real meaning in the Israelite religion. It's not an esoteric concept to struggle with; it is God's power to rescue us from impossible situations in this

---

[a] Incidentally, the name Yeshua` does not mean 'salvation'; Yeshua` is the Aramaic form of the Hebrew name Y^ehoshua` (Joshua), which actually means '**Yahveh** saves'.

life – situations you can see and experience for yourself. The Christian concept of 'being saved', translated into Yahwist language, actually means being 'atoned' – being cleansed of the blemish and injury of sin, having one's life-force and soul restored to wholeness, and having one's mind and spirit renewed by the fire of God's glory, and by the power of the Presence of God.

Line 9: And forgive us our sins,

Forgive us …

Do our sins separate us from God?

Those of us who have grown up in a Christian environment, still have the baggage of how Paullist Christianity views sin and atonement. If any of us hope to adjust to the Israelite way of seeing things, there are many concepts we need to unlearn – ideas we need to rid ourselves of, and relearn the Yahwist Israelite idea in its place.

Here are 3 Yahwist affirmations to consider:

1. There is nothing you can possibly do that can separate you from God.

We can turn our face from God, we can disobey God, we can even separate our minds and our ways from anything to do with God,[a] but there is nothing, *NOTHING* we can possibly do to separate God from *us*. Even in our darkest, most rebellious and most disobedient hour, when God withdraws His glory and withholds blessing[b] from us, or holds back from answering our prayer,[c] our heavenly Father is still closer to us than our own breathing. We cannot run away from Yahveh. We can separate ourselves from God, but we cannot make God separate from *us*.

2. There is nothing you can possibly do that can harm God's relationship with you[d]

Many think that it would go without saying that God is unharmable, yet we still persist in ways of thinking which imply precisely that. There are a few religious people who give the impression that, by sinning, by rebelling against God, we are hurting God's relationship with us. They'll say, 'If you do bad things, God won't love you anymore,' or 'God will

---

[a] Ezek 14:, Isa 59:2
[b] which is what the phrase 'hides His face from us' means.
[c] Isa 59:2
[d] Job 35:6 *'If you make a sinful error, how can you affect God? If your sinful crimes are many, what can that do to God?'*

abandon you.'

When we do wrong, we can harm our ability to relate to God, we can damage our view of God, but we cannot stop God from loving us, or wishing the best for us, or caring about us. We cannot break God's connection with us – Yeshua`'s parables on forgiveness teach us this, such as the parable of the lost sheep, or the lost coin; we are never lost to God.

3. God is not someone who stands permanently ready to beat us and crush us when we make mistakes.

There are a lot of unenlightened religious teachers who still have this image of God – 'If you're bad, God's gonna get you', as if God were some kind of divine boogieman, or a demon like Freddie from *'Nightmare on Elm St'*. The reality of this kind of thinking is, that it creates a negative image of God, and thereby desecrates the holiness of God's reputation.

Yes, Yahveh is a God of righteous discipline; Yahveh is a God of justice, and just retribution. But there is a difference between a parent who teaches and guides their child with love, and one who stands in anger with a whip or a stick ready to beat their child over the slightest mistake. The second kind of parent is a seriously disturbed – even psychotic – individual, yet there are some people who would stubbornly persist in painting God as such a psychotic individual.

Those who insist that our sin separates us from God, quote Isaiah 59:2 which says, *'But your iniquities are barriers between you and your God; your sins have hidden his face from hearing you.'*

Now, it seems that it is saying that if we sin, God cannot hear us. This appears to be a case of not being able to look at the bigger picture.

In the UK there was a TV commercial which was a good example of how our preconceived ideas shape how we interpret what we see. As I recall, it ran something like this: a Caucasian guy in his forties was being chased by a young Afro-Caribbean guy – all in slow motion. Some people might have initially thought that the black guy was a young thug chasing an innocent white guy. Then you are told that the black guy is in fact a plain clothes police officer. So you think, *Ah, the white guy is the criminal, and he has done something wrong, so the police officer is chasing him.* Then the camera angle pans out fully, and you see that both of them are running from a collapsing set of scaffolding on a building.

Going back to Isa 59:2, those of us from a Christian background, with the emphasis on us being separated from God, and the teaching that only the death of 'Jesus Christ' can reconcile such a separation, it makes us think, *either God doesn't want to be reconciled unless there's blood and death, or God is **unable** to be reconciled unless there is blood* *sacrifice.* So when we read something like Isaiah 59:2, we automatically think that by sinning, God is separating Himself from us; and that God is 'hiding God's face' from us.

But look at it again. It's not God separating from **us**, it's **us** separating from God. Our sins have caused us not to 'see' God's face. If you read further, you see that what this all implies is that we have become stubborn and unrepentant. For that reason, God will not hear us – i.e. will not answer our prayers until we actually do repent.

The biblical expression, 'God will hide God's face from you,'[a] occurs quite frequently. Most people misunderstand this as evidence of God's separation from us, because they do not understand the Hebrew use of 'face' when speaking of God.

The best way to demonstrate the meaning of this phrase, is to look at a *positive* expression containing it. When God's 'face' shines on you,[b] it means that good fortune and blessing are given to you in your life. So when God *hides* God's face, it means that having done evil and wicked things, we are not then going to be rewarded by blessings and good fortune.

The four stages of 'the forgiveness process'

In Paullist theology, salvation, forgiveness and atonement are all more or less the same thing. However in Yahwist theology, they are all distinct stages of what is called, 'the forgiveness process'. When one has done wrong, these are the 4 stages involved in the healing of our wholeness:

1. Repentance
2. Forgiveness
3. Reparation
4. Restoration ('atonement')

One has to first of all be genuinely sorry for what one has done, accompanied by the intent that one will try one's best not to commit such an act again. This is repentance – *t'shuvah* in Hebrew.

The act of repentance brings about God's forgiveness. If the repentance is genuine, then forgiveness is immediate, and it wipes the slate clean as if one had never sinned.

Now, when we sin, the wholeness – the healthy wellbeing – of our

---

[a] e.g. Deut 31:17-20, Micah 3:4, Ps 102:2, Jer 33:5
[b] e.g. Num 6:25, Ps 4:6, Ps 119:135

soul is damaged and diminished,[a] and needs restoring (that is what is so different about the Israelite understanding of the process, one that we need to grasp). The psychological effect of this damage is that we feel guilt and pain at what we have done.

So the next step is to apologise or make reparation to the one sinned against – the one harmed willingly or unwittingly by one's words or actions. If one is unaware of the person whom one has hurt, then general acts of charity have the same effect.

This brings about the restoration or healing of the wholeness of one's being, and the 'forgiveness-process' is complete.

The last stage – restoration – is actually what atonement is. In Judaism, 'to atone' means 'to cleanse and remove the stain caused by sin'. This applies to objects (e.g. Ex 29:36) as well as people (e.g. Lev 4:20). With regard to people, atonement also restores the healthy wholeness of one's being or life-force – this is an important aspect to realise, something that is always forgotten.

Forgiveness does not come as a result of atonement; in the Israelite way of thinking, if you are not sorry, then there is no forgiveness, and no point in seeking atonement. Atonement is only possible *after* forgiveness, and forgiveness is only possible *after* repentance. Therefore, when we read Leviticus 4:35b, it cannot be saying that forgiveness comes as a result of atonement, because in the Israelite religion, that is simply not the case. Something is _completed_ at the end of atonement; therefore, one way of translating the verse is: *'In this way, the priest shall perform the atonement ritual (*ve-khipper*) for the sin that he has sinned, and the forgiveness-process will be completed (*ve-nislach*) for him'.*

So on the Day of the Atonements, we are not there to reconcile God with us, or make ourselves 'at one' with God, because you cannot separate yourself from God in the first place – you cannot break or harm God's relationship with you. On that day, you are not apart from God. Yahveh is right there with you, listening to you – the Great Counsellor, the Great Healer. Yahveh is there beside you, listening to you opening up your heart, admitting to your faults and failings, so that you can be healed and made whole again.

Everything in the Talmidi way of approaching *Yom ha-Kippurim*[b] is designed to heal, to restore, and to make whole again. It is a psychological and spiritual process that removes our hurt, takes away our anger and pain, and prepares us to approach the throne of our God to be

---

[a] see section on 'Wholeness and Perfection' in chapter 2, and the section on wholeness and shleimut later in this chapter.
[b] The biblical name for the Day of Atonement.

cleansed and made whole.

Yom ha-Kippurim – the Day of the Atonements – is a day for examination, for healing, and for restoration. On this day we draw near to the glory of God, so that our souls can be restored to full health.

Here is a summary of all the terms I have discussed in this chapter so far, giving their definitions from a Yahwist Israelite perspective:

Salvation *(y'shu`ah)*	when God rescues you from an impossible situation, or from a destructive state of mind
Redemption *(ge'ulah)*	when God delivers you from a physically bad place to a good place; or when God delivers you from a mentally bad state of mind to a good state of mind
Repentance *(t'shuvah)*	when a person has true sorrow and remorse for the wrong they have done, and returns to God's ways
Forgiveness *(slīchah)*	comes as an immediate consequence of repentance, when God cancels the penalty due to a wrongdoer for the wrong they have done
Reparation *(pitsuy)*	when a penitent person does something to make good on the wrong they have done, so that God can heal the injury of their soul; the act enables the soul to come into the presence of God's glory
Atonement *(kippur)*	when God cleanses a penitent soul of the stain and injury of its sin, and restores a soul to full health, and renews the soul; atonement occurs as a result of the soul being cleansed by the fire of God's glory

What forgiveness is for

The Paullist teaching is that sin separates us from God, but the Yahwist understanding is that we are never separated from God. The question then arises, why then does God need to forgive us? If our relationship with God was never broken, then why does God need to forgive us?

It's important to bear in mind that the forgiveness is for *our* benefit, not for God's (well, I guess that it indirectly affects God in that it heals us so that we can fulfil our individual part in God's plan, but that's another thread)!

Let me tell you a parable:

> *There was a young Roman soldier who took part in the*

destruction of the Temple in Jerusalem, in the killing of hundreds of Jewish people, and in taking thousands more into captivity as slaves. When he returned to Rome, he took some of these Jewish people as slaves for himself. While in his service, these Jewish people maintained the practice of their faith. He was moved by the strong sense of their compassion for others, and in the ethical conduct of their lives even under hardship. As the months and years went by, he learned more and more about the Jewish faith from their example.

Many years passed, and he grew old. As an old man, he eventually came to realise the full enormity of what he had done to the Jewish people, and he began to feel the pain he had caused them. He felt truly sorry for what he had done. He then felt the burden of his guilt, and reached a point where that guilt was so unbearable he became severely ill. It was so bad that his whole life came to a halt.

He finally had an opportunity to meet the descendants of those he had killed in Judea, and showed great remorse for what he had done. He told them how he could not do enough to make amends for his past wrongs. His victims were unusually moved by his words of remorse and apology, and they forgave him. When they expressed their forgiveness, the old man fell on his knees and broke down in tears.

The former soldier was no longer crushed by his guilt. He had been released by those who had forgiven him. He had been made whole, and he could go forward with his life, his slate clean. Thereafter he released all his Jewish slaves, and secretly gave regular donations to the synagogues of Rome.

When we do wrong, we damage ourselves and those around us. **We** suffer, and society suffers. God doesn't suffer, and God is not damaged. When we turn back to God in repentance, with the intent to do better, God forgives us **in order to heal us and enable us to move forward**.

I approach *Yom ha-kippurim*[a] with this kind of thing in mind, and it really is an emotional experience – to feel God's forgiveness is a joyous release. You really do feel that a burden has been lifted off your shoulders, and sometimes you end up in tears.

Whenever we mention 'our relationship with God', and 'forgiveness putting right that relationship', it's not God's part of the relationship that needs to be put right, it's ours. Once the 'us' in the 'us

---

[a] The Day of the Atonements (or Day of Expiations), the Jewish day of fasting, when one contemplates ones sins, and asks God for forgiveness and healing.

and God' relationship is put right, we are able to function correctly – our hearts, minds and souls work in the way that God intended them to work, and we are better able to do God's will.

'Vengeance is Mine, says Yahveh'

On occasion, when I try to share with certain people who are not of the Jewish faith, saying that as a Jew I also believe in a loving and compassionate God, the response from these people is, 'No you don't; the God of the Old Testament is a wrathful and vengeful God. Our God, the God of the New Testament, is *the* God of love. We therefore worship different gods'.

The best verse to illustrate this accusation is Deut 32.35a:

'Vengeance and retribution are mine.'

Many times, the Miqra speaks of Yahveh taking vengeance, and being wrathful. But these English words give entirely the wrong impression of the mind of God. When we speak of vengeance, we think of the associated human feelings of anger, hatred, a desire for the suffering of one's enemies, for one's enemies to die horrible deaths, and so on. But this is not God's attitude. God says,

'Do I take any pleasure in the death of the wicked?' declares Yahveh of the heavenly battalions. *'Rather, am I not pleased when they turn from their ways and live?'* [a] Yeshua`'s parables were reflecting this very Jewish way of looking at God.

And Yahveh is not a slave to the human extremes of vengeance, such those who punish a slap with a knife or a gun. God repays wrongs justly:

'It is time for Yahveh's vengeance; God will pay her what she deserves.' [b]

Although the Hebrew word *naqam* literally does mean 'vengeance', we have to translate this according to what we know of Yahveh's true heart and personality. The English word 'vengeance' is associated far too much with the unpleasant human extremes of the word. It would be better to understand the phrase, 'to take vengeance' as, 'to deal out divine justice' – at least when speaking of God.

When we understand the word like this, a number of biblical verses become more balanced and make more sense; Yahveh's reputation as a just God is no longer impugned:

'But you, O Yahveh of the heavenly battalions, who judges

---

[a] an unrepentant and intentionally sinful life is a form of spiritual death even in life (the way of death), and a penitent, blameless life is true life (the way of life) – Jer 21:8, Deut 30:19

[b] Jer 51:6

*righteously and weighs the heart and mind, let me see your **divine justice** upon them, for to you I have committed my cause.* '[a]

When a crime is committed, we are meant to leave it up to the police and the justice system to handle things, and not take matters into our own hands. The same principle applies with social and moral injustices committed against us; we are meant to leave the matter for God to deal with. The young David understood this concept when King Saul treated him unjustly:

*'May Yahveh be the judge in our quarrel. And may Yahveh **mete out divine justice** for the wrongs you have done to me, but as for me, my hand will not touch you.* '[b]

David was saying that he would leave it up to Yahveh to be the judge and jury in their case, but as for himself, he would not lay a finger on Saul.

I want to look again at the verse in Deuteronomy that I opened with. Here's a free translation giving the sense of the verse:

*'Vengeance and retribution are My responsibility, i.e. **not** yours.'*

Vengeance – that is, divine justice – is God's job, God's responsibility, *not* ours. Our responsibility is to forgive.

When we are wronged, we feel angry, bitter, enraged, hateful and vengeful. In the Yahwist mind-set, we bundle that all up and hand it over to God – because it's God's job, not ours, and because Yahveh is a just and righteous God. God's wrath is not hateful but righteous anger, and God's vengeance is not human vengeance but divine justice. The prophet Yeshua` understood this about God when he taught us not to fret over evil, or seek to get even when we are wronged.[c] Hatred and anger cause the mind to go to a dark place, but forgiveness heals the soul.

Let me tell you a short story. There was an elderly lady who got on the same bus every morning, and was already on the bus when two Urdu-speaking shop-workers got on at a later stop. The two workers, not being able to speak much English, reverted to their native Urdu once they were seated and began chatting with each other. The elderly lady would tsk and tut every morning; it was obvious that she was irritated by hearing the foreign language being spoken. But eventually she could take no more. One morning she turned round and told them to shut up. They weren't even speaking loudly, and there were other people on the bus speaking English to one another at the same volume. Every morning after that, if she heard them speak Urdu, she would tell them to shut up.

One day, as the elderly lady was getting off the bus, she tripped and

---

[a] Jer 11:20
[b] 1Sam 24:12
[c] S.Yesh. 71:1 – cf Prov 24:19

fell, and one of the Urdu-speakers was right behind her. Now, he could have thought to himself, 'I'm not going to help a racist like you, it serves you right.' Instead, he helped her to get up. He could have thought, 'Not helping you would be my revenge against you', but he obviously left vengeance and punishment to God.

So also in the Hebrew mind-set, there is the opinion that to rejoice in the misfortune of one's enemies is to invite trouble, because your own justness will be diminished, and God's righteous anger will be turned away from your enemy who has wronged you.[a] That is why people in Israel do not generally rejoice when they score minor victories over their enemies; the justness of their own cause will be diminished if they do.

God's anger is not what it seems

The God of the 'Old Testament' is not a wrathful and vengeful God, but a God who feels righteous anger at wrongs committed against God's innocent children, and deals out divine justice in just measure with the wrong committed.

I remember my great-aunt telling me about her first visit to her Italian relatives, and her experience when they all sat down to dinner on her first evening there. They became very loud and expressive, with lots of gesticulating and wide-eyed faces. She grew very uncomfortable, and eventually had to ask them why they were arguing. Her relatives were most surprised; they weren't arguing at all; they were just very expressive – that was how they normally spoke.

We might understand the words of another language, but if we do not understand their cultural norms, we will get the wrong end of the stick completely. This often happens with the portrayal of God's so-called 'anger' in the Miqra. In the Book of Exodus,[b] God says, *"Leave me now, so that my anger can blaze out at them, and I can put an end to them ..... but then Yahveh relented over the disaster that God intended to inflict upon God's people."*

On the face of it, this is an amazing outburst from God, threatening to destroy Israel, and make of Moses's descendants a great nation instead. But Moses reminds God of what God had promised to Abraham, Isaac and Jacob, and that if God were to destroy Israel, God would be breaking that promise. Thereupon God renounces God's wrath and relents.

The first thing we should think of, is not that Yahveh is an angry and vengeful God, but rather, 'Is God so dumb and stupid that God would

---

[a] Prov 24::17-18
[b] Ex 32:10, 14

forget what God had promised for generations, needing to be reminded, and then relent, saying, "Oh yeah, I *DID* make such a promise, didn't I!"

If we read Numbers 23:19, we learn that God does not make a promise and then change God's mind. God had absolutely no intention of destroying Israel. If we want to understand the real meaning behind this outburst, we must step back a little in the story, and look at what God said to the Egyptian Pharaoh:

"I could *have stretched forth My hand and stricken you and your people with pestilence, and you would have been completely wiped from the face of the earth."*[a]

The whole exchange between God and Moses on Mt Sinai is an ancient Hebrew literary device, intended to say, "This is what I *could* have done, were it not for what I have promised, for I am powerful enough to erase the memory of your small, insignificant people from the face of the earth, and from all human memory. *But I'm not going to.*"

And why isn't God going to? For the same reason given to another people:

"I have spared you for this purpose: in order to show you my power, and in order that my fame may be proclaimed throughout the earth."[b] (God's explanation for ultimately sparing Pharaoh and his people).

Our God – Yahveh – who is not a man,[c] nor a human being, is a holy God. God doesn't do things in a human way. If Yahveh were a man, and thought like a man, God would say, 'I will strike them down, for they have disobeyed me! I will crush them and wipe them off the face of the earth!'

We as humans, expect God to act like a mafia boss and strike those who disobey him and obliterate them; but Yahveh is holy, and not like false, pagan gods. Human gods are portrayed this way, and when we try to portray Yahveh in this way, God is naturally upset.[d]

God is not a tyrant, and does not behave like one. When we are told that the Jewish God is a God of wrath, that the God of the 'Old Testament' is an angry, vengeful God, it is often because some people don't understand the cultural norms of the Israelites. Such people always forget that the 'Old Testament' also says of the Jewish God:

"Yahveh will judge (= defend and save) *God's people and have compassion on God's servants"*[e]

"You are a forgiving God, gracious and compassionate, slow to

---

[a] Ex 9:15
[b] Ex 9:16
[c] Num 23:19, Hos 11:9b
[d] Job 42:7
[e] Deut 32:36

anger and abounding in love. "[a]

What mere mortals see as anger, is in reality the cleansing and purifying fire of Yahveh's divine radiance, which naturally pours out whenever evil is present. God's glory is there to protect the innocent, and pull down the hateful, the oppressor, the human tyrants and the unfeeling hearts that delight in human suffering. Yahveh is the Great Defender of the weak against the strong.

'The measure you give will be the measure you get'

There is a Yahwist principle that, whatever wrong you do to others, Yahveh will ensure that exactly the same wrong will be done to you[b] – even in this life.

In the *Book of Job*, Elihu says, *'For God repays each person for their actions, treating each as his own conduct deserves. '*[c]

We go through life committing small, almost inconsequential misdeeds against other people. Sometimes we make some really bad foul-ups in our dealings with others. In the end, we have to realise that whatever small or large thing we do, God will ensure that the same will be returned to us in full measure. As Yahveh tells us through the prophet Isaiah,[d] *'I will pay them back in full – I will pay them right back into their laps.'* Whatever wickedness we do to others, God will repay the same wickedness back to us.

So when someone does something wrong to you, do not seek vengeance against them, or deal with them as they have done to you. You are not with that person 24 hours a day – you do not know what God has done or will do to that person in retribution for what they have done to you. Leave judgment and retribution to God, and stick with your job of spreading the light of God's kingdom in your words, thoughts and actions.

There is a phrase you might have read in the Miqra: *'May Yahveh judge between you and me!'*[e] When we take the principle of divine payback to heart, and then someone wrongs us, we are tempted to cry out, 'May Yahveh do to you what you have done to me!' However, such a cry would be a curse[f] – wishing ill on another person (even if that

---

[a] Neh 9:17
[b] implied by Prov 24:12
[c] Job 34:11; see also Proverbs 24:12 'Will He not repay each person according to what they have done?'
[d] Isaiah 65:6
[e] Gen 16:5, 1 Sam 24:12, 15 – in Hebrew: *yishpot Yahveh beyni u-veyneykha*
[f] cursing is avoided in the Israelite religion; cursing was considered the practice of evil people (Ps 10:7); and an unjust or undeserved curse may even

person *has* wronged you). The compromise to such a cry would be to call on Yahveh to be the just and righteous judge of the situation. So when someone has wronged you, the appropriate prayer would be, 'May Yahveh judge between you and me.'

You must therefore not do evil to the person who has wronged you, or seek to get even. Let Yahveh enact judgment, and pay your wrongdoer back for what they have done to you.

... our sins,

As with every one of the petitions contained in the 'Our Father', there was a contemporary reason for including this line. However, I want to leave the reason for this one until the next chapter, when I discuss the word 'trial'. For now, I want to examine the concept of sin itself in Israelite theology.

The different types of sin in Hebrew thought

The English word 'sin' is wholly inadequate to describe what the Hebrew concept means. There are in fact, many Hebrew words to cover what we call sin, and not all of them have the meanings that English ascribes to each word.

There are 3 basic types:

1. The minor infraction committed without knowledge of it – the misstep, the stumbling off the right path, the error. Even though these were not what we moderns would call 'evil', they still needed to be atoned for. These were such things as ritual infractions against God's holiness, or hurting someone with ones deeds or words, without knowing that such deeds or words were hurtful.

2. The wrong committed with full knowledge that it was wrong

3. The wilful and grievous rebellion against God.

Most of us can understand why the second two types of 'sin' needed to be atoned for, but it is difficult to understand why the minor 'sin' committed inadvertently without knowledge of it *still* needed to be atoned for.

But what is atonement? The Paullist view of atonement is in fact a pagan view of the concept. It causes us to think that the purpose of atonement is to restore God's relationship with us – to reconcile 'God

---

fall back on the person who spoke it (Gen 12:3, Prov 26:2), and so it became better to avoid cursing altogether.

with man'. But the Yahwist view is that you cannot possibly harm God's relationship with you.

This is why the word 'sin' is inadequate. We need to have another way of looking at this – the Yahwist Israelite way. I have previously explained the Yahwist concept of 'wholeness of being.' Well, what all these 3 things have in common, is that they *diminish* the wholeness of one's being. They are 'diminishments' or 'injuries' to one's being or life-force (*néfesh* in Hebrew).

So instead of looking at 'sin' as harming God's relationship with us, and atonement as reconciling God's relationship with us, we need to see these things as harming ourselves, and atonement as restoring our own wholeness; we cannot harm God, we can only harm ourselves and others. 'Sin' is an injury to *our* wholeness, and atonement is a restoration or healing of *our* wholeness.

The first kind of 'sin' is therefore like a minor injury – caused by an ethical trip-up, a spiritual misstep, missing the mark of the ideal. The second type is like running headlong into an accident with full knowledge that such actions will hurt us; and the third is like grievous bodily self-harm.

Many people still think that it was the blood of the animal sacrifice that was supposed to effect atonement, but if one had done wrong, one had to make reparation *before* one made the sacrificial offering. If one simply offered the sacrifice without repentance or reparation to the injured party, then there was no forgiveness or restoration of wholeness.

If the Temple were restored, Talmidis would be opposed to the restoration of animal sacrifices. It would be a step backwards. I suspect that God will not give us a Temple until we as a people understand that animal sacrifices are unnecessary for the forgiveness of sin, or for the restoration of the wholeness of our souls.

The purpose of worship in the Temple

Many Reform Jewish synagogues are called 'Temples', especially in the US. However, by the definition of what the Temple was for in Israelite worship, these are not strictly 'Temples', but rather 'houses of prayer'. To understand this difference – and the relevance of the Temple in the matter of sin and atonement – one has to understand precisely how worship in the Temple differs from worship everywhere else.

It is very true that we can pray anywhere, and that God's living Presence is everywhere. However, worship in the Temple is different, because it is meant to be the place where a doorway is kept open between heaven and earth – a doorway through which Yahveh's protective blessing and purifying radiance can come through permanently, just like with the Tabernacle in the Sinai desert. And there can only ever be one of these.

This stipulation can be well illustrated by the Qorachite rebellion,[a] when some Levite clans decided to have an alternative Tabernacle (*Mishkan*). The *Mishkan*, and its successor the Temple, was not merely a place of worship. It was not simply a place of prayer. Prayer can be conducted anywhere, because Yahveh is everywhere. The one single Sanctuary was the only place where the divine radiance (the 'glory' or *kavodh*) could come through safely from heaven; it was the only place from where the priests could diffuse its power and filter it through to the people and the world to become a blessing and a benefit.

This is the ancient Yahwist understanding that modern Judaism has lost entirely, but was central to understanding ritual worship in Temple times: priests could open up a safe doorway between heaven and earth, if they conducted worship with a right mind, and in the right way. Before Jerusalem was chosen, that single place was Shiloh. The ark had also rested in other places too, and wherever that Ark was, that was the single place of worship. Being a place where God's Name was established, meant this was precisely the place where God's Divine Radiance was to come through, where God's authority and divine reputation was to be established – the 'House of Yahveh'.

That is the huge difference between a Temple and a synagogue: the Temple and its specific forms of worship, bring God's Divine Radiance permanently through to this world from heaven, at near full force. Sanctuary worship is different from synagogue and home worship; its purpose is completely different, and failure to grasp this leaves us without an understanding of why there can only be one place of Sanctuary-worship. Simply calling a synagogue 'a Temple' doesn't make it a Temple; what makes a Temple is the unique form of worship within it, and the fact that a doorway between heaven and earth is kept open there.

The forms of Sanctuary-worship are also different to worship everywhere else. Incense cannot be burned elsewhere; altars cannot be set up elsewhere; sacrificial offerings could not be made elsewhere, and designated tithes cannot be eaten elsewhere. Another difference was that although Levitical singing and music could be performed in the outer courts of the Temple, there was *total silence* within the Sanctuary itself (i.e. the court of the priests); the priests went about their business without any verbal communication *whatsoever*. This was to combat the pagan notion that one could magically manipulate God or nature through sacred words in Temple worship.

---

[a] Num chs 16-17

Temple worship was designed to enable a doorway to be kept open between heaven and earth, so that the positive, cleansing and protective benefits of close contact with the Divine Radiance could be maintained – so that God could 'dwell' with Israel to protect her and bless her. Abandoning God's ways would close off this pipeline of sorts to heaven; God's presence would as a result be closed off. If God did not close off that doorway, the natural and automatic ability of God's glory to seek out and purify wrongdoing would kick in, and prove disastrous. God would rather do no harm; God would rather close off His glory than let it harm or destroy us.

Understanding the awesome power of God's radiance helps you to understand the 'hierarchy of holiness' – the concentric walls of holiness leading up to the approach of the Temple. It helps you to understand why only the High Priest was allowed into the Holy of Holies, why the priests had a greater holiness than the Levites, who in turn had greater holiness than Israelites, and so on. It also helps you to understand that restricted access to the Temple is not about restricting access to God, but rather about protecting human lives from the overwhelming power of God's *kavodh* or Divine Radiance. Not being able to understand this, the early Catholic church kept its priestly worship away from the people, creating the false impression that God was distant from the people. Protestant Christians rightly rebelled against this notion, but unfortunately also failed to understand this hierarchy of holiness – what Temple ritual was for.

The ritual worship of the Israelite priests created a psychological state of holiness within them, which in turn enabled them to withstand the effect of God's *kavodh*. Priestly service and Israelite worship is designed to enable a small group of people – the priests – to be in a state of permanent holiness, so that they can absorb and slow down the rushing torrent of God's glory out into the world. They surround the doorway to heaven, so that God's *kavodh* comes through to us *safely*.

However, when a sudden breach in these concentric walls is made, like when people rebel against God's ways and cause suffering and injustice, then it is in the nature of the Divine Radiance to rush forth to blot out the evil. A prophet or a *tsaddiq* – because of their closeness to God – their lives are filled with the glory of God, and so they are in a state of permanent holiness. They can step in, in a sense, to absorb the shock of the Divine Radiance so that it does not cause destruction.

In ancient times, a priest had to know how to prepare himself to approach the glory of God. By living a certain way, by observing certain disciplines and principles, a priest could withstand small doses of exposures to the searing glory of Yahveh. The way of life of the High Priest enabled him to endure the greatest amount of exposure to

Yahveh's raw glory; then the priests, then the Levites, then ordinary Israelites, and lastly the Gentile nations. This hierarchy does **not** mean that God views Gentiles with the least regard, but rather that, by the time Yahveh's purifying glory reaches Gentiles, it no longer has its destructive power; its power can be directed for blessing and guidance.

By the time God's glory reaches those nations who do not live a way of holiness, it is a gentle stream that blesses us and gives us life – a 'river of life'. That is what the increasing levels of holiness are for; as you get further away from the Sanctuary, there are lesser and lesser levels of ritual holiness required, so each level is protected from the strength of God's *kavodh* by the level above it. The High Priest takes the most, the priests next, then the Levites, then the ordinary Israelites, and by the time it reaches the Gentile nations, it has slowed down enough to become a gentle river of life.

I have said that the priests live a way of life that enables them to approach God's glory. In a sense, we too can create this state of mind by seeking God's will always, and by being ever willing to carry out God's sacred designs and plans in the wider world. Creating within ourselves a psychological state of holiness, enables us to withstand more of God's purifying radiance in our daily lives, so that it acts as a life-giving and protective blessing to us.

Dt 10:12-13 asks and responds, *"Now, O Israel, what does Yahveh your God require from you, but to revere Yahveh your God in awe, to walk in all His ways and love Him, and to serve Yahveh your God with all your heart and with all your soul, and to keep Yahveh's commandments and His statutes which I am commanding you today for your good."*

By doing this, Israelites and Godfearers create within themselves a state which absorbs and houses God's Divine Radiance. We then carry that radiance to the world for its blessing and benefit.

The process of 'atonement' or expiation

Knowing the purpose of the Temple, we can now get into the mindset of how it helps us in the process of atonement – and how atonement can be achieved even without a Temple.

The first thing I need to point out, is that the English word 'atonement' for the Hebrew word *kippur* needs to be re-evaluated. The word was coined as a result of the Paullist belief that the death of 'Christ' made us 'at one' with God. It literally means, 'at-one-ment'. This is NOT the Yahwist Israelite understanding of the process of *kippur*. It therefore follows that we need to be very careful in how we use the English words 'atone' and 'atonement'.

Yahveh is a holy God. That means that our God is able to purify and cleanse us of our sin simply by the awesome power of God's glory, once we have repented. Insisting on the principle that 'God cannot forgive without blood being spilt', implies that God is either a heartless being who is unwilling to forgive without blood being shed, or a puny weak being who is incapable of forgiveness without the shedding of blood.

Let me illustrate this by telling you a parable:

> *There were two moneylenders, a Roman moneylender, and a Jewish moneylender. Now, the Roman moneylender was the most notorious throughout all the Mediterranean. One day, one of his debtors came to him and said, 'The debt that I owe you can never be paid off in my lifetime; I beg of you, please have pity on me.'*
>
> *So the Roman moneylender said to him, 'I will forgive your debt, even though you are unworthy and don't deserve it, but only if the debt is paid in blood, and the price exacted in someone's death.'*
>
> *The debtor was incredulous, but the Roman moneylender said further, 'Yes, and I am sending my henchman to make sure that you wash yourself in that person's blood. That's the only way I am able to forgive your debt – my rules; I am after all the son of an Empire built on blood and death.'*
>
> *Now that same day, a debtor came to see the Jewish moneylender. In great distress he said, 'The debt that I owe you can never be paid off in my lifetime. Please, I beg of you, help me – I don't know what to do.'*
>
> *Seeing the depth of his anguish, and the gravity of his need, the Jewish moneylender had great pity on him, so he took the bill of debt, and tore it up.*
>
> *Surprised, the debtor said, 'But what about my debt?'*
>
> *The moneylender replied, 'I will remember your debt no more. Now go; your debts are forgiven.'*
>
> *There is no God like Yahveh.*

Yahveh did not intend blood sacrifice to be part of the faith God gave at Sinai. However, the episode of the Golden Calf showed God that the Israelites were not yet ready to give up sacrifices; if animal sacrifice had been forbidden from the outset, they would only have gone over to a pagan god that *did* allow sacrifices. So Yahveh allowed sacrifice, but only to Yahveh, and in the way Yahveh prescribed.

Yahveh only tolerated sacrifices.[a] God only permitted sacrifice to be made to *Yahveh*, and they had to be done in a holy way (which is what the book of Leviticus is all about). The whole sacrificial system was to impress upon Israel the awesome holiness of Yahveh – by avoiding the pagan uses and meanings of sacrifice and blood, and by strictly controlling sacrifice in a way that was holy and distinctively different from pagan ways.

You see, the gods of pagan Mystery Religions could not forgive people unless individuals actually believed in these gods, and blood was shed; apparently they were not strong enough to forgive otherwise. Yahveh is infinitely more powerful than any pagan God, because our God *can* forgive without animal sacrifice or blood.

King Solomon – the wisest king of Israel – realised this implicitly. He foresaw a time when the people of Israel might be exiled from their Temple, and sacrifices could no longer be made. This is what he prayed at the dedication of the First Temple:

"When they sin against you .... and their captors carry them off to a country be it far away or near .... if they come to their senses in that country ... saying, 'We have sinned ....' and turn back to you with all their heart and soul ... then listen to their prayer from heaven .... and forgive your people."[b]

King Solomon understood that our God is so powerful, that God is able to forgive without the need for blood sacrifices. This shows that Yahveh, unlike the pagan gods, forgives sin once genuine repentance is made – just like that. If a person repents and is truly sorry for what they have done, then Yahveh forgives without condition, and no blood is necessary. Remember that according to Torah, the scapegoat, upon whose head were placed the sins of Israel, was supposed to be sent away *alive* into the desert.[c]

In the ancient world, animal sacrifice was part and parcel of religious ritual. From their time in Egypt, the Israelites had grown used to the Egyptian way of accepting animal offerings as part of the process of atonement and forgiveness. In an ideal world, Yahveh could have taught the Israelites a completely new way of looking at atonement – the

---

[a] This is the view put forward in the ancient *Clementine Literature*. In the section which has now become known as the *'Ascents of James'*, ch. 36, referring to the Golden Calf episode, it says, *'because of this, [Moses] did permit them to sacrifice; but he told them that they could only do this in the name of God, so that he could cut off and bring to an end if only one half of this sickness [of blood sacrifice].'* I include this, not as proof against animal sacrifice, but as proof that rejection of blood sacrifice is not a modern view, rather a belief also held by *ancient* Followers of the Way.

[b] extracts from 2Chr 6:36-39

[c] Lev 16:21-22

way I have been describing to you in these last few pages. However, the old pagan Egyptian way of looking at animal sacrifice was so ingrained, that this connection between death and atonement could not so easily be broken. If the ancient Israelites could not let go of the idea of atoning sacrifices, then Yahveh would give them a new way of performing them, so that they might someday understand that they were not necessary.

God therefore instituted ritual worship based around the Tabernacle, whose form and structure was to be a symbolic representation of Heaven and Earth. The symbolism of the constituent parts of the Tabernacle would one day give Israelites an understanding of the power of God, and how God forgives and heals.

For example, the fire of the altar, on which sacrifices were consumed, represented God's glory on earth, just as the Ark of the Covenant represented God's glory (and throne) in heaven. Those sacrifices which were wholly consumed in the flames of the altar, were intended to show us that if our physical selves were to approach God's glory, they would not survive.[a] Paullist theology mistakenly thought that we could not approach God *at all* without blood sacrifice.[b] Rather, the sacrifice itself 'covers' (not 'atones') for the person making the offering i.e. it symbolically takes the place of the offerer before God's glory. It was meant to show us that our physical bodies cannot approach God's brilliant glory.

You also have to separate in your mind the actual offering from the blood of the offering. When an animal offering was consumed on the altar, the emphasis was on the animal's *body* being consumed, not on its blood. The blood was instead dashed against the altar, since it was sacred and belonged solely to God. The life of the animal was therefore symbolically returned to God in the form of blood. Blood is life, and all life belongs to God; the blood is returned to God, just as all life ultimately returns to God. The blood was supposed to symbolise how our souls can approach God spiritually without harm and be cleansed.

Before a sin offering was made, you had to repent and make restitution to the one you had sinned against. Yeshua` understood this concept implicitly:

'If you're making a sin offering in the Temple, and there you remember that your brother has some disagreement with you, leave your offering there with the priest. First make peace with your brother, and only then can you return and make your sin offering.'[c]

---

[a] Ex 33:20

[b] If you compare Yahwist thought with Paullist thought, you can see that there is a *huge* difference. Either Paul did not understand Jewish teaching, or he deliberately chose to ignore it.

[c] S.Yesh 125:1-2 – cf Mt 5:23-24

This shows us that all we have to do is bring our souls into God's presence, and the power of Yahveh's glory alone is enough to cleanse our souls. Even if our bodies cannot approach God's glory, our souls can. They are not destroyed, but restored.

In modern everyday parlance, atonement means 'paying for one's sins', but in the Israelite way of looking at things, that is simply what penance is. Atonement, in its original Israelite context, is being cleansed and purified of the stain of sin. Atonement also restores the healthy wholeness of one's being or life-force. These are the two aspects of atonement it is vital to understand – purification from the stain of sin, and restoration of the health of one's life-force.

Wholeness or 'perfection' (shleimut) – the health of the soul

Armed with all this wealth of information, that there is no connection between animal sacrifice and God's forgiveness, one will then ask, so what was the purpose of the sacrifice? To understand the answer to that question, you first have to understand the ancient Israelite attitude to both sin and sickness. *Both* resulted in a diminishment of the wholeness of one's being or life-force. One's wholeness therefore had to be restored, in order for you to function healthily on a spiritual level.

Repentance brought immediate forgiveness from God. Once someone had repented, then their spiritual, psychological and physical wholeness could be restored (all these things were one and the same in Israelite theology). If you can grasp this, you will understand why sacrifices were made even for offences committed unintentionally, or which didn't actually 'offend' God.

You then have to understand sacrificial symbolism. The fire of the altar represents the fire of God's cleansing and healing glory. The sin-offering represents the soul of the offerer. The Hebrew verb *lᵉ-khapper* is usually translated as 'to atone for' or 'to make expiation for'. The simple form of the verb literally means, 'to cover' for someone, in the sense of it being done on someone's behalf. The sacrifice was therefore offered on behalf of the offerer – that is the intrinsic meaning of *lᵉ-khapper*. However, in the active form of the verb[a] it means, 'to cleanse or free someone (that is, from the guilt/stain of their sin).' The ritual is therefore performed to impress upon the one who has repented, that the glory of God has cleansed their soul, healed it and restored it to wholeness.

The Book of Leviticus says, *"Thus the priest shall perform the expiation ritual for the sin which he had committed, and the forgiveness-*

---

[a] i.e. the Piel form of the verb + the preposition 'al (upon)

process will be completed for him".[a] In other words, they have been taken through an entire, symbolic, spiritual healing process. They repented, were forgiven by God, and now they have finally been freed of their guilt; they have now been cleansed and made whole by spiritually bringing their souls into the presence and glory of Yahveh.

The concept of healing - Marpei

The ancient Israelite art of healing (*marpei*)[b] understood this concept of the wholeness of one's life-force (*shleimut néfesh*). When you became physically ill, in ancient times it was thought that the wholeness of the blood diminished. Just as the blood is the life of the body,[c] so also the *néfesh* ('life-force') is the life of the soul. For the body to remain healthy, the blood had to remain 'whole'; and for the soul to remain healthy, the *néfesh* had to remain whole (or 'perfect').

Priests were ministers of both soul and body. Whereas Far Eastern religions teach that one's energy has to be kept in balance, Israelite religion taught that the soul had to be maintained in a state of *wholeness* or 'perfection' – a state of spiritual health. When you sinned, or became ill, your wholeness was diminished. Priests were the representatives of God, and through them, God dispensed God's healing of the body.

Operating side by side with priests were healers – *merappim*[d] in Hebrew. Both Naziriteship and healership allowed someone who was not a descendant of Aaron – any lay person – to do what a priest did outside of the Temple. While Naziriteship allows a lay-person to practise the ritual and pastoral duties of a priest, *merappim* took on the healing duties of a priest – they practised the Israelite art of healing, *marpei*. This used herbs and other plants to effect healing of the body,[e] as well as the laying on of hands and counselling to heal the mind and soul; a person was dealt with as a whole being. As well as healing the body, the soul and mind had to be healed as well.[f]

---

[a] usually translated as *'and it will be forgiven to him'.* The niphal form of the verb seems to have been a technical phrasing among priests for the entire forgiveness-process; it only occurs in the context of the expiation ritual – the ritual that impresses upon us that the glory ('Divine radiance') of God has cleansed our soul of the stain of sin, and restored its wholeness.
[b] pronounced maar-PAY
[c] Gen 9:4, Lev 17:11-14, Dt 12:23
[d] singular *merappei*, pronounced mair-rap-PAY (feminine: *merappah*, pronounced mair-rap-PAA).
[e] Ecclesiasticus 38:4
[f] The art of healing seems to have been one of the old Israelite practices the early Talmidi community sought to restore – see Ig. Yq. 12:2 – cf Ep. James 5:14

The Yahwist attitude to healing, was that the healer was a messenger of Yahveh,[a] and the process of healing was a blessing from Yahveh – Yahveh alone was the Great Healer, not the *merappei* him- or herself. Unfortunately, by the time of the rise of the Pharisees, healers had come to claim that the healing process was as a result of their *own* skill, and even that their art was a magical art. At this point, rather than reforming *marpei*, the Israelite art of healing was effectively banned by the Pharisees.

The result of the ban was that the spiritual awareness and knowledge of *shleimut néfesh* – the 'wholeness of being' that had to be maintained for spiritual and physical health – was lost. The concept of *shleimut* – wholeness – is now completely absent from modern Judaism. However, it was an intrinsic part of the Israelite understanding of one of the purposes of repentance and good works – that they restored the wholeness of one's being.

Now, 'to be in a state of wholeness' is 'to be perfect'. If you followed God's ethical and moral laws, you could maintain this state of wholeness or perfection. The Aramaic for 'whole', 'complete' or 'perfect' is *g^emir*. When Yeshua` told us to be perfect like our Heavenly Father,[b] this is what he meant; he was teaching us to be whole and complete like our Heavenly Father.

Yeshua` was not telling us to be sinless like God; such a thing is not possible. The Yahwist outlook acknowledges that none of us are sinless.[c] It is not possible to be permanently sinless, but it *is* possible to try and maintain this wholeness of being. Your being won't always stay whole, but the goal of a righteous and ethical way of life, is to maintain this wholeness – this state of 'perfection'.

Summary of the process of sacrifice and atonement

Talmidaism is categorically opposed to the reinstitution of animal sacrifice, but it is important nevertheless to understand the symbolism behind it.

The sin offering covers for (i.e. takes the place of) the offerer, to symbolise how our physical bodies cannot approach God's glory and live. Repentance brings immediate forgiveness from God; we were meant to repent before the offering was given, to show that repentance brings us into God's presence, and that our souls are thus cleansed by God's glory. The blood was dashed on the altar to symbolise this

---

[a] Ecclesiasticus 38:1-2
[b] Mg. Ms. 10:1 – cf Mt 5:48, Lk 6:36
[c] Prov 20:9

approach of the soul to God, and how it is thereby cleansed and purified by God's glory. The intent of the sacrifice was to symbolically restore the wholeness of the offerer's being, and thus remove the stain or guilt of one's sin (this being what 'atonement' or expiation means). Other than providing food for the priests, animal sacrifices and blood are entirely unnecessary in the process of forgiveness and atonement.

The Outer Darkness [a]

Have you ever read that phrase, 'the outer darkness' in the teachings of the Prophet Yeshua`, and wondered what they meant? The Gospel of Matthew equates it with Hell, but Israelite religion has no belief in hell, so what can it mean?

Not every aspect of Hebrew culture is contained in the traditional canon of the Miqra. Certain basic ideas are often not explained or even mentioned, because it is assumed that everyone is aware of and familiar with them, and so are not worthy of note or explanation. For example, the prophet Yeshua` mentions 'the outer darkness',[b] but he never, *ever* explains what he means by it. Since there are a number of ideas and beliefs like this that are never explained, as a result, those ideas and concepts were lost over time. To recover their meaning, you have to look *outside* the Miqra at other ancient Jewish writings, where such ideas were explored and discussed.

In the *Testaments of the Twelve Patriarchs*,[c] the writer describes the ascent of the soul into the presence of God by going through various levels of 'heavens'.[d] The lowest or first heaven is where souls are purified of their sins – ones they never repented of in life – before they can continue on to the second heaven.

This 'lowest heaven' was where human souls lamented their sins in

---

[a] The concept of Sheol was an early introduction to this idea. Other terms for 'the Outer Darkness' are: the Fortress of Shadows [Proto-Semitic *Azza Zeil*, Lev 16:8; the Hebrew would be `*Azzat Tzeil*], Place of the Shadow of Death [*Tzal Mavet*, Job 38:17], the Place of Perdition [*Abaddon*, Job 26:6, 31:12], the Darkness [*ha-choshekh*, Ps 88:12], and 'the Land of Oblivion' [*ha-eretz nesiyah*, Ps 88:13].

[b] eg Mt 8:12, 22:13, 25:30. People normally assume that it means the darkness outside a house at night. Indeed, it is the image that the phrase is taken from, but the allusion is to this place after death where one pays for the sins one has not repented of in life – 'a place of weeping and a gnashing of teeth'.

[c] This was a document that is thought of by some to have been written by an Ebionite writer in the 2nd century CE. The form it has now has a few later Christian additions.

[d] Testaments of the Twelve Patriarchs, Levi 2:6

darkness *('The lowest heaven appears for this reason gloomy to you.').*[a]
This is where there is 'a weeping and a gnashing of teeth'[b] – an Aramaic
idiom meaning 'a great and terrible lamentation'.

Reading the words of the Psalms when they speak of *She'ol*, it
becomes obvious that it too is a place of darkness,[c] where God's
Presence is absent. The souls of the dead cannot cry to God there,[d] and
God cannot hear them.[e] In such a place, our individual journeys to let go
of our sins have to be done completely on our own;[f] we have to have
remorse for our sins there, and understand the true gravity of them,
before we can then enter heaven.

Once we have been purified of our sins, we move on to heaven,[g] to
face our final purification by the fire of God's glory in the presence of
God; for nothing of this imperfect world on Earth can be allowed to touch
the holy Presence of God.

Thanks to the words of the Prophet Yeshua`, we have a historical
record of the actual Jewish name for this 'lowest heaven' in everyday
speech: 'the Outer Darkness' (in Aramaic, *chashokha baraya*; in
Hebrew, *ha-choshekh ha-chitson*). Once you understand that this term is
important, and not just a trivial, throw-away phrase, you gain an insight
into Yeshua`'s personal theology (from Common Judaism, rather than
Pharisaic/Rabbinic Judaism, where the concept is absent or
undeveloped).

In Yeshua`'s parables, do you recall the one about making peace
with your accuser while you are on your way to court? And how if you
don't, he will take you to the judge and you will be thrown into prison,
and *'you will not get out of there until you have paid the very last
prutah'*.[h]

This parable can be interpreted as a lesson in making peace before
we die with those we have wronged (or at least, a lesson in repenting of
our wrongs, or resolving painful issues). If we don't, we won't get out of
the Outer Darkness until we have paid fully for every last sin we have
ever committed against others and not repented of. What this tells us, is
that Yeshua` actually envisioned this as a place that someone would
eventually get out of – notice that he says, *"'you will not get out of there*

---

[a] *Testaments of the Twelve Patriarchs,* Levi 3:1
[b] S.Yesh. 110:6 – cf Mt 25:30
[c] Ps 88:7, 13 (Christian bibles 88:6, 12)
[d] Ps 6:6 (Xtian: 6:5), 88:11 (Xtian: Ps 88:10)
[e] Ps 88:5 (Xtian: Ps 88:4)
[f] Ps 88:11 (Xtian: Ps 88:10), although Hebrew tradition allowed for the
existence of archangels who guided our journey, such as Sariel the archangel
of death, and Rea'el the archangel of God's judgment.
[g] Ps 49:15
[h] S.Yesh 77; cf Mt 5:25-26, Lk 12:58-59

until *you have paid the very last prutah'.*

The Hebrew term *ha-choshekh ha-chitson* also gives us a deeper insight into the Israelite mind-set with regard to the Outer Darkness. The Hebrew word for 'outer', 'exterior' or 'external' is חיצון *chitson*. In biblical Hebrew it also had another usage – to mean 'secular' (as opposed to what is holy and sacred).

If you recall, when the Israelites were encamped in the Sinai desert, they were not allowed to foul their camp.[a] If they needed to relieve themselves, they had to go outside the camp and do it (i.e. not just away from their tents). Also if someone had a skin disease, or was ceremonially unclean, they had to remain outside the camp until they were ritually clean. The main part of sin offerings was also to be burned *outside* the camp.[b] These commandments are all meant to give us the sense that what is unholy is to be kept away from what is holy.

Also, if you recall offenses that were punishable by being 'cut off', such as eating bread made with yeast during the Festival of Unleavened Bread, or working on the Sabbath, or making sacred incense into regular perfume, or eating blood etc – all these are offenses against holiness,[c] and such a person is 'cut off' from contact with the Israelite people until they are ritually purified. As a punishment, the formula *'and he shall be cut off from his kin'* occurs again and again.

To understand this spiritual punishment, *karet* in Hebrew, we need to learn where the expression comes from. The primary image is that of a tree being cut off from its roots – from its life-giving sap.[d] Such a tree will either wither and die, or it will grow, but never again with the same strength or vigour.

If a person is 'cut off', they are therefore cut off from their 'life-giving sap' – the benefits of following God's ways. While they are cut off, they will not prosper. In the context of prohibitions in Leviticus,[e] a person who desecrates the holiness of God is cut off from the benefits they would normally be due as a faithful follower of Yahveh.

All this was designed to give the Hebrew mind a sense that what was outside and external, was ordinary, not holy, and a place *cut off* from what is holy. It is vital to understand the symbolism of Israelite ritual, otherwise you will see the symbol but not the meaning of the ritual. It is important to realise that in this world, such symbols in the Israelite

---

[a] i.e. they weren't allowed to go to the toilet within its boundaries - Deut 23:12-14

[b] e.g. Lev 4:21; it was an allusion to the fact that nothing unholy can enter heaven.

[c] Lev 19:8

[d] see Jer 11:19.

[e] see Lev 7:19-27

religion were deliberate and purposeful, designed to instruct us on the structure and nature of their counterparts in the Next World.

So if we return to Yeshua`'s sayings, he told us that the unrepentant would be sent to this '**outer** darkness', where there would be a 'weeping and gnashing of teeth'. He tells us how they wouldn't get out until they had paid 'the very last prutah' – until they had been purified of the very last trace of their sin.

In the *New Testament*, you also have the term '*Gehenna*' used. In the Israelite religion – the original one, that is – there is no concept of hell. However, in pagan religions, there is a concept of a place of eternal fire where one pays for one's sins, but *without* hope of being saved or taken out of that place.

The nearest image that Jewish culture had for this was *Gei Hinnom* – the valley of Hinnom. In Yeshua`'s day it was where Jerusalem's rubbish was burnt. No one would go there for any other reason. It was *outside* the city walls of Jerusalem, and it also had a sinister past. It was where Israelites, attracted by the religion of the Ammonite god Molekh, would sacrifice their children in fire, in order to gain permanent salvation from their sins. It was therefore an unholy place associated with fire and evil – the nearest image that Jewish culture had to the Christian idea of hell, a concept whose origins ultimately lay in pagan religion.

When Yeshua`'s sayings were being transmitted to a Gentile audience, they would not have understood what this 'outer darkness' was (just as most people today have no idea what the outer darkness is). I suspect that the instances where Gehenna is mentioned, were merely attempts to replace the Jewish term 'the outer darkness' with the nearest Jewish equivalent to Hell – a concept that Gentile pagans *were* familiar with. Even the parable of Lazarus and the Rich Man[a] was probably one composed by Luke himself (i.e. not by Yeshua`), in order to explain to Gentiles the concept of reward and punishment; it does not otherwise fit in with either Yeshua`'s personal theology, or with Jewish ideas of the afterlife.

Theologically, the likely origins of the Outer Darkness lie in the original Yahwist beliefs about what happened after death. As I mentioned in chapter 4, originally the Israelites did not have any concept of heaven. They thought that people dwelt in a dark, shadowy underworld after death called *She'ol*. If we want to know what it is like in the Outer Darkness, then all we have to do is look at how *She'ol* was portrayed; the idea of *She'ol* evolved into the Outer Darkness, and all the ideas connected with *She'ol* were transferred onto it.

So, as with *She'ol*, there is no contact between God and those in the

---

[a] Lk 16:19-31

Outer Darkness;[a] it is a place away from God,[b] and the only place that God's Presence is absent from.[c] Our voices cannot be heard by God in the Outer Darkness.[d] It is therefore a dark,[e] cold and frightening place. However, it is fortunately a place that the soul can be released from, to eventually enter heaven. Once we have realised the full gravity of our sins, and felt true remorse for them, we can move on to heaven.

The symbolism of the animal offerings made on the Day of the Atonements, may also reflect what happens to the soul on its journey in the afterlife. On that holiest day of the Israelite year, the sins of the High Priest and priesthood were confessed over a bull. The sins of the people were then 'confessed' over the scapegoat. The blood of the bull and a second goat was taken into the holy of holies, but curiously, their carcasses were taken *outside* of the Temple and burnt[f] – they were *not* burnt on the altar. And the scapegoat was to be taken out and released *alive* into the wilderness.[g]

We know that the blood of these animals represented the life-force being returned to God – the soul approaching God to be cleansed and purified. The bull and the second goat burnt outside the city, represented the fact that our bodies do not enter heaven; they remain 'outside' on earth, and return to the soil. The scapegoat represented the little-known belief that, while our sins are eventually separated from us after death, they remain imprisoned in the Outer Darkness like mindless spirits.[h]

The very word we translate as 'scapegoat' could in fact be an extremely ancient, proto-Semitic term for 'Outer Darkness'. In the Hebrew word, עֲזָאזֵל *Azazel* (more properly, `azza zeil), we could in fact have an early Semitic, pre-Hebrew word for the concept of the Outer Darkness.

---

[a] Ps 28:1

[b] Ps 88:5

[c] Ps 143:7; it is God's choice to be apart from the Outer Darkness. When God's kingdom is fulfilled, not only will heaven break through and shine on earth, but God's light will shine in the Outer Darkness, and do away with it, since it will no longer be needed.

[d] Isa 38:18

[e] Nahum 1:8, Lam 3:6

[f] Lev 16:27

[g] so says Lev 16:22. However, the Pharisees insisted that this be changed. As a result, the goat was taken to a cliff and thrown off, so killing it (and disobeying what God taught in Torah).

[h] This is how they are described in the *Testaments of the 12 Patriarchs*, Levi (Bk 3) chapt 3 verse 1 (cf *Ts. Yh.* 1:15). In the Book of Revelation, this is what is alluded to metaphorically when an angel opens the gates of the abyss (i.e. the gates of She'ol or the Outer Darkness) and releases the spirits of sins there (Rev 9:1-3; cf *Ch. Sh.* 8:1-3). The spirits of these sins then cause suffering to the people of Judah in the form of physical trials and misfortune.

Many people think (but incorrectly so) that the final element in the word, -el, is the Hebrew word for 'God', and therefore must be the name of something or someone. However, the Hebrew word for God, אל *El*, is actually not there – the letter א *alef* is missing. We have always assumed the word is Hebrew, and tried to interpret the word as if it were Hebrew. What if, like the term *El Shadday*,[a] it too was a Sinaitic, proto-Semitic word, and not Hebrew at all?

Given the Hebrew lettering, the word does not divide up conveniently as *azaz el*, and is therefore not a personal name – there is, in other words, no being or entity called Azazel. It actually divides up either as `*az azeil*, or `*aza zeil*. The first interpretation has given us the traditional word, scapegoat – 'the goat (`*eiz*) who departs (*azal*)'. The second way of dividing up the word suggests a possibility of a much more ancient word. `*Aza* could be related to `*azza*, 'fortress', and *zeil* could be related to Hebrew *tzeil*, 'shadow' or 'darkness'. If this is correct, then `*aza zeil* could have originally meant, 'Fortress of Shadow(s)' in a proto-Semitic Sinaitic language. In which case, Lev 6:8 should read, *"Aaron shall cast lots for the two goats, one lot for Yahveh and the other lot for the Fortress of Shadow* (i.e. the Outer Darkness)."

This momentous new interpretation, tells us the true meaning of the symbolism behind the two identical goats. The goat that remains and is sacrificed, represents the dead human being. Its body burnt outside the city represents the human body returning to the soil, and the blood of the goat represents the soul returning to God. But the goat sent away into the outer wilderness represents our sins which are sent into the Outer Darkness, to remain there.

To summarise, the Outer Darkness is a place of purification which the human soul goes to, in order to be cleansed of the sins one did not repent of or make up for in life, before one can enter into the holy Presence of God in heaven. In Israelite culture, what was outside was secular, apart and separate from the holiness of God. It was a place where one lamented greatly of one's sins – where one 'wept and gnashed one's teeth' – until one was purified and cleansed, so that one's eternal soul

---

[a] The word *Shadday* does not look Hebrew; the termination *–ay* would normally indicate a plural noun with the possessive 'my' (eg *elohay*: my God), but as a Hebrew noun, it sounds odd. It may be connected to the Akkadian word *shadû*: mountain (an idea first proposed by W.F. Albright?). If *shadday* is a proto-Semitic word meaning 'mountains', then the title *El Shadday* probably meant 'God of the Holy Mountains', i.e. the holy mountains of the Sinai. In Hebrew it came to mean 'God Almighty', and this is how it is usually translated. For example in Job, *Shadday* is used on its own, to mean 'the Almighty'. In Ancient North Arabian dialects, such as Thamudic, the termination *–ai* exists; the inscription of *alshaday* has even been found.

could approach the great glory and light of Yahveh in heaven.

The destructive myth of evil spirits

If you adhere to the logic of pure Yahwism, then there are no such things as demons or evil spirits *per se*. In the spiritual realm, nothing can **wilfully** disobey Yahveh, so there are no such things as Satan, demons, devils or evil spirits – nothing is ruled over or directed by an evil demiurge, or created by that demiurge in order to do evil in this world. This subject therefore requires the application of careful discernment; to the novice or untrained mind, these matters can easily be misconstrued; money-hungry charlatans often use the subject of evil spirits to fool vulnerable people, and lure them into accepting false beliefs.

In the period between Abraham and Moses, proto-Hebrew belief viewed *iyim*[a] (mythical, supernatural wild beasts) as the cause of all misfortune in the world. These included *sheidim* (ox-demons),[b] *śe'irim* (goat-demons),[c] and creatures such as the leviathan[d] and the behemoth.[e] They weren't thought of as actually evil in and of themselves; like real-world wild animals, they were neither good nor evil. It used to be believed that they did what they did, because that was their nature. Nothing and no one had any power over them except God.[f]

Even after the revelation of true Yahwism at Sinai, some Israelites came to worship these mythical *iyim*, building altars to them in fields and desert places, and offering sacrifices to them[g] – all in the hope of averting any misfortune they might cause. Kabbalah[h] has built up whole back-stories and legends about them, even giving these demons powers and individual names (such as Ashmodai, Lilith, and Shabriri).

After the Babylonian exile, Jewish mysticism became heavily influenced by Babylonian, Chaldean and Persian mythology. Persian mythology particularly was the source of the division of the demon world into good and bad spirits. After the exile, myths about demons proliferated wildly; pagan beliefs resurfaced, so that illnesses, accidents and even misbehaviour all became the domain of one demon or another.

---

[a] pronounced *ee-YEEM* - see section entitled, *'From wild beasts to Satan; pagan intrusions into Yahwism'*, in chapter 8.
[b] Dt 32:17
[c] Isa 34:14
[d] Job 3:8, Ps 74:14
[e] Job 40:15
[f] Ps 74:14, Job 41:1-2
[g] Lev 17:7, Dt 32:17
[h] a form of Jewish mysticism ultimately derived from pagan religion.

This way of thinking characterises the Second Temple Period.[a] However, this was in *total* opposition[b] to the theology of pure Yahwism, which teaches that Yahveh **alone** is sovereign over all.

According to the beliefs of many pagan peoples in the ancient world, skin diseases, sexually transmitted diseases, and death were all caused by demons. However, in the world of Yahwist monotheism, there are no such things as demons. Even in Yeshua`'s time, ordinary Jewish people still persisted in believing in evil spirits and in the power of demon-possession. Early Rabbinic literature is replete with tales of illnesses and misfortune caused by evil spirits (which I won't go into here). It became such a pervasive part of Jewish culture, that even some of Yeshua`'s followers believed that one could become possessed by evil spirits.

However, if we were to clear our heads, return to the revelation at Sinai, and recognise that demonology has *no place* in true Yahwism, then we would realise that certain sayings of Yeshua` actually *mock* the logic of demon possession:

> 'When an unclean spirit leaves a person, it wanders through waterless places in search of a resting-place. When it doesn't find any, it then says, "I'll return to the home I left". It then returns and finds it swept and refurbished.[c] Next, it goes out and brings back with it seven other spirits even more vile than itself, who enter and settle in there. So that person ends up being worse off than when they started!'[d]

The stories of Yeshua` casting out demons are therefore most likely apocryphal and so made up; Yeshua` was either a true prophet, in which case he would have known that there are no such things as demons, or he *did* believe in demons himself, in which case he was *not* a prophet of the One, true, living God who is Sovereign over all; there's no in-between.

The Shadows of Sin in the Outer Darkness

In the section on 'The Outer Darkness', I mentioned that one's sins

---

[a] A very good book on this topic is: *"Evil Within and Without: The Source of Sin and Its Nature as Portrayed in Second Temple Literature"*, by Miryam T Brand.

[b] even Kabbalist mysticism believes in these demons, which is why it is not Yahwist.

[c] i.e. implying someone who has repented and changed their ways.

[d] S.Yesh. 114:4-7; cf Mt 12.43-45, Lk 11:24-26

left one's soul and remained in the Outer Darkness. What now follows comes from the beliefs of the Ebionite writer who wrote the Jewish portions of *'The Testaments of the Twelve Patriarchs'*, which I also mentioned in that section. The Miqra is largely silent on what happens to us in the afterlife, so I have had to go outside of the Hebrew Bible to learn what our ancient spiritual forebears believed about these things. The *Testaments* speak of the 'shadows of the spirits of sin' and what they might be.

The best way for me to explain what happens in the Outer Darkness, is to use modern imagery and analogy. When you commit a sin, it is as if that sin remained inside you as a kind of recording or spiritual memory – a blemish on your soul until you repented of it, made reparation for it, and were 'atoned' or cleansed of it. As for unrepented sin, in the Outer Darkness those 'recordings of sin' have to be removed, since nothing imperfect can enter heaven into the presence of Yahveh. The process of purification involves 'replaying' these 'recordings' over and over, so that you experience yourself the wrongs you have done to others;[a] once you feel remorse and true sorrow for what you have done, then you are ready to enter heaven. These 'recordings' or memories of sin remain forever in the Outer Darkness.

In the *Testaments of the 12 Patriarchs*, these 'recordings' are called the spirits or 'shadows' of sin (which would be *tselaley cheit* in Hebrew).[b] These *tselalim*[c] have no will or mind of their own; they are simply 'recordings' of sinful or evil human deeds. They are like poisons that are removed from the soul before our purified souls can enter heaven. They have no will, they are just non-sentient recordings of human evil. They are simply poison that has been removed from human souls after death, like soiled water left behind after clothing has been washed clean.[d]

In the *Book of the Visions of Shim'on*,[e] a star descends to earth, and releases smoke from the Outer Darkness. This covers the Land like locusts. This is a ***metaphorical*** reference to the poison of the *tselalim*; their similarity to the proto-Hebrew, pre-biblical *iyim* – supernatural

---

[a] implied by Isa 65:6, Prov 24:12

[b] see the apocryphal *Testaments of the 12 Patriarchs*, Book 3, ch 3 verse 1: "the spirits of all the unrighteous deeds and of all the iniquities of humankind" – see also Ts. Yd. 1:15

[c] pronounced tsuh-laa-LEEM (*uh* like the **a** in Tina, *aa* like the **a** in father, *ee* like the **ee** in feel)

[d] cf Ps 51:2-7; also symbolised in Ex 40:12, & 40:32 when priests have to wash themselves before they come into the Tent of Meeting.

[e] Ch. Sh. chapter 8; cf Revelation chapter 9, which Christians usually interpret as Satan unlocking Hell, and so releasing demons and evil spirits. This may actually reflect a scantily recorded part of ancient Hebrew myth.

'wild beasts' that supposedly cause misfortune and tribulation – is deliberate. The seer used ancient Hebrew imagery there to get across his warnings of a tribulation soon to come – the images of a dark poison coming through to this world in dark times.

This is also an appropriate juncture to point out, that if a whole country or organisation indulges in doing evil – engaging in beheadings, suicide bombings, cruel and arbitrary punishment, and generally creating an atmosphere of fear – then not only will the Presence of God withdraw from such an area, but so also will the poison of the Outer Darkness seep through and compound any evil they perpetrate. Evil begets evil, and the human beings who indulge themselves in evil acts need to realise that. When we do bad things, we cannot say that 'the devil made me do it,' or 'evil spirits made me do it', because true evil comes from the minds of human beings.

Now the good news is, we have the radiance of Yahveh which can come through to us from heaven, which feeds and nurtures us, healing the malaise that ails society. It is the goal of the follower of Yahveh to allow oneself to be influenced and purified by the *kavodh Yahveh*, rather than be laid low by the poison of the mindless *tselalim* from the Outer Darkness. By doing good, we allow the radiance of Yahveh's glory to purify and lead us; by doing evil, we make our souls vulnerable to spiritual ill-health.

I want to close this section by saying that any continued personal belief in demons and evil spirits is dangerous and destructive to the soul. It will give you a wholly false and futile image of how God and heaven work. Most of all, it prevents you from realising the true, awesome power of Yahveh, and will lay you open in times of vulnerability to some pretty unpleasant individuals, who will actually harm you spiritually, and whose only goal is to take advantage of you and control you.

Yahveh alone is our God; if we believe in the living power of Yahveh, and concentrate on the goal at hand in this world, we need have no fear of whatever comes our way. We can walk through the valley of the shadow of death, and we will fear no evil, for Yahveh is with us; Yahveh's power and presence will comfort us.

The Journey of the Soul in Pre-Life, Life and the Afterlife

Everyone will have their own views about what happens in the afterlife. This difference should be respected, because the emphasis of Yahwist Israelite spirituality is on **this** life in **this** world. What I present here is my own *personal* view of the afterlife, based on everything I have learned of ancient Israelite spirituality from many different sources, and from my understanding of the underlying theological symbolism of the

Hebrew bible. I have brought together those concepts which work, and discarded those ideas that do not work.

You are here on earth, not because you fell from grace or disobeyed God. On the contrary, you are here because God valued you *so much*, that he thought you strong enough and worthy enough of working alongside God to bring God's kingdom to fulfilment; God ultimately wished to reward you for your service by setting you at God's right hand after death. You are here on this earth because God felt you had something really amazing and valuable to contribute to God's Kingdom, and trusted you enough with God's work to be sent here to earth – yes, that's right – you were sent to earth by God!

We are created and born in heaven[a] as non-corporeal, spiritual beings. In Israelite mysticism, the term 'son of man' represents perfected heavenly humans or 'holy ones'[b] once they have been returned to heaven. Those heavenly beings who have ever been born on earth – including all human beings alive today – are, I believe, those particular spiritual beings who volunteered to help God fulfil God's work in this world. God needs our assistance[c] – God uses us – to maintain the order of the Universe, and more importantly, in implementing God's Great Plan. Yahveh sends us to Earth in human bodies, but because the knowledge we had during our heavenly lives would otherwise overwhelm our earthly minds, most of us are born without knowledge of where we have come from. However, holy and pious people are those who retain some connection with the mind-set of their former heavenly selves – I am certain of it.

Most of the spiritual beings (or 'Holy Ones') in heaven never get to become human; I believe it is only the bravest, strongest and most heroic souls that God sends to Earth. That's right! It's not just people like Yeshua` and the saints that got 'sent' here – you and I got sent here too!

The first stage of our lives here on Earth is to evolve spiritually, so that we can return our souls back to such a state of mind, whereby we understand what our individual purpose in life was – to recall the reason why we were sent. To do this we need to train ourselves and grow spiritually. We then come to a point where we either recall our purpose, or we attain a sufficient level of spiritual development, whereby we fulfil

---

[a] 'Before I formed you in the womb, I knew you.' (Jer 1:5). Also, when the Covenant was renewed with the Israelites on the plains of Moab, it was also sworn with those who were not present (implying it was sworn with the souls of people yet to be born – Dt 29:15)

[b] *qedoshim* in Hebrew, see Ps 89:5-7, Dt 33:2-3, Job 5:1, Ps 34:9; *qadishayya* in Aramaic, see Dan 7:18-27.

[c] e.g. God asks of Israel to be alight to the world.

our purpose anyway, without ever having to be fully conscious of it; but all of us have a mission given to us by God.

Once we have fulfilled our individual missions, at our appointed time we leave this world, and return to our heavenly home, becoming spiritual beings once more. When we came to Earth, we were pure and unblemished, but because of the bad choices we made in this world, we need to be purified of the wrong we have done – nothing bad or impure can re-enter heaven; it's physically impossible because of the power of Yahveh's glory. So we spend some time apart from God being purified of our wrongdoing.

Those who have done *good* things, will see their lives over as a brilliant spectacle of astounding beauty, and these good things will add to the magnificent sum of the splendour which is already inherent in heaven. At this time, I believe we will experience all the happiness and love we ever gave to others.

However, those of us who have made bad choices and done bad things, will need to be purified of that bad, until such a time as we fully repent of the wrong we have done. Once we have been cleansed of our wrong, our souls are cleansed whiter than a fuller can bleach them, and we can then re-enter heaven. The time we spend apart from God, is for the removal of any impurities and spiritual toxins we may have accumulated within our souls during our time here on Earth. This is achieved by reliving all the pain and hurt we ever caused others, to feel it *ourselves*, until we experience true remorse for it.

Now I suspect that those who have led utterly wicked lives – the ultra-cruel who enjoyed inflicting suffering and pain on others, or greedy and ruthless sociopaths who stepped on and crushed others to achieve their goals – those who never showed any remorse or sorrow for their wickedness – probably do not get to enter the *sodh Yahveh*[a] (the inner council of Yahveh), which is the ultimate reward for serving God in life. When they have been purified and leave the Outer Darkness to enter heaven, they merely re-join those pre-existent human souls who have never yet been to earth (i.e. they sit at God's 'left hand'), and will therefore have missed their one and only chance to attain unity with God.

Furthermore, the teaching that those who desecrate the holiness of God are completely cut off[b] and are never forgiven,[c] suggests that unrepentant people who do violence and kill in God's name, for example, can never leave the Outer Darkness for what they have done – not until

---

[a] see Jer 23:18-22; for a fuller explanation of this, see the article near the end of this book entitled, 'The heavenly royal court'.
[b] Num 15:31
[c] Isaiah 22:14

the day when the veil between heaven and earth is torn down,[a] when heaven reigns on earth and there is no longer a need for the Outer Darkness. On that day all evil faces oblivion, because there will no longer be any need for the Outer Darkness. Therefore, the fate of the unrepentant who kill and do violence in God's Name is not paradise, but eternal oblivion.

The most obvious example of religious people desecrating the reputation of God, is ISIS, or the self-styled 'Islamic State'. They believe that by killing in God's name, they will be rewarded by resurrection and an earthly paradise. But people like them have to be warned, that their reward is not paradise, but eternal oblivion of the soul.

Once a soul has been cleansed in the Outer Darkness, a soul has two possible destinations in heaven: God's Right Hand, or God's Left Hand. A soul whose destiny is God's Right Hand, will be blessed with union with God.[b] The ultimate destination of a righteous soul in heaven is union with Yahveh. However, for a soul whose destination is God's Left Hand, their reward is simply to return to the same estate they had before they left heaven to come to earth.

However, someone who kills in God's Name and is unrepentant, is eternally cut off from God; they can never find union with God. If a violent and hateful religious person repents of their sin before death, then they will have to suffer the pain of their wrongdoing in the Outer Darkness, and merely return to the same estate as they had before their earthly birth; in effect, they will have wasted their one and only time on earth. To reach even this, they will have to work the remainder of their lives to undo the evil they have done. For a violent, cruel or oppressive religious person who does not repent, their ultimate fate is oblivion of the soul.

In heaven, all knowledge is available to us – the greatest knowledge and wisdom being accessible in the inner council of Yahveh; in other words, when we are in heaven, we know everything, we are perfect, and we are close to that perfect wisdom which is Yahveh. Therefore while we are on Earth, our purpose is not necessarily to gain or access all the esoteric knowledge of the Universe – because we will have that access *anyway* to an even greater degree once we die and return to God. All we need while we are here, is sufficient knowledge for each individual to become one who will carry out God's work efficiently in this world. The knowledge we should strive for while here, is that knowledge that

---

[a] so that the light of God's glory shines through from heaven, Isaiah 60:19-20. See also Rev 22:1-5 / Ch.Sh. 23:1-5

[b] that is, admittance into the inner council or *sodh* of Yahveh. This will mean that one beceomes privy to Yahveh's innermost thoughts, one will know and see everything that Yahveh sees and knows.

enables us to grow spiritually, in order to improve ourselves to such a point, whereby we can fulfil our individual missions. Perfect knowledge and understanding of the Universe is not required to be gained while we are here, since an infinity of knowledge and perfect wisdom will be fully available to all of us once we return to heaven. While here, some souls will need more spiritual knowledge in order to fulfil their missions than others. Your spiritual hunger will let you know how much knowledge is necessary for you.

I suspect that the Covenant relationship between God and Israel in this world, reflects the deal that God cuts with human souls who volunteer to come to earth. If we enter human bodies to carry out God's plan on earth, then when we return to heaven, our reward is to be allowed into the inner council of Yahveh – to be privy to God's will, as well as all the wisdom and knowledge in the universe.

The Great Plan – the eventual purpose, and the overall design for sending people to Earth – is first to eventually enable God's kingdom to fully function on Earth (for *"God's will to be done on Earth, just as it is in heaven"*), and then enable the barrier (or 'veil') between heaven and Earth to be torn down,[a] allowing God to do away entirely with the need to put us in earthly bodies in order to do God's will on earth.

At present, in order to do God's work, we need earthly bodies while we are here. It is only in heaven that God's will can at present be perfectly done, because in heaven, there is no choice. God knows the consequence of imposing God's will on the world – loss of choice, loss of free will, and beings who love God only because they have to.

In this world, our collective goal is to develop to a stage where all of us willingly do God's will. When a sufficient proportion of humanity willingly carries out God's will, then God will no longer need to put us in earthly bodies; we will remain pure spirit. In the far, far distant future, when God's Kingdom is fulfilled, and the veil between heaven and earth has fallen away, we will be able to come to Earth with full pre-knowledge of heaven, do God's work, and return to heaven when we are done.

Becoming more like our heavenly selves while on earth

A lot of people think that, all we are here for is to acquire knowledge and become perfect, so that we can get to heaven. However, heaven is where we all originally came from (not just Yeshua`), and in heaven we were already perfect, and had access to *most* heavenly knowledge; our emphases and perspectives are currently all wrong. When we finally understand the bigger picture, we will come to realise

---

[a] Isa 60:19-20. See also Rev 22:1-5 / Ch.Sh. 23:1-5

that we are not put on Earth primarily for our individual benefit; also, because we were already perfect in heaven, our emphasis is not necessarily on becoming perfect while here (because no human being can be absolutely perfect), but rather on reacquiring knowledge of our heavenly perfection – remembering the way we once were in heaven – and tap into that while on earth, *so that we become more like our heavenly selves*. If we can do this, we can better do God's will on earth.

We are here to do God's will – it's not about 'us', it's about God's Kingdom. We are all fellow servants of our Heavenly Father, working towards the fulfilment of that kingdom. Our ultimate reward is to be admitted to the inner wisdom and knowledge of God's inner council – the *sodh Yahveh*, and be privy to God's will and purpose.[a]

Knowing this will refocus the emphasis of our spiritual lives. The question is not, "What am I here to do so that my soul can grow?" or, "What am I here to learn for my spiritual benefit?" but rather, "How can I live, improve myself and grow, so that I am better able to understand the work God has sent me here to do?"

To summarise: we are born in heaven as spiritual beings or 'holy ones'. In heaven we have access to most knowledge and wisdom, but in order to become privy to the inner will and wisdom of God, and so become unified with God's glory, we must serve God's kingdom on earth – and our ultimate reward is union with God's glory. Those who have done their best to walk God's ways in life will have this reward. Those who have lived thoroughly wicked lives for most of their time on earth, but who repent of their sin before death, need to be purified in the Outer Darkness before returning to heaven, but will not be blessed with this reward of being privy to God's will; this is in fact the difference between those who are metaphorically seated at God's right and left hand; the 'left hand of God' is not hell, or even the Outer Darkness.

The 'right hand of God' is an exalted state of the soul, while the 'left hand of God' is not.[b] Those who do evil most of their lives and never repent or feel remorse, these will spend time in the Outer Darkness and serve time there according to what they have done. On leaving the Outer Darkness, they are denied access to the ultimate reward of unity with God, and merely return to what they were before they came to earth – to stand *outside* of the council of Yahveh, 'at God's left hand'. This state of affairs is alluded to in Isaiah 65:13-14, when God relates how the wicked will be denied a place at the final wedding banquet.

The day when the barrier[c] between heaven and earth is dissolved,

---

[a] implied by Jer 23:8
[b] S.Yesh. passage 134; cf Mt 25:32-46
[c] The veil in front of the Tent of the Presence was supposed to represent this barrier.

this is the day when

> *"the wolf shall live with the lamb, and the leopard lie down with the kid – the calf and the lion and the fattened lamb together, and a little child shall lead them. The cow and the bear shall graze – their young shall lie down together, and the lion shall eat straw like the ox. The nursing child shall play over the hole of a cobra, and the weaned child shall put its hand on the adder's den. They will not hurt or destroy anywhere on my holy mountain, for the Earth will be full of the knowledge of the glory of Yahveh, just as the waters cover the sea."*[a]

These things – which, after all, go against all the normal laws of the *present* order of the natural world – are only possible when the veil between this world and the next is torn down, the glory of God shines on earth,[b] and the kingdom of God is fulfilled.

The place of Knowledge and Wisdom in Israelite spirituality

The entire Book of Proverbs comes from King Solomon's observations of life.[c] He contrasts the wise person with the foolish person, because without wisdom, religion becomes an exercise in human stupidity. It is guided only by human desires, prejudices, vanity and spite. Wisdom, which comes from Yahveh, teaches you to bring together what you have learned from God, as well as from life, and bind them together with scripture, so that you will be able to figure out what to do in any circumstance of life – even in those things which are not mentioned in scripture.

A discerning person will soon realise that there are great lessons to be learned from the observation of life – from going through the highs and lows of life, and gaining new perspectives from them that one would not have gained otherwise. A spiritually-minded person will interpret these life-lessons as being directly from God. Therefore, rather than become cynical, bewail their fate and struggle bitterly through the daily grind, a discerning person – someone who is hungry for God, and thirsts after the wisdom that God delivers to all God's children – will strive to ensure that he or she will come out of each and every life-experience all the richer and wiser.

A wise person is someone who learns and grows through life's

---

[a] Isaiah 11:6-9
[b] Isa 60:19-20. See also Rev 22:1-5 / Ch.Sh. 23:1-5
[c] truisms derived from the observable wisdom of God in life are called *liqachim* in Hebrew.

lessons; a fool is someone who does not – this is King Solomon's very definition of a fool. Religious fundamentalists, who accept only the literal words written in scripture *and nothing else*, close themselves off from the observations of life, which God gives to us as a way of connecting directly with Yahveh. Starved of this living connection with God, this is why religious fundamentalists lack any godly compassion or a merciful heart. They are like the foolish and wicked servant who buried his talent of gold, and did nothing with it.[a]

Another way of looking at this is to see the puzzles and complexities of life like a connect-the-dots picture. A fundamentalist – someone who only looks at the words of the bible and nothing else – will only ever see life as a series of dots. Being blind to the lessons of life, and deaf to the wisdom of God, they can only connect the dots in a haphazard way, and end up with a picture that bears no resemblance to what God intended. However, someone who learns from life's lessons will be able to connect the dots in the way God intended, and someone who listens to the wisdom of God in a living relationship with God, will see the whole picture brightly painted in living colour!

Jewish wisdom literature is essentially a record of human experience under God's guidance, regarding how to approach the complex events and difficulties of life – it is what the *Book of Proverbs* ultimately teaches us (if anyone bothers to read it)! People who thirst for such knowledge soon find that they reach a point where the trials of life no longer frighten them. The more knowledge they acquire, the greater understanding they have. And the greater the understanding, the wiser decisions they are able to make in life.

Wisdom teaches you that there are no blanket solutions which can be applied to every single problem in life. Without wisdom, religion becomes essentially an exercise in displaying one's stupidity for all the world to see. One can read and know the whole Miqra off by heart, but it does not mean that one is wise. Wisdom comes from a living relationship with Yahveh;[b] without it, religion is just doing things by rote, acting only on one's desires, presumptions and prejudices. The Miqra more often than not tells us what we cannot do, and what we should do; between those two boundaries, we can use the wealth and spirit of the Miqra to live life and resolve our problems.

Wisdom, which comes from Yahveh, teaches you to bring together what you have learned from God, and life, and bind them together with scripture. Wisdom from Yahveh helps us to decide what to do even in circumstances that are not even mentioned in the bible. Wisdom teaches

---

[a] S.Yesh. 80:3-15; cf Mt 25:14-28, Lk 19:12-27
[b] Prov 2:6, Prov 9:10, Ps 111:10

you how to best apply scripture to life, without being an embarrassment to God, and a fool to the world.

Wisdom also comes from the study of nature and the physical universe around us; the Convener (the one known as 'Ecclesiastes') wrote: *'I set my mind to study and to explore through wisdom **all that takes place under the heavens.** '*[a] Again, understanding the world around us makes us less afraid of it. It makes us all the more appreciative of the handiwork of Yahveh. In contrast, those who hate knowledge and despise wisdom, sow the seeds of their own trouble and disquiet.[b]

Wisdom Mysticism in Israelite religion

Ancient Israelite sages found that this sense of calm gave them an almost spiritual serenity.[c] On a higher level, it almost felt like the more knowledge, understanding and wisdom one acquired, the closer one came into the Presence of God. The acquisition of knowledge and understanding therefore became a legitimate spiritual pursuit for a Follower of Yahveh. Proverbs 30:3 says, *'I have not learned wisdom, nor have I attained to the knowledge of the Holy One.'* This implies that the opposite must also be true – that learning wisdom brings one closer to Yahveh.

In time, there came a struggle to understand the precise nature of wisdom – that is, what was its relationship to God? Influenced by Greek thought, and Mediterranean pagan religions that worshipped goddesses of wisdom, Wisdom itself became personified and anthropomorphised by Hellenist Jewish sages. It first became the female aspect of God (since the Hebrew word for 'wisdom' – *chokhmah* – is grammatically feminine in gender). Then, in the time of Philo (20 BCE – 50 CE) it even became the daughter of God. From this, it was just a short skip and a jump to becoming the 'divine word'. Personification of wisdom was ultimately a serious mistake, because it allowed that wisdom to become detached from God, and then incarnated in the second person of the Christian trinity. Jer 17:5 actually warns against those who trust in supposed human incarnations of the divine.

I see myself as a humble practitioner of biblical *Kavodh* mysticism – that form of mysticism that comes from raising one's soul to bathe in the glory (the fire of the Divine Radiance) of Yahveh. The mysticism of wisdom is part of that practice. My own personal perception of wisdom is this: just as a fire gives off heat, and just as a flower gives off scent, so

---

[a] Ecc 1:13
[b] Prov 8:36b 'All those who hate me (wisdom) are in love with death.'
[c] Prov 19:11 – 'A person's wisdom yields patience'.

also Yahveh gives off wisdom. As we breathe air on earth, wisdom fills the very atmosphere of heaven. It surrounds the throne of God, and infuses every heavenly being. A soul that approaches the throne of God, breathes in the breath of wisdom.

When I travel in the spirit into the Presence of Yahveh, it is as if one is bathed in the knowledge and wisdom of the universe. You feel as if all that can ever be known becomes available to you. You feel a serene sense of peace and calm. That is what is retained when you return from God's immediate presence, because the wealth of that wisdom cannot be brought into this world; it is too much for the human mind to handle.

Once you are back here in this world, what you gain is a permanent sense that there are far more important things in life than the little pettinesses and squabbles we are too often distracted by. You retain an awareness that there is a higher purpose and a greater plan than what we mere mortals can imagine or perceive. And you retain this overwhelming sense that you need to realign your priorities to gain the most from your daily walk in the Presence of God.

Ha-Davar: The Word or 'Message' of Yahveh

The Christian concept of the divine logos was very much influenced by Hellenist philosophers, such as those who followed the views of Heraclitus, and the writings of the Greek Stoics. In their teaching, the logos was the creative force of the divine that permeated all things, and ultimately governed them. In Greek philosophy it was seen as an intermediary force between the divine and the human world, and it is this aspect of the Hellenist logos that was passed over into Christian theology – 'Christ' becomes the logos incarnate, the mediator between God and humanity. The Christian Logos is a Greek concept, not a Jewish one, and is the reason why the 'Jesus' of the Gospel of John sounds more like a Greek philosopher than a Jewish prophet.

Long before Heraclitus in the 5th century BCE, Israelite theology *also* possessed a type of mysticism in relation to 'the Word' or 'Message' of Yahveh – '*ha-Davar Yahveh*' in Hebrew. It stood for the entire body of teaching, principle and goodness that was identified with Yahveh.

There isn't one single English word that can translate this meaning[a] of *davar*. It's a combination of 'message', 'revered teaching', 'all-encompassing philosophy', 'just precepts', and 'wise advice'. Henceforth, I shall use the word 'Message' to represent what the Yahwist

---

[a] the word *davar* has an *enormous* number of meanings; other meanings in other contexts would include 'thing' or 'spoken word', hence 'proclamation' or 'edict'.

idea of *davar* stands for.

In Yeshua`'s time, the two views – the Hebrew and the Hellenist – had become intermingled. When it was taken over by Paul and his Christian Believers, instead of trying to reclaim the purely Jewish ideal of the *davar*, Rabbinic theology abandoned it, so that *ha-davar* (or 'the word') no longer plays any part in modern Rabbinic thought. This section is therefore an attempt to excise the Hellenist aspect of the Greek logos, and reassert the original, authentic Hebrew *davar*.

When the Message (or 'word') of Yahveh comes to the prophets, it is not merely a set of words that is given to them, but an entire body of understanding of what Yahveh is, as well as the values and principles God stands for. As a result, when a prophet is questioned or tested, they can draw on the wellspring of this message and speak further.

The Message is everything that Yahveh is – God's holiness, power, purpose, justice, moral law, wisdom and love – the sum total of everything that comes from Yahveh and has an active effect on this world; that is *ha-davar*, the Message.

The Message is so powerful, that it can almost be experienced; on Mt Sinai, God's glory passes before Moses, and Moses witnesses God's goodness, love, graciousness, compassion, justice and mercy.[a] This was the essence of Yahveh which was revealed in the glory to Moses – *ha-davar*, the Message.

When the prophets experience the Message for the first time, they are terrified by it, because the full force of its power becomes apparent. They are awed by its purifying holiness, and they come to realise that no human word they can produce can even come close to the Divine Message that they have witnessed. They realise that they can only sublimate their own words to this Message; the only response possible when God bestows the Message on your soul, is to follow it with humility and the spirit of service.

When you accept the Message as your spiritual foundation, turning against it is like turning against the air that you breathe, the food that you eat, and the water that you drink. To reject the Message is to reject life itself and be cut off from it.[b]

Ha-davar is a philosophy – one that is so powerful that it almost achieves a life of its own, a power to change and move the hearts and minds of all human beings. However, you cannot separate the Message from Yahveh; to do justice to the Hebrew vision of *ha-davar*, you cannot turn it into a disparate entity. The Message is Yahveh, and Yahveh is the Message.

---

[a] Ex 32:18-19, 34:6-7
[b] cf 1Sam 15:23, Num 15:31

Consider this: a woman teaches a philosophy of life and being. She not only teaches it, she lives it as well. In fact, she lives her message so completely and perfectly, that she becomes her message. Now, look at Yahveh's Message. God doesn't need to become God's Message; God is the Message already. So if you teach Yahveh, you are teaching the Message, and if you teach the Message, you are teaching Yahveh.

The Message of Yahveh is so strong and powerful that it is able to effect and change the world; through the prophet Isaiah,[a] Yahveh says, *'Just as the rain . . . comes down from the sky, and does not return before having watered the earth, . . . so it is with my Message (davar); . . . it will not return to Me unfulfilled, . . . nor fail to achieve what it was sent out to do.'* It has the power to heal, and rescue us in times of distress;[b] the power to provide and to sustain.[c]

A lot of people confuse the Message of Yahveh with the message of the bible – with its written word. The Message (or ethos) of Yahveh is the sum of God's values, principles, precepts, ethics, morals, as well as the fundamental essence of the nature of Yahveh. These things are unchangeable. The biblical text is the letter by letter, word by word literature that is written on parchment, separate and distinct from the overall and underlying message, which is far greater. Fundamentalists are unable to make the intellectual distinction between the two. Evangelicals in particular, because their religion is about belief rather than practice, rely heavily on the literal letters on the page, and ignore the context and underlying meaning of the words. For both right-wing Christians and right-wing Jews, the word of God is merely the letters on the parchment; for a true Yahwist, the Word (more properly, the Message) of Yahveh is the entire sum of what Yahveh is and teaches.

So in Yahwist thought, the Message is not a separate person or being; *the Message is Yahveh.* Yahveh imparts a portion of that Message to those who show humility to the Message. Our humility and service of that Message enable us to do things out of all proportion to our own, innate abilities. If a quiet, unassertive person accepts the Message, and does not change it, he or she is able to achieve far more than his or her own retiring personality will allow. And if an outgoing personality resists the temptation to inject the Message with ideas that are alien to it, such a person will avoid the dangers of the sins of pride and ego.

In this way, the Message is passed from generation to generation, and God's Presence is thus able to dwell with each generation. The Message guides us in wisdom and understanding – *Yahveh* guides us in

---

[a] Isaiah 55:11
[b] Ps 107:20
[c] Ps 147:15-18

wisdom and understanding through this powerful philosophy that God is, as a positive and active force in our world.

A true follower of the Way of Yahveh is called to carry forward this Message into the world, planting its seed and allowing it to grow; and allowing it to fundamentally change the world like yeast in dough. Become bearers of this Message, therefore; internalise it so that it travels with you wherever you may go; draw from it like a spring of water, and bring forth its treasures as you would from a depository.

Become apostles of the Message, without changing it or amending it, and you will see a miracle before your very eyes, as it changes the world around you, not failing to achieve what it was sent out to do.

Line 10: Just as we should forgive our debtors

Just as ....

The prophet Yeshua` said, *'When you stand praying, forgive anything you have against anyone, so that your heavenly Father may also forgive you your sins. For if you forgive others their offences, how much more so will your heavenly Father forgive you!'* [a]

This teaching gives us an insight into the thinking of the prophet. If we wish to be forgiven our sins, the first thing we should do is forgive others. How can we expect God to forgive us, when we are unwilling to forgive others?

These two Aramaic words also say much about our relationship with God. If we are to forgive our debtors, and those who sin against us, it assumes that God will do the same – forgive us our debts and sins. It implies a two-way relationship, with obligations on both God and God's people.

In the Yahwist Israelite way of thinking, every relationship has unwritten obligations and mutual responsibilities. In the ancient hospitality laws, there were unwritten obligations both on the host, as well as the guest. The host was not to be disrespectful, unwelcoming or abusive to the guest. However, at the same time, the guest was not to take advantage of the kindness or openness of the host. A similar code existed with gleaning rights. Landowners were to allow passers-by to take what they needed to sate their hunger, but passers-by were not to deliberately set off on their journey empty-handed, or take more than they needed; the people were to respect the king and not curse him, but a king also had the responsibility to stand up and defend his people, to treat them fairly and act as a role model; in the relationship between parent and child, just

---

[a] S.Yesh. 35:1-2 – cf Mk 11:25, Mt 6:14, Lk 6:37

as a child was to be obedient to its parents, so also a parent had a responsibility not to be cruel or abusive to their children, or give their children an evil or immoral command to follow. So also with the rich and the poor – the rich had a responsibility of charity towards the poor, but the poor also had a responsibility to be honest and not take or demand more than they and their families actually needed, as well as the responsibility to do whatever they could to improve their own circumstances.

This same kind of mutual responsibility and obligation is inherent when we talk about the Covenant. In fact, it is vital to understand that mutual responsibility and obligation is what a covenant is all about.

The Covenant

A big deal is made, especially in evangelical circles, of the relevance of 'the Covenant' for Gentiles. However, if you were to ask most modern Christians, 'What is a covenant?' they probably would not know. If they did, the overwhelming majority would not know what the actual *wording* of that Covenant was. Once you, my readers, know what the wording of '*the* Covenant' is, you will start to ask yourself why Paul of Tarsus made such a big deal out of his Gentile Believers having to be part of this Covenant, which actually only needed to be between just God and Israel.[a]

If we look at God's relationship with Israel, we see that God's care for us as a nation has *obligations*. Without intending any disrespect to those who do not follow a Jewish lifestyle, I get the impression that what non-Jews who want to belong to *the* Covenant seem to ask, is that they want all of the blessings, but none of the responsibilities. They want all the good stuff – love, community, salvation, good fortune – but they don't want to do any of the hard, spiritual work that is inherently required with a covenant.

A covenant is basically any pact or agreement between two parties, with mutual obligations and responsibilities on *both* sides. One major type of covenant in the ancient Middle East was that between the central royal authority of an empire, and a subject nation. Such agreements stipulated that as long as the subject nation abided by the central

---

[a] Having asked several Christian friends, and received various answers from each, I get the impression most Christians think that the Covenant is: 'If I do good, then God will love me and I will go to heaven.' When I say that Gentiles are not part of '*the* Covenant', Christians get either really angry or really distressed, thinking that I am saying, 'God doesn't love you, and you won't go to heaven.' When the real wording of the Covenant is explained, it becomes obvious why non-Jews don't need to be part of such a Covenant.

authority's laws, then that nation would have the central authority's protection. In return for their loyalty and annual tribute of gold, animals, grain etc, the subject nation would be protected. However, if the subject nation rebelled against the central authority and disobeyed its laws, then the subject nation would be reprimanded accordingly.

The relationship between ancient Israel and Yahveh was built on such a pact or agreement. It is a *huge* part of Israelite theology. If you cannot or will not understand what that Covenant relationship means, you will not understand the turbulent relationship between God and Israel.

For example, when the Israelites were entering the land of Canaan, they were told not to take the goods of the Canaanites for themselves. Some of them disobeyed this command, and surreptitiously pocketed a few trinkets for themselves. When this happened, their disobedience meant they were no longer able to stand up against the Canaanites, and were roundly defeated. Their greed marred them spiritually, and weakened them. This disobedience was only fully rectified when the Israelites reaffirmed their adherence to the Covenant.[a]

Another important thing to realise about covenants, is that they cannot be revoked or nullified. Nor can a present covenant replace a former one: *"Whatever God declares shall be forever;"*[b] *"The word of Yahveh shall stand firm forever;"*[c] *"And it shall be a law for all time;"*[d] *"I will not annul my covenant with them;"*[e] *"I will not violate My Covenant, nor change what I have uttered."*[f] Covenants can be expanded and appended to, but not annulled or changed. You can renew a Covenant, but you can't have a new one replacing the existing one.

So, what then is the wording of the Covenant between Yahveh and Israel? Basically, Yahveh's obligations are: to be Israel's God forever, to give Jacob's descendants the land of Canaan forever, to keep them as a people and a nation forever, and to protect them forever. Israel's obligations are: to worship Yahveh alone forever, and to follow only God's laws and teachings forever.[g] Everything else is terms and conditions, blessings and benefits, stipulations, provisos and addenda.

You will notice one word that crops up time and time again: **forever**. If God could maintain this people and this religion forever, throughout every generation and for all time, in spite of persecution,

---

[a] Josh 6:17-19, 7:1-26, 8:30-35
[b] Ecc 13:14
[c] Isa 40:18
[d] Num 19:21
[e] Lev 26:44
[f] Ps 89:35
[g] Gen 17:1-21

calamity and the attempts by insidious missionisers to convert the Jewish people, then it would be proof of Yahveh's power – that Yahveh is a living God.

The Covenant is not about us, it's about Yahveh. Given the purpose of the Covenant, that much should be obvious. To paraphrase a famous quote of President Kennedy: 'Ask not what your God can do for you; rather, ask what you can do for your God!' A Gentile Godfearer should not say, 'I want the blessings of the Covenant'; rather, 'I want to join the Covenant because I want to help raise the fame and renown of Yahveh, and to help Yahveh's reputation to increase and spread'. Belonging to the Covenant is a job; Covenant-holders are there to be a vehicle of witness to Yahveh's holiness and reputation *throughout all eternity.*

You can see then, if that concept of eternal witness is endangered in any way, for whatever reason, then Yahveh has no choice but to take firm action. God's good reputation depends on the fulfilment of the terms and conditions of the Covenant forever.

On God's part, God has promises to fulfil for the sake of his good reputation (usually rendered as 'for the sake of God's Name'). God has an obligation to forgive the penitent sinner. And so, just as we should forgive our debtors, and those who sin against us, so also God has an obligation to forgive us when we return to God and repent of our sins.

The practical implications of the Covenant

Being part of the Covenant does not mean that we are automatically protected from harm and misfortune, in spite of what we do; we cannot claim descent from Abraham, and then go and commit all kinds of unkindness, misdemeanour and transgression. Through the prophet Amos,[a] Yahveh said, *'You alone I have favoured from amongst all the clans of the earth.'* The people who originally heard these words would have been jolted by what followed: *'. . . that is why I will punish you for all your iniquities.'*

In the time of Amos, there were many among the wealthy elite who believed that all they had to do was offer the correct blood sacrifices, and perform the correct rituals and customs, and they would be all right – they would be protected from all harm. There are also those today who celebrate their salvation through faith alone, and I have met such people who then go on to speak with great unkindness and cruelty, are corrupt, are manipulative, walk by or *over* the poor, and are judgmental, hateful and malicious. Neither of these two groups of people – the shallow rich of Amos's day, or the malicious religious people of our day - realise that

---

[a] Amos 3:2

their actions would have to be accounted for one day, even in this life.

God spoke those words through Amos, because for someone who is part of the Covenant (and today, for someone who believes they are saved through faith alone), a higher standard is expected of such people. People who are part of the Covenant should know better, and should therefore behave in a better way.

The Covenant does not mean that we are given a 'get out of jail free' card; it means that we will be monitored with greater strictness and vigilance, and disciplined with greater severity than anyone else.

Therefore, do not think that just because you are Jewish or Christian that you automatically deserve God's favour, or that God's blessing is a foregone conclusion. Because Yahveh will raise up the Hindu who gives food to a destitute foreigner, and will grant blessing to a Muslim who strives to be a benefit to the country where he is an alien, but Yahveh will be blind to the Jew who rocks and sways as he davens[a] fervently, yet who also stones the innocent who seek only to pray with their spouses, or the Jew who spits at children on their way to school because they don't conform to a strict dress code; God will be deaf to the Christian who sings 'Glory halleluiah!', and then ignores the penniless who struggle in the cold, or the plight of the poor who succumb to illness and death because they cannot afford medical attention.[b]

Your ancestry and your faith guarantee you nothing, if your actions do not match what your God requires of you.

God's firm guidance

For those of us who believe primarily in a loving and compassionate God, the very idea of a God who disciplines or even punishes us is a terribly difficult idea to even contemplate. There is a Hebrew word, *musar*, that is often translated as 'discipline' in English bibles. However, it doesn't convey the true intent of our Heavenly Father in this discipline. A better translation would be, 'firm guidance.'

The parent who constantly punishes every small fault is a cruel parent. The parent who is firm but caring is a responsible parent. This is how God deals with us. God guides us through the experiences he gives us in life – both the good and the bad.

One basic Yahwist principle is that the wrong we do to others will be returned to us by God, *even in this life*. Many religious people today concentrate so heavily on punishment after death, that they ignore the

---

[a] 'prays'; from Yiddish *davnen*
[b] here I am not advocating any particular medical aid scheme; I am criticising those who believe that nothing should be done – that the poor should be left to die.

fact that our wrongs also come back to bite us even while we are still alive. Our Heavenly Father is emphatically a God of bountiful love, but a parent who *only* shows love and gives no direction to their children, providing no instruction or discipline of any kind, is not only a weak parent, but an ineffective one.

We will all have both good and bad experiences in life, not all of them from God. However, those who learn from their life experiences will mature into wise and caring adults.

The *Book of Joshua* is a story of how things go right for Israel when she is faithful to God's ways, and how things go horribly wrong when she deliberately ignores and turns her back on God. The writer of *Joshua* tends to see the misfortune as a direct punishment from an angry God, but I look at it in a different way. The situation is more a case of us, metaphorically, ignoring the instructions on the box, and we shouldn't blame the manufacturer or the ingredients if the cake doesn't turn out right. Or if we cut corners, scrimp on safe materials and ignore building codes, we shouldn't be surprised if the building falls down.

God promises us blessings, but God also has requirements of us to follow. Living under God's protection comes with it the prerequisite that we have to follow certain guidelines – which are there for our good. Yahveh's *love* is absolutely unconditional, but the blessings of God's Presence among us *do* come with conditions. The Covenant has requirements as well as advantages.

A son who doesn't know how to drive, is told by his father not to take his car keys. He disobeys, takes the car and is involved in a serious crash. A mother tells her daughter not to go out with a notorious thug from the neighbourhood. She disobeys and is violently raped. In the same way, there are consequences for going against God's wise and purposeful instructions. God's firm guidance is there, not to punish us or keep us under God's thumb, but to protect us and make sure, not only that we are safe, but that we prosper. God's guidance is firm but kind.

However, if we end up thinking that God is *only* a disciplinarian, then we end up being resentful of God. We have to remember that God is loving and cares greatly for us. If you remember the story of the Prodigal Son, you will remember how the father ran to greet his son upon his penitent return.

You can imagine how this wealthy Jewish landowner would usually be quite staid, with a calm exterior that demands respect. However, when he sees his son he drops all decorum, picks up his skirts and runs down the road to greet his son – he doesn't even wait for his son to come to him!

So it is with our heavenly Father. When we repent, and show a willing heart to return, God doesn't wait until we have completed the journey; God doesn't require any death or sacrifice to bridge the distance that we have created for *ourselves* by our disobedience.[a] God rushes immediately to our side and journeys with us the rest of the way – so great is God's love for us. There is no greater love.

... we should forgive ...

In the ancient Greek manuscripts, there are variations in the tense of this verb: 'we forgave', we have forgiven', 'we forgive' etc. I think this reflects a Semitic language problem behind the attempts at translation. You see, both Aramaic and Hebrew are written without vowels. If you don't know what vowels are supposed to be inserted between the consonants, then the only way you can tell what tense a verb is supposed to be in, is from the context. Sometimes, however, even that is not possible.

In Aramaic, 'we forgive' (*shabaqnan*), we forgave / have forgiven (*sh^ebaqnan*) all look the same: שבקנן This would be the reason why the Greek translations are unsure of which tense this should be.

If the verb is supposed to be in the present tense, then it would imply that God forgives us, in the same way that we forgive others. If the verb is in the past tense, then it implies that God forgives us only when we have forgiven others (i.e. God would not act on simple penitence alone).

However, putting the verb into the obligatory mood of the verb – 'should forgive' – reminds us of the Covenant relationship that exists between God and Israel. Just as we are obligated to forgive our debtors, and those who sin against us, so we ask God to remember God's promises, to uphold God's part of the deal, and forgive us when we repent.

The cancellation of sin

How often have you read about famous people in the tabloid press, when journalists have found out some unsavoury or regrettable act in their past and expose it. As a result, the reputation of the celebrity is tarnished, and their misdemeanour is held against them forever. Even if the celebrity is not the same person as they were when they committed the questionable act – if they have since changed their ways, and become better people – the press seem to have no sense of forgiveness. In their eyes, a sin is a sin forever.

Not so with God. In Aramaic, the verb 'to forgive' also means, 'to

---

[a] i.e. the distance is not on God's side, but on ours.

abandon'. In Hebrew, the verb *salach* has the idea of the lifting of a burden. When God forgives, the sin is remembered no more. If a person truly repents of what they have done, promises to God to strive to be a better person, and not to commit the sin again, then God wipes the slate clean. God abandons the remembrance of the sin, and lifts the burden of the sin from that person's soul. It is not held against them by God, and they do not have to pay for their sin twice.

As Yahveh proclaimed through the prophet Isaiah, '*I – and I alone – am the one who blots out your transgressions, for my own sake, and remembers your sins no more.*'[a]

Consider now another scenario: A middle-aged woman is catapulted onto the world stage, because she has an amazing message to deliver to the world. It is no less than the ultimate meaning of life itself, an unmistakeable message direct from God. It is a plan for the betterment of human society, an end to war, poverty and disease. It has a huge impact on the people of the world – as the flame of her sect spreads all over the world, and people start living the message, it has a profound effect on the quality of all human life on earth.

People begin praising her wisdom and abilities, and proclaim her the saviour of the world, but she tells them that she is completely unimportant. She protests vociferously and insists that she is no one; the message is from God, and it is to God that the public should focus all their attention.

However, there are some people who are aggrieved that these life-changing answers and results did not come through *their* religion. They become suspicious as to why she should not want attention to be focussed on her. So they decide to go digging into the woman's past. They find out that when she was younger, she used to be a prostitute. Even though she turned her back on her past, and has not followed such a profession for decades, this fact is brought to the public's attention. There is a huge scandal, and because of who she *once* was, the majority of the human race abandon the way of life and the saving message she tried to deliver. God attempted to give humanity the answers it sorely needed, but because the *messenger* was imperfect, they did not listen; human beings judged the message according to the person who delivered it, and not the One with whom it originated.

It was God's intent that people should conclude, 'Such a message could not have come from such a person; therefore it must be from God.' However, what actually happened was that people said, 'Such a message must be false, because the messenger was once a sinful and imperfect person.'

---

[a] Isa 43:25

271

Not only are human beings incapable of separating the message from the messenger, and examining solely the content of the message, sadly human beings are also unable to forgive and forget.

Not so with God. Yahveh says, '*I will forgive their iniquity, and remember their sin no more.*'[a]

... *our debtors*

In Aramaic, the word for 'sin' is the same as the word for debt – *choba*. However, because God forgives sins and not debts, the meaning that an Aramaic-speaker would think of first would be 'sin'. They would only realise the play on words when they heard the next line, which speaks about either 'sinners' or 'debtors' – *chayabayya*.

The forgiveness of debt would have been a major issue in Galilean culture, and indeed a big deal. It didn't happen too often; since most poor Galileans were in so much debt, to have one's debt cancelled would have been truly a wonderful thing. Galileans did not earn very much, but the overall tax burden was very high – some historians calculate it as much as 60 or 70 per cent. People had to pay out money to landlords, to the king, for fishing rights, tolls and customs duty at ports, and to tax collectors collecting for the Romans – all in addition to the 10% tithe payable for the upkeep of the Temple and priesthood in Jerusalem, and for the relief of the poor.

The tax burden was horrendous. Many people found it an impossible struggle, and in desperation turned to moneylenders. These men were a hated but typical part of Galilean society – usually landlords, officials of the royal court or chief servants ('stewards'). Even though Jewish religious law forbade the charging of interest, many families found it impossible to pay off what they had borrowed. And when that happened, they fell afoul of the moneylenders.

So then moneylenders made recourse to the courts to get their money back. Inevitably, the poor had no means by which to repay the money, and debtors – sometimes with their whole family – were put in prison until such time as the debt would have been paid off.

As a Galilean, Yeshua` understood how debt was crippling his society. Debt pushed his fellow countrymen and women further and further into poverty. That is why he urged moneylenders to forgive those it was hurting most.

In addition to moneylenders, tax collectors were another hated group of people. Not just because they often collected more in taxes than they were supposed to, and not just because the high taxes caused misery

---

[a] Jer 31:34; see also Isaiah 1:18

in itself. Tax collecting was a franchise; it was a right sold by the Roman occupiers to individuals, who collected taxes on behalf of their imperial masters. This made the profession doubly traitorous; it was bad enough to having an occupying force make someone collect taxes, but to actually have someone say to their oppressors, 'I would like to buy the right to collect taxes on your behalf', was seen as deliberate greed, a betrayal of one's people, and worst of all, collaboration with Rome.

Poverty in the Galilee

The Galilee had a great deal of natural wealth – it had green and fertile countryside, and a hard-working population. However, bad economic management, debt, tolls, taxes and dues ground its people into misery. No wonder they longed for someone to come and save them from it!

People often imagine that the economy in ancient times operated in a somehow more natural, market-driven way. However, for the Galilee, this was anything but the case. The economic system existed for the sole benefit of the ruler and the aristocracy; nothing was ever done for the benefit of the ordinary citizens. As a result, there was no improvement of infra-structure, no civil progress and no development. Building projects were only carried out if they furthered the aggrandisement of the elite, and the fortunes of the wealthy.

Ordinary Galileans had so little money that taxes and tolls were often paid in kind – agricultural produce went directly to pay off taxes and debts, which were then sold by the rich to fill their coffers.

Very often a poor peasant would sow seed he had borrowed, on borrowed land, using borrowed animals, and borrowed tools and equipment – even living in a borrowed house. All this of course had to be repaid, or at least rent paid for them. Some people owed so much that they could never hope to pay off their debts in their lifetime, and their whole family became debt slaves. They had to work for their creditor – usually a landlord – and become their tenants, farming their land, and giving over *most* of what they harvested. You can guess that they often had very little left to feed themselves with.

People usually only had one set of clothes – usually a simple tunic and a mantle. They would wear, wash and repair them, and repair them again and again, darning them and patching them up, until they couldn't be patched up any more. The poorest had no shoes, and lived in dwellings of one room. However, even that one room always had an oil lamp burning, even through the night while everyone was asleep. A person was considered to be living in abject poverty, if they couldn't even afford oil to burn in their lamps at night.

Work was often difficult to come by. As well as the marketplace being somewhere to buy and sell wares, it was also somewhere the unemployed would hang around, waiting for someone to hire them for a day's work – longer if they were lucky. Temporary, daily work was typical in the Galilee. People would hire themselves out as field labourers, or even as servants. People would do field labour mostly during the summer months. If they were lucky, they would get longer term work as servants. Because of the temporary nature of work, and because Jewish law stipulated it,[a] everyone was paid daily.

Poverty produced another problem – prostitution. Because men were often the sole breadwinners, if a woman had no husband, sons or brothers, she might turn to prostitution to make ends meet.

Many prostitutes came to their profession, not out of desire but out of dire need. What caused even bigger problems for these women was whom they were turning to for business – usually the only ones who could afford to pay: Roman soldiers, as well as the aristocracy, who were the stooges of the Romans. Prostitutes were therefore naturally seen as collaborators with the Romans. They were shunned as a result, and sometimes murdered by Zealots.

Yeshua` took a different line. By his words and actions, he showed his followers that what these women needed was not hatred and condemnation, but rather forgiveness for their past, and support to enable them to escape the very circumstances that had forced them into prostitution in the first place.

Yahveh, our compassionate God, put laws in place to ensure that the widowed and the fatherless would not be abandoned financially by Jewish society.[b] We can be sure that these are the very laws that the prophet Yeshua` would have reminded his people of, and exhorted them to observe.

Biblical solutions for the relief of the poor

Anyone familiar with the Torah and Jewish tradition would be reading all the above problems, and they would know at once that there were solutions in religious law to resolve these injustices. The difficulty back then, was that many of the rich and aristocratic members of society were ignoring these religious laws.

Jewish law was structured in such a way that debts were not forever. The wisdom and compassion of Yahveh comes out in the Jewish poor laws. I would even go so far as to say that no human could have

[a] Lev 19:13
[b] e.g. Ex 22:22, Dt 10:18, 14:28-29, 24:19-21 and others

come up with them; no human would have had the balanced sense of justice and fairness – that is, without being punitive towards those with money, together with a sense of compassion for the suffering of the poor – to create laws which were fair to everyone.

Take one of the simpler laws: *'If you take your neighbour's mantle*[a] *as a pledge, you must return it before sunset, because his mantle is the only covering he has for his body. What else will he sleep in? When he cries out to Me, I will hear, for I am compassionate; do not revile God.'*[b]

Jewish law also has the concept of *ts*^e*daqah*. In the context of the poor, it is most often translated as 'charity'. However, in Hebrew it also contains the idea of justice, mercy, righteousness, welfare and deliverance. All these ideas are present in the Israelite concept of charity to the poor.

Whereas in the western world, charity is a choice, in Jewish society it is an obligation. It is the way by which God helps the poor and needy in society. God commands us, saying, *'There will never cease to be needy people within the Land. For this reason I command you and say, open wide your hand towards your brother – towards your poor and your needy in your land.'*[c]

The Sabbatical year and Jubilee year laws

I previously mentioned the Sabbatical and Jubilee Year laws. The most radical and revolutionary laws to help the poor were part of the Sabbatical and Jubilee year laws. Rich people in our society today will be horrified today to learn about them.

Every seventh year, just as the land is allowed to rest in a Sabbatical Year, so also the poor and needy are given respite from their debts. Any debt they have is cancelled outright, and never asked from them again. Anyone who was bonded to serve out their debt was to be freed from such labour. And they were to be provided with the means to get themselves back on their feet.[d]

In addition, the year after the seventh Sabbatical year[e] was

---

[a] a mantle (*salmah* or *g*^e*lom* in Hebrew) refers to a long oblong cloth, usually made of cotton. It was one of only two items of clothing that a poor person would have (the other being a single-piece tunic). It was not the same as a religious tallit ('prayer shawl'); the mantle was an everyday item of clothing. At night it was used as a blanket.

[b] i.e. do not blaspheme God by oppressing the poor (Ex 22:25-27a – Christian bibles Ex 22:26-28a); see also Prov 14:31 – 'He who oppresses the poor shows contempt for their Creator.'

[c] Deut 15:11

[d] Deut 15:12-14

[e] which, in effect, was the first year of the next 49-year cycle.

proclaimed a Jubilee Year – during which time any land lost through debt was to be returned to its original owner (or rather, 'tenant'), for Yahveh teaches, *'the Land shall not be sold into perpetuity, for the land is Mine; with Me you are but resident foreigners and My tenants.'*[a] And through the prophet Isaiah, Yahveh speaks against those *'who join house to house, who add field to field, until there is room for no one but you, and you are left to live alone in the midst of the land!'*[b]

Torah legislates against the gathering of more and more land into fewer and fewer hands. The purpose of the Jubilee law is to return land to its original owners every 50 years – land lost through debt. The original ideal when the Israelite tribes entered the land of Canaan, was that land was to be distributed fairly among the tribes. Because the Land was how God provided for God's people, everyone had to have equal access to it. The Prophets protested bitterly against those who strive to accumulate land that rightfully belonged equally to everyone. Land is the source of life, the vital means for the poor to make an independent living. It therefore cannot be treated or sold like a commercial commodity.

So to summarise, if land could not be bought and sold, it could be lost through debt. If land was lost to its original owners through debt, then it was to be returned during a Jubilee year.

Non-Jews rarely understood the motivation behind the laws on debt release, or the strong passions aroused in pious Jews for them; this is why, in my opinion, neither the laws nor the motivation behind them are very well articulated by the gospel writers in the reported sayings of Yeshua`. The forgiveness of debt therefore features large in Yeshua`'s teaching. It is a fundamental part of Yahveh's plan in Torah to help the poor. Yeshua` was not calling for anything new, but rather something long forgotten and ignored.

One might think that these laws cannot work, but a society that operates under these laws – if it has the will to do so – will find a different and better way to function.

God of the poor, who are all 'God's people'

Through the prophet Isaiah,[c] Yahveh declares that all the poor are *'My people'*. As you read above in the quote from the Book of Exodus, where we are commanded to return a mantle given as a pledge and not keep it overnight, there is a deliberate follow-on saying, 'Do not revile God'. This gives us a deep insight into how Yahveh views the poor and

---

[a] Lev 25:23
[b] Isa 5:8
[c] Isa 3:15

needy.

In the Hebrew mind-set, to ignore the poor and disadvantaged is to revile God. An ancient Hebrew proverb says, *'He who oppresses the poor shows contempt for their Creator.'*[a] Yahveh is the champion of the poor, the despondent, the weak, the powerless, and those without a voice. Therefore, if you abuse those whom Yahveh champions, you revile Yahveh. As Jacob the Pious wrote, *'Are [the rich] not the ones who blaspheme the good Name which has been called down upon you?'*[b]

The Book of Psalms[c] says, *'God will deliver the needy who cry out, the oppressed who have no-one to help.'* *'Because of the oppression of the weak and the groaning of the needy, I will now arise* (i.e. and take action)*, says Yahveh.'*[d]

God stakes God's reputation on God's compassion and concern for the poor and the least of society. So in Yeshua''s day, when the laws designed to help the most disadvantaged in society were being ignored, God wasn't going to stay idly by and do nothing.

Debt and charity

I have previously mentioned the Jewish concept of *ts*[e]*daqah,* or charity, and how in Jewish society such a thing is an obligation, not a choice. It is interesting to note that a community[e] that actively practises giving the full 10% of its income before tax as *ts*[e]*daqah,* is a community that finds ways to pay better attention to its spending. Individuals in such a community are more careful of how they use their money. One is actively discouraged from falling into debt. The assurance to the poor of the receipt of *ts*[e]*daqah,* gives them a fall-back; knowing that in hard times you will receive this second-hand help from Yahveh, enables you to say no to borrowing and debt.

As a society, we need to work towards a way of living which does not function on the continuance of debt, and where profit is not the one single, overriding rule of life. If we work towards this, we will begin to operate on a different level. If we cannot give of our money as *ts*[e]*daqah,* we can give of our time and skills instead.

I remember when I was in heavy debt, the members of the

---

[a] Prov 14:31 – see also Prov 17:5 – where it implies that to mock the poor is to insult the Creator.

[b] Ig. Yq. 4:3 – cf Ep. James 2:7

[c] Ps 72:12

[d] Ps 12:6 (12:5 in Christian bibles)

[e] Such as the Orthodox and the Haredim. In their communities, there is no such thing as someone living in abject poverty, because the poorest among them receives assistance through *ts*[e]*daqah*

synagogue I attended practised this *ts^edaqah* with their time and skills. In order to get out of debt, I had to sell my house. They therefore helped me to get my house into a saleable condition. They repaired my leaking hot water tank (one of them was a plumber), they rewired my house (one of them was an electrician), they helped me clear up my unsightly, overgrown garden (one of them was a tree surgeon), and they gave me advice on money matters (one of them was a financial advisor).

The point is, I was able to get back on my feet, because others gave their *ts^edaqah* not in the form of money, but in the form of their skills, knowledge and time. I was released from debt, because of the salvation of God's law of *ts^edaqah*.

Illustrations from the words of the prophet Yeshua`

Yeshua` said:

'When you stand praying, forgive anything you have against anyone, so that your heavenly Father may also forgive you your sins. For if you forgive others their offences, how much more so will your heavenly Father forgive you!'[a]

'Be conciliatory towards your accuser, and settle matters with him quickly while you're on the way to court. Or else your accuser will hand you over to the judge, and the judge to the officer of the court, and you'll be thrown into prison. Let me say this to you: There's no way you're getting out of there until you've paid back the last *prutah*.'[b]

'There was a landlord who wished to settle his accounts with his servants. When he began his calculations, one servant was brought to him who owed him ten thousand *kikkarin*,[c] and as he couldn't pay, his master ordered him to be sold, together with his wife and children and all that he had, so that he could recover his money. So the servant fell on his knees, saying, "Master, have patience with me, and I'll repay you everything." And out of pity for him, his

---

[a] S.Yesh. 35:1-2 – cf Mk 11:25, Mt 6:14, Lk 6:37
[b] a *prutah* was the smallest value of Jewish coinage, so this is the equivalent of the English phrase, 'the last penny'; S.Yesh. 77:1-2 – cf Mt 5:25-26, Lk 12:58-59.
[c] a *kikkar* was a specific weight of silver or gold. In monetary terms, it would represent about 30 years wages. 10,000 kikkarin therefore represents a huge amount of money that could never be repaid in anyone's lifetime.

master released him and cancelled his debt.

But that same servant, as he went out, came upon one of his fellow servants who owed him one hundred denarii.[a] Seizing him by the throat he said, "Pay me what you owe me." So his fellow servant fell down on his face and begged him, "Have patience with me, and I'll pay you." The first servant refused and had him put in prison until such time as the debt would've been paid off.

When his fellow servants saw what had taken place, they were greatly distressed, and they went to report to their master everything that had happened. So his master summoned him and said, "You wicked servant! I cancelled your whole debt because you pleaded with me. Shouldn't you have shown mercy to your fellow servant, just as I had mercy on you?"

And in anger, his master delivered him over to the jailers, and had him put in prison until such time as his debt would've been paid off.'[b]

---

[a] A denarius was one day's wage, so this amount represented a little over 3 months' wages.

[b] S.Yesh. 31:1-11 – cf Mt 18:23-34

CHAPTER EIGHT: Protect us from the tribulation, and deliver us from our accusers

וְאַל תֵּעִילָן לְנִסָיוּנַא
אֶלָא אַצֵילָן מִן בָּאִישָׁא

we'al ta`eylan le-nissayuna
ela atseylan min bisha

And do not bring us to trial
Rather deliver us from evil / our accusers.

Good times and bad times

A while back, I was handed a leaflet from a member of a minor Christian denomination. The leaflet explained that the reason why so many bad things were going on in this world, was because the true ruler of this world was Satan.

As you will know by now, in Israelite theology the Sovereign Ruler of everything – of heaven and earth – is Yahveh, and Yahveh *alone*. In Yahwism, there is no separate ruler of all evil, equal and opposite to the God of Abraham; Yahveh is supreme over both the good and the bad.

Our Heavenly Father knows that our lives will consist of many good things – times of happiness and great joy – as well as times of sadness – times when our sadness is unbearable and our pain seems unending. This mix of good times and bad times is the nature of the world in which Yahveh set us down in. We cannot expect any more or less than this.

I was once told by an atheist that the reason why he could not believe in God, was because if God did exist, God would be a magic-wand type of God, who would ensure bad things *never, ever* happened; if God really existed, then life would be perfect, accidents would never happen, and no one would ever be born with disabilities. He couldn't believe in God, simply because God permits evil things to happen, and makes babies who are disabled. But God is not a puppet-master or an authoritarian who controls every single minutia of our lives – someone who suspends the laws of Nature and Science to ensure bad things never happened to us.

None of us deserves the tragedies and misfortunes that befall us. Sometimes they are so traumatic that they are all we can focus on. The way some of us cope is to create this magic-wand god and pray fervently to it, because we think that God would deal with the universe's problems in the same way we humans would do if we had unlimited power – by controlling everything, and by making bad things disappear with a magic wand. But this god is only a divine magician. This god does not exist.

God's kingdom here on earth is furthered, not by focussing on the tragedy, but on *how we deal with it* – on how we strive to remain decent people and retain our dignity in spite of what happens to us; and on how we selflessly help those around us less capable than ourselves. God's Kingdom is not about the woe of misfortune, but rather *how we handle that misfortune.* Yahveh is the powerful force that we draw our strength from, who enables to get through hard times when we would rather just give up.

When the prophet Elijah was on the run from Queen Jezebel, he hid in a cave. The divine Presence visits Elijah, but it does not manifest in a way that any human would expect:

> God said, *"Go forth and stand on the mountain before Yahveh."* For behold, Yahveh was passing by! Now, a mighty and strong wind was rending the mountains and breaking in pieces the rocks before Yahveh; but Yahveh was not in the wind. Then after the wind there came an earthquake, but Yahveh was not in the earthquake. After the earthquake came a fire, but Yahveh was not in the fire; and after the fire the sound of a gentle breeze. When Elijah heard this, he wrapped his face in his mantle and went out and stood in the entrance of the cave. And behold, a voice came to him..."[a]

God was not in the violence and power of the weather, or in the disasters and misfortunes going on around him, but in the gentle voice that spoke to Elijah.

God does not force or control us like puppets – God is not a puppet-master; God does not control us with fear – God is not a mafia boss; and God does not have a magic wand to wave – because God is not like a

---

[a] 1Kgs 19:11-13

magician. When innocent children are killed by extremist terrorists, it was not God's will that killed the children, it was human evil. When innocent children die from cancer, it was not God's will that caused the children's disease, but the natural course of how Nature functions, which acts without favouritism or capriciousness. God's will is not enacted in having people die in cruelty or suffering, but in how we react and respond to what happened to those children. When disaster befalls us, God's will is not shown in the storm or the flood, the earthquake or the fire, the misfortune or the illness, but in how we react to the disaster and help others.

Yahveh knows that good and bad are both integral parts of the nature of this world. Unfortunately, our modern society is just not set up to handle it. Atheists take their view of God from the naïve and unrealistic views of blinkered religious people, who expect God to stop all bad things happening and prevent all suffering – the existence of evil is therefore proof for atheists of the non-existence of God. However, the anger of atheist criticism is usually directed against a type of god which actually doesn't exist! The puppet-master, the mafia boss and magic-wand type of gods really don't exist.

Our modern, materialistic society trains us to expect that if we work hard, we will all be rich and earn lots of money, and if you don't, well, you just weren't trying hard enough. We are brought up to believe that if we are careful with our money, we will never fall into debt, that we will always be able to pay our bills on time, and that if we always do the right thing, our lives will go smoothly, we will all get everything we ever wanted, and we will all be happy. We will get exactly what we want, when we want it, and how we want it.

But even those who work hard lose their jobs, even those who are careful with their money are visited by unexpected expenses that they can't cope with; some of the things we want, we will never have; and tragedies happen even to good people.

Our society's expectations are not realistic, our view of God is unrealistic, and I think that is why we get so demoralised and become so miserable when even minor things go wrong – we seek to place blame on someone or something for those wrongs; we always look for the 'why' when something bad happens. But often there isn't a why; things just happen.

There are times of hunger, and there are times of fullness. It is unrealistic to pray that bad things will *never* happen to us – because they inevitably will. However, what is realistic is to pray that Yahveh will give us the strength and courage to deal with whatever comes our way; that people will be around us to help us cope; or that God will lead us into circumstances where we can make contact with people who can help us out of our difficulties – or even, where we can use our own strengths to help others.

Fundamentalists cope with the complications of life by over-simplifying and limiting things to what they want to see. Religious liberals cope by limiting what they see of the world to only the good things, and set themselves up for being utterly unprepared when the nastiness of life overtakes them. There is light and darkness, there are tragedies and there are wondrous things, sadness and happiness.

Yahwism takes a pragmatic approach to life. It doesn't see the world through rose-coloured glasses, but then neither does it see life pessimistically as a cosmic battle which will be brought to an end at some mythical point in our own lifetime. It tries to give us hope by letting us know that *God is with us in our struggles.* Yahveh is there for us to draw strength and courage from, to gain wisdom and understanding from, and to be inspired and uplifted by. The most practical and sensible way to deal with the inconstancies of life, is when we see darkness, tragedy and sadness, to remind ourselves of the light, the wonder and the happiness that lies around the corner.

Yes, good is fleeting, but then so is the bad. That is the nature of this universe we have been sent into to do God's work. The tides of both good and bad ebb and flow, and both light and dark wax and wane. We do not waste the night waiting for the dawn, and we do not waste the day ever fearful of the night.

God's laws take both the good and the bad into account. They envision a society where the weak would be supported, the rich would be obligated to help the poor, and where the under-privileged and disadvantaged were entitled to be helped by others, if they needed it. God set up a system whereby the least able in our society would not be left behind, or discarded like trash.

And if tragedy and misfortune should befall any of us, God's laws were designed to have a profound psychological effect on us. They would create human beings who would realise their own vulnerability, frailty and impermanence, and be moved to recognise that in others, and thereby have compassion on others and help them. God's laws take misfortune into account, and *that* is how Yahveh is Sovereign even over the bad.

The Israelite religion accepted that Yahveh was supreme over every aspect of the events of our lives; not that misfortune was a judgment or a punishment for sin, but rather that everything that happened was ultimately to be overcome by God's mercy and kindness. Yahveh is our refuge to whom we run in the most difficult of times, and from who we draw our strength. The ancient Israelite religion envisioned that we had to become individuals – no, a community – that would grow and learn how to cope with the good and the bad together. This profound attitude is expressed in the timeless line from the Book of Job:

'Yahveh has given, and Yahveh has taken away; blessed be the Name of Yahveh!'[a]

Line 11: And do not bring us to trial

Theologians have found this line the most puzzling out of the whole *'Our Father'*. The traditional English words for the line read: *'And lead us not into temptation'*. This has led generations of the faithful asking why God would lead someone into temptation? Hours have been spent in debate, and lifetimes in study, trying to figure out the hidden meaning behind these words. We should have been guided by the words of Jacob the Pious, who wrote, *'No one being tested should say, "I am being tempted by God." For God cannot be tempted by evil, and God Himself tempts no one.'*[b]

Now, I actually found this the *easiest* line to gauge the meaning of. All it needed was to realise that in Jewish poetry, lines parallel each other, and that neighbouring lines have connected imagery. Knowing a little bit about the social background of Galilean life also helps.

and ….

I have previously mentioned that the word '*v[e]-*' in Hebrew and Aramaic can sometimes mean more than simply 'and'. This is just such an occasion. In this instance, it means, 'and so [in other words]', as in: 'forgive us our sins/debts, and so in other words, don't bring us to trial.' The implied meaning is: if God forgives us our sins, we don't need to be put on trial for them. Remember the parable about making the effort to be reconciled with our accuser before we get to court?[c]

… bring …

The ultimate image being presented in this line, is that of someone being brought to trial in a court of law, not of being tempted into sin. The Syriac and Hebrew versions of the *Our Father* both use similar verbs, which are translations of the Greek, *me eisenengkis eis*, which literally means 'may you not bring [us] into'. The Jewish Aramaic and the Syriac literally mean, 'may you not cause [us] to enter into', and this can be

---

[a] Job 1:21
[b] Ig. Yq 2:9 – cf Ep James 1:13
[c] S.Yesh. 77; cf Mt 5:25-26, Lk 12:57-59

interpreted as meaning 'may you not *lead* us into'. However, knowing what image is being presented by Yeshua` in the words of his prayer, helps us to decide the meaning.

... *trial,*

Syriac and Hebrew use similar words to translate the Greek *peirasmon*. The Aramaic word *nissayuna* can mean 'trial', 'examination' or 'test'. It can mean a test to try someone's spirit or character, but it can also mean a trial in a court of law. However, the Greek word means both a 'trial in a court of law', and also 'temptation' (from the Greek verb meaning 'to try', 'to test' or 'to tempt'). We need to be aware that the Greek word *peirasmon* has this **additional** meaning of 'temptation', which the Aramaic and Hebrew verbs **don't** have. In the Hebrew and Aramaic way of thinking, to test someone does not mean to tempt them. Therefore, when God tested Abraham at Mt Moriah, Abraham was not being tempted; it was his character and the strength of his faith that was being examined.

I think this is where the problem in understanding the line has arisen. To complicate matters, at the time the prayer was originally translated into English, the English word 'tempt' had the additional meaning of 'to test' or 'to try' (e.g. someone's patience or resolve), a meaning the English word no longer has. Some older, 18th century dictionaries still have 'tempt' in their definition of the Hebrew *nasah*.

The story about Yeshua`'s forty days of fasting in the desert[a] is therefore about testing and examination (to see if he was worthy to be a prophet), and *not* about temptation.

Jacob the Pious in his letter,[b] mentions his take on temptation: *'No one being tempted should say, "I am being tempted by God." For God cannot be tempted by evil, and God's own self tempts no one.'* Now, something must have prompted this comment on the matter, and I think it was the fact that the Greek has this additional (and misleading) meaning of 'to entice or induce to do something bad'. Greek-speaking Followers needed to be put straight on this matter, and I think that this is the reason for Jacob's comments. God sometimes tests and tries us, but God does not tempt us into sin.

This line of the prayer therefore, is not about temptation, but rather trial and tribulation.

---

[a] S.Yesh. ps 136 – cf Mt 4:2-11, Lk 4:2-13
[b] Ig. Yq 2:9 – cf Ep. James 1:13

Taking debtors to trial in ancient Galilee and Judea

I have previously mentioned how the Aramaic word for 'sin' also means 'debt', and how the word for 'sinner' also means 'debtor'. This play on words does not exist in Hebrew; you can either connect the two lines of the prayer by using the Hebrew words for 'sin' and 'sinner', or you can use the words 'debt' and debtor'; these double meanings cannot be conveyed in Hebrew (or in any other language as far as I'm aware). The pun (which only exists in Aramaic) leads to the build-up of a specific image with this line, which mentions a *trial*, not a temptation. The metaphor gives us a picture from real life in those days. This is the depth of understanding that you can get with the Aramaic, and not with the Hebrew (or any other language for that matter).

Significant numbers of people in the Galilee were always getting into debt, and indeed many were *permanently* in debt. When a debtor could not make a repayment, their creditors were constantly taking them to court for non-payment. When they had no possible means of paying, the debtor was thrown into prison until such time as the debt would have been paid off. Since the man of the house was usually the sole breadwinner, this sent his wife and children even further into poverty. Many couldn't cope.

In many instances, the burden of debt was so great, that it simply was not practical to expect someone else to pay the debt off for them. Besides, there would always be the nagging suspicion that something would be required at a later date in return for the favour. Therefore, the greatest hope for any debtor was for the debt to be quite simply cancelled or 'forgiven'. If the debt was completely forgiven, then there was no need to go to trial.

It would have been a great blessing to have one's debts forgiven. And the greater the debt forgiven, the greater the joy for the debtor. For someone living under the weight of worry over debt, the release would have been a great mercy.

Trials and tribulations

On hearing this line, the image of the debtor's trial would have been the first obvious thing to come to mind for a poor, rural Galilean. However, there was a second, even more serious image underlying that one.

Israel's history is one of living amongst hostile nations – it's not anything new. God's people had twice before experienced the misery of exile. The first one, which took place between 734 – 715 BCE, was imposed by the Assyrian empire. They removed the nine[a] northern tribes into exile. Only a tiny proportion were able to return, and their descendants became the Samaritan people.

The second exile took place between 597 – 582 BCE, and was carried out by the Babylonian Empire. It deported the three southern tribes.[b] A proportion of them returned after 538 BCE, and their descendants became the Jewish people.

At each exile event, Israelites asked themselves, 'Why is this happening to us? What did we do to deserve this punishment from God? Their general conclusion was that they had done something to disobey God – for example, by worshipping other gods, or by living immorally.

This fear of exile was ingrained in the Israelite national consciousness. There was a constant awareness that any serious rebellion against God's ways would incur God's judgment. Prophets such as Hosea and Amos called the northern tribes to repent before they were exiled; prophets such as Micah and Zephaniah did the same to the southern tribes before their exile.

The Roman occupation of Judea was a most dangerous time for the Jewish people. For any astute political analyst of the time, it was obvious that the signs of the times pointed to an impending conflict and war. For such a small nation, under such a cruel occupier, the outcome could only mean one thing: exile from our sacred and beloved land.

Some religious groups, such as the Essenes, had already examined the situation within a spiritual context. They had identified the moral decline and corruption of the Sadducean priests as a sin against the holiness of God, one that would be the trigger for a day of reckoning, and would require drastic action on God's part to prevent. Their solution was to take themselves off into the desert and keep themselves morally and culturally pure.

In my first book, I described something that the Miqra calls, 'the Day of Yahveh'. This would be God's reaction to the injustice perpetrated by transgressors within Israelite society. It would be a terrible day of reckoning – a tribulation for all the people. During previous such events, prophets called the guilty to repent, and good people to remain true to God.

So there we have it: the main theme contained in this line of the prayer, therefore calls for the sins that invite tribulation to be forgiven, so that the tribulation does not happen: 'Please do not put us through

---

[a] People usually say ten, but this is because Manasseh was divided into East and West Manasseh.

[b] Judah, Benjamin and Simeon. By the time of exile, the two smaller tribes had become completely subsumed into the tribe of Judah, and were indistinguishable from them.

tribulation; forgive us our sins, so that we don't have to suffer tribulation.'

The place of 'Apocalypse' in Jewish literature

To most western Christians, the word 'Apocalypse' conjures up images of destruction, death and the end of the world in one final, cosmic battle. However, in its original context, apocalypse was actually a particular type of Jewish literature. It unfortunately gave the people of Yeshua`'s time a way of looking at the world and its problems which was particularly unhelpful – and self-destructive.

I have mentioned several times before that the Pharisees banned prophets. They effectively told God that if things were going wrong, God was not allowed to choose a prophet to warn people about it – to therefore repent and amend their ways. From the time of the last official prophet (Malachi in about 450 BCE), until the time of the prophet Yeshua`, the Jewish people experienced several, potentially disastrous episodes in their history.[a] Since prophecy was banned, God's messengers had to find another way to warn people about the dangers to come.

Thus was born the apocalyptic genre. In order to get round the rabbinic ban on prophecy, writers never put their own names to their prophetic works. Instead, it was the accepted practice to choose a famous biblical figure who lived *before* the rabbinic ban on prophets, and put *that* figure's name as the author of the book instead. Another way was to set the events in a book in a time before the rabbinic ban (such was the case with the *Book of Daniel*).

Apocalyptic books typically contained frightening images of the future. Just as a prophet of God would normally have said things like, 'If you don't repent, your cities will be destroyed, and you will be carried off into exile,' so also an apocalyptic writer would describe vivid and terrifying scenes, as a warning of terrible consequences if the current situation did not change.

The most unhelpful result of this apocalyptic genre, was that it personified the forces of evil and the forces of good. The struggle between good and evil was portrayed as a cosmic battle between Satan's demons battling God's angels (whereas pure Yahwism does not believe in evil spirits); and instead of seeing the march of time as a succession of ages – as one age ends, another begins – the apocalyptic writers saw all of history as only one age, which would end in one final cosmic battle,

---

[a] such as the near extinction of the Jewish religion under the Syrians, which led to the Maccabean revolt in 167-160 BCE. The victorious outcome of the revolt is celebrated in the festival of Lights (Chanukkah).

when the world would end.

This was not the view of the biblical prophets. The prophet Malachi understood that yes, there would be times of tribulation, but at the end of each tribulation, people would still be alive, and the righteous would leap about in joy 'like calves released from the stall'.[a]

This is why I encourage people to shy away from the Hellenist-influenced theology of the Second Temple period – the theology that gave people in Yeshua`'s time a view of the world that was not God's – and instead, stick to the cosmology of biblical Yahwism. Interpreting the world in a Hellenistic way resulted in messianism, cosmic battles, and end-of-the-world thinking; sticking to the world-view of biblical Yahwism will give you a much more realistic view of the world – one that accords with what human beings actually experience of it, and what actually happens in real life.

Apocalypse and the Book of Revelation

When the Book of Revelation is mentioned, what comes to mind? The four horsemen of the Apocalypse? The release of Satan after 1,000 years and the final apocalyptic battle? Armageddon? The Lamb of God and the breaking of the Seven Seals? The seven bowls of plagues?

How strange! And how revealing! It is notable how people today focus on the non-Ebionite portions,[b] and completely ignore what the Ebionite portions say.

The Ebionite portions contain a warning to flee Jerusalem,[c] because Jerusalem would be destroyed; that many would die – including many righteous people. But the righteous who died would be rewarded by an eternity in God's immediate presence. The perpetrators of that destruction – Rome – would eventually be punished and fall.

If you consider that the *Book of Revelation* – which covertly compares Rome with the devil – has survived through the life of the Roman Empire, you can put that down to the fact that it had to be written in a kind of code.

There are many verses in *Revelation* that seem to have been lifted directly from various books of the Hebrew prophets. It is possible that

---

[a] Xtian bibles Mal 4:3, Jewish bibles 3:20

[b] Some writers, notably Hugh J Schonfield (*The Original New Testament*), believed that underlying the Christian *Book of Revelation*, was the work of an Ebionite prophet who had 3 visions. These are Rev chapters 7-14, 17-18, and 21-22.

[c] *"The members of the Jerusalem church by means of an oracle, given by revelation to acceptable persons there, were ordered to leave the city before the war began and settle in a town in Peraea called Pella."* (Eusebius: Historia Ecclesiae, Book III, 5:4)

the recipient of the Ebionite visions actually received a less complicated version of them. Knowing that they contained undeniable criticism of the Roman Empire, the visions could not be openly transmitted. So it is possible that the Ebionite seer deliberately cut and spliced the words of the prophets, in order to hide from the uninitiated the true meaning of the visions.

For this reason, once you understand the biblical and cultural references contained in the visions, it becomes obvious that much of the imagery cannot be taken literally. For example, the mention of locusts in Rev 9:3-7 are actually a symbolic call to repentance.[a]

The Ebionite visions warned ancient Followers of the Way to leave Jerusalem (which is what the part about the woman giving birth and fleeing with her son into the desert was about – the woman is Israel, but the son is the community of Followers, not a messiah). It warned that some good people would die. But the righteous who died would have the consolation of their reward in heaven – eternity in God's presence. They are also consoled by the knowledge that the Roman Empire would eventually fall in their distant future – our past. Then they are told of the fulfilment of God's kingdom – the heavenly city, when the division between heaven and earth will be taken away, and the fact that God's glory will be its sole light – which is also in *our* future.

If you stick to the Ebionite portions of Revelation, you will see that ultimately it is a book about hope, consolation and the purifying presence of God, not about demons, destruction and apocalyptic battles. Because it mostly describes events that have already taken place, we can read this and understand that for those who persevere and follow God's ways of justice, mercy and compassion, and remain faithful to God's witness, then there is a great reward awaiting us in heaven. And the time of the heavenly city also awaits us!

Prophecy is not about predicting the future

I have long noticed people in the world today, trying to discern what will happen in the future from the words of prophecy, as if their faith and their very lives depended on it. There is no difference between this kind of person, and the one who goes to a fortune teller in order to know the future. They use the books of the Prophets as if they were some kind of Almanac!

Why do people do that? That's not what prophecy is for. Prophecy is not about foretelling the exact sequence of events in the future – that's not its primary aim. It's not there to give you a running commentary on

---

[a] cf Joel 2:2-5

what is going to happen in the months and years to come; prophecies are not horoscopes. There are some who will say, 'But I need to know for certain what is going to happen in the future!' To which I have to respond, 'No, you don't!'

There are people who trawl through the books of the prophets in an attempt to understand and reconcile all the events that will happen in the future. As a result, when that understanding doesn't come, and they can't make any sense of the logic of prophetic events, they become frustrated and anxious. I have met people who have become really distraught when they discover they cannot comprehend what is going to happen in the future.

This is because they do not approach prophecy in the spirit in which it was given. Prophecy contains warnings and consolations. If you follow God's ways, and set your heart on a righteous path of mercy and justice, then *you do not need to worry about what will happen;* you don't need to put together any kind of time-line of the future. All you need to know, is that your reward will be great in heaven. All you need to do, is remain a good person, and work towards influencing others around you for the good.

The only people that need to be worried about what will happen, are those who have set their hearts on the **wrong** path, and have turned away from God's teachings. They need to know what will happen, because **they** need to be aware of the consequences of their injustice, cruelty and lack of consideration for others.

If such people repent, then they will avert the calamities prophesied. If not, then the warnings will affect the innocent too.

The true purpose of prophecy in the Israelite religion

I have previously mentioned that although most people today think that prophecy is about giving new revelations, that is not the purpose of prophecy in the Israelite religion. Yahveh often appoints prophets in times of great trial to give fore-warnings, guidance and consolation, as well as in times of peace to provide good counsel when things are unclear.

Banning prophets (which is what modern Judaism and Islam has done) has **disastrous** consequences. If there had been prophets around in the 1930's, the Jewish people could have been warned about the impending Holocaust. Just think – if we had 'allowed' God to send us a prophet, maybe six million lives could have been saved, and their descendants would be with us today. And today, a Muslim prophet could warn his or her people of the dangers of extremism, and actually prevent much of the modern world's fear of modern Islamist terrorism.

The ban on prophets prevents God's ongoing guidance of humanity, forcing us instead to rely on fallible human decisions. I reiterate once again: in the Israelite religion, prophecy is about warning humanity when things are going wrong, and about calamities that *might* happen if wrongs are not corrected; prophecy is **not** about delivering a new revelation that completely countermands previous revelations, or about predicting the future, blow by blow, centuries in advance. Such a way of looking at prophecy is a pagan one, treating prophecy as if it were an oracle of the gods, or a horoscope.

Many of us in the Jewish community are happy to just sit back on our hands and recite the mantra that we can't do this and that or the other, 'because it will be sorted out when messiah comes'. This is complete nonsense. **Prophets** were meant to be God's *ongoing* method of guiding us throughout the centuries,[a] giving us God's decisions about things which are unclear, but mainstream Judaism has banned prophets. However, God is fully able to give us a prophet *at any time*, to relay God's message *any time* that people are ready to listen to a genuine prophet.

When you forbid prophets, you have no option but to put all the burden of hope on messiahs.[b] People are so obsessed with coming messiahs in the future, because they have no faith in God's desire to choose and call prophets in the here and now. Others may long for a messiah, but I personally long for God to guide us through a prophet. Hope in messiahs to solve all our problems is not sanctioned by God, but hope in prophets *is*.

Any serious student of Torah will eventually come to see that there are indeed gaps in what Torah covers. However, that is what sages, judges, a council of elders, and prophets are for – to fill in those gaps as and when necessary, based upon *what is already in the written Torah*; adding to Torah as the Oral Law does, is not an option.

Dt 18:15-22 covers the place of prophets in Israelite life. Verses 18:15 and 18:18 in Hebrew use the singular 'prophet':

> *"Yahveh your God will raise up a prophet like me from amongst your brothers; you must listen to him. ... I will raise up for them a prophet like you from amongst their brothers; I will put My words in his mouth, and he shall speak to them everything that I shall command."*

---

[a] Dt 18:15-22
[b] The Oral law describes a messiah in such impossible terms, that consequently no one in the mainstream community would ever accept a real messiah when God chooses one.

This has led Christianity and Islam to use this verse as biblical justification for their respective primary prophets. However, just as Dt 17:14-20 uses the singular 'king' to refer to *all* Israelite kings, so here also, the word 'prophet' is what is known in Hebrew grammar as 'the collective singular', used to refer to *all* prophets. The singular word 'prophet' refers to prophets *as an institution*, not to just one single prophet.

So instead of listening to astrologists, soothsayers and mediums, we are to listen to genuine, God-appointed prophets as the chosen messengers and mouthpieces of Yahveh. No future prophet would ever be like Moses.[a] Only Moses spoke directly to God in heaven, as one person speaks directly to another. He alone was ever able to have discussions, question and answer sessions face to face with God. No future prophet was ever to be held as equal to Moses – lawgiver, minister of Yahveh[b] and direct intermediary and negotiator for God's message.

We are also told here that Israel's future prophets would be from among our own kin,[c] so that means that we are not meant to listen to prophets who are not Israelite/Jewish. We are also given advice on how to recognise a true prophet – that what they say comes true. This is only practical advice if it refers to prophetic warnings that come true in the lifetime of the prophet's audience;[d] if biblical prophecies were about warnings that referred to things in the far distant future, then the advice is utterly useless to the people to whom the warnings are being given.

Evangelical scaremongers often ignore this simple fact, which should otherwise be staring people in the face: warnings of disasters centuries in the far future, would have been utterly useless to the people of the prophet's time, to whom prophecies were actually being delivered. Prophecy is about warning the people of the prophet's own generation, so that they will be prompted to change. If they repent and change, *the disasters prophesied **will not happen**.* It seems to me that fundamentalist scaremongers highlight prophesy not with the spirit in which it was given – to make people repent and change heart, so that tribulations can be avoided – but rather to scare people, so that they will follow the preachers who are playing on people's fears, and thereby give them more money. Real prophecy is given so that tribulations can be avoided; scaremongers abuse prophecy, hoping that tribulation will happen. Scaremongers will claim they are turning people back to *belief* in God, but the true aim of prophecy is to turn people back to God's *ways*.

Warnings contained in the books of the Prophets therefore only

---

[a] Dt 34:10
[b] Num 12:7-8
[c] Dt 18:15
[d] Dt 18:22

refer to things that occurred within a short space of time from when they were spoken. Only prophecies of consolation (i.e. peaceful, positive prophecies) refer to things in the far future. Pawing over the books of the Prophets for negative predictions of events in the 21st century is therefore futile.

This is one of the reasons why the prophet Jonah was afraid of speaking for God. He was afraid that the people would repent, God's warnings would therefore not need to come true (because God was a merciful God), and he would then be accused of being a false prophet.

I have also noticed that many evangelicals think their own background thoughts are actually prophecy – but that is not what prophecy is. Claiming one's own thoughts are God's words, is a recipe for misfortune (Dt 18:20). We therefore need to be 100% certain that a message is from God before claiming that it is.

Jacob the Pious seemed to have had an additional test of a true prophet – that such people had to endure much suffering in their lives.[a] Perhaps such an additional test became necessary, because times were so urgent. Because of this air of urgency, another test was needed. It seems that Jacob the Pious held with the idea that, if the prophet had had a difficult life, and was made to suffer hardship by others for the sake of his or her message, then this seems to be a good enough method of testing whether a prophet was real or false, and more importantly, whether their message required immediate attention or not.

There are many things that make us fearful today, and we need God's guidance. Banning prophets stymies God's ability to counsel and guide the human race, not just the Jewish people. But Yahveh is Yahveh; God will find a way to speak to us. Following on from Jacob the Pious's words, a true prophet will have undergone much suffering for the sake of the message; a true prophet will be a man or woman of humility, unconcerned with his or her own reputation or influence. If we learn the personality of Yahveh, we will be able to recognise that personality coming through in God's message. A prophet does not therefore need to claim that he or she is a prophet; prophethood will be obvious from the character and content of the message, from what the prophet has gone through for the sake of that message, and from the humility of their character, claiming nothing for his or her self. Yahveh will find a way to speak to us.

---

[a] Ig. Yq. 2:12, James 5:10 – *"My brothers and sisters, as an example of long-suffering and patient forbearance, take the prophets who spoke in the name of Adonai."*

The consequences of cosmic pessimism

What we believe has consequences. If we believe that there is an end-time battle between supernatural forces of good and evil, then it makes us think that the battle is out there, beyond our control, and there is nothing we, as mere mortals can possibly do for God. It makes us think that we just have to sit back and let the heavenly beings knock the ever-so-holy crap out of each other until the good guys win. We end up feeling powerless, and that there is *nothing* we can do here on earth for this 'cosmic battle'.

This way of thinking also allows unscrupulous religious people to control ordinary men and women, because it gives them permission to become interpreters and commentators for this other-worldly battle that we can actually *know nothing about ourselves*. It can be used as a threat: if we do not do as these people say, then this supernatural battle might take a turn for the worst.

There are people whose very foundation of faith depends on the world being destroyed in one final, cosmic conflagration, when all 'born-again' Christians will go to heaven, and all non-Christians will suffer and then go to eternal damnation in hell. There are some fundamentalist evangelicals who even pray for wars to take place, who pray against world peace – and even saying that anyone who brings about world peace is an instrument of Satan! There are even politicians who hold these destructive and crazy beliefs, people who are in positions of power and influence, yearning for WW3 to take place!

Stories of supernatural conflicts might make for bestsellers, blockbuster films and prime time TV, but the truth is, *there is no cosmic, end-time battle.* It is all up to us. *We* spread the kingdom of God, *we* work for God, *we* are God's agents on earth – *we* are, us, human beings. The coming fulfilment of God's kingdom, when the veil between heaven and earth will be taken away, when God's glory comes through the clouds of heaven,[a] it all depends on what *we* do. *Our* actions, *our* words, *our* deeds and *our* thoughts – they all matter. *We* are responsible for what happens. If we sit back and do nothing, then that is precisely what will happen – *nothing* – at least, nothing *good* will happen. People will lose respect for life and property, society will start to unravel, violence will increase, and when it all comes to a head in one big implosion, this time period will end, another one will begin, and we will do it all over again.

In the Paullist way of seeing the future, the end is a battle between good and evil, between light and dark. The two sides are equal enemies, and one has to win out against the other. This is a Gnostic dualist way of

---

[a] Isa 60:19-20. See also Rev 22:1-5 / Ch.Sh. 23:1-5

looking at the future. This outlook comes from Gnosticism, not from God.

The Yahwist way of understanding the future is entirely different. Supreme over both good and evil is Yahveh. And Yahveh presents this choice to us: the battle is not outside of you up in heaven; the battle is within you. *You* have to choose between good and evil, between light and dark, and between peace and war. When you have lain down your anger, your hatred, your bitterness and your weapons of war, only then can Yahveh's light sweep away all the darkness, and give us all an eternity in light.

This radical shift in perspective is what made the ancient Israelite religion different from all the other religions of the world at the time. Now, I have had an interest in the many different mythologies of the world since I was eleven years old. I took an interest in Anglo-Saxon mythology, because it was the ancient religion of this country. I also read about Norse religion and their mythology, as well as Greek, Egyptian and Roman mythology. In many pagan religions, there is this almighty end-time battle – like Ragnarok in the Norse religion. In pagan religions, humans are basically helpless against the gods, and there is nothing we can do while they fight it out. According to pagan religions, we can only learn to control our immediate fates, using magic and incantations.

Israelite religion was different. It saw an optimistic future, one that humans had a *crucial* role to play in. We are vital participants in God's plan to create paradise – we serve God's purpose on earth. Heaven is peace, not war. Heaven is the ultimate destination of the Hebrew mystic, who journeys in spirit to a place of calm.

Over time, the Jewish religion has imported a lot of pagan beliefs, such as king-saviours, end-time battles, second comings, and we need to rid ourselves of all that. Prophets remind us of God's original plan. Over the years, I have had some really anxious people hit back at me, saying, 'But I need to know that I will see Jesus when I get to heaven!!!!' To which I usually reply, 'My friend, you will! You will also see Moses, and Abraham – also your loved ones, and indeed anyone who has gone before you to their rest in our heavenly Father's presence!'

One purpose of the community of the Way, was to restore the Israelite religion to its 'original factory settings', so to speak.[a] We need to cleanse ourselves, and get rid of pagan ways of looking at the world of the spirit, and of the mortal realm. We need to renew our souls, so that they return to Yahveh's way, reminding us of our original purpose,

---

[a] see S.Yesh. 13 (which speaks about sewing new cloth on old garments, which ends up tearing the old), & S.Yesh. 14 (which speaks about putting new wine into old wineskins – the old wine is good enough) – cf Mk 2:21-22

setting us back on the path, so that we once again take up our God-given missions – to work each day for the spread of God's kingdom on earth.

The Israelite view of the future

Some people seem to need a fear of destruction, oppression and persecution to help them keep their faith; remove these things, and the entire *raison d'être* of their faith disappears. When they perceive everyone to be against them, their faith is strong, but when their foes no longer actively work against them, they are lost. So then they create enemies. They begin seeing the devil and other imaginary enemies around every corner, and the hand of Satan in every misfortune. Life is a struggle, a tedious chore to be endured. Death becomes preferable, a 'blessed release' from their woes. They begin to see signs of the end of the world in everything, and in every world event around them. But fear is not faith.

The sayings of the prophet Yeshua`, and the passages in the *Book of Visions*[a] which speak about an end to come, refer to the end of a *very specific period of time*. To any student of that period of Jewish history, familiar with the political, religious, and social events of the time, it becomes obvious that Yeshua` and the prophetic author of *Visions* are referring to the ravaging of Judea and the destruction of Jerusalem and the Holy Temple; the 'end of the age'[b] does not refer to the end of the world, nor to the end of time, but to the completion of their present era (and the beginning of a new one). Even Yeshua` said that, *'This generation will not pass away until all these things have happened.'*[c] You see that? He fully expected everything he talked about to happen within the lifetime of his audience, and not in the far future. Modern-day scaremongers never even listen to the man they claim to represent!

Whenever Yeshua` said, 'the Kingdom of God is at hand,'[d] I think the intellectual blockage that has prevented most theologians from understanding this one phrase, is because they assume that the tribulation is *(a)* a one-time event, and *(b)* that it will *only* happen at the end of the world. The mistake is thinking that the tribulation brings about the end of the world – it doesn't / didn't. It only brings an *era* to completion (and

---

[a] which is basically the *Book of Revelation* with all the Christian additions removed.
[b] S.Yesh. 169:3 – cf Mt 13:50
[c] S.Yesh 163:3; cf Mk 13:30, Mt 24:34, Lk 21:32
[d] The best way of translating this is, "The *kingship* of God is fast approaching". In referring to God's kingship (the same word in Aramaic as 'kingdom'), Yeshua referred to a time when God would intervene in human affairs in His position as our King and Judge.

ushers in another one).

Yeshua` often uses the phrase 'at the end of the age'.[a] The Greek actually means 'at the completion of the present era/epoch'. The Aramaic equivalent for the Greek *aiōnos* (age/era) would have been `*iddana*.[b] This is a *portion* of time – an era or epoch, *not* the end of time itself.[c] All of time is divided into these epochs or eras, and Yeshua` was referring to the end of the current era in which he was living. In the ancient world view of history, when one age ends, another age begins.

Tribulations will happen whenever human society gets to a point of no return, when the only option is for God to actively intervene to put things right. Those religious people who long for the world to end, who pray for tribulation to increase so that God will hurry up and get it all over with, so that they can get to heaven – these people don't understand that calamitous tribulations only end one period of time, and another one starts. They don't understand that tribulations (catastrophic divine interventions) take place *whenever* the moral and social standards in a particular society reach an alarming low, beyond a point which human remedy alone can rectify.

As for the *real* end of time, instead of death, destruction and misery, Yahveh tells us through the prophet Isaiah[d] that the far future holds peace for us, not apocalypse:

> *In the last days, the mountain of Yahveh's temple will be*
> *established as the highest of the mountains;*
> > *it will be exalted above the hills, and peoples will stream*
> *to it.*
> > *Many nations will come and say, 'Come, let us go up to*
> *the mountain of Yahveh, to the temple of the God of Jacob.*
> > *God will teach us God's ways, so that we may walk in*
> *God's paths.'*
> > *For Instruction will go out from Zion, and the word of*
> *Yahveh from Jerusalem.*
> > *God will judge between many peoples, and will settle*
> *disputes for strong nations far and wide.*

---

[a] eg Mt 13:39-40, 49

[b] The Hebrew equivalent would have been עת `*eit* (a fixed period of time), or דור *dor* (generation).

[c] This confusion arises from the Greek habit of using *aiōnos* to translate both Aramaic `*iddana* (epoch) and `*alma* (world). The English translation of the Greek 'in this age, or in the age to come', would actually be in Aramaic: דאתא בעלמא הדין או בעלמא *b*ᵉ`*alma hadeyn o b*ᵉ`*alma d*ᵉ`*ata* – literally, 'in this world, or in the world to come'.

[d] Isaiah 2:2-4

> *They will beat their swords into ploughshares, and their spears into pruning hooks.*
> *Nation will not take up sword against nation, nor will they train for war anymore.*
> *Everyone will sit under their own vine and under their own fig tree, and no one will make them afraid.*

A lot of people don't realise that in order for much of the Israelite vision of the real future to come about, the *first* thing to happen has to be the return of the exiles of the northern kingdom. If they haven't come back, then there is no point in watching for a son of David, or for the rebuilding of the Temple. From the Book of Ezekiel, this is the preliminary order of events before the time of universal peace (notice at what point we get an anointed descendant of David):

- **the exiles of Ephraim will return** *[36:24],*
- *Israel will be cleansed by the glory of God [36:25-26],*
- *Ephraim and Judah will be reunited [37:15-19],*
- **a descendant of David will then be chosen** by God to be king over Ephraim and Judah *[37:24],*
- *the Covenant will be renewed [37:26a],*
- **the Temple will be rebuilt** *[37:26b-28].*
- *Then there will be a period of peace while reunited Israel is consolidating [implied by 38:11-12],*
- *then a country (Magog) to the far north of Israel will try to conquer Israel [38:15-16],*
- *but they will not succeed in conquest, because they are being led by the nose by God [38:4, 39:2]*
- *this is in order that the great power of Yahveh will be revealed [38:16b, 39:6-7];*
- *Magog will be resoundingly defeated [39:3-4, 39:20].*
- *Finally, the glory of God will be poured out on the now reunited nation of Israel [39:29],*
- *and no one will be left in any doubt among the nations that Yahveh is God [39:27].*

There are certain religious people who believe that there will be one final, almighty, devastating conflict in the Middle East, that the world will come to an end, and only those who belong to their faith will go to heaven. This unfortunately misguided way of thinking has led certain individuals to endeavour to actually *create* conflict, in order for a destructive war to take place. Israeli police regularly arrest people who arrive in Israel to encourage violent discord between its communities. These people have come in the hope that what they do will lead to explosive conflict. In the minds of these individuals, conflict means the end of the world, and the end of the world means that only they, and those who belong to their faith, will go to heaven. But Yeshua` taught us, *'Blessed are those who create peace, for they shall be called, 'the children of God.'*[a] And Jacob the Pious taught us, *'righteousness is the fruit of the seed sown in peace by those who create peace.'*[b]

What misguided people like this need to realise is that they cannot force God's hand. **They cannot speed up the time when 'the end' will come.** No one can make events run faster; if the time is not right for God's plans, then there is absolutely nothing any human being can possibly do to make God's promises come any quicker.

The Talmidi Israelite view is that if humanity works for peace, and encourages others – of all faiths and of none – to do the same, then the kingdom of God will be fulfilled; there will be heaven on earth, and there will be no more war, disease or poverty. It is not our job to speed up the so-called 'end-time'; it is our job to create the right conditions for peace, and for God's kingdom to be fulfilled. But in the end, the decision to take the final step belongs to God, and to no one else. *We* prepare the groundwork for God by the lives we lead, but it is Yahveh our God who ultimately makes things happen when God is good and ready to make them happen.

So when you see calamity or war coming, your job – even if you are only able to influence people's attitudes around you – is to **prevent** it, not encourage it or look forward to it – remember, Yeshua` told us that peacemakers (i.e. not warmongers or disaster-seekers), are held blessed by God.

You do not need to scour the Miqra to find out what terrible things will happen in the future. All you need to know is that living a good, decent and moral life will bring on its own reward – even in this lifetime. Calamity is avoided by repentance, and prosperity is brought on by living God's ways, and encouraging others by your example to do so as well.

The definitive response to those who look through prophecy in order to figure out what will happen in the future was given by the prophet Yeshua` himself: *'But concerning that day or hour, no one knows, not the angels in heaven, nor this son of man; only our Father in heaven.'*[c]

---

[a] S.Yesh 3:6 – cf Mt 5:9
[b] Ig. Yq. 7:6 – cf Ep. James 3:18
[c] S.Yesh. 163:4 – cf Mk 13:32

Maintaining one's dignity in the face of suffering

In the mid-1970's, I travelled up to London with my mum and my brother to Great Ormond Street Hospital For Sick Children. My brother Edward used to have very bad eczema, and he would go up to London every so often for review and adjustment of treatment.

There was one occasion which was the only time I ever accompanied them – I simply wanted to see the big city. When we arrived at the hospital there was a boy in a cot – one of those children's beds with bars around it. And although he was apparently about ten years old at the time, he only looked about five. He had an illness that was described to me at the time as one whereby his skin was so thin, it would tear and come off. His hands were permanently bandaged. I recall him greeting my mother by name in a northern English accent. What struck me most about him though was that, despite what was obviously a very painful illness, he sounded remarkably cheerful, warm-hearted and happy.

That was about 40 years ago. About 7 years ago I learned the boy's name – Jonny Kennedy[a] – and what happened to him.

The Discovery Channel[b] broadcast a programme called, *'The Boy Whose Skin Fell Off'*. If you ever get a chance to see this documentary, I strongly recommend you see it. He had a condition called *Epidermolysis Bullosa*. If you can imagine two pieces of Velcro and how they stick together, well, that's how your skin is on your muscles. Normal skin has a layer that allows the skin to stick to muscle. In people with E.B., this layer is missing, so the skin tears and comes away, and inevitably blisters and bleeds.

Every day, his mother had to change his bandages, and it was a painful process for him. He lived with excruciating pain constantly, every day of his life, yet he still managed to retain a cheerful disposition. He always had a kind word to say to people; he was never bitter or resentful. He was quite a spiritual man, and his faith kept him going through everything he suffered.

What I felt in my heart, was that God was supremely present with him, throughout every second of his suffering. In spite of everything, he maintained his human dignity. When he learned that the constant blistering and tearing of his skin had caused his skin to develop cancer, he decided to make a documentary of the last six months of his life.

In those last few months, he displayed such extraordinary human dignity and nobleness, with no bitterness or anger. I also believe, that

---

[a] b. 4 November 1966, d. 26 September 2003.
[b] also shown on Channel 4 in Mar 2004

when the power of God fills you to bursting and overflowing, it shows, and it showed so much in this young man's life. He showed a simple, genuine, humble piety and devotion towards God. He showed us who his heavenly Father was (and he was neither Christian, nor Jewish).

And such people can inspire our faith too. I was so impressed by his courage, it made me realize that *nothing* I can ever go through in my life, could possibly ever compare to his experience of life. I still get a lump in my throat when I remember him and think about him. It is good to learn about such people, because they give us an insight into the greater universe around us, and ultimately God. When we look into the eyes of someone like Jonny, we get a glimpse of the enormous and boundless power, love and mercy of God; of God's infinite kindness; and of God's overwhelming concern for each of us even when we suffer indescribable pain.

The reward in heaven for the endurance of the righteous who suffer

In the *Book of Visions*,[a] the seer is shown a number of people dressed in white. He is asked who they are by an angel. He responds that the angel already knows who they are, and the angel proceeds to tell us:

> 'These are the holy ones who are going to go through the great tribulation. Their robes have been washed and made white in the fire of the trials they will endure. Because of this, they will come before God's throne; day and night they will minister to God in God's Temple, and the One who is sitting upon the throne will spread His tent over them. Never again will they know hunger or thirst; no more will the Sun or its heat beat down on them. For Sovereign Yahveh, who is in the midst of the throne will shepherd them – God will lead them to living springs of water. Yahveh our God will shelter them forever, and wipe every tear from their eye.'

Formerly, only the *serafim*[b] could come close to the throne of God, but now as a reward, the righteous who died during the tribulation (and indeed, any future tribulation, such as the Holocaust) would stand in this privileged position – right next to the throne of God, at God's metaphorical 'right hand'.

And not just those who suffer religious persecution. *Any* good

---

[a] S. Ch. 6:6-7 – cf Rev 7:14-15
[b] the fiery winged serpent-angels who dwell in the immediate presence of God. They sing the praises of God's holiness (see Ezekiel chapter 1)

person who suffers in this life, and endures with dignity in spite of the bad things that happen to them, has the reward of dwelling throughout all eternity in the immediate presence of God.

According to the beliefs of the early Talmidi community,[a] their final suffering is enough to pay for whatever wrongs they may have done and not had the chance to repent of. When they leave this life, they will be taken by God's angels into the very presence of Yahveh, to dwell in eternal blessedness.

'Blessed are the pure in heart, for they shall see God'

In the Miqra, there are a couple of instances where the phrase, 'pure in heart' means 'to be pure or clean'[b] in a moral sense i.e. to show moral rectitude. The Hebrew implies someone who manages to stay on the right path in life.

However, the list of Beatitudes on the whole is speaking about people who consider themselves hard done by in life – the poor, the meek, the lowly, the mourning, the hungry, and the thirsty. So this line cannot be talking about someone who is necessarily morally upright, since such people have no reason to fear their standing in religious communities. And the reward of those who live good lives is assured by God. This has to refer to a certain type of person who does not normally see themselves as being blessed in life.

I feel that the stress on this is on the meaning of 'to be innocent of heart'. I think Yeshua` is referring to people who have a gentle, unassuming and trusting spirit. They are people who do not become cynical or bitter about life. Because they also have no natural guile or cunning, and no wariness about others, they do not really prosper in life financially, and often get trodden on by others in life. These people are 'pure in heart' i.e. they have a naturally innocent outlook on life. Yeshua` is saying that they should not worry that they are not hardened men of steel or tough-nuts, because 'they will see God'.

So what does this mean exactly? You can't 'see' God, because God cannot be seen. Prov 22:11 says, *'He who loves a pure heart and whose speech is gracious will have the king for his friend.'*

The phrase 'A pure heart will have the King for his friend', suggests, 'a pure heart will be allowed in to see the king'.

The English phrase, 'to be shown into the presence of the king' in Aramaic is literally 'to be caused to see the face of the king.' I think the original of 'for they will see God', may have been, 'for they will be

---

[a] S. Ch. 8:6b – cf Rev 9:6b
[b] using the Hebrew verb *zakah*

caused to see the face of God' – which means, 'for they will be shown straight into the presence of God'.

You will also recall I mentioned that that if God's face shines on you, this phrase means that you will be shown good fortune and blessings. This also suggests that the pure in heart should be happy in this life too, because even in this life, God will give them good fortune and blessings.

Line 12: Rather deliver us from our accusers / Evil

Moral evil and physical evil

We have a tendency to lump everything bad that can happen to us as 'evil'. As a result, we are unable to make a distinction between the evil we have control over, and the evil we cannot control. We then blame either God for all the evil that happens to us, or 'Satan'; we are unable to see that much of the really sickening and terrifying evil we witness around us, is actually the sole preserve and creation of human beings alone.

When a wild animal does something harmful, it is not morally evil; when a human being does the same thing, it is evil. For example, if a lion kills its offspring, it is not moral evil; if a human being kills his or her offspring, it is morally evil. There is therefore the precondition that one or both parties involved must have a moral aspect to their being, before an action is considered evil or not. When God gave us self-awareness, God gave us the ability to be aware that some of our actions will harm others – to be able to discern the difference between good and evil; other animals do not have this ability.

The Hebrew word *ra'*, normally translated as 'evil', comes from the root *ra'a'*, the intrinsic meaning of which is 'to be harmful' or 'to be hurtful'. That is why the basic meaning of *ra'* is 'evil' – because evil is harmful and hurtful. When we 'do evil', not only do we harm the physical, mental and spiritual wellbeing of others, but also the wholeness of our *own* being (*shleimut néfesh*, the 'perfection' of our life-force). In Yahwist thought, doing evil harms *us*, as well as the person whom we are being evil towards.

In Yahwist thought, **moral evil** involves wilful – and at worst, malicious – rebellion against God's will, and against God's created order. It is therefore the remit of religion to give human beings a code of behaviour and a set of moral guidelines, so that if we follow them, we will prosper spiritually, our society will have peace, and the evil of suffering as a result of *human* action or inaction will be reduced.

Most human beings would consider misfortune and suffering as a *physical evil* – such as when we suffer mentally or physically, or when accident or natural disaster befalls us, or when we go through illness. However, in the early Israelite tradition, this was not considered evil in the modern moral sense – we must not confuse physical evil with moral evil, since it does not always necessarily happen out of retribution for wrongs that have been committed (for more biblical examination of this, read the *Book of Job*).

Later, the post-exile Judaism of the Second Temple Period strayed away from this earlier Israelite understanding. It forgot the concept of blamelessness, it forgot the concept of the trembling of heaven and earth, and it forgot the concept of the glory of God as a fire that punishes wrongdoers, while purifying the righteous. As a result, it came to believe that *all* misfortune was a consequence of what we have done as individuals or as a nation; that *all* our suffering was as a result of retribution from God – that if we are suffering misfortune, then we *must* have done something wrong. This attitude does not help us cope with misfortune.

We are moral beings who unfortunately look for a reason behind everything, as if misfortune is easier to bear if there is a reason for it. Instead of leaning on the power of God to overcome, we lean on a hastily grasped reason for our misfortune.

I have previously mentioned that some misfortune comes as a result of being in the wake of God blazing a trail to right wrongs, and to correct injustice and oppression. However, sometimes that it not the case, as with most natural disasters. Sometimes there isn't an actual reason for the misfortune. Sometimes misfortune is simply the absence of good – just as order is the absence of chaos, darkness is the absence of light, and cold is the absence of heat. Sometimes misfortune just happens. The process of creation is the process of making order out of chaos. Good may be characterised by order, and evil may be characterised by chaos. God didn't end creation in the beginning; God is still creating, still making order out of chaos.

Where was God in the Holocaust?

The systematic murder of 12 million people, including 6 million Jews, was the most traumatic event in living memory. Modern theologians often talk of 'post-Holocaust theology'. It caused spiritually-minded people to ask, how could God allow such a terribly evil thing to happen? It forced many people of faith to re-examine their spiritual points of reference.

Some people, who are of the mind-set that 'all misfortune is punishment for sin', come to the conclusion that we, the Jewish people, must have collectively done something wrong to deserve it. I personally find this way of thinking unjust, as well as offensive to the memory of those who were murdered.

In October 2004, I visited the sprawling complex of Holocaust Museums and monuments near Jerusalem, known as *Yad va-Shem*. I had always avoided it on previous visits to Israel, because I knew that it would be a very upsetting, emotional experience for me.

The name *yad va-shem* ('a monument and a memorial', literally, 'a hand and a name'), comes from Isaiah 56:4-5,

> *'To the childless ones who keep my Sabbaths, who choose what pleases me and hold fast to my Covenant – to them I will give within my Temple and its walls* **a monument and a memorial** *better than having sons and daughters; I will give them an everlasting memorial that will never be destroyed.'*

For those who died in the Holocaust, many of them have no descendants – no children to carry on their names as their everlasting memorials. But there, within the boundaries of modern Jerusalem, within the 'walls' of the Holy City, I feel they have an eternal monument to their memory.

One stunning monument at *Yad va-Shem* was an interconnected series of artificial canyons and valleys. If you were able to look down from above, you would see that these canyons formed a map of Europe and North Africa. At various intersections were the names of towns and villages where there used to be Jewish communities, some of which had existed for over a thousand years, but were obliterated during the Holocaust. It is aptly called 'the Valley of the Lost Communities.'

Perhaps the most stunningly beautiful and poignant memorial was to the 2 million children who lost their lives. It is in a dark hall, which is in reality lit only by a few candles in orange-coloured glass holders, but with the clever use of mirrors, those candles are reflected and multiplied, until it looks like there are thousands of small candles, like myriads of stars lighting the sky. As the stars themselves go on for millions of years, so too the memory of these innocent little souls will live on forever.

The main memorial in the complex, is the building which contains the eternal flame to the 6 million dead, with the names of the concentration camps placed in geographical relation to each other. As I was walking into the building, it did not immediately hit me that this was the main memorial – the one place I knew would upset me the most. Once inside, it was a profound shock to realise, 'This was it'. I just broke down in floods of tears. I just could not control the feeling of grief – it was so overwhelming.

"My God, my God, why did You abandon us? We called out to You, 'Deliver us!' and You did not hear us. You did nothing! Where were You when we needed You most?"

"My beloved children, I did not abandon you. Would a mother desert her children when they cry out in bitter agony, day and night? Would a father not come to the aid of his children who cry out to be saved? I was frantic and beside Myself – I desperately went among the nations and I called out to them, saying, 'I am Yahveh, God of Israel. My children are suffering terrible affliction. Will you help them?' And the answer from the leaders of those nations came back to Me. 'No; what Germany does to its own citizens is an internal matter. We will not help.' [a]

"Then I went to the politicians of the nations, and I spoke to them, saying, 'Listen, I am the God of the Congregation of Jacob; my children are being persecuted beyond endurance. Will you not help them?' And the answer came back to Me: 'No, we should not interfere in the affairs of others. We will not help.'

"Then I went to the peoples of the nations of the earth, and I cried out to them, 'The Jews are being slaughtered in their millions, I'm begging you, please, please, please, will you not help My children?' and the reply came back to me, 'Such a thing cannot be happening. Besides, it's not our problem. No, we will not help.'

"I did not abandon My children; humanity did'.

The real wrongdoers in the Holocaust

If we remain aware of ancient Yahwist concepts, a natural conclusion would be that the Holocaust was some kind of 'Day of Yahveh' – remember, this is a calamitous, earth-shaking 'punishment event' – a day of reckoning when God punishes wrongdoers. However, if we are also aware of the concept of the 'trembling of heaven and earth' – where good and *innocent* people experience God's punitive presence first as misfortune – then we begin to suspect that the true objective goal of this 'Day of Yahveh' was *not* the Jewish people. The Jewish people of that time were no worse and no better than anybody else.

---

[a] These are actual, verbatim responses by the global community when asked to help deal with what was going on in Germany at the time, as reported in the international newspapers of the period.

So what or who were the wrongdoers destined for punishment? If the innocent suffered in God's wake, then it must have been the people they were living amongst – the Germans – or more specifically, the Nazis.

You see, the 'Day of Yahveh' isn't only intended as a day of reckoning for the Jewish people. In Jonah's day, such a punishment was due to be visited on the Assyrian people in Nineveh. To prevent this, God called Jonah to deliver a message of repentance to the Assyrians – all of them Gentiles – so that they would be spared.

The sins of the Nazis were too numerous to recount, but I think one sin in particular tipped the balance. Apparently, the Nazis were planning on restructuring the religious life of Germany after the war. Religious values would be turned on their head, and corrupt Nazi values would replace the 'weak' spiritual values of traditional religion. Church ceremonies, such as marriage and baptism, had already been given a Nazi counterpart.

The new Nazi religion would be a corrupt form of neo-pagan Germanic religion. It would become a religion where the less able were done away with, the just and compassionate would be suppressed, and moral right would be based on power and ruthless cruelty.

I now believe that God felt that this would be *the* supreme abuse of religion, and therefore an indirect tainting of God's reputation. Even though such a Nazi religion would have no connection to Yahwism, I believe that Yahveh could not allow such a heinous corruption of human spirituality to stand as a threat to the holiness of Yahwist values in the world – perhaps if left unchecked, the Nazi corruption of spiritual values would have eventually infected all religion. It was inevitable that Yahveh would act against Nazism. It *had* to be destroyed from the face of the earth.

In the wake of God's action against the Nazis, the Jewish people and other innocents were caught up in the horror of the time. Did God call a prophet at the time, one that warned the Jewish people to flee? If God did, his or her voice was never heard; after all, we are told that there are no more prophets!

I have said before that when innocent people suffer because of God's actions to right wrongs, then God compensates us, often by giving us wisdom from what we learn in the experience. I think that God compensated the Jewish people for their suffering in the Holocaust by allowing the modern State of Israel to come into being.

The Holocaust was a terrible wound, a grievous injury to the Jewish soul. It remains a trauma, blighting the Jewish psyche even today. It can never be forgotten. But we do need to heal, and move past it. Jewish life cannot become what Yahveh intended it to become, until the wholeness of the Jewish soul – our collective *shleimut néfesh* – recovers from the horror of the Holocaust, and returns to full health:

> *"Cry no more My people,*
> *Weep no longer, My children;*
> *For the many who were put to death*
> *are with Me now like lights in the firmament.*
> *They are beside Me like the stars in the heavens -*
> *They live, they are not gone;*
> *They walk in light,*
> *they are not dead.*
> *Move beyond your grief, for I have comforted you,*
> *Let your pain be no more, for I have healed you.*
> *Rejoice, for they are clothed in white,*
> *They are bathed in the fullness of My glory.*
> *I have given them honour and dignity,*
> *I have crowned them with the Way of Chaff,[a]*
> *And lifted them above even the serafim,*
> *for My Name's sake.*
> *They stand in praise by My throne,*
> *And sing throughout all eternity in joy,*
> *'Holier than the holiest holiness*
> *is Yahveh of the heavenly battalions;*
> *Heaven and earth are full of Your glory.'*
> *Be comforted and know that I remember them forever,*
> *So that you are freed once more to remember Me."[b]*

'Do not fret over evil'

When we are wronged, we feel angry, bitter, enraged, hateful and vengeful. Hatred and anger cause the mind to go to a very dark place indeed. If we allow our anger over the evil that happens to us in this world to fester unchecked, then we will end up ruining our *own* lives.

'Don't be afraid!' Yahveh constantly tells us this in the Miqra. Do not be afraid of what you don't know. If you are the type of person who thinks that you are constantly surrounded by sin, evil and death, you are going to end up in a psychiatric institution! If you think that the imperfections of this world and this life are going to overtake you, then they will. If you constantly think that 'Satan is out to get you', then you will end up a paranoid wreck. Some religions will want you this way so

---

[a] the Milky Way
[b] S. Kit. Oracle 1:3

that they can control you more easily, but that's not how Yahveh our God wants you. Step back; do not let these matters eat away at your soul. Your heavenly Father wants you strong. God wants you courageous. God wants you to realise how wonderful you are, that you can succeed, that you have a worthy life, and a purpose given to you even before birth. If you look only to your imperfections and weaknesses, then you will stumble at every turn; if however you look to every good thing that God presents you with, then you will succeed.

Proverbs[a] says, *'Do not fret over those who do evil.'* There is a particular teaching of the prophet Yeshua` which ably demonstrates this Jewish way of thinking Unfortunately, in a non-Jewish environment, it has been misinterpreted.

Yeshua` said, *'if anyone strikes you on the right cheek, present them with your left cheek as well! If someone sues you, and demands your mantle, give them your tunic as well! And if anyone conscripts you to go one mile, go with them two miles!'*[b]

Outside of the Jewish culture and historical setting in which this saying was given, it has been interpreted to mean, 'Do not resist or fight against evil'. 'Turn the other cheek' has been taken to mean, 'Ignore evil', and 'going the extra mile' has come to mean, 'doing more than is expected of us'. None of these ideas are anything even close to what was originally intended in front of a Jewish audience. In fact, if you had been present amongst Yeshua`'s original Jewish listeners, you would have seen them rolling about in stitches!

For me, the funniest line is, *'If someone sues you, and demands your mantle, give them your tunic as well!'* Well, it does become funny when you are aware that poor people only had two items of clothing! If your mantle is demanded of you as a pledge for a loan, then if you give your tunic as well, you would be naked!

Take a look at the other two situations. Now, the Romans were often forcibly conscripting Jewish men to carry their belongings for them. So if you were conscripted to go one mile, do more and go two – which in fact would take you *way past* where the Roman actually wanted you to go (and seriously annoy the Roman you were being forced to serve). And the thing about turning the other cheek? Well, this is where knowledge of Jewish social customs comes in. The manly way to slap someone across the face is with the back of your right hand on their right cheek. However, presenting your left cheek would force them to slap you with the front of their right hand – which in those days was actually considered a sissy slap.

---

[a] Prov 24:19 – also Ps 37:1, 8
[b] S.Yesh. 71:2-3

Now that you know all this, you can see that Yeshua` was being light-hearted. He was purposefully taking things to the point of silliness.

The message of these words of Yeshua` therefore, is not 'Do not resist evil', but rather, 'Don't take evil seriously – don't let it get to you.'

... *deliver us* ...

The Aramaic word has the sense of 'to deliver from physical or moral evil'. It also has the sense of 'to set free' or 'to release'.

In a legal trial, the person being accused would sometimes cry out to the judge, 'Deliver me from my accuser!' In such a situation, the accused would be asking to be found innocent, and be set free from the stress and misery of a trial.

As I will shortly be describing to you, at that time some people used to believe that the accusations of 'the Accuser' brought suffering in this life. Therefore, the petition of this line is asking, rather than putting us through the pain of tribulation, set us free. Rather than putting us through the trial that is to come, deliver us from the suffering that tribulation brings.

... *from our accusers / the Evil One / evil*

I'm going to make a leap of intellectual supposition here, and theorise that, in the original spoken prayer that Yeshua` taught his followers, he did not use the term 'evil' or 'evil one'. If, in the last four lines, he was creating the image of a court of law, where the innocent are accused, and plead for deliverance from their accusers, then the word(s) 'evil' or 'evil one' would be completely unsuitable and incongruous (remember, in Jewish poetry, *ideas* are repeated in line couplets). Besides, you have to remember that at that time, the Persian-influenced, post-exile Jewish idea of 'Satan' was not as the lord of all evil, but as the heavenly prosecutor – 'the Accuser' – who recited our sins before God.

I think that it is more likely that he used the Aramaic term for 'accuser' – or more probable, given its poetical metre, 'our accusers'. There are various alternatives[a] for 'accuser', 'adversary' or 'enemy' (all the same concept in Aramaic), but the most likeliest might have been *b^e'el d^esana*. I say this because it fits in with the rhythm and metre of the last two lines. If Yeshua` were trying to play on the image of a courtroom, then 'our accusers (*ba'^elan d^esana* in Aramaic), fits perfectly.

I have provided scope for both possible translations in *The Exhortations*. In *The Book of the Preaching*, I have given the translation

---

[a] such as *b^e'el d^esana*, *b^e'el d^ebaba*, or *b^e'el dina*

of, "but rather deliver us from our accusers". However, in *The Book of the Prophet Yeshua`*, I have given the translation of "but rather deliver us from evil". This latter form is the one which is said in the Talmidi Israelite community, when reciting the prayer.

Now, I have to say here that I personally do *not* believe in 'the Accuser'; it is an idea that crept into Judaism after the Babylonian exile. Besides, I believe that God Himself is adequately aware of what we have done, and what we have failed to do; God does not therefore need an 'Accuser' to recite our sins to God. In modern Talmidi prayers, the line is always recited in English as 'deliver us from evil'; it avoids so many pitfalls in understanding that way (and is closer to God's reality, since there is no 'accuser'). However, I am not letting my own beliefs get in the way of my 'theological archaeology'. I am willing to acknowledge that this was a belief that was generally held at the time. So in Aramaic, Yeshua`'s version may have been:

w^e *'al ta 'éylan l*^e*-nissayuna*
ela atséylan mibba 'layn d^e*-sana*

You can see that this actually rhymes sound-wise in Aramaic. In English, this would give the following:

And do not bring us to trial
Rather deliver us from our accusers.

I suspect that in the very first translation of the prayer by the scribe who compiled the Q-Gospel, and put the Aramaic words into Hebrew, *ba 'layn d*^e*sana* ('our accusers') would be rendered simply as *sataneynu* ('our accusers') – because that is what *'satan'* means: Accuser. When it came to translating the prayer from Hebrew into Greek however, the translator may have read 'satan' as a singular ('our Satan' / 'our Accuser') instead of plural ('our accusers').

Understanding it only as a singular ('Satan'), he would then have been faced with a dilemma. The non-Jewish, Greek-speaking world would not have been aware of what 'satan' meant to a Jewish audience. There would have been no Greek word that could convey the full imagery of the Hebrew or Aramaic original. I think that the writers of both Greek *Luke* and Greek *Matthew* decided to go with the easiest and most logical word to replace *satan* (Accuser), and that would be *tou ponerou* ('the Evil one').

From wild beasts to Satan; pagan intrusions into Yahwism

In my first book,[a] I mentioned that in the period of the Patriarchs, there was the general belief that the misfortune of the good and righteous was caused by mythological wild beasts such as the leviathan, the behemoth, rahab and other similar creatures.[b] We now know that there are no such things, but in those days, it was believed that the world was populated by these invisible creatures. Just like normal wild animals, they were neither good nor evil; they acted according to instinct, and did what they did simply because that was how they behaved. They caused problems in the real world, just as real wild animals do. However, they were still considered creations of Yahveh, and were still subject to God – God alone was able to control them.[c]

If you are aware of early Israelite mythology, then you will know that the leviathan, the behemoth and the ziz / simurg are all 'heavenly wild beasts' (or *iyim*,[d] the 'howling creatures' of Isaiah 34:14 and Jeremiah 50:39). Similarly in Isaiah 24:21, the 'host of heaven' being referred to can cover any supernatural beings, and not necessarily the angels in heaven: *'On that day, Yahveh will punish the supernatural creatures in the sky, as well as the kings of the earth on earth.'*

In early Israelite tradition, 'wild beasts' came to represent the unpredictable, random forces of the supernatural. According to Yahwist thought, animals are neither good nor evil; what they do is not subject to moral judgment. When Adam and Eve ate of the tree of knowledge, they became aware of what good and evil was, thus separating themselves from the other animals.

According to primitive Israelite mythology, metaphorically in this world we were subject to the random actions of these *iyim*, but the way God gave us to protect ourselves from them was by living a way of holiness. It was this holy way which protected us from these supposed 'heavenly wild beasts'. Just as Israelites built walls around their cities to protect themselves against earthly wild beasts, God's ways became a kind of 'city wall' to protect us against these supernatural 'wild beasts'.

Now, not for one second do I personally believe that such mythical creatures actually exist. Of course, this way of looking at things is purely mythological and not real, but it was a way of helping our ancestors understand, that the bad things that happen to us are not the result of a cosmic battle in heaven, but things that only God has control over –

---

[a] see Chapter One, the section on, 'The trembling of heaven and earth'.
[b] see Job 40:15 – 41:26; these supernatural, mythical creatures are collectively known as *iyim* (pronounced ee-YEEM).
[c] Job 40:19-20
[d] pronounced ee-YEEM

forces that are random in this world, but which are ultimately not random in the eyes of heaven.

I acknowledge and fully accept that this is what the ancient Hebrews believed at that time. It affected how they behaved towards the supernatural, and it is an important factor to understand when reading the literary imagery that such ancient beliefs engendered; it helps us to understand otherwise strange and obscure biblical passages.

The Israelite experience at Sinai changed this way of thinking. In the time of the original *Book of Job*, which predates the Exodus, people thought that misfortune was caused by supernatural wild beasts – creatures from which we could protect ourselves only by living God's ways. However, at Sinai, the Israelites learned about the glory ('divine radiance') of Yahveh, and of the trembling of heaven and earth – how the very fabric of the universe shook when God's presence moved to correct injustice and wrongdoing.

This understanding lasted all through later Israelite history, from Sinai until the Babylonian exile. After that, the Jewish people came into contact with the Zoroastrian religion, and through that contact, they developed the alien and detrimental belief in Satan. If you feel the need to defend your belief in Satan, just because he is named in the Hebrew Bible, then you will also have to defend the existence of the Leviathan in the sea, the Behemoth on the land, and the Ziz in the sky – because, after all, are they not also named in the Hebrew Bible as real?

Satan is not the ruler of all evil

In Christianity, Satan is the name of the supreme, controlling being who directs all the evil that happens, as the 'lord of all evil'. However, in post-exile Jewish tradition, it is evident from the artificially inserted prologue in Job[a] that Satan has no power of independent action, but requires the permission of God, which he is not allowed to transgress. He cannot be regarded, therefore, as an opponent of God. He is 'the adversary', the prosecutor of human souls, the 'counsel for the prosecution' – a minor, powerless being subject to the infinite will of God.

This view is also retained in Zech. 3:1-2, where Satan is described as the adversary of the high priest Yehoshua`, and of the people of God whose representative the High Priest is; and he opposes the 'angel of Yahveh,' who ultimately orders him to be silent in the name of God. In

---

[a] It is likely that the portions in the Book of Job that mention Satan (Job 1:6-12, and 2:1-7a) are in fact late post-exile additions to the text (c. 6th – 4th century BCE), and not from the *original* text from the Patriarchal period (c. 17th century BCE).

both of these passages, Satan is a mere 'accuser', who acts only with the express permission of God.

After the Babylonian exile, because of the dualist[a] influence of the Persian religion, books of the bible edited *after* that date begin to show Satan as an independent agent. For example, in I Chron. 21:1, he appears as one who is able to tempt and provoke David to destroy Israel. The Chronicler (third century BCE) regards Satan as a being with independent will, a view which is all the more striking when we look at the much older, pre-exile source he drew his account from (II Sam. 24:1), which speaks of God *Himself* as the one who moved David against the children of Israel. Since the older, pre-dualist narrative attributes all events, whether good or bad, to God alone,[b] it is probable that the Chronicler was influenced by Persian Zoroastrianism, even though Israelite monotheism strongly opposed Iranian dualism.

The evolution of Satan into an independently thinking being, strong enough to be capable of opposing God, is derived directly from dualist Zoroastrianism; the character of Satan is based directly on its evil god, *Angra Mainyu*. It is inconsistent with native Hebrew concepts of evil. Zoroastrian dualism influenced Gnosticism,[c] and through Gnostic theology, dualism entered Paullist beliefs.[d]

Satan as the Accuser

When the very idea of Satan itself entered Hebrew thought in about the 6th century BCE, originally it was merely an angel whose power was very limited. It acted like the 'counsel for the prosecution' in the heavenly court, where God was the judge, and individual human souls were put on trial for their sins. Satan was supposed to point out our sins to God. The title for this job was 'The Accuser' (which is what the word

---

[a] Dualism refers to the concept that there is a good god and a bad god; that these two deities rule the universe as equals and opposites. This is in complete opposition to Yahwism, which holds that Yahveh *alone* rules both good fortune and bad fortune, and that Yahveh has no equal or opposite.
[b] I Sam. 16:14; I Kings 22:22; Isa. 45:7; etc.
[c] an independent system of religious thought that influenced Judaism in the late Second Temple period, as well as early Christianity. It held that all things in this world were evil, that the ruler of this world was the devil, and that salvation could only come through secret knowledge or '*gnosis*'.
[d] such as 'this world is the realm of the ruler of evil, Satan, and we will only be saved at the coming of a king-saviour from the world of light.' The Yahwist way of looking at the same statement would be, 'This world and the next is ruled by Yahveh alone – who is always with us – and we will be strengthened against the evil that other people do, when we repent and return to God's ways.'

'Satan' literally means in Hebrew).

The idea eventually developed that the very act of Satan accusing us in heaven – even before our deaths – was the cause of our misfortune here on earth. If the Accuser loses its case in the heavenly court, it is 'rebuked'. This is the mythological imagery behind the verse in the *Book of Visions*:

> *'For the accuser of our sister Israel,*
> *who accuses her before our God day and night,*
> *has been rebuked.*[a]
> *She won her case against him*
> *by the word of her testimony.*'[b]

In Gnostic-influenced theology, it was the accusations of Satan that caused us misfortune. Most times, misfortune just happens, and we turn to our heavenly Father to get us through the worst of times. On rare occasions, as I have explained in my previous book, it is the movement of the fire of God's glory when God moves to right wrongs, which shakes the fabric of the Universe – not the accusations of 'Satan' the Accuser. The effect of this for us in this world is that the misfortunes and trials of life increase for both good and bad people. God compensates good people in such times by enabling us to gain insights and wisdom from our troubles.

The incongruity of obedient angels and fallen angels

There is something I find curious about the arguments of certain religious people who defend the existence and status of Satan. They believe that angels can 'fall' through disobedience to God. This is based on several passages in the Miqra which *actually* refer to Gentile kings who were once paragons, and had since fallen from moral grace.[c]

As I have mentioned previously, in Yahwist thought, angels *cannot* disobey the moral will of God. They can act independently and make their own choices, since they are not entirely puppets, but they cannot ultimately disobey the moral rulings or instructions of Yahveh; nothing in heaven can disobey God.

The idea of fallen angels proliferated after the Babylonian exile,

---

[a] The Hebrew verb *ka'ah* can mean 'expel' or 'cast out', but it can also mean 'rebuke' in a court of law – see Zechariah 3:1-2
[b] S. Ch. 5:10b-11 – cf Revelation 12:10 'For the accuser of our brothers, who accuses them before our God day and night, has been hurled down. And they overcame him by […] the word of their witness.'
[c] eg Isaiah 14:12 (King of Babylon), and Ezek 28:11-19 (King of Tyre).

and was heavily influenced by the mythology of the Persian religion, Zoroastrianism. The apocryphal *Book of Enoch* contains many references to fallen angels, and was written during this period. However, this idea of fallen angels is in reality a deviation from the Yahwist standard,[a] and is alien to any true understanding of how our living God Yahveh works in heaven and on earth.

Take for example the idea of the *Nephilim*. After the arrival of Paullist Christianity, this word came to mean, 'Fallen Angel'. However, in Greek and Aramaic translations before Paul of Tarsus, this Hebrew word was translated as 'giant'. Indeed, in the Greek Septuagint translation of the Torah, which was made long before Christianity and therefore knew nothing of fallen angels, this is how the word is translated.

Many people interpret *Nephilim* as meaning 'fallen', since it is similar to the Hebrew word for 'fallen ones'. It's true that the word *Nephil* is connected to the Hebrew word *nafal* (to fall), but we only associate that with 'fallen from grace' because of the influence of Christian teaching (i.e. if Paul's Christianity had never existed, we would never think of *Nephilim* being connected with 'fallen from grace' or 'fallen angels').

Pagan religion is choc-a-block with stories of gods and divine beings that have intercourse with human women and produce super-humans. I think that this idea has crept back into monotheism under the guise of supposedly 'fallen angels' who had intercourse with women.

However, if the *Nephilim* in reality had been a non-Semitic race, then the word 'Nephil' may have been their native name for themselves, and could have meant something entirely different in their own language. You see, whenever the ancient Hebrews encountered a people who spoke a completely different language to Hebrew, they had a tendency to take the foreign ethnic name, and then find a similar word in Hebrew and so rename them. In Hebrew, every single word means something (like in English and some other European languages, the word 'telephone' literally means 'far sound'). To a Hebrew speaker, every word has to mean something, so if a foreign word is unrecognisable as it is, then it is given meaning by finding a similar-sounding Hebrew word.

---

[a] the baseline theology of the original Yahwist faith revealed at Mt Horeb. The Hebrew Bible sometimes deviates from this, including beliefs from other religions and traditions (eg Satan, war in heaven, fallen angels, supernatural animals causing misfortune etc). In order not to be distracted by these additions, one has to remember the 'Yahwist standard – what the baseline Yahwist beliefs are, and realise that often, references to these other traditions are for literary purposes only.

Who is to say there wasn't some other reason why their name was connected with the verb 'fall'? Was it due to some notable physical characteristic they had? Or some manner of their speech? Or was it simply a Hebrew version of their own name? (as I say, there was a fondness in ancient Hebrew of connecting foreign words to Hebrew ones, even though there actually was no connection). Whatever may have been the case, the existence of *Nephilim* in the Miqra is false evidence of fallen angels.

The irony of defending Satan instead of defending God

There are certain religious people today who spend more time defending the existence of Satan than they do exalting the power and majesty of God. They would rather diminish the power of God and defend the power of evil, than raise and magnify the majesty of our Heavenly Father, and thereby render evil powerless. To such people (who are often more interested in their bank balances and their own power over others than serving God), it is more important that the power of Satan be maintained.

The power of Satan is so great in these people's minds, that he becomes an all-consuming bogeyman, who lies in wait round every corner. Their lives are run by the fear of Satan, rather than by the reverent awe of Yahveh. If their belief system is dependent on maintaining the power of Satan, then I would seriously question the foundations of such a belief system! The reverent awe of Yahveh leads to life in abundance; fear of Satan can only lead to mental illness.

I have heard people say that you can't have God without the Devil – that if God exists, then logically, the Devil must also exist. However, this assumption is based on a false premise, because such a notion assumes that the essential character of such a god is either Zoroastrian or Gnostic – dualist in nature. But if you were to ever grasp and fully comprehend the infinite magnitude, and all-encompassing majesty of Yahveh, you would surely realise that the Devil – as ruler and instigator of all evil – cannot *possibly* exist; if such a Satan did exist, the power of God is automatically cut in half, and the omnipresent sovereignty of God is diminished. If Satan exists, *then the God of Abraham does not.*

The danger in making Satan the centre of your spiritual fears, is that you eventually begin thinking that human beings are no longer responsible for their evil – because it is Satan who is directing it all. The criminally insane will then proclaim that 'Satan made me do it!' – and indeed, they do, frequently. The falsehood about the supreme power of Satan facilitates the concealment of a terrible truth: that no one is to blame for the proliferation of moral evil except for human beings themselves. The greatest achievement of religious people who defend Satan's power, is that they have succeeded in crippling the ability of the human race to deal effectively with the *true* cause of evil actions and wicked deeds throughout history – humanity itself.

When we are faced with the choice to do either good or evil, many religious people say that we are being tempted by Satan. But this is what Jacob the Pious had to say on who was doing the tempting – it isn't God, and it isn't the devil either: *'rather each one is drawn away and enticed, tempted by his own desires.'*[a] Satan just wasn't part of early Talmidi theology – and shouldn't be now.

Early Israelite religion severely limited the power of evil, in the respect that Yahveh is mightier and more powerful than any evil. There is no controlling 'lord of all evil' who directs all the evil things that happen; such a way of thinking is Gnostic dualism. Our souls profit more from the study and love of good, than they do from the study and fear of evil. Modern religion has attributed to Satan *too much power*, making people believe that he is greater than he actually is (i.e. nothing), allowing evil to keep them in a constant state of fear. The sole result is to make people afraid in order to control them.[b] However, Yahveh is the only Supreme Power, and everything is subject to *God's* will. There is nothing even remotely equal to Yahveh; there is nothing in creation so great that it cannot be overcome by the power of Yahveh.

To summarise, the original Israelite religion did not have any concept of Satan (as lord of all evil, equal and opposite of God). The idea only entered Judaism after the Babylonian exile in the 6th century BC, influenced by Zoroastrianism and Gnosticism, when the bible's "Satanic passages" were inserted.[c] Originally in Israelite theology, Yahveh is supreme,[d] and has no equal or opposite.[e] In the Patriarchal period when books like Job were written, misfortune on earth was thought to be caused by supernatural wild beasts (*iyim* in Hebrew), like the leviathan and the behemoth;[f] even the serpent in the Garden of Eden was actually one of these *iyim*, not an incarnation of Satan. However, Yahveh was still in complete control.[g] Then after the revelation at Sinai, when the theology surrounding the glory or 'divine radiance' was given,[h] we

---

[a] Ig. Yq. 2:10 – cf Ep. James 1:14
[b] I suspect that this is the real goal of preachers who otherwise have no moral force or intellectual weight behind their message.
[c] eg Job 1:6-12, 2:1-7a; 1Chr 21:1 - see the original, equivalent passage in 2Sam 24:1
[d] Dt 4:39, Isa 43:11, Isa 45:5
[e] Isa 40:25
[f] Job 41:1
[g] Ps 74:14
[h] Ex 16:10, 24:16-17

learned that God's glory has the power to cause both misfortune[a] and good fortune.[b]

As for cosmic battles, there is no war or discord in heaven,[c] and angels cannot disobey God or fall (anything that suggests they can has been taken out of context and misused; in heaven nothing can disobey God's will). Then, during contact with the Persian religion, the idea of Satan entered Judaism, as well as the idea of fallen angels and wars in heaven, (but even then, *ha-Satan* was still an agent of God). These things were not part of the original Israelite faith; to suggest there is a Satan is basically saying that God is not all-powerful.

Seek to know Yahveh, not Satan. In order to fully comprehend suffering, temptation, sin, 'Satan' and evil itself, you need to take yourself to a very dark place, a harmful domain that we as sons and daughters of Yahveh were not meant to go to. It is enough to have our trust set and locked firmly in the light of Yahveh's Presence; it is sufficient to acknowledge Yahveh as our great shield and defender, and not to fret over evil.[d] Seek to know enough to enable you to cope with misfortune and discomfort, but no more. I have come to realise that there are things that we were not meant to know or understand, because there are some things that are too terrible or too damaging to understand.

Illustrations from the words of the prophet Yeshua`

Yeshua` said:

'The good person out of the storehouse of good in their heart brings forth good, and the evil person out of the storehouse of evil in their heart brings forth evil; because from the abundance of plenty in the heart, so the mouth speaks.'[e]

' . . . but the things that come out of a person come from the heart, and these things defile you – acts of murder and adultery, false witness and theft, greed, malice, deceit, envy, arrogance and blasphemy. 'All these evils that come from inside are what make a person unclean.'[f]

---

[a] 2Sam 6:6-7
[b] 2Sam 6:12
[c] cf the book of Ezekiel's visions, which portrays heaven as peace
[d] Prov 24:19, Ps 37:1
[e] S.Yesh. 53:2-3 – cf Mt 12:34-35, Lk 6:45
[f] S.Yesh. 160:7-8 – cf Mk 7:15, 20-23

CHAPTER NINE: Summary of the Second half of the prayer

Overview

The second half of the prayer depicts Yahveh our heavenly Father first as our Provider, then as our Saviour, and finally as our Defender. The overwhelming message that comes across is to trust in Yahveh – trust in God to provide for us, to care for us, to lift our burdens, to deliver us, to save us and to protect us.

If you were fortunate to have a good relationship with your earthly father or mother, I can bet there were times when you were proud of being in your father or mother's care. You would hold their hand, and think to yourself, 'Nothing bad can possibly happen to me, because I'm with my father, or because I'm with my mother.'

So it is with Yahveh. The issue here is trust. We need to trust Yahveh, our protector and defender. The ancient Israelites were told not to make alliances with other nations, but to trust in the ability of Yahveh alone to protect and defend them. Instead, when danger came, they sought help from one empire against another,[a] thinking that such a tiny nation could only survive by being under the hegemony of a greater human power. History shows that in Israel's case, such alliances *never* worked.[b]

On a personal level, we often do not trust in God to guide and teach us in life. We do not trust the ability of God to be there for us in the future. We trust instead in fortune-tellers, horoscopes, astrologers and mediums. Abandoning these superstitions will enable us to lose our fear and dread of the future, and have faith and confidence in our heavenly Father in the present.

'Become passers-by'

The enigmatic words in the title of this section come from the Gnostic *Gospel of Thomas*.[c] It is purportedly a saying of the prophet Yeshua`. When scholars met in the mid 1990's to discuss the sayings of Yeshua` in 'the Jesus Seminar', this saying equally divided the scholars.

---

[a] Isaiah 30:1-3, also Jer 2:36
[b] Isaiah 20:6
[c] Gos. Thom. 42:1

Some felt it sounded like it could have come from Yeshua`, some not.

In the New Age community, it has become a mystical catch-phrase, and has even been made into a catchy song. There are many webpages on the internet discussing its possible meanings; few of them however can agree on a unified interpretation.

I last visited this saying in the mid-90's myself when I was compiling and editing the *Sefer Yeshua`*.[a] If this *was* a genuine saying of Yeshua`, at the time I could not myself think what it could possibly mean. The fact that it only appears in the *Gospel of Thomas* should not in itself preclude the possibility that it was once in the *Q-Gospel*, since there are many sayings there which have parallels in the gospels of *Matthew* and *Luke*. If the authors of *Matthew* and *Luke* did not understand the saying either, they very well could have left it out for the same reason I did.

At its face value alone, it implies walking on by, not participating in the world. This suited Gnostic themes well, since they saw the real world as having been spawned by Satan, and that only the spiritual was from God. They interpreted it as a call to disassociate oneself from the flesh and from material things in general, and concentrate on the spiritual.

I had forgotten all about this saying over the years, and thought nothing more of it. Then one Shabbat recently, while reading the sidra[b] for that week, several verses concerning gleaning rights leaped out at me:

"If you pass through your neighbour's vineyard, then you may eat any grapes as you wish until you are sated, but you may not put any into your basket. If you pass through your neighbour's field of grain, then you may pick kernels with your hand, but you may not put a sickle to your neighbour's standing grain."[c]

In ancient Israel, fields were joined together i.e. with no access paths or lanes between them. In order to get to one's own field, or simply to get to one's own property, one had to pass through other people's fields. This was not seen as trespass in those days, since all land belonged

---

[a] This is a complete collection of the Jewish and re-Judaised sayings of the prophet Yeshua`. It is used to teach others within the Talmidi community about the ethics and emphases of the prophet, as well as inspiring his ideals in others. It thus avoids the need to use the New Testament, which has been heavily influenced by Paul's teaching and theology.

[b] a weekly Torah portion. A *sidra* (pronounced see-DRAA) is a short portion of Torah to be read on the Sabbath. It is not to be confused with a *parashah*, which is a longer portion. Short *sidra'ot* enable Torah to be read in 3 years (the ancient custom of the Galilee and Judea, and the practice of the modern Talmidi community), and long *parashot* enable Torah to be read in 1 year (the practice of the mainstream rabbinic Jewish community.

[c] Deut 23:24-25

to God. When Yeshua''s followers passed through fields and took grain to rub in their hands and eat,[a] notice they weren't accused of stealing, only of harvesting on the Sabbath.

Anyone who worked the land, who farmed or harvested anything, was doing so on behalf of their landlord, who in effect was really Yahveh. The grapes and the grain belonged to God, and it was a charity on behalf of God, and a measure of Yahveh's kindness, to give to hungry travellers on their way to and from their homes.

The ancient sages pointed out that if every traveller were to take from every field, many farmers would be ruined, so they limited this right to farmworkers. However, this misses the point of the mitzvah. It was not about providing for *every* traveller or taking from *every* field; it was rather for the *hungry* and *poor* traveller, who did not have enough money to buy provisions sufficient for their whole journey.

In the ancient hospitality laws, as I have previously mentioned, there are unwritten obligations both on the host, as well as the guest. So it was with gleaning rights. You were not meant to set off on a journey thinking, 'Oh, I don't need to take any food with me, because I can take from other people's fields'. This would have been an abuse of the gleaning laws. The key to understanding this is the single Hebrew word *sav`ekha*, which is usually translated 'until you are sated,' or 'until you are full'.

Only if you are hungry are you to glean. As a passer-by, you have the obligation at the outset to take what you can for your whole journey, but if you are poor, and don't have enough food to last you the whole way, then Yahveh will provide for you *if you run out*.

Now we return to the enigmatic saying from the *Gospel of Thomas* – 'Become passers-by'. With knowledge of the culture surrounding the gleaning rights of passers-by, the meaning becomes clear. As a passer-by, *you trust in Yahveh to provide for you.* If you run out of food on your journey, do not fret or worry, because God, as the provider of the poor, has made adequate provision for you.

It all suggests to me that there is an attitude that was supposed to have been engendered by this mitzvah from Deuteronomy – the attitude of trusting in Yahveh to provide for our needs. Remember how Yeshua' told us, *'Don't be anxious, saying, "What will we eat?" or "What will we drink?" or "What will we wear?" Because even the Gentiles look for these things, and yet your heavenly Father knows that they need them all. Rather, look for the kingdom of God, and you'll see, all these things will be yours as well.'*[b]

---

[a] *New Testament*, Mk 2:23-26
[b] S.Yesh. 45:1-3 – cf Mt 6:31-33, Lk 12:29-31

To become a passer-by suggests becoming someone who has this attitude. If this is a genuine saying of the prophet Yeshua`, then he was telling his followers to become people who did not worry or become anxious about where their next meal would come from. Become a passer-by, and trust in Yahveh to provide for you.

This is the meaning of the phrase when seen from a Jewish perspective. Perhaps this is the attitude Yeshua` tried to inculcate in his followers when he told them not to worry about where their next meal was coming from, or how they would be clothed, or what they would drink.

There is no mystical, New Age or Gnostic, this-world-denigrating purpose behind the words, 'become passers-by'. Perhaps there were landowners and farmers in Yeshua`'s day who were not following this law – not allowing passers-by to take from their fields. Perhaps Yeshua` was also reminding them that this was for their benefit too.

Trust in your heavenly Father

Let me tell you a parable.

> *There was a young boy in a village who was very disobedient and rebellious towards his parents, and did not honour his mother or his father. His father would tell him to do one thing, and he would do another; his mother would instruct him to go one way, and he would head off in a different direction.*
>
> *So one day, his father called this son and said, "My son, I need you to go on an errand for me to the neighbouring town over the hills. Now the path is a winding way, so I will give you instructions and you must follow them carefully, veering neither to the right, nor to the left. You must go there and return to me straight afterwards."*
>
> *But the son on leaving the village went off on his own way, and in time, he found himself hopelessly lost. So he sat down on a rock along the way, and when he heard wolves and leopards nearby, he began to cry out of fear.*
>
> *Presently he felt a hand on his shoulder; he turned round and saw his father's kindly face of concern looking down on him.*
>
> *So the son said, "Father, I have been foolish. I have strayed and become lost, and thereby put myself in danger."*
>
> *But the father said, "My son, you were never really lost to me, because I always knew where you were. I knew you would*

disobey me, so I followed you, because I love you and don't want to lose you. You may have strayed from the path I had set for you, but I accompanied you close by, and I was always there with you. "[a]

We sometimes resent that religion gives us all these rules to adhere to. They often seem unnecessary and trivial. We tend to view them as restricting our freedom, and as holding us down. However, rules that are truly from Yahveh are there for a reason. They are there to protect us. They enable Yahveh to extend God's guidance and loving care to every aspect of our lives, and because Yahveh only wants the best for us.

Yahveh alone is our Saviour

Through the prophet Isaiah, Yahveh told us most emphatically, *'I – and I alone – am Yahveh, and beside Me there is no other saviour.'*[b] *'I – and I alone – am the one who blots out your transgressions, for my own sake, and remembers your sins no more.'*[c]

There is no power greater than the power of Yahveh to forgive us, to cleanse us, and remember our sin no more. We do not need to turn to messiahs to save us, or to the sacrifice of blood for forgiveness, because it is by the power of God's purifying glory alone that Yahveh is able to wash us clean of sin.

We can either believe in a God who forgives and restores by the power of God's merciful love, or we can believe in a small, weak god who is only able to forgive if blood is shed; we cannot believe in both. *We have to choose.*

Talmidaism chooses Yahveh. Talmidaism chooses a powerful, living God who is able to cleanse us and make us whole, when we approach God's Presence in the spirit of repentance. Talmidaism chooses a holy God before whom evil and wrongdoing cannot endure.

I remember reading a book many, many years ago entitled, 'Our God is Too Small'.[d] The God we worship is often limited by our perceptions of God. When I was in my teenage years (and still a Christian), I remember a Catholic priest saying to me that he took great comfort in the belief that God needed to become human – become a baby and grow up with us – in order to truly know our suffering. Without intending any disrespect to Christians or the Christian faith, this statement actually sowed the seeds of my doubts about the Christian

---

[a] S. Kit. 3:11
[b] Isaiah 43:11; see also Isa 45:5
[c] Isaiah 43:25
[d] by John Young

deity, because it made me think, 'If the God I am taught about were truly God – all-knowing and all-seeing, all-feeling and all-present – then surely, *wouldn't He already know the suffering of humanity?* If such a God didn't know, then the only logical conclusion was that he wasn't God.'

Yahveh alone is our true Deliverer, our hope in times of darkness, our sure and constant rock when we are in doubt, the One we can turn to when we are troubled and afraid. Yahveh is our one, true Champion who has no failings or shortcomings, who is constant and unchanging – the One we can always trust.

I hope that by now, after reading my first two books, that Yahveh has become real for you. My fervent prayer is that you have come to know the *real* Yahveh, the real living Being who loves you, cares about you, and would never do anything to endanger the salvation of your soul.

CHAPTER TEN: The meaning of the whole prayer in brief, and a summary of the petitions

Our Father, who is in heaven,
Sanctified be Your Name!

Beloved Heavenly Father, may the way we live our lives – how we think, speak and act – bring fame to your good reputation (the line was phrased this way because people were calling religious leaders 'Father', and living lives that were desecrating God's Name).

May Your Kingdom be fulfilled!
May Your will be realised –

May You intervene soon and speedily to act against wrongdoers, and vindicate the innocent and the righteous; may we all come to live your ways, so that heaven may one day reign on earth; May your divine plan, rather than human designs, be carried out and followed.

Just as it is in heaven,
So also upon the earth.

Just as we carried out Your will perfectly as Holy Ones in heaven, so may we also do the same on earth.

Our bread, which is from the earth,
Give us day by day.

As our Provider, give us the bread of the earth, our food, our shelter and our essential needs, day by day; help us to get by from one day to the next.

And forgive us our sins,
Just as we should forgive our debtors.

Forgive us our sins, especially those that put us in danger of a tribulation; release us from our sins, just as we should release those who are in debt.

327

And do not bring us to trial
Rather deliver us from the Evil One.

Do not bring us to trial for our sins, or take us through tribulation, but rather deliver us from the accusations of the Accuser (don't put us on trial – rather set us free; protect us and keep us safe from harm).

APPENDICES A: The 'Our Father' in Aramaic, Hebrew and various modern languages

Appendix 1: The 'Our Father' in Jewish Aramaic

The 'Our Father' in Standard Jewish Aramaic. This is the form it is said within the modern Talmidi Israelite community.

אבון דבשמייא

יתקדש שמך

תאתי מלכותך

תהי רעותך

היכמא דבשמייא

כין אף בארעא

לחמן דמארעא

הב לן יומא דין ומחרא

ושבק לן חובין

היכמא דאף שבקנן לחייבין

ואל תעילן לנסיונא

אלא אצילן מן באישא

This transliterates as:

abbun d^ebishmáyya,
yithqadesh shmakh,
titey malkhutakh,
tihey r^e`utakh,
heykhma d^ebishmáyya,
keyn af b^ear`a.

lachman d^eme'ar`a,
hab lan yoma deyn u-machra,
ushbaq lan chobayn,
heykhma d^eaf sh^ebaqnan l^echayyabayn.
w^eal ta`eylan l^enissayuna,
ela atséylan min bisha.

(th - not an English 'th' like in 'path', but a t-sound with the tongue pressed against the front teeth
kh & ch – as in Scottish loch

Phonetically, this is pronounced as follows:

aah-BOON duh-bish-MY-yaa,
yeet-kaa-DESH SHMAAKH;
tee-TAY maal-khoo-TAAKH;
tee-HAY ray-oo-TAAKH,
haykh-MAA duh-bish-MY-yaa,
kayn AAF bay-aar-AA.

lakh-MAAN duh-may-aar-AA,
haab laan yoh-MAA dayn oo-makh-RAA;
oosh-BAAK laan khoh-BINE,
haykh-MAA duh-AAF shuh-baak-NAAN luh-KHY-yaa-BINE;
wuh-AAL taa-AY-laan luh-niss-SY-yoo-NAA,
ell-LAA aa-TSAY-laan min bee-SHAA

(the stressed syllables – the syllables where the emphasis falls – are written in capital letters
uh – like the 'a' in Tina)

Appendix 2: The 'Our Father' in biblical Hebrew

The corrected, reconstructed Our Father *in full biblical Hebrew, with vowel pointing:*

אָבִינוּ אֲשֶׁר בַּשָּׁמַיִם

יִתְקַדֵּשׁ שְׁמֶךָ

תָּבֹא מַלְכוּתֶךָ

יְהִי רְצוֹנְךָ

כְּבַשָּׁמַיִם

וּכְבָאָרֶץ

אֶת־לַחְמֵנוּ אֲשֶׁר מִן־הָאָרֶץ

תֵּן לָנוּ יוֹם בְּיוֹמוֹ

וּסְלַח נָא לָנוּ אֶת־חַטֹּאתֵינוּ

כַּאֲשֶׁר נִסְלַח לַחוֹטְאִים לָנוּ

וְאַל־נָא תְּבִיאֵנוּ לְנִסָּיוֹן

כִּי אִם הַצִּילֵנוּ מִיַּד הָרַע

Transliteration:

(Standard Talmidi Roman phonetic)

> āvînu ašer ba-šāmáyim
> yitqadeish šᵉméḳā
> tābo malḳutéḳā
> yᵉhī rᵉżónḳā
> kᵉ-ba-šāmáyim
> uḳ-bā-âreż
>
> et-laḥméinu ašer min-hā-âreż
> tein lânu yom bᵉ-yomo
> u-sᵉlah nā lânu et-ḥaṭotéynu
> ka'ašer nislah la-ḥoṭīm lânu
> vᵉ-al-nā tᵉbi'éinu lᵉ-nissāyon
> kī im hażīléinu mi-yād ha-rāʿ

(Anglicised phonetic)

> aa-VEE-noo aa-SHARE baa-shaa-MAA-yim
> yith-kaa-DAYSH shuh-MEKH-aa
> thaa-VOH maal-khoo-THAY-khaa
> yuh-HEE ruh-TSON-khaa
> ku-vaa-shaa-MAA-yeem
> ookh-vaa-AA-rets
>
> eth lakh-MAY-noo, aa-SHARE min haa-AA-rets
> tayn LAA-noo yom buh-yo-MO
> oo-SLAKH naa LAA-noo eth khaa-to-THAY-noo
> kaa-aa-SHARE nee-SLAKH la-kho-TEEM LAA-noo
> vay AAL-naa tuh-vee-AY-noo luh-nee-saa-YON
> kee im haa-tsee-LAY-noo mee-YADH haa-raa

Appendix 3: The Talmidi version of the 'Our Father' in various modern languages

The reconstructed 'Our Father' in various modern languages. What appears below is the form the prayer is said in the modern Talmidi community.

English:

Our Father, who is in heaven,
Sanctified be Your Name!
May Your Kingdom be fulfilled!
May Your will be realised –
Just as it is in heaven,
So also upon the earth.

Our bread, which is from the earth,
Give us day by day.
And forgive us our sins,
Just as we should forgive our debtors.
And do not bring us to trial
Rather deliver us from evil.

French:

Notre Père, qui est aux cieux,
que ton nom soit sanctifié;
que ton règne soit accompli;
que ta volonté soit réalisé
tout comme il l'est dans les cieux
donc aussi sur la terre.

Notre pain, qui est de la terre
donne-nous jour après jour;
et pardonne-nous nos péchés ,
tout comme nous devrions pardonner nos débiteurs.
et ne nous amène pas à l'essai,
mais délivre-nous du mal.

Spanish:[a]

Padre Nuestro, que estás en el cielo
¡Santificado sea tu nombre!
¡Cumplase tu reino!
¡Llevese a cabo tu voluntad -
como en el cielo,
también en la tierra!

Nuestro pan, que es de la tierra,
Danoslo día a día.
Y perdónanos nuestros pecados,
así como debemos perdonar a nuestros deudores.
Y no nos traigas a juicio
mas bien líbranos del mal.

German:[a]

Unser Vater, der im Himmel ist,
geheiligt werde dein Name!
Möge dein Reich erfüllt werden!
Möge dein Wille realisiert werden,
Ebenso wie im Himmel,
so auch auf Erden.

Unser Brot, das von der Erde kommt,
gib uns Tag für Tag;
Und vergib uns unsere Sünden,
ebenso wie wir unseren Schuldigern vergeben sollten.
Und bring uns nicht vor Gericht,
sondern erlöse uns von Bösen.

---

[a] with thanks to Mauricio ben Zipporah of www.ebionim.org for the Spanish and German versions.

Appendix 4: Translation notes for future translators

For the second edition of this book, I hope to include more translations of the prayer into other languages. If you wish to help translate this new version of the prayer into any modern language, email me at *shmuliq.parzal@googlemail.com*

To help you in this endeavour, here are some notes I have put together for you:

Our Father, who is in heaven,
Father: the normal word for father, not 'dad' or 'daddy'
who: In Aramaic, the little word *dᵉ* ('the one who') is a qualifier, simply identifying which 'father' we are talking about.
is: There is also no verb 'to be' in Aramaic ('is' or 'are'). The words 'who is in heaven' are not addressed to God, but identifying which father is meant for the benefit of the one praying, or for the audience hearing the prayer.

Sanctified be Your Name!
sanctified: we sanctify God's Name by living a life which brings honour to the reputation ('name') of God. If you have a word which implies this (and not just one that means 'make holy'), then that word would be preferable. Otherwise, 'make holy' will do.
name: God's Name is not just what God is called, it is also God's *reputation*. If you have a word which means both, then that would be preferable; otherwise 'name' will do.

May Your Kingdom be fulfilled!
Kingdom: in this instance, 'kingdom' means **kingship** – what God has planned for us as our King – the end result of the laws he asks us to follow.
be fulfilled: the Aramaic would literally be 'come'. However, in Aramaic and Hebrew, a prophesy 'comes' (to its fulfilment), and a careful plan 'comes' (to its fulfilment). This is the sense conveyed by the Aramaic word 'come'.
May your will be realised –
be realised: the Aramaic verb is literally 'be' or 'become'. It conveys the sense of what God's wants for us, coming about, or coming into being. At creation, God wills light, and light 'becomes' or comes into being. The sense of the line is, 'may what you want come about / come into being'.

Just as it is in heaven,
So also upon the earth.
Just as . . . so also . . . : Here the comparison is what is important

Our Bread, which is from the earth,
bread: In Aramaic and Hebrew, the word 'bread' does not just mean the bread we eat, but everything we need to sustain us. If you have a word that conveys that, then use it; otherwise, the simple word for 'bread' will do.
which is from the earth: As in the first line, this is a qualifying clause, clarifying which 'bread' is being referred to. 'Bread' also was slang for 'money'; it also meant 'God's teaching'. While we need God's teaching each day, that is not the immediate need of the poor; more than money, the poor need food and clothing. So this clause clarifies which 'bread' is being prayed for.

Give us day by day.
(this line should be self-explanatory)

And forgive us our sins,
sins: the Aramaic word for 'sins' is the same as the word for 'debts'. If you have a word that can also be used for both, use it; otherwise in this line use your normal word for 'sins'.
Just as we should forgive our debtors.
debtors: The Aramaic word also means 'sinners', but the idea of 'debtor' is also implied because of the imagery of the trial which follows.

And do not bring us to trial,
trial: the Aramaic word means both 'trial in a court of law', and 'trial in life'. If you have a word that conveys both meanings, then use it; otherwise use the word you have for a court trial. The overt image is 'please don't bring us to trial for our sins'. but the underlying image intended is 'please don't put our people through tribulation for the sins of our society'.

Rather deliver us from evil.
deliver us from: When someone was brought to trial unjustly, especially for a crime they didn't commit, the traditional plea from the defendant

was, 'Deliver me from my accuser!' This is the plea that is brought to mind by the line.

evil: Please use the general word for 'evil' here.

APPENDICES B: General Notes On The Talmidi Israelite faith

Appendix 5: Main Talmidi Beliefs

The Kingdom of God plays an important part in Talmidi outlook. We teach that the Reign of God exists here and now, and that we all play our small part in spreading the justice, compassion and peace of God's reign. However, there is also a hope in what the kingdom of God can become in the future – a time of universal peace,[a] where *'nations shall hammer their swords into ploughshares, and no one shall know or learn of war anymore'.*[b] It will be a time when the veil that exists between heaven and earth will fall away,[c] and the glory of God will cover the earth.[d]

Talmidis do not believe in a personal messiah – that a messiah will come to save us. Rather, we teach that God Himself will act in human affairs to guide the future and save us, and that an anointed, faithful and righteous descendant of David will simply be one of the end-products of God's actions, together with the return of the descendants of the lost northern tribes, and the rebuilding of the Temple in Jerusalem *in peace*. In short, we accept the idea of a Davidic messiah-king, but not a messiah-saviour; we view Yahveh as our sole Saviour and Redeemer, not any messiah. We look not to a messiah, but rather to God who puts him there.

Talmidi beliefs in which there is absolutely no compromise would be: that Yahveh has no physical form;[e] that Yahveh is indivisible;[f] that Yahveh alone is our Saviour,[g] rather than a messiah; that Yeshua` was a fully human prophet,[h] not a messiah or Son of God; that we do not accept the authority of the Talmud; and that we do not accept the teachings of Paul of Tarsus. *These things are not negotiable.* If one does not accept these beliefs, then one cannot call oneself a Talmidi – a Follower of the Way of Yahveh.

The following are the most basic Talmidi beliefs and affirmations:

---

[a] Hosea 2:20 (2:18 in Xtian bibles), Isa 65:25
[b] Isaiah 2:4
[c] Isaiah 60:19-20. See also Rev 22:1-5 / Ch.Sh. 23:1-5
[d] Hab 2:14
[e] Dt 4:12-15
[f] Dt 6:4
[g] Isa 43:11
[h] Mt 13:57, 21:11; cf Num 23:19

Basic tenets of the Talmidi Israelite faith

The Twelve Central Attributes of Yahveh:[a]

1. the Oneness of Yahveh
2. the Incorporeality of Yahveh
3. the supreme Sovereignty of Yahveh
4. the Wisdom of Yahveh[b]
5. the Holiness[c] of Yahveh
6. the Kavodh[d] of Yahveh
7. the Davar[e] of Yahveh
8. the compassionate Love of Yahveh
9. the righteous and merciful Judgment of Yahveh
10. the Creatorship of Yahveh
11. the Saviourship of Yahveh
12. the Redeemership of Yahveh

The Four Cornerstones of Israelite Culture:

1. Torah and the commandments of Yahveh
2. the Miqra and the principles of Yahveh
3. Yahveh's eternal Covenant with Jacob and his descendants[f]
4. Houses of prayer – the Temple and the Synagogue

The Seven Pillars of Piety:

1. Faithfulness to Yahveh alone, as our only Saviour
2. Regular Prayer (directed to Yahveh alone)
3. Charitable giving (*tsedaqah*) and good works

---

[a] These are all intrinsic qualities of the very nature of God, not separate parts – one attribute cannot be separated from the other

[b] that not only is Yahveh the source of all wisdom and knowledge, but that Yahveh is Wisdom itself.

[c] that nothing evil, wicked, sinful or profane can approach the glory of Yahveh, without being harmed or destroyed.

[d] *Kavodh* literally means, 'glory'. However, in the context it is most often used in Torah, it is describing the fiery, purifying and atoning radiance of God – a central concept in Israelite theology.

[e] *Davar* literally means, 'word' or 'message'. This attribute is the belief that Yahveh embodies and encapsulates the whole corpus of ethics, teachings, principles, judgments etc. The Message is not a separate entity – Yahveh IS the Message, and the Message is Yahveh.

[f] this would include things such as the Land of Israel, the people of Israel, and circumcision as a sign of the Covenant.

4. Observance of Shabbat
5. Fasting on Yom ha-kippurim
6. Observance of the three Pilgrim Festivals
7. Repentance for wrongdoing

The Twelve Major Negative Injunctions:

1. Do not worship any other god or name but Yahveh
2. Do not make or worship idols or graven images
3. Do not use the Holy Name for false, common or evil purposes
4. Do not consume flesh with the blood still in it
5. Do not engage in sexual immorality
6. Do not commit murder
7. Do not commit adultery
8. Do not steal
9. Do not give false testimony
10. Do not seek to have for yourself that which rightfully belongs to someone else
11. Do not follow pagan forms of religious custom or superstition
12. Do not practise witchcraft, divination, or augury

The Twelve Words of the Prophets:

1. that Yahveh alone is our Saviour and Redeemer
2. that faithfulness to God's ways will be rewarded, and widespread rejection[a] of God's ways will result in exile
3. that God will one day restore the Land, the tribes, the Temple and the Davidic monarchy
4. that one day, when God's Kingdom is fulfilled, there will be universal peace
5. that God will forgive and deal compassionately with those who return to Him
6. that to revere Yahveh in awe is the beginning of wisdom
7. that we should never forget the needs of the poor, the orphan, the widow or the alien among us
8. that religion practised with humility is the true Way
9. that ritual without intent is meaningless
10. that personal fasts without charity are pointless

---

[a] i.e. by oppressing the lowest and poorest in society, ill-treating non-Jews in the Land, allowing injustice to become commonplace, turning to other gods or other customs, corrupt ministers bringing disrepute to the good Name of God etc.

11. that we are to have just judgments in our courts
12. that we should deal and trade fairly with one another

In detail: The Basic beliefs of Talmidaism

On God:

1. that Yahveh exists, and is a living God
2. that Yahveh is One and indivisible
3. that Yahveh has no equal or opposite[a]
4. that Yahveh has no incarnation or physical form;[b] Yahveh cannot therefore be born or die
5. that Yahveh has no gender – God is neither male nor female
6. that Yahveh is holy, before whose glory evil and wrongdoing cannot stand, and whose Presence purifies good
7. that Yahveh is different and distinctive in nature and personality to what is portrayed of pagan gods: Yahveh is a just, merciful and compassionate God; the Creator, and the Author of all the laws by which the universe functions; omniscient, omnipresent, immanent and transcendent
8. that Yahveh alone is our Saviour and Redeemer[c]
9. that all worship and prayer is directed only to Yahveh – no one and nothing else; we worship Yahveh, and *only* Yahveh
10. that we pray in Yahveh's Name alone – we use no one and nothing else's name in prayer or worship
11. that the Name of Yahveh is holy, and cannot be given to anyone or anything else
12. that we should not make any image or representation of God in any way, or for any purpose
13. It is by God's merciful love that God forgives the penitent soul
14. It is by the glory ('Divine radiance') of Yahveh that Yahveh atones our souls (i.e. cleanses them of the stain of sin, and restores them to health and wholeness)

---

[a] Isaiah 40:25 – ' *"To whom will you compare Me? Or who is My equal?" says the Holy One.'* Also Isaiah 46:5. In practical terms, what this implies is that we reject dualism – that there is a good god and a bad god; and that we reject a belief in Satan as an evil power equal and opposite to God.

[b] Jer 17:5 warns against trusting in mortal flesh, and so by extension in human incarnations of the divine – of God incarnated in flesh. cf also Dt 4:12-15

[c] Isaiah 43:11 *'I, and I alone, am Yahveh, and besides Me there is no other saviour.'*

On Torah and the Covenant:

15. The relationship between God and the people of Israel is guided by the maintenance of the Covenant: 'If we worship Yahveh alone forever, and observe Yahveh's commandments, principles and precepts forever, then Yahveh will give us the land of Canaan forever, and preserve us as a people forever.'[a]
16. We are to follow not only the commandments of God, but also the principles of God[b]
17. The commandments and principles of our way of life are those contained in the Torah, and expanded upon in the books of the Prophets and Writings.[c]
18. The Miqra (*Torah, Prophets and Writings*) is the sole authority to our cultural, moral and ethical heritage.
19. As a sign of the Covenant – that we and our descendants have an inheritance in the Land – all Israelite males are circumcised. However, uncircumcised Godfearers are accepted as part of our wider community – the Assembly of all Israel.
20. Our holy and distinctive way of life was intended to serve as an eternal witness to the power and presence of Yahveh
21. Moses was the greatest of all the prophets, who alone spoke to God face to face[d]

On the viewpoint of the Talmidi Community:

22. We follow the Jewish teachings of the prophet Yeshua' of Nazareth, as long as they are in accord with Yahwist Israelite beliefs, values and principles
23. Yeshua' was a fully human prophet
24. His calling as a prophet was to restore the original ideals, principles and values of the 'Way of Yahveh' (the original Israelite religion), and through his call for repentance, to warn the Jewish people of the destruction of Jerusalem, and of the

---

[a] That is why gross breach of the terms of the Covenant results in exile from the Land.

[b] gleaned from Ps 119:4, Ps 103:18 – God's moral precepts are to be fully obeyed.

[c] We do however use other books to inspire and teach us, as long as they do not contradict the basic principles contained in the Miqra.

[d] that is, he spoke directly to God, not through visions; in the Mishkan, there was an opening into heaven, and God was able to speak directly to Moses. Moses was therefore able to hear God, as one human being speaks to another.

impending exile under the Romans

25. Yeshua` was born of normal human parentage, the son of Miryam and Yosef

26. Yeshua` was not a messiah, or a god, or Son of God

27. Yeshua`'s death did not serve any salvific or redemptive purpose; it was an unjust Roman punishment for a crime he did not commit (messianic rebellion against Rome)

28. After Yeshua`'s death, his cousin Ya'aqov son of Qlofas ('James the Just' / 'Jacob the Pious') was elected to serve as pre-eminent leader of the community of Followers

29. Yochanan the Immerser ('John the Baptist') was a prophet who taught in the spirit of Elijah, thus warning people of an impending 'Day of Yahveh' if wrongdoers did not repent and return to God's ways

30. Although we accept that Yahveh will set a descendant of David on the throne of Israel at some point in the future, he will not be our saviour, but a servant of God; Yahveh alone is our Saviour

31. We do not accept the authority or infallibility of the Oral Law; it is a collection of human opinions and decisions

32. We do not accept the authority of the New Testament

33. Any official record of Yeshua`s teachings and the ancient Talmidi community, shall only have the status of 'esteemed commentary' or 'respected sermons' on the Israelite faith; it shall not overrule Torah

34. We do not accept the authority of the teachings of Paul of Tarsus, and reject the claim that he was an apostle[a] of Yeshua`

35. We follow biblical customs and traditions, as far as is possible and practical in the modern age

36. We can use God's Holy Name when speaking of faith in reverence, or in private or congregational prayer, or when teaching Followers about God, or when discussing God peacefully

37. We should not use God's Name in anger or argument, or in everyday, casual conversation (thus making it empty, profane and ordinary)

38. We do not follow Kabbalist teaching or study it, since much of it is of pagan origin and outlook

---

[a] The quintessential definition of an apostle is that they repeat verbatim the message of their Master. Since Paul clearly did not do this – he never quotes the words of Yeshua` - he cannot be called an apostle.

Some Basic Talmidi affirmations:

39. Yahveh is above all a just, loving and compassionate God
40. The Kingdom of God is here and now
41. The Kingdom of God is within us – God's ways have already been written on our hearts
42. The fulfilment of God's Kingdom won't come by watching and waiting for it; God will bring about the fulfilment of His Kingdom only with our active participation
43. The Kingdom of God will be fulfilled gradually, like a small portion of yeast leavening a large quantity of flour; even a small act of kindness furthers the cause of God's Kingdom
44. The Kingdom of God is likened not to a battlefield, but to a farmer tending his field, or to a gardener tending his garden
45. The kingdom of God is not fulfilled by violence
46. To do violence in God's Name defames the holiness of God's Name; it is an affront to God
47. Practising justice and mercy, and living a good and honorable life, are of far greater value to God than how far we go to observe the minutiae of custom and tradition
48. It is the heart and intent with which a mitzvah is carried out that matters, rather than the perfection with which it is performed
49. We show who our Heavenly Father is by the compassion, consideration and dignity that we show to others
50. By sincere repentance we are immediately forgiven by God
51. Atonement comes through prayer, reparation and good works, by which our soul is cleansed, restored and made whole
52. It is not blood or death that brings about atonement for a soul, but rather the glory ('Divine radiance') of Yahveh
53. One cannot serve both God and wealth
54. Those who work for peace are the children of God
55. The Sabbath was created for the benefit of human beings, not human beings for the Sabbath
56. 'Seek, and you will find'[a]
57. 'The old wine is good enough' – the Israelite religion is sufficient for our spiritual needs
58. Those whom human beings have unjustly put last – the outcast and the rejected – God will put first
59. To oppress the poor is to revile God
60. Performing religious acts simply to extract praise from others is hypocrisy; such acts are meaningless, and gain no merit or

---

[a] Seek answers, and God, and you will find answers and ultimately God

favour with God

61. Spiritual defilement of the heart and soul are of greater concern than ritual defilement of the body
62. Faith without works is dead

Some Basic Talmidi values and emphases, derived from the teachings of the prophet Yeshua` and of Jacob the Pious:

63. Doing to and for others, as we would have them do to and for us
64. Doing good even to those who have wronged us
65. Helping others without want of thanks or return
66. Honesty, not swearing oaths; 'let your yes be yes, and your no be no'
67. Keeping a reign on our tongue – not being violent or malicious in speech
68. Training ourselves not to be selfish or possessive, or obsessed with our belongings
69. Storing up for ourselves treasure in heaven, rather than storing up things of this world
70. Righteousness and justice take precedence over mammon (wealth)
71. Living a good and decent life in witness to our Heavenly Father, so that we can be strengthened to endure the heat of life's trials
72. Bearing good fruit – showing the value of our ideals by our positive way of life and outlook
73. Practicing our faith with humility and compassion
74. Practicing mercy, repentance and forgiveness
75. Concern for the poor and the least of society
76. Awareness and vigilance for the stability of society
77. Being mindful of the gap between the rich and the poor
78. Not to ill-treat, oppress or exploit the poor or the weak in society
79. Treating all human beings with equal dignity and respect
80. Dealing with others without judgment or condemnation
81. Trying not to worry about things we cannot change; trying not to fret or allow evil to make us lesser people
82. Guarding our souls from the destructive effects of wrongful thought or intent
83. Guarding the tongue, not gossiping about others or spreading malicious rumours
84. Guarding against religious hypocrisy in ourselves; we should examine ourselves first before criticising others

85. Not making ostentatious or vain displays of piety
86. Guarding the fence of the mind – resisting lesser evils so that greater evils may be avoided[a]
87. Avoiding divisiveness amongst one's own, discussing differences and problems in the spirit of seeking; avoiding contentiousness for its own sake
88. Avoiding indecisiveness, wavering to and fro in our opinions
89. Not to take advantage of another's kindness
90. Mutual responsibility: each party in a given situation has their own responsibilities (host and guest, parent and child, government and citizen etc); not to take advantage of one another
91. Both rich and poor should contribute to the society from which both hope to benefit
92. If someone repents completely of the wrong they have done, amends their ways, and makes reparation to those they have wronged, then their past wrongs should not be held against them; we should rejoice over the lost who are found
93. As we are shown mercy and are forgiven, so should we also be merciful to others and forgive
94. Not treating people any differently according to their outward appearance or social status
95. Not to follow the majority when they do wrong
96. Not to follow a commandment or precept so literally that its heart and intent are lost
97. To acquire knowledge with humility, so that we might find the light of Yahveh's Wisdom

Some Voluntary Acts of Piety [b]

98. To lend to the poor, knowing that one will not get anything back
99. To live only according to one's needs
100. To seek out the company of the pious, so that we might emulate them
101. Accompanying any personal fasts with acts of charity, justice and kindness

---

[a] Such as resisting anger and hatred, so that murder may be avoided, or resisting jealousy and lust so that adultery may be avoided
[b] These are ideal acts which are not expected of everyone, but are reserved rather for those who wish to grow spiritually, and train themselves to become better servants of God and His Kingdom.

Some Yahwist beliefs held by Talmidis

102. God's will is knowable – not completely or perfectly, but nevertheless knowable; Yahveh is not an unknowable God
103. There is no such thing as permanent salvation; if a good man sins, then his previous good actions do not count in his favour. If a sinful man repents fully, then his previous sins do not count against him (i.e. there is no scorecard system of reward and punishment)
104. Whatever willful wrongs we do to others, God will return the same to us if we do not repent of them.
105. There are no such things as 'fallen angels'; angels cannot rebel or sin against God, since God's holiness prevents it
106. There is no such thing as 'Satan' – a supreme ruler of all evil who directs evil people and evil spirits, equal and opposite to God
107. There are no such things as demons or evil spirits – supernatural beings whose sole reason for existence is to make evil happen, or make people do evil
108. Evil comes instead from the hearts and minds of human beings; people alone are responsible and answerable for evil
109. If we return evil with evil, then we negate our own righteousness, and we turn our backs on God's help
110. God returns an unjust curse back to the one who pronounced it
111. We should not rejoice at the suffering of our enemies[a]
112. To see humanity and the world with a right mind, so that we might be led to a greater understanding of them
113. We should not seek signs of God's plans in the stars or movements of the celestial bodies
114. Places of the dead are not suitable places of worship
115. Holding that the Bible is perfect, infallible and without fault is elevating it to an equal status with God, and is therefore idolatry
116. Worshipping the Bible and putting it above God is idolatry

---

[a] Prov 24:17-18

Appendix 6: About The Mission Of Talmidaism

The essential mission of Talmidaism is to spread the Kingdom of God – to encourage other human beings, regardless of their religion, to live with an awareness of the nature of their heavenly Father, and change their lives accordingly. Christianity would see its mission as 'to make disciples of all nations' (i.e. to convert everyone to Christianity). However, Talmidis would see part of their mission as 'to spread the Kingdom of God to all nations' (i.e. to create peace and encourage understanding and tolerance between nations, cultures, political parties and religions).

There is a principle in the Israelite religion that God allows Gentiles their religions[a] – Yahveh does not expect everyone to become Israelites. However, what God *does* expect is that everyone should endeavour to reach a certain standard of ethical and moral behaviour within their own society. It is in this sense that all humanity will come to 'know Yahveh'. There are today many serious problems facing society, and most of them would be nipped in the bud if we simply encouraged a certain standard of respect towards our fellow human beings.

Below are the full articles of mission of the Talmidi Faith:

Articles of Mission of the Talmidi Faith

Our basic mission is to restore the best ideals and principles of the Israelite religion ('The Way of Yahveh'), and to proclaim the good news of the Kingdom of God to the House of Israel and to the Nations.

In detail:

With relation to God:

-   To imitate God in God's ways, by exercising the same compassion and mercy to others that God shows to us, and thereby demonstrating who our Heavenly Father is;
-   to bear witness to the power and presence of Yahveh by our

---

[a] Deut 4:19 "And when you (i.e. Israelites) look up to the sky and see the sun, the moon and the stars – all the heavenly array – do not be enticed into bowing down to them and worshipping the things that Yahveh your God *has apportioned to all the nations under heaven.*"

holy and distinctive way of life, culturally, ethically, and in our outlook on life;[a]

- to restore the theological supremacy of Yahveh;[b]
- to restore the good reputation of God's Name, demonstrating that God is above all a loving and compassionate God;[c]
- to restore the best of the original ideals and principles of the Israelite religion;
- to make people aware that the Kingdom of God is here and now;
- to bring the good news of the peace of God's kingdom to Israel and all the nations[d]
- to sow the seeds of the fulfilment of God's Kingdom.[e]
- to make people understand the importance of the social and ethical stability of society (the 'kingship of God'), and how God is given no option but to intervene when society fails into moral lawlessness, and brings God good reputation into disrepute ('Day of Yahveh')

With relation to the Houses of Israel and Judah

- to help our people to realise why we are called to do what we do, and what our cultural and ethical distinctiveness is for;[f]
- to encourage our people to change, to become a nation that other nations would want to be inspired by – a 'kingdom of priests and a holy nation';[g]

---

[a] See 1Chr 16:24, Ps 96:3 'Declare His glory among the nations, His marvellous deeds among all peoples.' Isa 49:6 'I will also make you a light for the Gentiles, that you may bring my salvation to the ends of the earth.' We do all this by our distinctive culture, outlook, and ethical way of life.

[b] For example, by re-examining beliefs that diminish the absolute supremacy of Yahveh, such as belief in a messiah-saviour, the role of Satan as the equal of God, the rulings of rabbis overturning the rulings of God etc.

[c] not the wrathful, vengeful god of religious fundamentalism, which advocates killing and violence

[d] This does not mean converting people to one religion, but rather restoring the image of God as a loving and merciful Sovereign where Israel is concerned, encouraging our people to practice their faith with compassion; and to spread tolerance and understanding among the nations, in an attempt to bring peace between different faiths and cultures.

[e] In order to prepare humanity for the day when the veil between heaven and earth is taken away, God's glory shines on earth (cf Isa 60:19-20), and God's will be done on earth as it is in heaven -,

[f] to be an eternal, physical, visible witness to the power and presence of Yahveh

[g] This way the peoples of the earth will see that we are called by the Name of Yahveh, and they will respect us.

- to help our people to realise our collective mission, so that we as a people become better able to carry out the work that God has given us to do in the world – to minister to the nations as a kingdom of priests;
- to encourage our people to act justly in our dealings and treatment of other peoples, so that we will become a people *'set in praise, fame and high honour among the nations'*,[a] by being a people holy in our ethical behaviour and outlook, for the sake of Yahveh;
- to remind our people who are in the Land not to oppress those among us who are not of our own people;[b]
- to ever remind our people of our obligation of *ts'daqah* towards the poor;
- to encourage our people towards a living and vibrant relationship with our God;

With relation to the Gentile nations:

- to be a light to the Nations, so that by our example, they will be inspired to build just, righteous and stable societies according to their own cultures;[c]
- to be a benefit and a blessing to the Nations;
- to spread the Kingdom of God among the Nations, by encouraging them to follow a way of righteousness, and to practice tolerance and understanding between faiths and peoples;
- to remind the rich of the God-given right of the poor to social justice, since all the poor are God's people;
- to bring healing to humanity, and encourage people towards a wholeness of spirit;
- to encourage humanity to realise their stewardship of creation, and so not abuse it;
- to encourage others to work for the social, moral and spiritual stability and betterment of their society;

With relation to one another:

---

[a] Deut 26:19 – *'He has declared that he will set you in praise, fame and honour high above all the nations he has made and that you will be a people holy to Yahveh your God, as He promised.'*
[b] Ex 22:21 – *'Do not mistreat a resident foreigner or oppress him, for you were foreigners resident in Egypt.'* Also Ex 23:9
[c] It is this way that God's salvation shall be brought to the ends of the earth.

- to strive to love our neighbour as ourselves;
- to do to and for others that which we would want others to do to and for us;
- to encourage others to change and better themselves by not judging or condemning others;
- to so change ourselves that we become more effective citizens of God's Kingdom, and better instruments through which the Kingdom of God shall be fulfilled;

With relation to Torah:

- to promote a simple, direct approach to Torah;
- to provide a way of internalising Torah, of 'writing it on our hearts';
- to remind people of the true heart of Torah, which is justice, mercy, compassion, charity, repentance and forgiveness;
- to encourage a culture in which the Hebrew scriptures are studied and interpreted honestly and responsibly;
- to teach people the original Yahwist Israelite mind-set and outlook, so that understanding of *Torah and the Prophets* comes more easily and naturally;

With relation to Yeshua` and the Jewish tradition of his ancient followers:

- to restore his humanity, and his proper place as a Hebrew prophet;
- to help people to focus on the real Jewish aspects of his original message – that in his day he warned of the destruction of Jerusalem and eventual exile; and that this could be avoided (or if not, the time of tribulation shortened) if people changed and lived a just, merciful and compassionate life;
- to help people to refocus on his teachings, and not on him;
- to remind people of the social aspect of his message with regard to the poor, debt, charity etc;
- to make people aware of the honoured and respected place Jacob the Pious played in the ancient community of his followers, and who he was;
- to work for and to enable the restoration of the succession of Nasis of the community one day.

Appendix 7: Cultural Differences With Other Israelite/Jewish Communities

Talmidi Israelite observances are based on our understanding of the culture of 1st century Galilee and Judea, and on our understanding of Torah. Our observances therefore differ from those of rabbinic Judaism in many ways.

These are our main differences based upon our rejection of the Oral Law, and are customs shared with Karaites:

- we observe New Moon festivals (since they are biblically enjoined observances)
- our months begin on the evening of the sighting of the first sliver of the New Moon
- we observe the New Year Festival at the beginning of the first Hebrew month, not the seventh
- New Year begins in Aviv (determined biblically by the finding of *aviv* – that is, ripe barley – in Eretz Israel)
- the counting of the period of 50 days after the wave offering of omer[a] is started on the first Sabbath after the *pesach* meal[b]
- our *Shavu'ot* always falls on a Sunday,[c] and is celebrated as the 'Festival of First Fruits',[d] not of the giving of the Torah
- at *Sukkot* we don't wave a *lulav* – the bunch of 'four species' of greenery; we build our booths out of the greenery (only a palm branch is waved during the festivities)
- we wear *techelet* (blue cords) on the corner fringes of our *tallitot* (prayer shawls)
- we don't wear *t'fillin* (phylacteries or prayer boxes) on our foreheads; we feel this practise is an over-literal reading of idiomatic expressions in the passages following the Great Commandment)
- the first day of the seventh month (Tishrei) is observed as *Yom Tru'ah* (Day of Shout & Trumpet), and not *Rosh ha-Shanah*

---

[a] Lev 23:11
[b] Lev 23:10-14
[c] Lev 23:15-16, Deut 16:9
[d] Ex 23:16, 34:22, Num 28:26; also called the Festival of Weeks, and the Festival of the Harvest

(New Year); this is the day we celebrate our joy in Torah, when the whole of the Book of Deuteronomy is read in public between daybreak and noon

- we don't have *Simchat Torah* (Rejoicing of the Law) (see previous item on *Yom Tru'ah*); instead, the day after *Sukkot* is observed as 'The Eighth Day of Closed Assembly' (*Yom Shmini ha-Atseret*), when we pray for rain in Israel, and for the needs of Israel and Judah

- we do use the Holy Name of Yahveh in our private and congregational prayer

- we don't have a ban on the eating of meat and milk together; we view this as a misreading of what not to do at the Festival of First Fruits[a] – forbidding Israelites to follow a Canaanite practise of actually boiling a kid-goat in its mother's milk

The following customs are today specific to Talmidaism, based upon our understanding of 1st century Galilean and Judean custom and tradition:

- we have elders (*z'qeinim*), scribes (*soferim*) and sages (*chakhamim*), not Rabbis

- we have a *Sanhedrin ha-shalosh* (Council of Three), not a Beth Din

- we don't require *ha-tafat dam brit* (ritual cutting to draw blood) of a male convert who is already circumcised; instead, the existing circumcision is sanctified with a prayer, and thereby its purpose is reassigned and dedicated to the Covenant

- our *Miqra'ot* (bibles) do not contain the *Book of Esther*[b]

- the order of the books of the *Miqra* (Hebrew Bible) is slightly different; it follows the 1st century CE Galilean canon described by Josephus, rather than the later Babylonian canon of mainstream Judaism; the order is the same up until the books of the *Kethuvim* ('Writings'). In our *miqra'ot* (Bibles), the last book ends up being the *Book of Psalms*

---

[a] Ex 23:19, 34:26, Dt 14:21

[b] Bibles in Eretz Israel at the time of Yeshua` did not contain the *Book of Esther*. Good examples of this situation can be found among the corpus of literature found at Qumran, which does not contain the *Book of Esther* at all. *Esther* is part of the Babylonian canon of Scripture, which mainstream Judaism uses now, but was not part of the canon used in Galilee and Judea at the time of the earliest Followers of the Way – which is the reason we don't include it. We were not part of the assembly which sat to decide on the Hebrew canon of scripture, and so stick with the one that was around in the 1st century CE.

Shmuel ben Naftali

- we don't observe non-Torah ordained festivals (apart from *Chanukkah* / the Festival of Lights, which we consider a national festival and a 'day of joy',[a] not a religious one)
- we don't observe *Purim*[b] (we believe it to have been originally a local Babylonian Jewish festival); we have no objection to the Rabbinic observance of this festival
- we count down[c] the candles at Chanukkah, not up (i.e. eight on the first night, one on the last)
- we don't wear *kippot* (or skullcaps – we view this as a Muslim practise adopted by Jews);[d] instead, conservative sects require only married men and women to cover their heads in public, women with a shawl or a woman's hat in local style, and men with either a Hebrew turban (*pe'eir*) or an ordinary hat in local style. Unmarried men and women would not be required to cover their heads. Moderate and Liberal sects tend not to observe these customs. However, we respect communal custom in wearing kippot when mixing with Rabbinic Jews.
- we don't rock when we pray, or bob when we say certain blessings;[e]

---

[a] See Num 10:10 – 'On your days of joy, at your festivals and at the beginnings of your months, you are to sound the silver trumpets ....' Local and national festivals are permitted by Torah as 'days of joy', as long as God is remembered as the Saviour and Deliverer of the Israelite people; as the same verse concludes: 'as a reminder in God's presence that I, Yahveh am your God.'

[b] The *Book of Esther* does not mention God, and only celebrates the power of the Jewish people. It is based on the Babylonian festival of the birthday of the god Marduk, which was accompanied by outlandish costumes, heavy drinking and outrageous behaviour. It is considered by Talmidis unbecoming of the reputation and holiness of God to behave in such a manner.

[c] This is the practice followed by the School of Shammai, who followed the older Jewish tradition. They reasoned that because the festival was a second Sukkot, and since at that festival the number of offerings decreased as the festival went on, so also the number of candles should decrease. The School of Hillel decided to do something new, by increasing the number of candles as the festival proceeded. They reasoned that one increases in holiness as time passes.

[d] or possibly a leftover from the ancient Middle Eastern practice of forcing subjugated peoples to wear a corded captives' hat; see 1Kgs 20:31-32, where these hats are called *chavalim*. It is therefore the difference between the headdress of a שְׁבִי shevi (captive) and the headdress of a חָפְשִׁי chofshi (free person).

[e] This rabbinic custom was based on a medieval rabbi making a connection between the two words 'to bless' (Hebrew *barakh*), and 'knee' (Hebrew *bérekh*). However, the two words are not connected etymologically, and have two entirely different origins.

356

- the ancient Israelite way of having both hands raised up is seen as a valid attitude in prayer, as is being seated with the hands clasped on one's lap, or held close to one's chest
- we read Torah in three years, not one
- our synagogues would reflect the ancient layout, rather than the current mainstream trend of mimicking a church: congregants would be sat around the side and back, rather than in rows facing the front; and the prayer leader would be at the back, rather than the front; also an east-facing curtain or 'veil' [*masakh mizrachah*] would be at the front, rather than the Torah ark [which would be mobile and be brought out only during the service and kept to the side]
- the Torah scroll would be kept in a *tiq*[a] in Middle Eastern mizrachi style, rather than wrapped in a cloth in European Ashkenazi style

A note on relations with the wider Jewish Community

Talmidis do not missionise other Jewish people, because we do not see our fellow Jews as needing converting – they are already Yahwists. We are strongly opposed to the missionising of the Jewish community by Christians. In fact, Talmidis have actually assisted former lapsed Jews to return to Rabbinic or Karaite Judaism, as well as assisting Gentiles and Messianics wishing to convert to mainstream Judaism. Since Talmidaism attempts to emulate what it sees as the pluralist, non-sectarian *Common Judaism* of the 1st century CE, Talmidaism is in favour of a varied and diverse Jewish community.

Talmidis accept all Rabbinic Jews, Karaite Jews, and even secular and atheist Jews of Jewish descent as Jews, whether of matrilineal or patrilineal descent.[b] We also respect and accept Samaritans as Israelites.

Talmidis feel a certain affinity with Karaite Jews, both our branches of Judaism being descended theologically from Common Judaism. Like Talmidis, Karaites also reject the authority of the Oral Law and Talmud.

---

[a] pronounced *teek*; it is a decorated wooden or metal case, in which the Torah scroll is housed.

[b] In mixed marriages, where only one parent is Jewish, Rabbinic Judaism only accepts the children as Jewish if the mother is Jewish. If the father alone is Jewish, then Rabbinic Judaism does **not** accept the children as Jewish (with the notable exception of Liberal Judaism). What this exclusion results in, is a closed faith that is not based on moral teaching from God, but on race. It results in many people who adhere to God's laws and principles, but are not accepted as part of the Jewish community – and consequently become lost to the people of God.

However, there are some practical differences between us: because we broadly follow the ancient custom of the Land,[a] Talmidis celebrate Chanukkah but not Purim, while Karaites observe Purim but not Chanukkah. Karaites do not have any light or heat in their homes on the Sabbath;[b] Talmidis in conservative sects by contrast extinguish lights not needed, and enkindle lights needed, well before the beginning of the Sabbath. On the whole, Talmidis also have a more flexible approach to Torah.

---

[a] the customs and traditions practised in the Land of Israel up until the 1st century CE. This was our choice, our distinctive witness to Yahveh. We should not, however, berate those Jewish communities that follow customs that originated outside of the Land (unless of course, they are un-Yahwist in principle).

[b] I understand that this custom was followed by Egyptian Karaites; European Karaites in cold northern climes did not follow this for practical reasons.

Appendix 8: Glossary & List Of Abbreviations Used In These Books

Word	Definition
Animism	the oldest human religion; the belief that spirits and gods dwell in everything around us - rivers, rocks, trees etc. All of these things are therefore worshipped and revered.
Aramaic	a Semitic language, related to Hebrew and Arabic. *Until the rise of Arabic in the 7th century CE, Aramaic was the international language of the Middle East, and there were many different varieties of it.*
Aramaicist	A person who involves him/herself in the study of the Aramaic language and its history
Asherah	main Canaanite goddess
Baal	the general title of respect for any Canaanite god; the word means 'lord'.
BCE	abbreviation: 'Before the Common Era', used with the western dating system. The academic equivalent of BC
Believers	self-appellation of the first Gentile Christians, (*Pisteuontes* in Greek); the followers of Paul of Tarsus; the Jewish followers of Yeshua` did not use this term.
CE	abbreviation: 'Common Era', used with the western dating system. The academic equivalent of AD
cf	compare with; from Latin *confero*

Ch. Sh.	*Chazoney Shim'on* (Visions of Shimon); 8th book of *The Exhortations*. It covers the Ebionite portions of the *Book of Revelation* in the New Testament
Christianity	the religious philosophy based on the belief system of Paul of Tarsus, and the ethical teachings of Jesus of Nazareth
Convention of Jerusalem, the	known as 'Council of Jerusalem' in the Orthodox and Catholic churches. Took place in about the summer of 49 CE to discuss the status of Paul's Gentile Believers, and their relationship with the community of Followers
Coptic	modern descendant of the ancient Egyptian language.
copyist	A man whose job it was to copy existing texts.
Covenant, the	the pact made between God and Israel: 'If you will worship me alone, and follow only My laws and teachings, then I will give you the land of Canaan forever, and preserve you as a nation forever'. Everything else are terms and conditions.
Ebionite	an ancient Talmidi sect. Even in the first 40 years after Jesus's death, there were several sects. The only one whose name we still know are the Ebionites.
El (or Eil)	the highest god in the Canaanite pantheon
Essenes	ancient Jewish sect. They were opposed to the priesthood in the Jerusalem Temple, whom they saw as corrupt, so they formed an isolated community in the Judean desert near the Dead Sea.

Exhortations, the	The Talmidi equivalent of the New Testament, covering approximately the same period and the same kind of material. However, it does not have the same authority as the Hebrew Bible. It is used for teaching and inspirational purposes only.
Exhs	abbr. for 'The Exhortations'
Followers of the Way	self-appellation of the first Jewish followers of Jesus of Nazareth; see also: 'Way, the'
free translation	a translation that gives the sense of the original, and is not necessarily a literal, word for word translation. This also gives the nearest vernacular equivalent of otherwise misleading, idiomatic expressions.
Galilee, the	region in the north of ancient Israel. *Its population consisted mostly of farmers and fishermen. Its capital was Sepphoris*
Gnosticism	Belief system that holds that there is a good and an evil god; that this world is controlled by the evil god, and only spiritual things are good. Attainment to the spiritual realm is only possible through secret knowledge or *gnosis*.
Godfearer	Non-Jew who follows the beliefs, principles and customs of the Israelite religion, without going through full conversion (in Hebrew: *yireh elohim* [for a woman, *yirat elohim*], 'someone who reveres God in awe'). Can also be called a *nilveh / nilvah* ('one who attaches themselves' i.e. to Yahveh)
Ig. Yq.	Iggeret Ya`aqov, or 'Letter of Jacob the Pious'. The 6th book of *The Exhortations*; it is the Talmidi version of the 'Letter of James' in the New Testament.

immersion	the Jewish version of baptism. It is carried out, not only for conversion, but whenever one needs to be ritually prepared for attending Temple. It was therefore not a one-time-only ritual.
Inquisition	The Portuguese Inquisition (1536-1674), like the Spanish Inquisition, sought out all those who secretly practised the Jewish faith, and gave them a stark choice: convert to Christianity or face execution. There was a brief window in the early 17th century when a third choice was given: to leave Portugal.
interlinear translation	a multi-lingual text, with the original language at the top, and a literal translation word for word in the second language below each line.
Jacob the Pious	St. James the Just, author of the 'Letter of James' in the New Testament. He was the leader of the ancient Talmidi community after Jesus died. He led the community from c.30 to 62 CE, when he was executed by stoning at the orders of the High Priest.
Jerusalem Council, the	the central ruling body of the ancient Talmidi community; not to be confused with what Catholics call 'the Council of Jerusalem', which was a great meeting (or *Convention*) convened specifically to decide the position of Paul's followers in relation to the ancient Talmidi community.
Jewish Aramaic	the dialect of Aramaic spoken by Jews – more accurately, Galilean Jewish Aramaic. *It was heavily influenced by Hebrew*

Josephus	Jewish historian who lived shortly after Jesus. He was a Galilean who witnessed many of the events that led to the destruction of Jerusalem and the Temple.
Jubilee Year	the year after every 7th Sabbatical year was a Jubilee year (i.e. the year after every 49th year, or in other words, the 1st year of every 49-year cycle). In this year, land lost through debt was to be returned to its original owner.
Kabbalah	a form of mysticism which is a mixture of pagan, Gnostic and Jewish thought. Not accepted in Talmidaism as being of pagan origin.
Karaism	The religious philosophy of Karaite Jews. They do not accept the authority of the Oral law, and rely on the freedom to interpret Scripture according to one's own learning and understanding.
Kavodh	lit. 'glory'; refers to the fire of the 'Divine Radiance' - the powerful and purifying aspect of God's nature.
kheruvim	(pronounced khair-oo-VEEM) a form of angel that, according to tradition, supports God's throne. They have the back end of an ox, the front end of a lion, the wings of an eagle, and the torso and head of a man. The Christian version of these angels are cherubs; Israelite *kheruvim* look nothing like the baby-faced Christian cherubs.
Koine Greek	the everyday form of Greek spoken by ordinary people *(in contrast to classical or literary Greek). The gospels were probably written in this form of Greek to make them easy to read by ordinary people.*

literal translation	a translation that gives a word-for-word translation of the original language. Literal translations don't give the real sense of idiomatic expressions, only the literal rendering of them.
marpei	the ancient Israelite art of healing, the using of plants and herbs alongside prayer and human care; it dealt with the human mind, body and soul as a whole unit.
Marranos	Jews who were forcibly converted to Christianity in Spain and Portugal in the 16th - 17th centuries.
merappei	(female: *merappah*) healer who practises the Israelite healing art of *marpei*.
Mg. M.	*Megillat ha-Musar* (Scroll of the Preaching); 1st book of *The Exhortations*
minuscules	small Greek letters *(the opposite of capital letters)*
Miqra, the	the oldest word for the Hebrew Bible or 'Old Testament'. Also called *the Tanakh*, after the rabbinic abbreviation for the 3 parts of the Miqra (T.N.K. - Torah, Nevi'im Ketuvim (Torah, Prophets & Writings).
miqveh	ritual immersion pool
Mishkan	Hebrew for the Tabernacle, the covered tent that was the central place of worship in the Sinai, and also in the Land of Israel until the Temple was built.
mitzvah	a religious commandment

Miz. E.	Mizmorey ha-Evyonim (Hymns of the Pious Poor); 10th book of The Exhortations
Molekh	Ammonite god, whose followers believed that the sacrificial death of one's child, especially an only-begotten son, could 'save' them from their sins, and bestow upon them permanent salvation.
Nazirite	a man or woman who has taken a particular vow not to consume anything derived from grapes, and to avoid contact with the dead. During the time of their vow, they had to live a life of piety, in accordance with the laws and principles of the Israelite religion.
Oral Law	a corpus of books that contain the debates and decisions of the ancient rabbis. It has greater authority in modern Rabbinic Judaism than the Hebrew Bible.
Outer Darkness	in Massorite Talmidi theology, a term used by Yeshua` to describe a place after death where the soul goes to dwell apart from God (also known as Sheol and Azza Zel). Here one has to work through one's sins by reliving what one has done to others as if they were happening to oneself. Once one has experienced and repented of all the sins one did not repent of in life, one then goes on to heaven.
Parallel panels	a particular form of Hebrew poetry. You have two lists of lines of poetry. The first lines of the lists will parallel each other in either ideas, form or language; then the second two, then the third two, and so on.
Paul of Tarsus	St Paul. His teachings and beliefs form the basis of modern Christianity (the atoning death of Jesus on the cross, original sin etc). He was not accepted by the ancient Jewish

	followers of Yeshua`
Paullist	adjective, describing a particular theology and outlook that originates from the teaching of Paul of Tarsus (or 'St Paul'), and not Jesus.
Pharisees	ancient Jewish sect from which the majority of modern Jewish sects (i.e. Rabbinic Judaism) are descended. They held the Oral Law in greater esteem than the Hebrew Bible
Q-Gospel, the (or simply, *Q*)	earliest hypothetical gospel, containing only the sayings of Jesus; it would have predated the Gospels of Matthew and Luke, and possibly even Mark.
Qin. Y.	*Qinot Lirushalayim* (Laments for Jerusalem); 9th book of *The Exhortations*
Roman alphabet	the alphabet that English and most European languages are written in; also called 'Latin script'.
S. Kit.	*Sefer ha-Kitbey ha-vney ha-Derekh* (Book of Talmidi Writings); 12th book of *The Exhortations*
S. Niss.	*Sefer Nissayunayin* (Book of the Two Trials of Yeshua`); 4th book of *The Exhortations*. It contains the stories of the trials of Jesus before the Jewish Sanhedrin and the Roman governor, Pontius Pilate, and of his death by crucifixion.
S. Yaq.	*Sefer Ya'aqov* (Book of James the Just); 7th book of *The Exhortations*
S. Yesh.	*Sefer Yeshua`* (Book of the Prophet Yeshua`); 3rd book of *The Exhortations*. It contains the detailed Jewish sayings and stories of Jesus.

S. Yoch.	Sefer Yochanan (Book of the Prophet John the Baptist); 2nd book of The Exhortations
Sabbatical Year	every 7th year was a Sabbatical year. The land was not to be tilled or harvested, and all debts were to be forgiven.
Sadducees	ancient Jewish sect consisting mostly of aristocratic priests. They only accepted the first 5 books of the Hebrew Bible, and did not believe in life after death.
Samaritans	Israelite sect descended from the northern tribes of Israel. In Jesus's day, Jews and Samaritans hated each other, and there were regular intercommunal clashes.
scribe	generally a professional who is paid to write or copy anything. In Yeshua`'s time, they were also trained, learned interpreters of Torah.
Second Temple period	Jewish historical period from 530 BCE to 70 CE. The period in which Jesus lived is referred to as the Late Second Temple period, or the Herodian period (after King Herod the Great, and the dynasty he founded).
seraphim	(pronounced sair-raff-FEEM); fiery, winged, serpent-like angels who are traditionally thought to exist in the immediate presence of God. In Jewish tradition they are gigantic, flying serpents, the colour of copper or bronze. They have three sets of wings, one with which they fly, another with which they cover their faces, and the third with which they cover their middle.
Shem Tov Matthew	rabbinic Hebrew translation of the Gospel of Matthew, dated 1385. The translator was Ibn Shaprut, who lived in Aragon, Spain.

She'ol	the underworld, place of the dead. *Before the Israelites believed in heaven, they used to believe that the dead went to a dark, unknowing underworld called She'ol. This later evolved into belief in a place Yeshua` called 'the Outer Darkness'.*
sidra	a portion of Torah. Differs from a *parashah*. A *sidra* is short, and the division of the Torah into *sidra'ot* enables the Torah to be read in 3 years (the division of Torah into longer *parashot* enables Torah to be read in 1 year).The *sidra'ot* represent the older custom.
sukkah	(pronounced soo-KAA, plural *sukkot*); a simple, rectangular structure, made with 4 poles, connected at the top by 4 pieces of wood. Used during the festival of Sukkot to dwell in. The roof is made of date palm branches, and the sides are decorated by fragrant or leafy branches and fruits.
Syriac	the Syrian dialect of Aramaic. *It is heavily influenced by Greek, and is used by Aramaic-speaking Christians. It is distinct from the dialect that Yeshua` spoke, Galilean Jewish Aramaic.*
T. Sh.	*Torat ha-Shlichim* (Teaching of the Emissaries); 5th book of *The Exhortations*
Tabernacle	the covered tent that was the central place of worship in the Sinai, and also in the Land of Israel until the Temple was built.
Talmidaism	modern term for 'Jewish-Christianity' (pronounced taal-mee-DAY-izzm, from the Aramaic *talmida*, 'follower', 'disciple'), and is synonymous with 'the Way'. It is an umbrella term for any Jewish sect that follows Jesus of Nazareth as a fully human prophet.

Talmidi	modern term for 'Jewish-Christian', (pronounced taal-MEE-dee; plural: Talmidis), and is synonymous with 'Follower of the Way'. *This term refers to those Jewish followers of Jesus of Nazareth who believe he was a fully human prophet. Although the word was only coined in 1996, the term is used retrospectively by modern 'Jewish Christians' to refer to ancient Jewish Christians too.*
Talmud	the Oral Law. *This is the collected debates and decisions of the ancient rabbis, and contains material which is often contradictory to books of the Hebrew Bible, and even with itself. For modern rabbinic Judaism, it has greater authority than the Hebrew Bible.*
Targum Onqelos	An Aramaic translation of the Hebrew Bible. *Targum* means translation, and Onqelos (or Onkelos) is the name of the translator. It literally means, 'translation by Onqelos'.
tithe	ten per cent of one's income before tax. This was given to pay the clergy, the upkeep of the Temple, and to help the poor.
trinitarian	adj. pertaining to belief in the Trinity.
Trinity, the	Christian belief that holds that God is made of three persons: Father, Son and Holy Spirit. Each person of this trinity is considered the same as each other, yet at the same time distinct from each other.
Ts. Y.	*Tsava'at Yehudah* (The Testament of Judah the Nasi); the 11th book of *The Exhortations*

uncials	the capital form of Greek letters. *In the 1st century, all Greek was written in capitals*
Unitarian	Liberal Christian denomination which believes Jesus was a human being, and that God is indivisible and without bodily form.
Way, the	short for 'the Way of Yahveh'. It was the original name of the Israelite religion, but came to be associated with the faith of the first Jewish followers of Jesus of Nazareth.
Yahwism	the pure form of Israelite theology, before it was affected by the beliefs of other religions. Yahveh is held supreme, without equal. Yahveh alone is Saviour (i.e. not a messiah), and has no equal (so Satan is not the 'ruler of evil').
Yahwist	someone who adheres to the purest form of Israelite theology; also adj., to describe the purest form of Israelite theology
Yeshua`	Jesus of Nazareth. This was his original Aramaic name (from Hebrew *Yehoshua`*, which means 'Yahveh saves'). Talmidis use it to emphasise the difference between the Christian 'Jesus' and the Jewish 'Yeshua`', and to point out that they are two distinct entities.
Yochanan the Immerser	John the Baptist. He actually led his own sect, the Nazorayyans. The Mandeans of Iraq claim descent from these Nazorayyans.
Zoroastrianism	The old religion of Persia (now Iran). It was founded by a man called Zoroaster (*Zardusht*). It believed in a good god (*Ahura Mazda*) and an evil god (*Ahriman*), and that a saviour from the world of light would come to save humanity. This religion influenced Judaism after the Babylonian Exile in the 6th century BCE, and introduced new beliefs

	such as a king-saviour, Satan, fallen angels and battles in heaven.

SELECT BIBLIOGRAPHY & RESOURCES

This list is by no means a complete record of every single book that has ever had influence over the material contained within these books. However, it is a list of those books which have had the most impact on the contents of this work. I apologise for the omission of any book.

GRAMMARS:

Grammatik des Jüdisch-Palästinischen Aramäisch
Gustaf Dalman
J C Hinrichsische Buchhandlung, Leipzig 1905

Manual of the Aramaic of the Palestinian Talmud
J T Marshall
E J Brill Ltd, Leiden 1929

A Short Grammar of Biblical Aramaic
Alger F Johns
Andrews University Monographs 1972

A Grammar of Galilean Aramaic
Caspar Levias
Jewish Theological Seminary of America, New York 1986

Grammar of Palestinian Jewish Aramaic
William Stevenson
Clarendon Press, Oxford 1987

A Grammar of Biblical Aramaic
Franz Rosenthal
Harassowitz Verlag, Wiesbaden 1995

An Introduction to Aramaic
Frederick E Greenspahn
Scholars' Press, Atlanta 1999

DICTIONARIES

A Manual of the Chaldee Language

D M Turpie
Williams and Norgate 1879

An Aramaic Handbook Part 1
Franz Rosenthal
Otto Harassowitz, Wiesbaden 1967

Hebrew-Chaldee Lexicon to the Old Testament Scriptures
Gesenius
Baker Book House, Grand Rapids 1988

A Dictionary of Jewish Palestinian Aramaic
Michael Sokoloff
Bar Ilan University Press 1992

Practical Talmudic Dictionary
Yitzhak Frank
The Ariel Institute 1994

A Dictionary of Judean Aramaic
Michael Sokoloff
Bar Ilan University Press 2003

The Comprehensive Aramaic Lexicon Project
http://cal1.cn.huc.edu/

DISCUSSIONS AND RESOURCES ON ARAMAIC

A Manual of Palestinian Aramaic Texts
J Fitzmeyer, D J Harrington
Biblical Institute Press, Rome 1978

An Aramaic Approach to the Gospels and Acts
Matthew Black
Clarendon Press, Oxford 1979

ANCIENT TEXTS *(related to the study of Aramaic)*

Gospel of Mark (Koine Greek text)
(Synopsis of the Four Gospels, Kurt Aland, German Bible Society 1984)

Gospel of Matthew (Koine Greek text)
(Synopsis of the Four Gospels, Kurt Aland, German Bible Society 1984)

Gospel of Luke (Koine Greek text)
(Synopsis of the Four Gospels, Kurt Aland, German Bible Society 1984)
Book of Revelation (Koine Greek text)
(NIV Interlinear Greek-English New Testament, Rev. A Marshall, Zondervan 1976)

Book of Daniel
(NIV Interlinear Hebrew-English Old Testament, J R Kohlenberger III, Zondervan 1987)

Book of Ezra
(NIV Interlinear Hebrew-English Old Testament, J R Kohlenberger III, Zondervan 1987)

Aramaic Targum of the Torah (Onqelos)
(Alexander Sperber, Brill Paperbacks 1992)

Aramaic Targum of the Prophets (Jonathan)
(Alexander Sperber, Brill Paperbacks 1992)

COMMENTARIES ON THE MIQRA & THE NEW TESTAMENT
I have not included every single commentary I have ever read on every book of scripture; I have merely listed those that have had a direct influence on the current manuscript.

Book of Exodus
N M Sarna,
JPS Torah Commentaries 1991

Book of Joshua
Trent C Butler
Word Biblical Commentary, 1983

The Book of Isaiah
S B Freehof
UAHC Press 1972

The Book of Jeremiah
S B Freehof
UAHC Press 1972

A Critical and Exegetical Commentary on the Book of Daniel

J A Montgomery
T&T Clark 1926

Gospel of Saint Mark
D E Nineham
Pelican NT Commentaries, 1986

Gospel of Saint Matthew
J C Fenton
Pelican NT Commentaries, 1985

The Gospel of Luke
E Earle Ellis
New Century Bible Commentary, 1983

The Book of Revelation
R H Mounce
Eerdmans Publishing 1997

CULTURE, HISTORY AND EVERYDAY LIFE IN JUDEA AND THE GALILEE

Wars of the Jews
Flavius Josephus
Milner & Sowerby, 1864

Life In Palestine When Jesus Lived
J Estlin Carpenter
The Lindsay Press, London 1949

Manners and Customs of Bible Lands
Fred H Wight
Moody Press, Chicago 1953

Everyday Life in New Testament Times
A C Bouquet,
B T Batsdord Ltd, 1953

New Testament History
F F Bruce
Pickering & Inglis, Basingstoke 1969

Jerusalem in the Time of Jesus

Joachim Jeremias
Fortress Press, Philadelphia 1975

Everyday Life in the Holy Land
James Neil
The Olive Press, London 1976

Jesus and the World of Judaism
Geza Vermes
SCM Press, London 1983

The New Manners and Customs of Bible Times
Ralph Gower
Moody Press, Chicago 1987

Jesus Within Judaism
James H Charlesworth
SPCK 1989

Judaism – Practice and Belief 63 BCE – 66 CE
E P Sanders
SCM Press, London 1994

Galilee – History, Politics, People
Richard A Horsley
Trinity Press International, Pennsylvania 1995

Archaeology, History & Society in Galilee
Richard A Horsley
Trinity Press International, Pennsylvania 1996

The Meaning of Jesus
NT Wright, Marcus Borg
SPCK 1999

Jesus the Jewish Theologian
Brad H Young
Hendrickson Publishers 1999

THE ISRAELITE RELIGION

Antiquities of the Jews
Flavius Josephus

Milner & Sowerby, 1864

The Jewish Encyclopedia
(online and printed versions)
1901-1906

Hebrew Religion – Its Origin and Development
W Oesterley, T H Robinson
SPCK 1952

Israel's Prophetic Heritage
B W Anderson, W Harrelson
SCM Press, 1962

Everyday Life in Old Testament Times
E W Heaton
BT Batsford Ltd, London 1966

Ancient Judaism
Max Weber
Free Press 1967

Ancient Israelite Religion
Susan Niditch
Oxford University Press 1997

Ancient Israel – Its Life and Institutions
Roland de Vaux
Eerdmans Publishing, 1997

Families in Ancient Israel
L G Perdue, J Blenkinsopp, J J Collins, C Meyers
Westminster John Knox Press 1997

Reconstructing the Society of Ancient Israel
P McNutt
Westminster John Knox Press 1999

Life in Biblical Israel
P J King, L E Stager
Westminster John Knox Press 2001

The Lost Testament

David Rohl
Century Random House Ltd 2002

A Final Note from the Author

On page 53, at the end of the section of the pronunciation of God's Holy Name, I made the bold claim that by the end of this book, you would know Yahveh. So, having read this book, I want to ask you now, **do you know Yahveh?**

Why do I do what I do? In my early twenties, when I was still a Catholic, God gave me a commission: 'Restore My Name, restore My Kingdom, and restore My people.' I had no idea what these words meant, and for many years, I did nothing about them.

At around the same time, God told me He would teach me new and wonderful things, that I would gain an understanding of God's Wisdom, and that I would write a book about God's Message. God also told me that in the future, religion would become despised for its violence and hatred. God promised me that these things would come to pass. And they have – nearly 40 years after I was told they would.

Any good thing that I have written here which has lifted your spirits and taught you wisdom has come from Yahveh, not me. And if you find here anything base and distasteful, then it has come from my simple and imperfect human heart. I pray the content of this book is worthy of the message God has given me to deliver.

It was never my intent to criticise any sect, denomination or religion, or make enemies of any religion. My job is and always has been to criticise negative attitudes and ways of thinking, that are an active hindrance to God and God's Kingdom. Sometimes it will seem as though I am criticising a specific belief, but I only say what I say because all beliefs have consequences, and some beliefs have distinctly unhealthy consequences.

If you have any constructive criticism of these books, or any useful comments, suggestions or information, I would be happy to hear from you. If you think I have made any factual errors, *please tell me*, so that I can correct them in the next edition. Genuine enquiries about the Talmidi faith can also be sent to the same email address. I can be contacted at:

shmuliq.parzal@googlemail.com

Please be aware that any hateful or missionising emails will be filtered out, and will not be read; similarly with junk or spam email.

For more information about the Talmidi Israelite faith, take a look at our website:

www.talmidi.co.il

Please make a donation to help me get my books translated into other languages. You can either send a donation through PayPal to

talmidi-donations@hotmail.co.uk

or visit my Patreon page, and support my work by pledging a monthly amount:
www.patreon.com/shmuelparzal

Made in the USA
Middletown, DE
22 June 2018